Deconstructing Communication

Deconstructing Communication

Representation, Subject, and
Economies of Exchange

Briankle G. Chang

University of Minnesota Press
Minneapolis
London

Portions of chapter 4 first appeared as "The Eclipse of Being: Heidegger and Derrida," *International Philosophical Quarterly,* 25, no. 2 (June 1985), 113–37, used by permission. Portions of chapter 5 are based on "Deconstructing Communication: Derrida and the (Im)Possibility of Communication," *History of European Ideas,* 9, no. 5 (1988), 553–68, copyright 1988, with permission from Elsevier Science Ltd., The Boulevard, Langford Lane, Kidlington 0X5 1GB, UK.

Published by the University of Minnesota Press
111 Third Avenue South, Suite 290, Minneapolis, MN 55401-2520
Printed in the United States of America on acid-free paper

Second printing 1997

Library of Congress Cataloging-in-Publication Data
Chang, Briankle G., 1954–
    Deconstructing communication : representation, subject, and
economies of exchange / Briankle G. Chang.
        p.   cm.
    Includes index.
    ISBN 0-8166-2644-8 (hardcover)
    ISBN 0-8166-2645-6 (pbk.)
    1. Communication—Philosophy.   2. Deconstruction.   I. Title.
P90.C48   1996
302.2'01—dc20   95-31241

Contents

Acknowledgments   vii

Introduction   ix

Part I. The Transcendental Economy   1

1 / Phenomenology and After   3
Crisis and Beyond: The Phenomenological Way —
Phenomenological Reduction: From Phenomenon to Eidos —
Phenomenology as Transcendental Egology — I and Others:
The Problem of Intersubjectivity — Phenomenology and
Philosophical Modernism

2 / Communication before Deconstruction   33
A Note on the Problematic — The Question Then . . . :
Communication and the Communicative Subject —
Communication as Mediation: The Postal Principle —
Metaphorics at Large in Communication — Rereading the
Problematic of Communication — *Ignotum per Ignotius;* or,
Theoretical Ventriloquism

3 / The Inaugural Relation: Toward an Ontology of
Communication   69
Reading the Circle and the Hermeneutic Return — You Must
Take for Granted the Taken-for-Granted — Grounding the
Life-World: Social Ontology — Fundamental Ontology: *Quo
Vadis?* — The *There* of Being — Being as Relational Totality —
Toward an Ontology of Communication

Part II. The Economy of Difference   113

4 / The In-Difference of Being   115
Like a Novel Commodity: What Is Deconstruction? — The
Odd Couple *Aujourd'hui:* Heidegger and Derrida —
Deconstruction and the Ontological Difference — From
Destruction to Deconstruction: Homecoming versus
Nomadism — Derridean Doubt and the Metaphysics of
Presence — Deconstruction I: Strategic Seduction and
Seductive Strategy — Deconstruction II: The Double
Science — Being and Its Void — Loose Play: *Différance* — Being
and/or Text — Beginning Ends?

5 / Deconstructing Communication: Derrida and the
(Im)Possibility of Communication   171
What Is the Message? *Positivity* as the Critical Dogmatics of
Communication — Two Roads Diverge after Positivity: The
Material and the Textual — Loud Voice versus Quiet
Writing — The Logocentric Scandal of Speech — The
Logocentric Scandal of Communication: Is It Possible? —
Signing Off: Signature, Communication, and the Postal Paradox

Conclusion   221

Abbreviations   229

Notes   231

Index   253

Acknowledgments

Writing always involves appropriation; it depends to a large extent on making others' ideas one's own. In writing this book, I have appropriated many ideas from individuals who have written on related topics. They include John Sallis, Christopher Norris, Rodolphe Gasché, John Caputo, Mark C. Taylor, Stephen Watson, Geoffrey Bennington, Irene E. Harvey, and many others whose names can be found in the notes. I must acknowledge their contributions and hope that they will not feel abused. On a more personal level, I wish to thank Larry Grossberg for being there from the very beginning and for his steadfast advice and encouragement. I am similarly grateful to Jesse Delia; were it not for his unceasing help and regular counsel, I would have remained unpropitiously elsewhere. Norman Denzin has always been more than generous as a teacher and friend; the example he set for me, though not always by design, has made my unusually long journey through Lincoln Hall that much easier. My deep gratitude also goes to Richard Rand, from whom I relearned the meaning of reading, writing, and, most important, the necessity of restyling the ideographic imagination my mother tongue, Chinese, affords me to the demands of English. Marty Allor read an early version of the manuscript; his timely input has made a difference to the outcome of this project. The anonymous reviewers from the University of Minnesota Press also offered useful comments on my manuscript. I am grateful for their suggestions and well-intentioned criticisms; all the infelicities that remain in the book are, of course, my own. I have no reason to believe (and some reasons to doubt) that the people mentioned above will approve of everything expressed in the following pages, but without their direction I would not have completed this book.

Special thanks are extended to Dr. Seymour Berger, the former dean of the College of Social and Behavioral Sciences, and to Dr. Jarice Hanson, chair of the Department of Communication, both at the University of Massachusetts, for providing aid for the final preparation of the text. I am indebted to Jeff Moen, Robert Mosimann, Mary Byers, and, especially, Janaki Bakhle at the University of Minnesota Press. Their patience and expertise proved to me that the arduous process of publishing can become a rewarding experience. Finally, to Mary Ann I can only say "thank you," for the time being, forever. As for the unnamed, only they know what they are owed.

Portions of this book are based on articles first published in the journals *International Philosophical Quarterly* (chapter 4) and *History of European Ideas* (chapter 5). I thank the publishers of these journals for allowing me to include these materials in revised form.

Introduction

Il faut parler. Parler sans pouvoir. — *Maurice Blanchot*

Those who talk about communication don't know what they're talkin' about. — *A passenger on the New York City subway*

Writing, despite poststructuralist suggestions to the contrary, is a transitive act. To write is to answer a call; it is, minimally, to respond to a need to make one's ideas public: to communicate. In this book, I cast doubt on this apparently innocent activity; I try to convey my deep skepticism about communication, about communicability in general, by subjecting a set of discourses addressing this issue to a rigorous critique. However, in problematizing communication in this way, in communicating to readers my doubt about the possibility of communication, I am confronted at once with an epistemological circularity: Any such attempt to make public my skepticism about communication can be realized only by and through communication (for example, in writing) — a fact that seems to nullify the basis of my inquiry, if only because the very subject matter I interrogate is employed as the medium of the interrogation. The apparent result is a tangible monument to communicability that, taken at face value, neutralizes — in practice at least — the significance and exigency of my project. I seem to be immobilized, unremittingly trapped in a hermeneutical circle even before I begin.

Such a predicament, however, is not unique to those who problematize communication; in fact, it characterizes the epistemic quandary of writers from diverse fields (such as philosophy of mind, philosophy of language, cultural anthropology) in which the act of the investigation is itself implicated in the object of inquiry as its condition of possibility. Undoubtedly, the presence of circular reasoning poses a methodological problem of considerable difficulty, but, as Martin Heidegger among others has assured us, it is not as pernicious as it appears on first blush. According to hermeneutical theories of understanding, the skeptical subject is always and already embedded in a structural whole of preunderstanding that mediates between the knower and the known. The knower is conditioned throughout the process by an interplay between part and whole, between focus and background, between implicit comprehension and explicit interpretation. In this view, to know X, including knowing one's lack of knowledge of X, is to stand squarely within a particular precognitive horizon, a preinterpretive forestructure surrounding X in which X achieves its minimal level of intelligibility as an object of inquiry vis-à-vis the inquirer. Once we replace the naive empiricist picture of the inquiring mind as a tabula rasa, or empty receptacle, with the hermeneutical principle of interpretive embeddedness, the task of gaining knowledge of X is not so much to escape or break free from the forestructure encircling X as to enter it at the correct angle.

The importance of entering the circle in the right way presents me with a challenge: It makes it imperative that I be explicit and reflexive about my point of entry and about what I think my intervention will entail. To that end, in this introduction, I shall first briefly forecast the trajectory of this book's argument, signaling the directions I will follow as well as those I will not. I will then provide a preliminary sketch of the critical perspective on which my analytic procedure rests.

The temptation to define communication is as persistent as it is notoriously difficult.[1] The word *communication,* thanks primarily but not exclusively to the rapid development of media technologies, is used today to cover so vast and diverse an area that the concept itself appears to defy clarification. Despite the word's uncontrollable overflow of referential boundaries, however, there is an identifiable common core beneath its apparent semantic excess, a conceptual invariant that can be readily uncovered etymologically. The word *communication* derives from the Latin *communicare* (to make common, to share). It can also be traced to *munia/muntare,* a root connoting mutual help, exchange (as in *munus, mutuus*), and interaction among those who belong to the same community (as in *communis, communitas*). To communicate is to participate in collective life, to perform service for a common purpose from which one can be exempt only under special circumstances (*immunis, immunity*). Conversely, to be excommunicated is to be purged from the community, to be barred from partaking in the Holy Sacrament (*communion*) that binds together those who hold something in common (*communier*). As can be discerned from this simple etymological tracing, the current semantic amplitude of communication can justifiably be reduced to the conceptual kernel "commonality," evidenced by a well-delimited pool of lexical units: *com/cum, munia/munus,* out of which the English word *communication* develops.

There is little doubt that the semantic core of "commonality" has persisted in our understanding and in our use of the term today. As a result, whenever the concept of communication comes into play — be it in the limited episodic context of mundane interpersonal interactions, in the relatively mediated situations in which distant parties exchange information with one another through writing or printing, or in the grandiose narratives of modern telecommunications replete with such utopian images as the "global village," "virtual communities," or "information superhighways" — the emphasis is always on the common sharing of material or symbolic wealth, on social intercourse, mutual exchange, or the imparting of feelings and thoughts to one another. In each instance, the correspondence between a sender and a receiver of messages stands unwaveringly at the center of the concept. And the built-in goal, the telos, of communicative events is always — at least for those who are involved — to arrive at a better mutual understanding or greater feeling of certainty and security toward one another, in short, the achievement of *common*wealth that reflects the triumph of sociality over individuality, of collective identity over individual difference.

In this book, I offer a systematic critique of this notion of communication as it is articulated differentially and often obliquely within modern communication theories.[2] I argue that the conceptualization of communication as the "transcendence of difference," reasonable as it may seem at first, reflects an implicit subjectivist thesis — what I call the "ideology of the communicative" — to which modern communication theories remain heavily mortgaged, notwithstanding the varying forms these theories may assume across rigidly demarcated disciplinary boundaries. I argue that this implicit subjectivist thesis causes communication theorists to view communicative events as moments within a teleological process, a foreclosing dialectic, eventually leading them to their unquestioned valorization of identity over difference, of the selfsame over alterity, of dialogue over polylogue, and most important, of understanding and the determination of meaning over *mis*understanding and undecidability. My book contests this romantic view of communication as organized exchange and advocates an inverted image of communication as the occurrence of Babel-like, *a* destinal sending (*envoi*).

I should point out without delay, however, that my skepticism toward the romantic scenario of communication as gratifying interlocution between subjects does not carry any unhappy consciousness or cynicism toward dialogism as such, which, as a principle of exchange, seems by all reckoning affirmed — though, as I will argue, never confirmed — by the events of communication. Regardless of its diverse purposes, an act of communication must, prior to its happening, surrender itself to a general economic determination, proceeding, as if observing a categorical imperative, on the principle of equivalence, translation, and circulation, and through this surrender, displaying itself as intersubjective commerce in which the self and the other refashion themselves through the passage of expressions and counterexpressions. Such display of communication as an intersubjective affair implies that before the message in question is sent, and certainly before that message can be properly received, the act of communication must communicate its communicability as the very foundation of message transfer. Logically speaking then, there is always a message before the message, a prior sending before the sending itself, which, despite the absence of the addressee, proposes itself as capable of being understood. I argue that this proposal, thematizable as the forwarding of a sending before its proper representation as the message, creates a curious and yet decisive logico-temporal dislocation, an *atopos* articulating itself as "performative contradiction," in the very happening of a dialogic exchange. It is to this disjointing proposal, a proposal — equally a thesis, a theme, and a rule — that simultaneously poses its own *ex-timate* counterthesis (not, I repeat, dialogism as such) that my analysis turns and seeks to unravel.[3]

Having said that, let me briefly discuss the critical perspective that enables and organizes my argument in this work: deconstruction. Despite checkered and varying interpretations of deconstruction as "playful," "open-ended," or "nihilistic," deconstruction is essentially a limited or, as Jacques Derrida describes it, a "parasitic" activity. In fact, even a cursory reading of Derrida, or any of the deconstructionists, is enough to repudiate the pandemic view of deconstruction as some kind of frivolous, unconditioned verbal free play. Popular misunderstanding to the contrary, deconstruction does not license uncurbed textual freedom, nor does it in any way lead to interpretive anarchy or moral relativism. Just the opposite: Like any serious critical analysis, deconstruction is unswervingly text specific; its apparent open-ended, exorbitant transgression of established textual borders is always relative to and rigorously structured by an unfree target text whose meaning structure delimits the uneasy horizon of all deconstructive activities.

Because I will address the question of deconstruction more closely in later chapters, it is sufficient at this moment to point out two related operations that Derrida claims deconstruction must execute: mimesis and castration.[4] To deconstruct a text, says Derrida, one must first "copy," or "mimic," it, passively and faithfully registering it in toto. Therefore, to deconstruct metaphysics, for example, one must begin by *citing* its texts. This can only mean that one accepts the lexicon and grammar of metaphysics and its regime of iterations and citations, and that one has no choice but to begin with a quotation that both retains and questions the remains and effects of one's metaphysical past and predecessors. Deconstruction, Derrida emphatically states, "ne veut rien dire" (does not want-to-say/mean anything).[5] The "ne veut rien dire" of deconstruction, however, does not mean a poverty of ideas; it is not the same thing as literally having nothing to say — a mutism that in light of its disciplined appearance would be at best suspect. Rather, by copying the text it engages, this self-professed silence indicates deconstruction's thoroughgoingly text-dependent character; it reflects the deconstructionist's initial circumspect "hesitation" in front of his objects, thus betraying a profound respect for the text and a willingness on the part of the deconstructionist to examine the text in all its particularities before conducting textual surgery.

Copying the text faithfully, however, does not automatically yield good analysis. To be deconstructive, Derrida goes on to suggest, mimetic reading must be extended to include "castration." Unlike mimesis, castration does not leave the text alone; it lacerates or deforms it. Castration refers to deconstruction's violent act of transgressive reading; it embodies deconstruction's unique strategy of counterreading, a way of dealing with the parent text that goes deliberately against what might be called our "logocentric habit" of reading. Castration destroys the identity of the text-body by slicing the text apart and reassembling it in unexpected ways, creating a surprise or crisis where it is least expected by the writer and the reader alike. But deconstruction's counterreading is not an arbitrary exercise. By focusing on the "relation between that which a writer commands and does not command of the patterns of language that he or she uses," the deconstructive counterreading seeks to show why and in what respect there always exists a discrepancy or asymmetry between a text's explicit "statement" and its implicit "gesture."[6] To mimic a text, the deconstructionist reads it slowly and carefully. To undo a text's coherence or unity, to transgress its boundary, the deconstructionist cuts the text open, finalizing his job by leaving a "wound" or "scar" on the text-body that bears witness to the violent act of transgressive reading. Reading deconstructively, as Harold Bloom reminds us, "is not necessarily a polite process, and may not meet the academy's social standard of civility."[7] A deconstructive reading is critical and clinical. It must strive to be a salutary act of textual violence; it must resist the desire of subjective appropriation and must respect not the author but the textual movement that provokes reading and observes no other desire than that of writing itself. Such is deconstruction's double play of mimesis and castration; the former retraces, prior to the incision, the "limit," the "border," the "margin," namely, the "liminal" area surrounding whatever is worthy of copying, whereas the latter creates an absence on the operated surface, an absence reminding the writer of an ingrown blind spot, an aporia that frames the body of his or her work only to frustrate the Icarian dream of *ousia*.

The double operation of mimesis and castration reveals the duplicitous nature of deconstruction. To the extent that deconstruction is parasitic upon (not symbiotic with) a host author-text, it does not and cannot exist in and by itself. Deconstruction, by implication, affirms the independence of the other, the authority of its object. Reduplicative in its operation, deconstruction must remain content with being a parody, if only because it needs an original in order to show the tragicomic illusion of origin. To deconstruct a text, therefore, presupposes two things: On the one hand, the host text must be (or be thought to be) coherent, unified, and meaningful, so that it is worthy of deconstruction. On the other hand, the text, despite its own claim, is not and cannot be coherent or unified; it must have always and already harbored, often unbeknownst to itself, a contradiction between what it says but does not know and what it knows but cannot say. It is this noncorrespondence, or slippage, between a text's overt statement and its covert gesture that opens the text to deconstruction.

These two assumptions reflect two kinds of desire and two corresponding economies of meaning/sense with reference to the Western metaphysical thinking that undergirds our conception of what counts as the proper object of reading and analysis. On the one hand, there is the desire of "reason" or logos, that is, the desire for presence and the consequent constructions of philosophical hierarchies based on transparency, identity, and totality. This desire, according to Derrida, is synonymous with philosophizing as such, in that philosophy has always been understood as the guardian of an original and originary truth. Assuming the task of fighting off "doxa" and refusing to accept reality as it is, philosophical reasoning has always been considered an operation of protecting and restoring the intact "kernel" (to use Walter Benjamin's metaphor) of truth, a pristine idea wrapped in an "arch–mother tongue" of *ratio* and buried beneath various historical and theoretical languages that dissimulated, disfigured, or mistranslated it.[8] Facing the threat of possible errors caused by historical, hence contingent, expressions, the project of philosophy is to set truth or meaning in a medium most natural to it. Philosophy thus becomes a fight against Babel, against any Babelian disorder or multiplicity; philosophical culture, as it were, is a culture in constant pursuit of a single pure language; as Stéphane Mallarmé put it sarcastically, "Ces langues imparfaites en cela que plusieurs, et cetera [These imperfect languages, imperfect in that they are plural...]." This reduction of, or mastery over, plurivocity for Derrida characterizes nothing other than the very passage into philosophy.[9]

Parallel to the desire for primitive meaning (*sens propre*), however, stands a contrary desire, a desire coming from the far side of reason. This is the desire of deconstruction, of Nietzsche, Heidegger, and Derrida, an antimetaphysical desire that disavows transparence, presence, totality, and everything that motivates and safeguards the logocentric diegesis. Instead of uncovering the virginal kernel buried beneath layers of historical sediment, this deconstructive, disbelieving desire realizes that there is no intact kernel; more than that, it does not think there has ever been one. In contrast to philosophy's totalizing economy that either reduces phenomena to the bifurcating categories of metaphysics or restructures reality in terms of rigid rules of veridical correspondence, the deconstructive desire goes against the logocentric imperative of "critical verisimilitude" by relentlessly chasing the rhetorical excess erupting from within philosophers' texts.[10] In so doing, as in the case of Nietzsche, it scandalizes the claims of reason by initiating, across diverse instances, a tropological movement that "reasonable" philosophy cannot control; and, as in the case of Derrida, it reenacts the movement of the *supplément*, where one word, be it *Being, Woman, pharmakon,* or *hymen,* "means two things *at the same time* and ... therefore cannot be translated without an *essential* loss."[11] Whereas philosophy's first desire for full presence creates a totalizing transcendental economy characterized by meaning-*fullness* and univocity, the second desire, ensconced in literature, arts, and various forms of *délire,* brings forth an economy of nonfinality and undecidability that detotalizes the former by placing its eternal aspiration toward self-foundation in serious question.

The relationship between these two economies provides the organizing principle of my analysis. Insofar as deconstruction parodies philosophy, that is, insofar as it presupposes a prior metaphysical system to be parodied, a deconstructive critique of communication by necessity requires that one identify the relevant conceptual apparatuses that produce and are in turn supported by various theories of communication. The first part of my analysis, therefore, traces the formation of the transcendental economy as it bears on the modern theorizing of communication. To that end, I choose to follow one specific vector of twentieth-century transcendentalism, Husserlian phenomenology. This choice, as I shall argue later, is made on the understanding that Husserl's "radical Cartesianism" articulates most forcefully the transcendental desire just indicated, and that the Husserlian transcendentalism (and its hermeneutic outgrowth) constitutes an "untranscendable horizon" within which modern theories of communication define their problematic by marking their conceptual point of departure in the Husserlian matrix of intersubjectivity. Phenomenology has often been thought to provide an alternative to positivist mainstream communication theory and research. One of the central claims of this study is that phenomenology does more than that. Phenomenology, I argue, forms the very foundation of modern theories of communication, a pretheoretical platform shared by both the positivist-empiricist and the interpretive-critical approaches in media and communication studies. On the basis of this claim, chapter 1 begins with a discussion of Husserl's transcendental phenomenology and proceeds to show how his project turns into a cul-de-sac when the question of intersubjectivity emerges. In chapter 2, I first reconstruct the problematic underlying modern theories of communication and then discuss a specific problem that any transcendentally based theory of communication necessarily faces and cannot solve. Chapter 3 proposes a Heideggerian solution to the problem identified in chapter 2 and argues for a rethinking of communication as an ontological issue.

In essence, the first part of this book traces the formation of the transcendental-hermeneutic foundation of modern communication theories, and the second part seeks to undermine it. By reading chosen ontological narratives (Husserl and Heidegger) against their own logic, against their own momentum, the chapters in the second part map, within the transcendental economy, "a variety of crossings, displacements, and substitutions, as inside becomes outside, outside inside, or as features on either side cross over the wall, membrane, or partition dividing the sides."[12] Chapter 4 juxtaposes Heidegger and Derrida and develops the reading of deconstruction as an antimetaphysical graphematics. Chapter 5 returns to the problem of communication and proposes the possibility of polylogism as an alternative to the deeply entrenched (hermeneutic) ideology of the communicative. Were I to summarize my book's objective in one sentence, I would say that it is to show how and why modern theories of communication fail, how and why theories of communication, like other communicative acts, come to "lie."

I wish to make it clear, however, that by accusing communication theorists of encouraging and perpetuating a teleological interpretation of communicative events, I do not mean to suggest that they deliberately choose idealist philosophies of the subject and meaning to promote social harmony, collective identity, or romantic interpretive practice. Such an explanation would be superficial, for it would circumvent the issue of analysis by submitting psychological diagnosis in lieu of genuine philosophical argumentation. My aim, rather, is to highlight the starting point of my critique: Modern communication theorists have indeed been held captive by an idealist-transcendental economy that circumscribes their moves and countermoves within a delimited space of subjectivism. My purpose, then, is not to denounce the vague charm of commonality, of dialogism, of the "fusion of horizons," of the "ideal speech situation," and the like; nor is it to descry errors in specific research programs in communication studies, whether empirical, interpretive, or otherwise. Rather, it is to scrutinize closely the idealist-transcendental economy in question, to push the logic of the idealist-transcendental argument to its extreme, and finally, to suggest a way out of the aporia endemic to transcendentalism by drawing out the philosophical implications of this subjectivist-based problematic.

During the past twenty years or so, the landscape of communication studies in the United States has been significantly reshaped by European critical theories. In fact, the change has been so drastic that topics that would have been resolutely cast aside two decades ago as the concerns of the sociologist, literary critic, or philosopher now fall well inside the purview of communication and media theory. This paradigm shift has resulted in a flurry of reactions ranging from denying its existence to embracing its consequences. Regardless of one's stance toward this shift, one thing seems certain: We can no longer refuse to confront the philosophical foundations of communication theories. How one confronts these philosophical foundations depends in great measure on where one stands in relation to the past and how one envisions the future. The substantive challenges made by recent Continental thought have called into question many of the assumptions underlying modern communication theories in the Anglo-American mode. My book confronts this issue by positioning classical communication theories of the past against the intellectual backdrop fashioned by recent massive reorientations within the human sciences, and it articulates a vision of the future enabled by post-phenomenological thinking, in particular, deconstructivism.

Finally, I must point out that I have no intention of constructing a theory (*thea, theoros* [viewing, speculation]) of communication in the classical sense, and I have no pretension of establishing protracted contact with various postmodern theories, each of which, I imagine, can easily be brought to bear on the questions I address. In keeping with the skeptical spirit informing my critique, I have attempted to track only what I take to be the most representative and revealing path traversing the conceptual underground of modern communication theories. If, as I remarked in the beginning, writing always embodies a desire to communicate, the desire behind this book is to unsettle the relation that exists between communication theorists and their beloved topic. I will consider my purpose served if I can manage to persuade some of these theorists that the "ideology of the communicative" can and should be fractured.

Part I

The Transcendental Economy

1 / Phenomenology and After

The Whole of modern metaphysics ... remains within the conception of
the existent and of truth initiated by Descartes. — *Martin Heidegger*

One's beginning remains always one's future. — *Martin Heidegger*

One will have understood nothing of the *age*... if one does not think
first the conceptual, dialectical, speculative structure of this *déjà-pas-encore*
[already-not-yet]. — *Jacques Derrida*

In Plato's *Phaedo,* Socrates, awaiting death, recalls how he came to be what
he is; how he was misled by his predecessors; how "traditional wisdom," instead of launching him on a journey toward truth and virtue, set him adrift;
and finally, how his rejection of past teachings put his philosophical voyage
back on track, making the love of wisdom truly worthwhile. Thus ended
the age of myth (*mythos*), as a new form of reflection and wisdom seeking
(*logos*) declared independence from that of the mythopoetic imagination.
Many centuries later, René Descartes, sitting comfortably by his fire, re-
counted a similar story. In both *Discourse on Method* and *Meditations,* Descartes,
too, began his narrative quest for certainty by discussing the necessity of
breaking with tradition, of breaking with influences exerted on him by past
philosophers, which must be exorcised by the earnest, thinking mind. At
least twice in history, philosophy has claimed to begin anew by turning
away from history to reason; both times, philosophy announced a new be-

3

ginning by trumpeting a rupture with its own past, its own memory, as if philosophy would not deserve its name unless it established an absolute discontinuity with what had been done under that name.

This turning away from tradition in order to inaugurate a new beginning was to become an integral part of the philosophical tradition itself, remaining definitive throughout the tradition, "definitive *of* the tradition."[1] Thus when Kant, for example, came to the scene, he was obliged to devote a few pages, "The History of Pure Reason," as the final chapter to his *Critique of Pure Reason,* although, by his own testimony, the few pages bearing that title address a relatively insignificant issue, merely marking an empty space in the architectonic so inessential that its filling out could with impunity be deferred. This tendency of philosophical beginnings to (re-)turn to reason eventually came to be coupled with a turn away from philosophy's own development; that is, "the turn from history tended also to suppress its own history, depriving that history of any positive constitutive role."[2]

It appears as if philosophy can only be born of repression, by forgetting or abandoning once and for all the "futile controversies that are taken, for the most part retrospectively, to have constituted its history."[3] From the very beginning, this suppression of the history of philosophy, of the historicity of thought, has accompanied all the voices of great thinkers, repeating itself *as* the beginning of philosophical thinking. Every philosopher aspires to be the "first" philosopher, and philosophy is thought to be worthy of its appointment only if it (re-)emerges as the "first philosophy." That being the case, it would make sense to perceive Descartes as constituting a radical break with the faith-oriented culture of the Middle Ages.

Descartes's *Meditations* is arguably the most widely read philosophical text of all time. Written in a semiconfessional mode, the six meditations represent a systematic attempt by the skeptic-meditator to purge himself of every belief that he has indiscriminately accepted on some external authority. By doubting the validity of all his previously acquired knowledge, and using as a criterion of validity the clearness and distinctness of ideas, the skeptical meditating I of the narrative discovers in the end one absolutely indubitable fact: *cogito,* I think. This is to be the foundation for—or the beginning of— all future philosophical thought and all scientific knowledge.

Apart from the discovery of an anchoring point for all future knowledge, the most important lesson of Descartes's systemic doubt is that the foundation of epistemological certitude (*ens certum*) cannot be found outside the doubter; the true location of certainty is inscribed within the I who questions everything. In the last instance, it is the skeptical I who is trustworthy, it is the I who should be in control, and following that, it is the I who brings his own hyperbolic doubt to a halt, charting the path of positive knowledge in an opposite direction. This self-certainty of the thinking subject—apodictically founded in the *cogito me cogitare*—becomes the unshakable cornerstone of modern philosophy itself. The essence of a human being no longer resides in things ontologically and theologically independent of that person; instead, it exists in the logically and ontologically prior phenomenon of the *cogito me cogitare*, in which the thinking self appears to itself as *me cogitare*. This Cartesian turning, culminating in the unquestionability of the *cogito sum*, is thus related to the absolute certainty of the *ego*, the distinctive *subjectum* (a certainty attainable at all times), and becomes in one decisive stroke the pathos and the arche of modern philosophy.

Making a debut through distinctive narrative arrangements, the indubitable Cartesian *cogito* inaugurates a new metaphysics, marking a new relation between thinking and being, the latter anchored within the interior clarity and infallibility of the former. When metaphysics is regrounded in epistemology and knowledge is thought to begin with a finite thinking being, philosophizing changes its character dramatically. The comprehensive theological order systematically articulated in Scholasticism and externalized in the grandiose Gothic cathedrals is thus replaced by or reconstituted as a rigorous rational science whose foundation is this-worldly clear and distinct ideas. Mathematics, specifically geometry, becomes the model of knowledge because its formal validity, reflected in the formulation of special axioms intuitively evident in and of themselves, best exemplifies the *mathesis universalis* of which any rational mind is in principle capable. With this foundation in place, philosophy is finally "rationalized," and the "age of reason" dawns with eloquent promises that until recently have had a firm grip on Western theoretical thinking.

If philosophy must always begin anew, if reason must always struggle to reassert itself, then any beginning of philosophy sooner or later comes to an end, for reason, aging with time, is always disappointed by its own "overgrowth."[4] Crisis, in other words, always haunts philosophical projects, every now and then signaling the need to do it all over again. This acute sense of crisis is exactly what Husserl experienced at the turn of this century, and his phenomenology set out to redress this problem by doing everything all over again.

Crisis and Beyond: The Phenomenological Way

When we reconstruct, we have universal ideas. — *Simone Weil*

In Husserl, the theme of crisis is explicit and constant. As early as "Philosophy as Rigorous Science," published in 1911, Husserl discusses two trends that in his opinion threaten the universal validity of philosophy: naturalism and historicism. According to Husserl, naturalism (positivism and sensationism) commits the error of reducing all phenomena to physical states, whereas historicism (for example, *Lebensphilosophie*) makes the mistake of reducing all phenomena to particulars. Symptomatic of a loss of faith in science and a consequent loss of meaning in life, these philosophies foster an irrationalism, furthering a disbelief in reason and creating a crisis not only in the sciences and culture at large but also in philosophy itself. In *The Crisis of European Sciences and Transcendental Phenomenology,* written close to the finish of his career and published posthumously, Husserl takes up this same apocalyptic tone again with an urgent plea for change.

Working under the European ideal of *humanitas,* of the veridicity, value, and intelligibility of human experience against epistemological and moral skepsis, Husserl takes upon himself the task of returning philosophy to its original vocation. "Philosophy as Rigorous Science" opens with the unhesitating declaration that "from its earliest beginning, philosophy has claimed to be rigorous science."[5] But how is this rigorous science to be achieved, given the crisis situation, the "unhappy present" that Husserl compares with the philosophical confusion lamented by Descartes in the early pages of the *Discourse?* The answer lies in rearticulating a First Philosophy in its original Aristotelian sense, a universal science that " 'in itself,' that is, in terms of inner and essential grounds, is first," and that therefore constitutes the "beginning" of all sciences in the most fundamental sense.[6] Understandably, this First Philosophy could not be found in the crisis-ridden European philosophical scene of the time; instead, it had to be (re-)constructed from the ground up, against specters of various dogmatisms nonplussing the European culture before the war. Such reconstruction is the objective of "transcendental phenomenology." "I am convinced," says Husserl, "that with the breakthrough of the new transcendental phenomenology a first breakthrough of a true and genuine First Philosophy has occurred."[7] With confidence and vision, he then proceeds to describe this First Philosophy as the

> science of method in general, of knowledge in general and of possible goals of knowledge in general, i.e., of possible knowledge in general in which all *a priori* sciences that have disconnected all types of the contingent (and also the con-

tingent and material *a priori*) show themselves to be branches which have developed from one and the same science. A *mathesis universalis* stands above all science...as a mathematics of knowledge-achievements.... This highest logic, illuminated by absolute intelligibility... moves within exceptional *forms of pure subjectivity and requires the study of pure subjectivity in its entirety.*[8]

According to Husserl's vision, if transcendental phenomenology is to secure an absolute foundation for philosophy, it must unfold in the form of a basic science of transcendental subjectivity and its constitutive accomplishments. In opposition to empirical sciences, which cling to constituted beings, transcendental phenomenology is concerned with the "region" of absolute being, "since everything we can in general speak of as 'being' (*Seiendem*) is being (*Sein*) for consciousness and must permit the justification for its being posited as being to be exhibited in consciousness."[9] In this way, Husserl reinvokes the exemplary Cartesian quest for the *fundamentum absolutum et inconcussum,* while radicalizing its operation beyond the epistemological self-evidence of the *ego cogito* to a transcendental science capable of justifying "all conceivable a priori sciences." Husserl further explains that

phenomenology [is] the science of all conceivable transcendental phenomena and especially the synthetic total structures in which alone they are concretely possible — those of the transcendental single subjects bound to communities of subjects is *eo ipso* the a priori science of all conceivable beings. But [it is the science] then not merely of the Totality of objectively existing beings, and certainly not in an attitude of *natural positivity*; rather, in the full concretion of being in general which derives its sense of being and its validity from the *correlative intentional constitution.* This also comprises the *being of transcendental subjectivity* itself, whose nature it is demonstrably to be *constituted transcendentally in and for itself.* Accordingly, a phenomenology properly carried through is the truly universal ontology, as over against the only illusory all-embracing ontology in positivity — and precisely for this reason it overcomes the dogmatic onesidedness and hence unintelligibility of the latter, while at the same time it comprises within itself the truly legitimated content [of an ontology in positivity] as grounded originally in intentional constitution.[10]

In this passage, one can discern the basic trajectory of Husserlian phenomenology. As a truly universal ontology, transcendental phenomenology is to move from the naive "natural positivity" embedded in the unreflective habitation in the world through a comprehensive analysis of the process of "correlative intentional constitution" to a final explication of "the being of transcendental subjectivity itself." Many of the key concepts of phenomenology can also be unpacked with reference to this trajectory.

To move beyond natural positivity, of course, does not constitute any new beginning, for every metaphysics begins by questioning, if not negating, the positivity of the natural world in one way or another. How then does phenomenology begin? In the midst of beings, where does the phenomenologist find a starting point whereupon one's naive cognition of reality can be elevated to the reality of cognition? As is well known by its call "to go back to things themselves [*zurück zu dem Sachen selbst*]," phenomenology begins by performing the "reduction," namely, by abstracting or reducing whatever is reducible in experience. But what is reducible in experience? And how does one reduce it? Without tackling the very difficult and multilayered question of phenomenological reduction, one might answer the question simply, still remaining faithful to its principle, by saying that whatever is "transcendent to" consciousness is reducible and hence must be reduced, and whatever is "genuinely immanent in" consciousness is irreducible and hence must be retained.[11]

In Husserl's phenomenology, transcendence and immanence are to be understood in strict relation to consciousness, characterized essentially by its *intentionality*. Consciousness is invariably a *consciousness of* .... The intentionality of consciousness means that consciousness is in the first place outside of itself, that it inescapably transcends itself toward the world, toward something other than itself. In this view, intentionality *is* consciousness, not just a property of consciousness, and as such can no longer be the object for anything else. Defined by intentionality, consciousness does not so much signify the individual unity of a "flux of subjective process" as it does the distinct nature of a mental act that always turns itself toward an intended object. Inasmuch as "all experiences (*Erlebnisse*) are conscious," all experiences are intentional; intentionality is constitutive of *all* forms of consciousness.[12]

Although, as previously stated, "everything we can in general speak of as 'being' (*Seiendem*) is being (*Sein*) for consciousness and must permit the justification for its being posited as being to be exhibited in consciousness," it does not follow that every instance of being is mind-dependent or consciousness-derivative: There are objects or phenomena that are *outwardly beyond* conscious processes. These objects or phenomena represent instances of the in-itself that, although not exterior to consciousness in that their presence depends upon noetic representation, nevertheless hold their opacity and plenitude in opposition to any particular intending act. These instances of being, including numbers, geometric shapes, other mental lives, and so on, are transcendent to the immanent stream of consciousness. They stand as objects that resist in their respective manners any arbitrary appropriation by the reductive consciousness. These objects, in other words, cannot be experienced in toto at any one moment but always involve something extra, another side, for example, toward which consciousness must subsequently advance, without, however, ever reaching completion. The totality of these objects constitutes the realm of transcendence, a region of otherness parallel to and irreducible to the immanent flow of intentionality. Phenomenologically speaking, transcendence does not entail metaphysical commitment, for it does not concern the de facto world but rather the insistent coherence (or coherent insistence) of certain objects against intentional appropriation.

Always intending toward something, consciousness is by its very nature bipolar and reflexive. Not only does it intend toward transcendent objects, but it can also intend toward intending acts themselves within the same conscious process. Being reflexive, consciousness can coil back on its own activities, so that one intending act can become, at a later moment, the "intentional object" of another intending act without any disruption of the conscious flow. The totality of these mental processes, ever ready for such reflexive intending, Husserl calls "immanence," designating not anything transcendent but the noetic constellation of recursively intended objects of consciousness in and by consciousness itself. To the extent that consciousness always stands in relation to an object, "immanence" refers to consciousness's own interior plenitude, while "transcendence" indicates the possibility of exteriority as the very "irreducibility of what is meant to the particular act or acts in which it is meant."[13]

Phenomenological Reduction: From Phenomenon to Eidos

Not only do we have what is intuited as noema, but also there takes place
a *grasping* of the essence. — *Edmund Husserl*

With the transcendence-immanence distinction, the reduction in Husserl's phenomenology unfolds in two steps. In its earliest moment, reduction is descriptively motivated in that phenomenology conceives of itself as radical empiricism in which objects are given the chance to show themselves as they truly are. Starting at the surface of things and surveying phenomena in their manifold presence, reduction at this stage means the suspension of the "transcendence thesis"; the existence of the transcendent objects must be "put out of play," even if the object is posited in "belief." Introduced as a method of registering phenomena exactly as they avail themselves to consciousness, reduction in its descriptive phase remains principally a means to an end. Resembling the archaeological effort to restore buried and distorted artifacts, reduction "brackets" the objective world as given in the "natural attitude," for the objective world is "transcendently posited" insofar as its nonbeing can be conceived. To overcome the natural "belief in being," the naive realist presumption of the in-itself characteristic of the "natural attitude" must be held off or parenthesized, at least until the meaning of the existence of the fact-world (*Wirklichkeit*) is properly understood. That is to say, insofar as the world is present to consciousness, it is retained with all its modalities of presentation (for example, possible, probable, actual, true, attentively noticed, marginally perceived, fantasized, intuited), but its assumed pregivenness is negotiated by the abstracting reflection into a "phenomenon of being." The empirical remains, but it is emptied of its ordinary, mundane, naturalistic investment.

Thanks to reduction, phenomenology becomes "critical," for like any good Cartesianism it rises above the sphere of unchecked assumptions and habits and sets sail on the Kantian-like project of explicating the "conditions of possibility" of knowledge. Facing a tree, for example, a phenomenologist must alter his or her ordinary commonsense reception of it and approach the tree as *noema*. That is, rather than perceiving the tree as existing in actual space and time and possessing all the physical qualities normally attributed to it, the tree may be regarded as an intentional object strictly correlative to the mode of consciousness in which it is given. Because of the change in the mode of reception, a tree in nature is now turned into a noematic tree in consciousness; it becomes a tree-phenomenon whose reality depends solely on the noetic act that intends it. This noematic tree is not the same object as that given originally in the prereflective visual perception, although one has to grant that there is only one tree in front of the perceiver. The object of the perception of a tree is a tree, but the *noema* of this perception is not the tree independent of or prior to being perceived, but rather the polar correlate of the perceptual act that apprehends the tree in that same act. Although the tree in question remains the tree it was, the status of the tree as an object changes from a thing in nature to an object in consciousness. The tree in nature can be burnt or processed for human needs, but the tree arrested in the noetic act certainly cannot. In this way, reduction purifies the perceptual object by neutralizing the prejudgments that under normal practical circumstances would consume it, and in so doing, reduction brings conscious cognition closer to the "reality" of the object in question.

To ground a universal ontology, however, phenomenology cannot be satisfied with describing transcendent surfaces. As can be seen from Husserl's programmatic statements cited earlier, phenomenology is not concerned solely with what actually occurs in conscious living as such; rather, phenomenology uses the method of reduction to uncover *essences*, which are the transcendentally warranting or de jure structures governing actual (de facto) conscious experiences. This is the moment of Platonism in Husserl whereby a descriptively based science of consciousness is expanded to involve an eidetic analysis of what descriptive inquiry first discovers. This Platonic twist causes a change in the direction of the phenomenological epoche, turning what in its inception is conceived as radical empiricism into a kind of essentialism. For essences are not phenomena, and what is essential might not be always phenomenal. An essence is a universal, an ideal entity; as such, it is related by its very nature to an open class of actual and possible *instantiations*. The essence of "two," for example, is related to any number of actual and possible instances of "twoness," such as the number of hands of a normal person, all "couples" of objects, thoughts about couples of objects, and the like. Though embodied in and appearing through manifold instances, essence itself is not equal to any one of its particular manifest embodiments. Instead, an essence must be seen as the *structure that governs* a range of actual and possible objects and as that which makes these objects *objects of the same type*. It is this self-identical structure underlying multiple phenomenal presentations that eidetic reduction seeks to uncover.

Because the essence of phenomena exceeds their particular instantiations, eidetic reduction becomes an inductively based transphenomenal pursuit. Rather than describing phenomena, eidetic reduction must subject noematic objects to a serial, repetitive anatomy, whose purpose is to render the transphenomenal essence present to "eidetic seeing." Since the essence of objects may lie behind their phenomenal appearances, description by itself is not sufficient; imagination becomes necessary. "Research in the region of the essence," suggests Husserl, "necessarily demands that one should operate with the help of fancy."[14] This help of fancy, more exactly known as *free variation in fantasy*, consists of three identifiable steps: exemplary intuition, imaginative repetition, and synthesis.[15]

For Husserl, free variation begins with the intuition of an "elucidatory example." For instance, if one looks at a white page and intends "a white page," the size or shape of the paper, the printed content, and the like are not parts of the de jure essence of "white page" but rather are arbitrary or optional de facto elements in the perception of any given piece of white paper. This intuition serves as a model or paradigm for the second step in the process of "ideational abstraction." Beginning from an exemplary intuition, one can (1) hold the intended object (that is, "a white page") in retention, and (2) vary in turn any of its many aspects. These repetitive variations generate a series of imaginative intuitions that are similar images, or copies, of the original intuition. If the variation is correct and proper, these imaginatively produced copies will have some elements that are different from the original image and some that are identical. As the instances of imaginative repetition are brought forth one by one, certain aspects of each instance may become more explicit than others. In the variations on "a white page," for instance, it is the whiteness and paperness of the imaginative repetitions that stand out and are focused upon, whereas the particular words or symbols on the page or its feel to the hand may be noticed only peripherally to the extent that they are accidental to the intended "white page." It is through this serial, repetitive autopsy that all the nonnecessary elements of the intended object, namely, "a white page," can be removed, thus enabling the phenomenologist-surgeon to inch closer to what is irreducible, that is, essential, to being "a white page."

Although they yield a multitude of interrelated examples, imaginative repetitions do not by themselves result in essential intuition if the final repetition is not *synthetically* related to the rest of the series. If free variation is to result in eidetic seeing, the examples in the chain of variations must not only be *maintained* in retention, but more important, they must also be grasped comparatively through an "overreaching act of identification," an act of "synthetic abstraction," which separates the necessary features of the examples from those that are contingent or accidental to them.[16] Given a series of imagined "white pages," to continue the example, one may ask what defines the white page as white page? Is it the shape of paper that does it? What if one alters the shades of its color? In other words, an active comparative reduction must be performed to isolate the invariant sense element(s) from their multiple imaginative reproductions. It is this play of the "what if" that peels off the optional features of the white page under examination, thus enabling one to identify the "core" (*Kern*), "the indissolubly identical," from among the different examples of white pages that are imaginatively reproduced. Through a step-by-step excavation, the phenomenologist gradually unearths a "universal singular," a "hybrid unity" from a multitude of phenomenal or representational white pages, namely, the pure essence of "white page," which remains selfsame across multiple phenomenal instantiations and without which a particular white page would lack the measure to be what it is. This fantasizing strategy completes the descriptive phase of reduction, a phase of "neutralization" in the phenomenological labor that approaches the real as an index of the phenomenon's essential character open to intuitive insight (*Anschauung*).

This combined effort of descriptive and eidetic reduction radicalizes phenomenology beyond its Cartesian point of departure. Beginning as a science of consciousness, phenomenology evolves into a theory of essence according to which the "I think" tells only half of the story. By separating the *positing* of consciousness from what is *posited by* consciousness, reduction not only recovers the structure of an object's presence but also develops an *analysis situ,* to borrow a phrase from the mathematician Jules-Henri Poincaré, of the cognizing consciousness, offering a structural topology of intentionality premised on the recognition that every *cogitatione* intends a *cogitatum.* Cartesianism is thus radicalized because (1) the moment of "I think" that institutes a simple split of the subject and object is unearthed as a tertiary *ego-cogito-cogitatum* more fundamental than the mind-body opposition, and (2) by bringing fiction into play, eidetic variation actively penetrates objects and facts to their essence (*eidos*), their "universal meaning structure." Such radicalization, of course, would not be possible without reduction. By uncovering layers of meaning strata in accord with their operative consciousness, reduction not only exceeds Descartes's hyperbolic doubt but also revives, in a productive way, the Platonic illumination of the true being of things. J. N. Mohanty describes this trajectory of reduction as follows:

> By bracketing existence so as to be left only with essence, then by bracketing all transcendence so that one is left with the purely immanent experience with its act-noema structure, and finally by suspending the natural world-belief so that what is left over is the domain of consciousness within which the "world" is intended as a noematic structure and the world-belief is recognized *as a belief,* the meditating philosopher finds himself *living* the life of a transcendental ego.[17]

Phenomenology as Transcendental Egology

Only someone who misunderstands either the deepest sense of intentional method, or that of transcendental reduction, or perhaps both, can attempt to separate phenomenology from transcendental idealism. — *Edmund Husserl*

As shown in the preceding passage by Mohanty, reduction has a more distant but definite telos in Husserl's phenomenology. Not only does reduction suspend the world-belief and map the structure of purely immanent mental processes, it also leads, in a positive way, to the confirmation of the primacy of a self-identical ego as the functional center, the terminus a quo, or counterpole, of the transcendent, analogous to the body as the center of orientation and vision.[18] To secure valid knowledge of the world, the origin of knowing must be justified in and for itself. Not content with the reduction of "other," the bipolar consciousness must find within itself an "absolute viewpoint" capable of justifying its various activities. In a progressive movement, reduction shifts its objective from purifying the presence of the world to privileging the performance of a centered and centering ego-subject. "When I regard my life exclusively as consciousness of this world," says Husserl, "I gain myself as the pure ego with the pure flux of my cogitations." "I gain myself" means that I appropriate for myself whatever is my "own" (*eigen*), that is, the for-me-ness of the world. Consequently, "the world is for me only what exists and has status for consciousness in such a cogito."[19] As if the ego wills it, the initial reduction *of* the world culminates in a reduction *to* the ego; everything other than consciousness becomes ego-dependent.

What occurs with this ego centering is that reduction surpasses the negative suspension of the world-belief and eidetic exercise and effects a positive recuperation by *positioning* the ego as the ultimate source of "sense-making" that oversees the "horizonal structure" of beings and guarantees the progressive determination of the indeterminate (*hyle*). That is, if the reduction is carried past its descriptive phase, the world appears not merely as a "phenomenon of being" but as a phenomenon-of-the-world-for-my-consciousness. Husserl continues: "The objective world which exists for me (*für mich*), which has existed or will exist for me, this objective world with all of its objects in me, draws from me (*aus mir*) all of its sense and all of the existential status that it has for me."[20] A metaphysical decision is made at this point, bringing about a glide from the *für* to the *aus*. This decision means that "there is no other dimension of being than the dimension of its being for me," and that "there is but one possible system of limitation," which is that of my reflexive consciousness.[21] Increasingly appropriating what resists interiorization, reduction here reaches a subjectivist closure, through the "for me" to the "from me," where phenomenological effort does not so much reduce as constitute the plenitude of being in terms of the *ego* pole of the *ego-cogito-cogitatum* schema. The *ego* becomes more than the Cartesian doubting-thinking subject; it is elevated above the level of the *res cogitans* and becomes a singular constitutive agent of the world—where the *ego* is, the *world* shall be.

Once the reduction has been performed thoroughly, one is confronted with the pure ego and its entire field of actual and possible consciousness. This pure ego exists for itself in continuous evidence, for it is the ego that constitutes itself as being, and "the *cogitatum* is grasped in the *cogito* and this in the ego which lives 'through' its thinkings."[22] In other words, the ego gets hold of itself not only as a flowing life and stream of experience but as an I, who lives this or that *cogito* as the same I:[23]

> The entire life of consciousness is dominated by a single universal constitutive a priori. Insofar as it is a universal intentional analysis of this life of consciousness, phenomenology cannot fail to lead to this universal a priori, which... is the transcendental ego itself, the transcendental presupposition as spontaneous and originary source itself.[24]

From a radical phenomenological point of view, the reductive process must be continued up to the transcendental ego, the only ultimate and hence irreducible foundation.[25] Anything short of this, argues Husserl, betrays the phenomenological principle and leads to nonsense:

> The attempt to conceive the universe of true being as something lying outside the universe of possible consciousness, possible knowledge, possible evidence, the two being related to one another merely externally by a rigid law, is *nonsensical*. They belong together essentially, they are also concretely one, one in the only absolute concretion: transcendental subjectivity.[26]

The pure ego, presupposing nothing but its own activities, becomes transcendental insofar as it constitutes itself while motivating objective or transcendent beings through its own intentional life. This pure ego thus becomes an absolute being in that it functions as the a priori abiding principle from which the universal ideality of all intentional unities stems. This, in turn, reflects nothing but the pure ego's own coherence in and through its substratal "position-takings." To the extent that it constitutes itself absolutely, this self-identical transcendental ego remains singular, self-originating, and self-justifying through its own active (that is, autoeffected) genesis. Metaphorically speaking, the life of the transcendental ego becomes extremely lonely, not for lack of events or activities but for the sheer absence of any equals; the transcendental ego is by nature solitary. Referring only to itself, the transcendental ego stands at the end of the road of reduction as the foundation of foundations, the presupposition of all presuppositions. For only this presupposition is presupposed legitimately, that is, justified by a thorough reduction. And "it alone," as André de Muralt argues,

> is to be genuinely criticized, it alone is to be by itself genuine and permanent self-criticism (since it is nothing but the transcendental consciousness of the ego by itself) — the transcendental ego being a primordial fact, the originary basis of my own world, and the only absolute presupposition, the presupposition which gives other presuppositions their sense. This ego is the adequate object of a philosophy, the first of philosophies, *first philosophy* or absolute knowledge, which grounds all metaphysics and all philosophy which would present itself truly as science. All the prejudices of the naive-natural world are indices of this fundamental presupposition and need to be intentionally justified by it. So far as they are grounded and criticized in and by it, these prejudices enter as objects into an apodictic and absolutely grounded science which fully realizes the idea of philosophy. Only in this way do the prejudices of the natural world lose their pejorative character by being grounded by intentional reference on the fundamental prejudice. Since as ultimate norm it judges itself, this fundamental prejudice — the transcendental ego — is the source of its own validity and can be called a presupposition or prejudice in a positive sense — i.e., in the sense that it is a necessary foundation, set down *a priori*. The transcendental criticism which it performs with regard to itself thus guarantees that the ego realizes the ideal of presuppositionlessness (*Vorurteilslosigkeit*) which genuine science requires. This is the radicalism of self-constitution by itself, by and in transcendental self-consciousness. The transcendental ego is therefore this originary *Leistung* of self-giving sense. Thus it is impossible to go beyond the ego in a transcendental philosophy.[27]

Descriptive, eidetic phenomenology finally yields to transcendental phenomenology; radical empiricism gives way to an idealism of the ego. All that exists for the transcendental ego becomes constituted in itself according to its own particular manner of constitution. The realist imagery of the absolute exterior, which a misunderstanding of intentionality might give rise to, is definitively removed. "Transcendental subjectivity is the universe of all possible sense"; every imaginable meaning and every imaginable being, be it transcendent or immanent, falls within the domain of transcendental ego as the origin that constitutes all meaning and being.[28] "The universe of true being (*Sein*)" and "the universe of possible consciousness" merge as one in and by the only "absolute concretion" of the transcendental ego. Constitution becomes, without exception, a gigantic project of progressively composing the signification "world." Once the ego is transcendentalized in this way, the for-me-ness of the world and all the noetic possibilities immanent to my consciousness become the "constitutive achievement" of the transcendental ego-subject, which is the only being that can fully grasp the a priori possibility of consciousness and is able to unify the manifold presentations experienced by the empirical ego *temporally.*[29]

According to this description, one can see that phenomenology's "leading back" (Latin *reducere*) to the things themselves does not end up in empiricism, not even transcendental empiricism. Quite the contrary: It ascends to a subjectivist idealist position with the enthronement of a transcendental ego-subject in whom the "world-constitutive" function of consciousness is articulated as that subject's very own performative achievement. Seen in this light, Husserl's transcendental philosophy, as Paul Ricoeur rightly argues, can be interpreted as a philosophy of "sense," giving this term the broadest reading possible. For "the exuberance of consciousness," "the gratuitousness of the 'I think,' " and the "superabundance of being" all find their justification as "sense," as "intentional meaning-units" in the realm of purified "irreality," accessible only to the transcendental vision. The world *for* me — when reduction is complete — "is the sense of the world *in* me, the sense inherent *in* my existence, and, finally, the sense *of* my life."[30] Only the transcendental ego-subject can truly speak of I, can truly claim the world as *mine.*

I and Others: The Problem of Intersubjectivity

In short, we still do not know if, when someone rings the doorbell, there is someone there or not. — *Eugène Ionesco*

You are in my dream, but then I am in your dream too. — *Lewis Carroll*

Husserl's transcendental idealism, relatively reserved in earlier works, finds its most radical expression in his *Cartesian Meditations.* In *Idea I,* for example, consciousness is called a "reminder," a "phenomenological residue," for it is the necessary medium of objects' presence; in *Formal and Transcendental Logic,* the notion of "transcendental ego" or "transcendental subject" is not yet fully thematized. In *Cartesian Meditations,* however, one observes a decisive transcendental turn by way of an empowerment of the ego, and phenomenology is fundamentally egologized. Consequently, what occurs is a total triumph of interiority over exteriority and of the immanent over the transcendent. Ultimately, to practice phenomenology of the ego is tantamount to practicing phenomenology itself, for the ultimate concern of phenomenology is now seen as the "self-explication of my ego, as subject of all possible cognition."[31]

Reduction, which originally is supposed to lead the philosopher back to things themselves, does not end in things but in the realm of transcendental consciousness, whose a priori certainty and apodictic clarity derive precisely from its distance or separation from the natural, mundane environment of things. The search for a presuppositionless First Philosophy finds its treasure in transcendental subjectivity, as the *first* presupposition is no longer relative to anything other than itself. Muralt's summary is worth quoting at length:

> In phenomenology, the process of reflective regress resolves into a transcendental self-normation or pure constitutive act of self-criticism. Transcendental subjectivity is also the ultimate foundation.... It resolves the reflective search for the ultimate foundation in transcendental consciousness, the pure act of self-giving of sense and pure self-constitutive spontaneity. Phenomenology as well as subjectivity thus has the possibility of turning back upon itself; this is the *Selbstnormierung* (self-normation) of the former and the *Selbstbesinnung* (self-giving of sense) of the latter. And this possibility heads off the danger of any *processus ad infinitum*...in the search for the last foundation. The iterative process is not eliminated; but the infinite regress which seems to result from it is, as it were, neutralized by this possibility of self-constitution.... The dynamic movement of constitution is not interrupted, but it is, so to speak, mastered or dominated (*beherrscht*, as Husserl says with reference to the universal a priori). Transcendental constitution shows itself as infinite.... it is an a priori system of determination of an infinite multiplicity, the a priori definition of a multiplicity.[32]

Phenomenological investigation now reaches a resting place in the transcendental subject that in fact is no different from the retroactive starting point of phenomenology's return journey. Driven by the imperative of reduction, phenomenology fulfills itself by becoming a retracing of the steps of an all-encompassing constitution centripetally effected by the ego. This is how Husserl closes off his critical efforts: The unity of the sciences is grounded in the unity of being, which in turn is univocally constituted by transcendental subjectivity.

As can be inferred from the two different functions that reduction plays in its progression, Husserl's phenomenology involves a struggle between two tendencies that might not be as easily reconciled as Husserl himself thought. This conflict (on which Heidegger and Derrida would later capitalize for their respective critiques of Husserl) can be traced to a duplicity inherent in Husserl's conception of phenomenology. Because of this duplicity, one can justifiably speak of two Husserlian phenomenologies.[33] The first one is a philosophy of "constitution," of the *production* of meaning and the constituted objects. For this first phenomenology, nothing is given apart from the labor of the transcendental life. The work of such a phenomenology is carried out by means of the epoche, the suspension of natural belief and the subsequent reduction of the object to transcendental subjectivity.

Parallel to this constitutive phenomenology is a second phenomenology — a philosophy of givenness, of intuitive contact, of the in-person presence of the things themselves. For this second phenomenology, phenomenological work is conducted under the principle of principles as the demand for what is self-presenting. Whereas the first phenomenology proceeds from a critical imperative that admonishes us to take nothing for granted, the second one has recourse to the rhetoric of the granted, given, self-presencing. It is in response to this dual, incompatible demand that phenomenological reduction is forced to play two different, incongruent roles.

On the one hand, as a descriptive endeavor restricted to explicating things as they are given, phenomenology is decisively empirical — not empiricist — because of its respect for the diversity of appearance, for the "quota of strangeness" of the mode (perceived, imagined, desired, willed, and so on) in which appearance takes shape.[34] On the other hand, because of the transcendental shift that causes an idealistic interpretation of its own descriptive moments, Husserlian phenomenology proves to be a post-Cartesian theory of the subject that modernizes the moment of certainty by reducing all otherness in the monadic life of the ego. In his return journey through reduction, the phenomenologist faces not so much the manifold forms of givenness but rather an ego that constitutes the plenitude of all the empirical givens. On the whole, the transcendental tendency overrides the descriptive impulse, and a philosophy of the subject completes its closure in transcendental solipsism.

The problem caused by transcendental solipsism is obvious. If phenomenology is the "elucidation of myself (egology)," how could the otherness of others be justified? "Having arrived at the ego," writes Husserl, "one becomes aware of standing within a sphere of self-evidence of such a nature that any attempt to inquire behind it would be absurd."[35] It may indeed be absurd to inquire *behind* the ego, but that does not mean that there is no problem *facing* the ego. The absurdity of any *behind* could not conceal the trouble that lies well *within* the ego's world of experience. This is the problem of *other* egos and other *subjects*, of the plurality of subjects, and finally, of the reality of the social and the question of tradition or history specific to social or collective life.[36]

It is not difficult to see why the problem of other egos poses a serious challenge to Husserl's transcendentalism. The ego is qualitatively different from other objects in the world. It is not a "tag-end of the world," and it cannot be inferred according to the principle of causality, as can other worldly beings; the ego's relation to the world and things in it is intentional, and it does not fit a niche in a causally interrelated whole.[37] In sharp contrast to this ego-subject, whose certainty is reflected in its own intentional activities and is therefore in constant evidence because of an absolute self-proximity, other egos as such, as David Carr rightly observes, are not *reduced* or *meant* egos (*cogitatum qua cogitatum*); they cannot be "a mere intending and intended (*Vorstellung und Vorgestelltes*) in me, but... precisely *others*."[38] Other egos, in other words, are intentional subjects, too. The problem facing transcendental phenomenology, as Husserl himself formulates it, is "how other egos—not as mere worldly phenomena but *as other transcendental egos*—can become positable as existing and thus become equally legitimate themes of a phenomenological egology."[39] This succinctly frames the central question of *intersubjectivity*, over which hundreds of pages have been generated by Husserl's critics and devotees alike, all attempting to rework the problematic relation between the Fifth Meditation and the four preceding it.[40] In the following I wish to examine this issue. The purpose of examining intersubjectivity is not to adjudicate various positions and interpretations of Husserl's text or to advance yet another argument. Rather, tracing how Husserl deals with this particular problem will bring into sharper focus a certain intrinsic difficulty of the transcendental problematic symptomatically betrayed in an *asymmetry* or *nonreciprocity* between the I and others.

Before we start, it is only fair to let Husserl speak for himself on the issue:

> Contrary to the false ideal of an absolute existent and the absolute trueness of an absolute existent, *every existent* is ultimately relative; not only everything that is relative in any usual sense, but every existent is relative to *transcendental subjectivity*. Transcendental subjectivity alone, on the other hand, exists "*in and for itself*"; and it exists, in itself and for itself, in a hierarchical order corresponding to the constitution that leads to the different levels of transcendental intersubjectivity. First of all, then, as ego I am absolutely existent in my self and for my self. I exist for another existent, only insofar as it is *someone* else, another ego, himself a transcendental subjectivity—who, however, becomes *necessarily posited in me* as the ego already existing beforehand for himself.[41]

One cannot fail to see in this passage a lack of reciprocity between the I and others: the I exists first, in and for myself, and the other ego, though existing beforehand for himself, is nonetheless *posited in me*. Given the priority of the I over the other whose reality depends on a positing act on my part, one can reformulate the question of intersubjectivity in sharper terms: How could a philosophy whose principle and ground is the ego of the *ego-cogito-cogitatum* account for that which is *other than I* as well as all that depends upon this fundamental difference (that is, the objectivity of the world insofar as it is the common object of a plurality of ego–subjects)?[42] If certainty is established only egologically, what happens to other egos, whose certainty is at best putative in relation to mine, not to mention various communities of ego-monads and the sociocultural sedimentations that constitute a distinct historical reality of those communities? The competing strands of reduction and description in Husserl's project are here played out again in the conflict between monadism and the transcendence of others. Should reduction be followed through to the end so that the sense of the alter ego is constituted *by* and maintained *in* me? Or should the originality and specificity of the experience of the other be registered precisely and faithfully as the experience of an ego radically distinct from but no less "certain" than the I? Differences in formulating the question notwithstanding, the answer hinges on whether and to what extent other egos, as other I's, capable of experiencing a world that also includes me, are reducible to what Husserl calls the "sphere of my ownness."

In keeping with the spirit of phenomenology, Husserl starts to tackle the issue by performing the reduction. Because other egos figure as special transcendence, "the temptation to hypostatize this transcendence must be thrust aside through an abstention appropriate to this temptation."[43] What Husserl is suggesting is that if one is to remain a good phenomenologist, one has to perform an initial reduction, the "reduction to sphere of ownness." He explains, "For the present we exclude from the thematic field everything now in question: *we disregard all constitutional effects of intentionality relating immediately or mediately to other subjectivity* and delimit first of all the total nexus of that actual and potential intentionality in which the ego constitutes *within himself a peculiar ownness.*"[44] That is, the special transcendence of others, their transcendence over against me, must be grasped through a transference of the sense "ego" from me to others. Through this transference, the other is regarded as other in the limited sense that it is recognized as something "alien," an alter ego. "In this very specific intentionality there is constituted a new being-sense that encroaches on the own being of my monadic ego. There is constituted an ego, not as 'I-myself,' but as mirroring itself in my own ego, in my monad."[45] This preliminary "reduction to ownness" enables the other ego to take shape in a mirror image of me; the world-for-me of the ego is duplicated with a new center by a reproduction through communicating or transporting to the other what is originally "mine."

It has to be noted, however, that the other ego becomes (that is, through transference) ego only in a derivative, secondary sense, because the sense "ego" is initially constituted in me and for me only. I first constitute the sense "ego," and then I transport the sense "alter ego" to the other. Despite the reduction, the ego is not in any real sense decentered; it simply constitutes another second-order, shadow center, another "being-sense" having a world of its own. Although the reduction indicates to the ego the superabundance of being—I experience myself as a "member of" (*Glied*) a totality of things "outside me" —the ego has yet to experience any real *other* as irreducible "factum."[46] Although the explication of "ownness" has sharpened the contrast between the same and the other and has revealed through the mirroring a transcendence that exceeds the sphere of ownness, the excess of sense attaching to the experience of the other as an alien-I is still rooted in a realm of immanence closed upon itself. To the extent that transcendence is extrapolated on the basis of immanence, all events remain *my* events, and the experience of the other is but an extension of *my* experience. The relation between the ego and the alter ego remains asymmetrical.

New questions now emerge: How does one achieve justified evidence of "a being which is not my own being and is not an integral part of it?"[47] How does one move from the sense "alter ego" to the other as a genuine and legitimate ego-subject? How does one move from the *cogito* to the *sum* who is not a *cogitatum* but another full-fledged *cogitans*? In short, how does one move from a *sense-being* to a real being whose sphere of ownness is "peculiarly his or her own" and is at the same time expansive enough to include me and my world, too?

To answer these questions, Husserl relies on the notion of "analogical apprehension," which is supposed to take into consideration both the primacy of the original experience of the ego and the additional substratum of the experience of the other located within the former. In essence, Husserl's strategy here is not very different from the "argument by analogy" advanced in response to the question of "other minds" in the analytic tradition (such as by David Hume or Thomas Reid).[48] Although his language differs somewhat, Husserl places the weight of the problem squarely on a kind of "analogical grasping," through which the other ego is to be apprehended in its fullness through the experience the ego has of itself. As already made abundantly clear in the debate over "other minds" and "personal identity" within the analytic tradition, the initial difficulty with analogical reasoning is that the experience of the other is never given in the original. I do not see and cannot experience the life of the other; if I did, the other would be me. In fact, the experience of the other is at no time "presented" immediately or directly, but is "appresented" through his or her physical body, which alone is "presented," because only the body *appears* in my sphere and can partake in my perceptual world. Husserl's argument by analogy, like any analogical argument, depends upon an inferential movement from one body, whose experience is given directly and immediately, to another body that *gives* the other but without ever disclosing its interiority. It is the material body, the only datum available in the "sphere of ownness," that forms the basis of the inference; it is the visible that motivates the leap toward the invisible:

> Let us assume that another man enters our perceptual field. Under the primordial reduction this means that in the perceptual field of my primordial nature there appears a body (*Körper*) which, so far as [it is] primordial, can only be a determining element of myself (an immanent transcendence). Since in this nature and in this world my owned body (*Leib*) is the only body (*Körper*) that is or can be constituted originally as an organism (*Leib*) (a functioning organ), that other body (*Körper*) over there — which, however, is also given as an organism (*Leib*) — must have derived it in such a way as to exclude a truly direct and primordial justification (that is, by a perception in the strict sense of the term) of the specific predicates belonging to the organism (*Leiblichkeit*). From this point on, it is clear that only a *resemblance connecting the other body (Körper) with my body* within my primordial sphere can provide the foundation and the motive for conceiving "by analogy" that body as another organism (*Leib*).[49]

The resemblance connecting my body with the other body makes possible what Husserl calls "pairing" (*Paarung*).

For Husserl, pairing designates a basic act of "passive genesis" by which one understands something new and unfamiliar by analogy with something already known and familiar; the new understanding emerges from an antecedent experience that proffers a sort of originary institution (*Urstiftung*). Husserl defines pairing as

> a *primal form of that passive synthesis* which we designate as "*association,*" in contrast to passive synthesis of "identification." In a *pairing association* the characteristic feature is that, in the most primitive case, two data are given intuitionally, and with prominence, in the unity of a consciousness and that, on this basis — essentially, already in pure passivity (regardless therefore of whether they are noticed or unnoticed) — as data appearing with mutual distinctness, they *found phenomenologically a unity of similarity* and thus are always constituted precisely as a pair.[50]

As a form of passive genesis, pairing occurs prereflectively. As Husserl describes it, it enables one to "apprehend at a glance" an object against a prior givenness, against a "*primal instituting,* in which an object with a similar sense became constituted for the first time."[51] In fact, "*each everyday experience,*" suggests Husserl, "involves an *analogizing transfer* of an originally instituted objective sense to a new case, with its anticipative apprehension of the object as having a similar sense. To the extent that there is givenness beforehand, there is such a transfer."[52] As an automatic achievement or act in intentional life, pairing furnishes an associative support for various transfers from the originary to the nonoriginary, from the same to the different, from the here (*hic*) to the there (*illic*), not the least of which includes that from my own body to the alien body.

Few would dispute the fact that individuals need to engage in some form of pairing or analogizing transfer in their everyday dealing with others. But this indicates a practical necessity for normal interpersonal interaction and does not constitute any phenomenological evidence to warrant elevating the paired being to the status of what effects the pairing. That is, the transference based on bodily similarity lacks the full force necessary for validating that the other body is a body of the alter ego and not simply a duplicated example of my own body. "The paired configuration," as Ricoeur points out, "is a universal structure, the initiation of a multiplicity or of a totality. In this respect it is an originary form of all passive synthesis."[53] To the extent that "passive synthesis" occurs in prereflective, antepredicative experience, pairing is a relation that lacks the fullness of a living experience. Because the transference by pairing furnishes only the supposition, the empty anticipation, of an alien life, it requires further confirmation. The body *over there* must be verified in such a way that the being-status (*Seinsgeltung*) can be conferred upon it, thus transforming it from being a paired body into another animate ego-subject.

For Husserl, the burden of verification of the paired body is dealt with in terms of the "concordance" or "harmony" of expressions emitted by the other body.[54] This verification is twofold. First, the supposition or anticipation of an alien subjective process must be subject to confirmation (or disconfirmation) by what that other body expresses. Bodily expressions are "indicative signs" of a nonoriginary presentation of another ego.[55] Second, these indicative signs must exhibit "a unitary transcending experience," and they must do so continuously. The continuation of unitary experiences is paramount to verifying that the other body is indeed as much an ego as the "originary institution" to which it is paired, because

> every experience externalized by the other animate body, points to further experiences that would fulfill and verify the appresented horizons, which include, in the form of non-intuitive anticipations, potentially verifiable syntheses of harmonious further experience. Regarding experience of someone else, it is clear that its fulfillingly verifying continuation can ensue *only by means of new appresentations that proceed in a synthetically harmonious fashion,* and only by

virtue of the manner in which *these appresentations owe their existence-value to their motivational connexion with the* changing *presentations proper, within my ownness,* that continually appertain to them. . . . The experienced animate organism of another continues to prove itself as actually an animate organism, solely in its changing but incessantly *harmonious* "behavior." Such *harmonious* behavior . . . must present itself fulfillingly in original experience, and do so throughout the continuous change in behavior from phase to phase. The organism becomes experienced as a pseudo-organism, precisely if there is something discordant about its behavior.[56]

It is through bodily expressions as indicative signs and through what might be called the "anthropological principle of concordant behavior" that the being-status of the other is verified. If the body in question demonstrates harmonious behavior continuously, it is validated — validation being the progression from the empty sense to the fulfilled sense, safeguarded by a certain "fulfillingly verifying continuation." That is, the fulfillment of verification, itself grounded in a kind of "verifiable accessibility of what is not originally accessible," makes it possible to recognize the other body as an animate ego-subject, even though the experience of that body remains "mediate," or indirect. Such successful verification alters the status of the paired being, elevating it from a physical being to an intentional being, an ego-monad. Just as the "past" in my memory, once verified in terms of the "harmonious synthesis of recollection" *as* my past, "transcends" my living present, the appresented other body, if so verified, would "transcend" my own being.[57] Harmonious verification, therefore, endows a veridical transcendence to the other; that is, "in showing himself as addressed toward me in concordant behavior, he truly becomes '*Other.*' "[58]

Is solipsism overcome or not? Is the "fulfillingly verified" organism in front of me a fully animate other who, if he or she so wishes, might in turn subject me to the same phenomenological scrutiny? Husserl seems to think so, for after demonstrating how other egos coexist with me, Husserl immediately goes on to discuss various higher-level intersubjective phenomena, all of which presuppose the multiplicity of ego-monads. A new dimension is quickly added to egology to form the basis for what Husserl calls the "intersubjective phenomenology," which includes as its major tenets not only intersubjective Nature but also "intermonadic community" and different forms of "social communalization," each possessing "the character of '*personalities of a higher order.*' "[59]

Is Husserl moving ahead of himself? Does egological phenomenology lead to intersubjective phenomenology as smoothly as Husserl makes it seem? Two observations can be made. First, according to the preceding discussion, one can see that Husserl's argument stands or falls with the plausibility of his "analogizing apprehension." But the argument of analogizing apprehension carries sufficient strength to prove that others exist *only if* one attributes equal validity to presentation and appresentation, to what is presented and what is appresented. That is, the experience of presentation and that of appresentation must possess equal credence so that, without diminishing certitude, one can move from what is given originally and immediately (presented) to what originally lies outside the sphere of ownness (appresented).

Second, and perhaps more damaging to Husserl, is the fact that analogizing apprehension and the subsequent verification in terms of anthropological regularity depend on a minimal level of similarity between the two bodies being paired; unless there is sufficient bodily resemblance between those who are being compared, analogizing would not be able to take its first step. Without specifying this minimal condition of similarity, Husserl's reliance on analogizing apprehension is at best circular; consequently, the test of "harmony" or "concordant behaviors" proves to be inconsequential. Could a healthy white middle-aged bachelor successfully pair himself with a deformed pregnant black teenager (not to mention the more extreme situations of anthropological encounters where apparent differences between the observer and the observed are compounded by behavioral discrepancies engendered by radically dissimilar cultural patterns)? Is there any objective standard for behavioral concordance? Where does the phenomenologist find the basis, the common denominator, for an analogical transference? Where does the phenomenologist obtain the criteria of verification? If phenomenological inquiry is ever to stay close to experience, one wonders if Husserl's abstract (and one might add, ethnocentric) reasoning lends any concrete support for his argument. In the absence of any clue as to how these problems might be addressed, there is no reason not to believe that all the others I have encountered and will encounter in the future are mere parts or scenes of my mental theater, which stages nothing but the self-variation of my ego.

To be sure, Husserl is not totally unaware of the problem. At one time, he indicated that "experience *can appresent only because it presents*...that, from the very beginning, *what this experience presents must belong to the unity of the very object appresented.*"[60] Unfortunately, this does not help him a great deal. Granted that there is a causal relation between presentation and appresentation, it does not warrant a slide from the ego (which is presented) to the other (which is appresented) such that the latter acquires exactly the same degree of certainty the former enjoys. At any rate, perception and apperception are two different intentional acts, with their respective correlates. Although perception is defined by a relation of visibility in the living present, apperception claims knowledge beyond perceptual visibility, involving protension and retention that transcend the punctual simplicity of the "impressional now."[61] Although it is true that the apperception of the perceptually unavailable back of a cube, for example, is simultaneous with the perception of the front visible to the perceiver, this simultaneity does not cancel the difference between the two intending acts. While the front of the cube is "authentically given," the back of the cube, as a *meaning more* intended by intuition, remains lodged in the modality of presumptive "cogivenness," subject to change and verification because of the inadequacy of its evidence. In the case of the other ego, what appresented experience of another animate organism achieves, according to Husserl's own testimony, is not so much a factual concretion of the other as an "intentional modification" of the ego:

> The character of the existent "other" has its basis in this kind of verifiable accessibility of what is not originally accessible. Whatever can become presented, and evidently verified, *originally*—is something *I* am; or else it belongs to me as peculiarly my own. Whatever, by virtue thereof, is experienced in that founded manner which characterizes a primordially unfulfillable experience—an experience that does not give something itself originally but that consistently verifies something indicated—is "other." It *is therefore conceivable only as an analogue of something included in my peculiar ownness.* Because of its sense-constitution it occurs necessarily as an "*intentional modification*" of that Ego of mine which is the first to be Objectivated, or as an intentional modification of my primordial "world": the Other as phenomenologically a "modification" of myself (which, for its part, gets this character of being "my" self by virtue of the contrastive pairing that necessarily takes place). . . . In other words, *another monad* becomes constituted appresentatively in mine.[62]

As a *modificatum* of my ego, the other ego could not be more than an ego-analogue and as such could never exist outside the "sphere of my monad." Although the sense "ego" can be transferred to an other, the privileged certainty of "my" ego cannot.

Husserl himself emphasizes the difference of certainty, if not in kind then surely in degree, between the I and the other. After claiming that he has dissipated objections made by skeptics against his solipsism, Husserl is quick to point out that

> at no point was the transcendental attitude, the attitude of transcendental epoche abandoned; and our "theory" of experiencing someone else, our "theory" of

experiencing others, did not aim at being and was not at liberty to be anything but explication of the sense, "others," as it arises from the *constitutive productivity* of that experiencing: the sense, "truly existing others," as it arises from the corresponding harmonious syntheses. What I demonstrate to myself harmoniously as "someone else" and therefore have given to me, by necessity and not by choice, as an actuality to be acknowledged, is *eo ipso* the existing Other *for me in the transcendental attitude: the alter ego demonstrated precisely within the experiencing intentionality of my ego.*[63]

According to this account, the accurate characterization of the phenomenological inquiry concerning the problem of the other is quite clearly that "it considers everything meant purely *as* meant (*cogitatum qua cogitatum*) and withholds any other attitude toward it."[64] As long as the transcendental attitude is preserved, the phenomenology of the other is "by necessity and not by choice" an analysis of the "sense" of the other that is its only delegate in the purified realm of transcendental consciousness. Insofar as the other is given, the task of phenomenological exercise does not go beyond arriving at a circumstantial account of its being-for-me. In the final analysis, the other amounts to no more than a moment in the "constitutive productivity" of the ego. Stated differently, it is the I who *constitutes* the other as constituting and understands itself as constituting and not constituted by the other, even though the fact that the other also constitutes me could be found in the sense that I attribute to the other *as constituting*, too.[65]

Husserl's failure now becomes apparent, for it can be recalled that the other ego as such has to be more than a sense, more than a being-for-me. The other ego, to repeat what was pointed out earlier,

cannot even be considered purely as meant; or, to the degree he is, he is no longer an ego. Thus the concept of the ego in general is incompatible with the phenomenological concept of something given, at least if the alter ego is to be considered transcendental and not merely worldly. *To the extent that he is given he is not a transcendental ego, and to the extent that he is transcendental he is not given.*[66]

Even though the appresented ego achieves the "sense" ego, it is still the I who gives this sense to that ego. Within the transcendental sphere there can be only *one* ego, which is then multiplied associatively. That being so, the I-other relation is essentially asymmetrical, or nonreciprocal. "The apodicticity of the existence of the Other remains derivative from mine."[67] "The alter ego does not *himself* exceed my actual and possible consciousness."[68] Inasmuch as the other ego is derivative from my ego, what Husserl calls the "illusion" of solipsism cannot be said to have dissolved.

Phenomenology and Philosophical Modernism

The System is almost finished, or at least under construction, and will be finished by next Sunday. — *Søren Kierkegaard*

What does this Husserlian failure mean? If the illusion of solipsism is not dissipated, what implication is there for transcendental phenomenology as First Philosophy? Throughout his career, Husserl maintained that phenomenology does not create but rather discovers — a hyperempirical principle no critical philosophy after him has been able to ignore.[69] But, as can be seen in the preceding discussion, the explication of the sense "other ego" serves only to confirm the I as the ultimate sense-giver. Although egology is qualified in that the alter ego is granted objectivity as constituted sense, the absolute status of the ego is never forsaken or compromised. On the whole, the Husserlian enterprise does more than explicate the sense-component of different strata of intentionality; in fact, reduction gives birth to a transcendental ego-subject as the last guarantor of objectivity. Driven by the desire to reach a *ground,* phenomenology begins as an archaeology of consciousness but ends as a universal science of the *sovereignty of the subject.*

Most philosophers agree that Descartes substantized the ego, substituting the dualism of two substances (*res cogitans* and *res extensa*) in lieu of the chasm between the ideal and the real instituted by Plato. For Descartes, however, "the privileged idea of the *cogito* secures no more than a tangential contact with the real, ever to be renewed and never expandable beyond the immediate present."[70] The *cogito* for Descartes is not an all-inclusive being, for it still recalls, at the risk of epistemic circularity, the principle of a benevolent God to protect it from illusions. Although the privileged *cogito* is endowed with the highest degree of certainty, the mind by itself "possesses no warranty of truth whatever."[71] In fact, for Descartes there is always a potential gap between the mind's cogitation of a state of affairs and its truth, a space in which doubt can lodge and be mobilized. Once universal doubt is declared, the burden of attaining truth (not certainty) "lies entirely in a deliberate, clearly conscious effort of the subject."[72] This is why epistemology achieves a status on a par with metaphysics. "The new rationalism to originate from Descartes' school," concludes Louis Dupré, "certainly resulted not from an initial confidence in reason, but from a cautious trust in the subject's ability to circumvent the obstacles in the path of reason by means of the more fundamental power of the will."[73]

The sovereignty of the subject in Descartes is therefore a limited and conditioned one. Although it establishes the ground for certainty, it leaves open the question of truth to which Kant's transcendental critique might be interpreted to represent a response. But Kant remedies the situation "by defining the objectively real itself in conceptual terms," leaving, unfortunately, "the residual reality of the *thing-in-itself.*"[74] Even when Kant dignifies the subject, at the withdrawal of God, as the center of knowledge, the subject is conceived above all as a "finite being," which in the final analysis amounts to no more than a "simple proposition." In fact, it is the very finiteness of the subject that makes possible the production of knowledge as *representations.*

With Husserl, the sovereignty of the subject is pushed to a new height. By means of the epoche, the Cartesian doubt is stripped of its damaging skeptical edge, and the Kantian mystery of the noumena is displaced by a descriptive-cum-genetic analysis of what displays itself to the relational consciousness. Husserl's ego, unlike the Cartesian "thinking thing" constantly embarrassed by its double, hence dubious, nature of being both a foundation of knowledge and concept and an object in the world definable by the same categories applied to physical objects, does not meditate on the world and truth but rather constitutes them. And the ego in Husserl, unlike the Kantian ego, does not merely regulate perceptions and understanding according to the principle of reason in a complex system of checks and balances among various faculties; it *constitutes* everything other than itself.[75] The ego becomes a *performing ego* that "as free before all reflection is always absolutely certain of itself beforehand," and correlatively, "the world in its 'holding sway' (*Walten*) is nothing other than the free play (*Spielraum*) of the transcendental subject."[76] In the Husserlian transcendental phenomenology, there is no longer any "residual reality," and the transcendental subject reigns without challenge through its constitutive productivity.

This is no small matter. For the absence of any residual reality means not simply that the ego is established as the basis of all possible truth but, more significant, that a certain unqualified and unqualifiable moment of simple presence — call it "transcendental subject" — now stands as the *ultimum subjectum* of total being. The return to origin in Husserl is a return to the absolute *concreta* of transcendental consciousness "in which all other regions of Being have their root, to which they are essentially related, on which they are one and all *dependent* in an *essential* way."[77] Determining others, the transcendental subject itself is beyond determination; making others present, it remains itself unrepresentable. It is, as it were, the subject's becoming God that remains at all times self-identical because of its autorepresentative structure built upon total self-transparency. It is in such an autoconception of a subject beyond determination that modern philosophy arrives at its hitherto unfulfilled telos. It is in such a subject-foundation that the stillborn Cartesian dream of supreme subjectivity as the autofoundation or autopositioning of a subject presenting itself as consciousness finds its final expression. And, last but not least, it is in the self-assuredness of this same subject-foundation that the "Cartesian anxiety" that has been tormenting philosophers for too long finds its effective alleviation.[78] In this regard, Husserlian phenomenology can certainly be read as the high point of philosophical modernism, a grand narrative of metaphysics that rewrites the principle of reason or logos in the form of a totalizing philosophy of the subject.[79]

To be sure, many themes are central to Husserl's thought: his apriorism, his intuitionism, his ahistoricism, his idealism, often indistinguishable from a metaphysical subjectivism à la Berkeley or Leibniz, and so on.[80] But it is his neo-Cartesian quest for certainty founded on an absolute subject that is decisive. And in Husserl, the paradigm of subject-object relation is explicitly thematized and formulated in terms of an intentional consciousness that functions as the permanent source of meaning and value. When the transcendental subject is enthroned as the *origin of all meaning and identity*, the break with the classical tradition is completed, and philosophical modernism comes to full fruition in the absolute singular sovereignty of the subject. Gone is the disquieting dualism; in comes a totalizing monism. In philosophical modernism, the objective finds its home in the subjective: *The objectivity of the object turns out to be nothing other than the subjectivity of the subject*. The last chapter of the modern philosophy of the subject is thus written, wherein *mathesis* (the universal science of measurement and order) and *genesis* (the temporal constitution of things), which up until now have had independent determination, articulate with one another harmoniously for the first time.

Husserl introduces phenomenology as an answer to the crisis-ridden European culture. As his answer unfolds, however, one is told that the crisis of culture has its root in the crisis of self. At the end of *Cartesian Meditations*, invoking the Delphic motto "Know thyself!" Husserl writes, "I must lose the world by epoche, in order to regain it by a universal self-examination."[81] "Noli foras ire," says Augustine, "in te redi, in interiore homine habitat veritas [Do not wish to go out; go back to yourself; truth dwells in the inner man]." After all, this might be what Husserlian phenomenology is all about: Go back to yourself and you will find the light. It is in the inner person that truth dwells. There is no need for others; the reflective I will do. After a long search for certainty, phenomenology ends not only in transcendental solipsism but also, to borrow Foucault's apposite words, in "transcendental narcissism," in which the self-responsible subject dreams up the truthful world during an uninterrupted "anthropological sleep"—well, at least till next Sunday.[82]

2 / Communication before Deconstruction

The end of a philosophy is the account of its beginning.
—*Maurice Merleau-Ponty*

Husserl's genius derives in large part from his determined pursuit of a genuine starting point for philosophical reconstruction. If the trajectory between *Logical Investigations* (1900–1901) and *The Crisis of European Sciences and Transcendental Phenomenology* (1936) appears to be punctuated by too many shifts and changes, it is because Husserl believed that every time phenomenology is practiced and regardless of the topic it pursues at that moment, it must start from the ground up. Consequently, each of his works is a radical "return journey" in which philosophy itself is always a major philosophical problem. It is to the relationship between a philosophy's beginning and end that the father of phenomenology devotes most of his energy, meticulously thinking through time and again what his student Eugen Fink aptly called the "paradox of the beginning of philosophy."[1] It is also in exploring and remapping the terrain between the beginning and end of its return journey that Husserl came to differentiate the transcendental and the empirical, making possible a reflexive project in which the transcendental unfolds as an archaeological inquiry into the empirical in "an ever-renewed experiment in making its own beginning."[2]

Although Husserlian phenomenology was severely criticized from the start, Husserl's vision of a First Philosophy did take root and became one of the more prominent exemplars of twentieth-century theoretical thinking. By the beginning of the second half of this century, phenomenology had developed into something more than a movement in philosophy; with increasing cross-disciplinary influences, it expanded—geographically and conceptually—well beyond its original context and established itself as a major conceptual edifice against which many other fields measured their critical advance. The spilling over of phenomenology into the humanities and social sciences was particularly noticeable during this period and had the far-reaching effect of disencumbering the received paradigms of many nonphilosophical disciplines. In sociology, for example, ethnomethodologists started to "describe" the everyday "life-world" from an "insider's" point of view—a perspective invoking a "discursive authority" rather different from that of the dominant positivist sociology.[3] Similarly, in literary criticism, what is now known as "reader response theory" can be traced to the groundwork of Roman Ingarden and Mikel Dufrenne—a perspective directly inspired by Husserl, which stands in marked contrast to the system building of Northrop Frye or the free-flowing "practical criticism" of I. A. Richards.[4] Although it is debatable whether phenomenology caused an irreversible paradigm shift in the social and human sciences, its wide-ranging influence in both domains seems beyond dispute. It would not be unfair to say that "contemporary critical theory is the legacy... of a desire to use Husserl in order to go beyond Husserlianism," a legacy one sees reflected in such contemporary concepts as "reduction," "presence," "transcendence," "the subject" (or its death), "the life-world," "temporality," "transcendental consciousness," and "deconstruction."[5]

The discipline of communication studies has not been immune to the influence of phenomenology. Although it is difficult to date precisely when the "philosophy of communication" emerged, unmistakable signs of its birth can be seen in the late 1960s and early 1970s, foreshadowing an emerging critical consciousness in a new generation of communication scholars who drew on phenomenology to examine the very conceptual foundation of their discipline.[6] Understandably, the concept of communication itself formed the focus of their reflection. To the extent that the term *communication* signaled the beginning of a whole new academic enterprise, the need to "go back to that beginning point itself" was immediately felt.[7] A return journey was embarked on, bringing about a distinctive philosophical turn in the short history of modern communication studies, a moment of radical self-critique that sought to reestablish the scene for future theory building.

In this chapter, I examine the meaning and significance of this philosophical turn within communication theory and research. My analysis proceeds in two steps. First, I describe how this philosophical consciousness, awakened by phenomenology, makes possible the clear articulation of a subject-based problematic that gives an underlying unity to competing theoretical discourses on communication. Second, I show how and why these theories, because of their indebtedness to an idealist theory of the subject, *necessarily* fail to answer the question of "mediation" prescribed by the problematic. I should point out that my purpose is not to offer a direct critique of any specific body of thought labeled "communication theory" in the relevant literature. Rather, by examining the effects of the "formal rule" that the problematic of communication imposes on theories, I offer a conceptual archaeology that traces not only the outer limit but also the internal fault lines of communication theories' discursive space.

A Note on the Problematic

The real foundations of his enquiry do not strike a man at all.
　　　　　　　　　　—*Ludwig Wittgenstein*

The light dove, cleaving the air in her free flight, and feeling its
resistance, might imagine that its flight would be easier in empty space.
　　　　　　　　　　—*Immanuel Kant*

Through the metaphor of a dove in flight, Kant cautions that pure reason without preconception is impossible, and that any attempt to develop pure reason by itself is doomed to fail. The flight of thought toward truth requires the assistance of preconception just as the flight of a bird needs the resistance of air—a Copernican idea clearly too difficult for a bird to comprehend. Autonomous as they appear to be, the activities of the mind depend nevertheless on a preexisting objective world upon which reason imposes its order. For Kant, the finitude of mind does not limit knowledge; instead, it makes knowledge possible by opening up the possibility of cognition as representation. This is the lesson Kant learned from reflecting on the meaning of the New Science of the seventeenth century, the century of Kepler, Galileo, and Newton; this is also the starting point of critical philosophy as we know it today.

Although "reason has insight only into that which it produces after a plan of its own," thinking is always thinking about *something,* however unthematized that something might be.[8] Knowledge, therefore, always has before itself—spatially and temporally—a preunderstanding of that which the thinking subject tries to grasp. The "hermeneutical circularity" incurred in this process of knowing, however, is not as vicious as some methodologists would have us think; on the contrary, the essential character of human cognition is that it always unfolds in a dialectic of question and answer, in a double movement in which experiences and concepts fold upon one another to form understanding.

If thought cannot proceed without a preunderstanding of the thought object, if scientific thinking is always directed by an implicit question, what is the preconception of communication that prompts inquiry, sustains theoretical reflection, and finally, leads to the construction of theories? Answering this question is not simply a matter of discovering one common definition of communication unconsciously held by communication theorists; nor is it a matter of reformulating an implicit preconception into an explicit problem and evaluating competing theories of communication as better or worse responses to that problem. Because the preunderstanding that guides theoretical activities remains always subterranean—that is, implicit, unthematized, and all too often ambiguous—any attempt to rewrite it too precisely runs the risk not only of reducing its vital complexity but also of overlooking the possible contradictions involved in the pretheoretical dialectic between preconception and theory, between experience and science. To recover the full significance of a particular preconception and its subsequent transformations through disciplined theoretical reflections, one needs to look beneath theories to uncover what Louis Althusser, building on Gaston Bachelard's notion of "epistemological field," calls the "problematic." To identify the problematic in question, one has to perform (again following Althusser's lead) a "symptomatic reading" of the available theories in order to reconstruct the system of concepts behind the words, that is, to discover the "discursive network" that predates specific theoretical maneuvers and that, as conceptual background, ordinarily escapes any surface reading of those theories.[9]

Althusser deploys the notion of the problematic in defense of Marx against his detractors. Denouncing historicist, idealist, and economist interpretations of Marxism, Althusser contends that there is a resolute shift in Marx's work, a theoretical rupture beginning in *The German Ideology* and maturing in *Capital*. To fully appreciate the significance of this shift in Marx and the subsequent formation of a new "continent of knowledge," namely, historical materialism, whose discovery Althusser considers comparable to Thales' contribution to mathematics or Galileo's to physics, Althusser argues that one must go further than the unmentioned presence of the thought of a living author to the presence of his potential thoughts, to his problematic, that is, to the constitutive unity of the effective thoughts that make up the domain of the existing ideological field with which a particular author must settle accounts in his own thought.[10]

For Bachelard, and for Althusser as well, an epistemological field does not mean a clearly defined disciplinary territory; rather, it means the unsaid horizon—a "pretheoretical neighborhood"—circumscribing discursive activities interrelated by certain shared concerns and themes. An epistemological field constitutes a "problematic" that functions as the latent thought-structure enabling the production of theories within its scope. As the unmentioned, silent, conceptual matrix underlying specific scientific researches, the problematic can be characterized as "the structural unconscious" of scientific discourse, for it offers working scientists, through nuanced suggestions, "the indispensable theoretical minimum" that makes their collective enterprise possible.[11] To the extent that scientific inquiry is a regulated activity, and given the fact that science does not and cannot study everything in the universe, scientific research necessitates a principle of relevance that determines for the scientific community "the forms of the posing of all problems and what is seen as relevant to the problem."[12]

Building on Bachelard's insight, Althusser uses the concept of the problematic to designate "the particular unity of a theoretical formation."[13] For Althusser, the problematic represents the overall framework of a system that puts the basic concepts of a theory in relation to one another, determines the nature of each concept by its place and function within that system of relationships, and last but not least, confers on each concept its peculiar, system-specific significance.[14] As a formative agency of theoretical production, the problematic makes possible an ordering of the pretheoretical chaos, creating a plan, a geo-structure that unifies multiform theoretical practices. Simply put, not only does the problematic grant legitimacy and viability to specific research questions, thus drawing forth theoretical exercises as topic-driven, coordinated interrogations and replies, it also endows these exercises with coherence and unity by setting the parameters of theorists' collective explorations. Indeed, it is the problematic's power to determine what counts as a legitimate scientific objective—that is, what comes into the *pre*-view of a given science—that enables Althusser to characterize the problematic as the "condition of possibility" of any theoretical production.

Because of its dual capacity of predefining for a theory the forms in which problems can be posed and of suggesting, prior to specific experiments or analyses, what kind of solution this theory is able to provide, the problematic can be viewed as a theory's internal mechanism of inclusion and exclusion. As a behind-the-scene decision maker over what can be problematized and what must remain unquestioned throughout a theory's development, the problematic brings into play the *first* determination a theory must undergo — instituting, without explicitly justifying itself, a structure of di-*vision* that predisposes the theorist's gaze as it opens up the theoretical or ideological field.[15] Althusser elaborates:

> What actually distinguishes the concept of the problematic... is that it brings out within the thought *the objective internal reference system of its particular* themes, the system of *questions* commanding the *answers* given by the ideology. If the meaning of an ideology's answers is to be understood at these internal levels it must first be asked *the question of its questions.*[16]

Since activities of theorizing presuppose a pretheoretical neighborhood delineated beforehand by the problematic — that is, since theoretical activities are fundamentally motivated by the system of questions prescribed by the problematic — the problematic emerges as the virtual commander of theoretical maneuvers. The problematic commands by speaking first; in fact, it must have spoken, through its own system of questions, prior to the theorist's response. Consequently, mapping out the problematic of a theory requires identifying *the question of its questions,* a *mother question* that not only articulates the theory's internal reference system with regard to a given topic but also determines theorists' practices as coordinated interrogations and replies. Identifying this mother question thus becomes a preliminary but necessary step in understanding the formation and transformation of a theory.

The Question Then . . . : Communication and the Communicative Subject

Questions are invented, like anything else. . . . The art of constructing a problem is very important: you invent a problem, a problem-position, before finding a solution. — *Gilles Deleuze*

Individuum est ineffabile.

What is the "question of its questions" underlying communication theories? What is the mother question to which different communication theories respond in fundamental unity? When communication scholars theorize about communication, what is the commanding question they *must* answer? If, as Gilles Deleuze remarks, questions are invented, what is the story behind the invention of this commanding question? How does this commanding question assume the problem-position it does, and how does it manage to have its demands fulfilled? In essence, how do communication theorists problematize their presumed subject matter such that their diverse presentations display a formal coherence and parallelism?

Despite its differing formulations, the central challenge facing all communication theories is the question of how individuality is transcended.[17] How is it that different individuals, isolated in their respective biographical experiences, come to understand one another? How do people resolve their differences, transcend their private thoughts, and render their subjective experiences shareable with others? In short, how is "shared meaning" or "understanding" achieved?[18] At first glance, this hardly seems to be a real problem, for nothing seems more certain and natural than the various communicative activities we engage in every day. Our lives as social beings are built upon an ongoing process of communicative events or activities, a fact so massively self-evident that it does not seem to need any analysis.

This commonsense confidence in communication is easily shaken, however, if we assume a skeptical stance toward the taken-for-granted in everyday life. The assumption of this contra-phenomenological posture subjects mundane experiences to a critical analysis that asks, How and when does communication occur? Such a critical stance unsettles our natural attitude toward communication by problematizing the taken-for-granted, by reframing our naive beliefs regarding the way communication works. The naturalness of an everyday occurrence and the certainty associated with it are suddenly cast into doubt; common sense is suddenly turned into a theoretical puzzle. As Ricoeur writes: "For an existential investigation communication is an enigma, even a wonder. Why? Because [it] . . . appears as a way of transcending or overcoming the *fundamental solitude* of each human being."[19]

The existential wonder of communication derives from the following: On the one hand, communication seems to be an indubitable fact, reflecting events that take place constantly in and appear to be confirmed by our ordinary, day-to-day existence; on the other hand, communication appears to be enigmatic, seeming to run counter to our deeply entrenched belief about selfhood, our intuitive (self-)understanding that a person's individuality is characterized by something only he or she possesses, a privacy or difference that sets that person apart from all others. This enigma reflects a tension, a conflict, between a natural certainty and the skepticism raised against that certainty by a reflective turn of mind.

As can be inferred from Ricoeur's remarks, communication becomes enigmatic only to the extent that individuals are conceived as essentially separated from one another—separated, in Ricoeur's words, by the "fundamental solitude of each human being." The question of the possibility of transcending individuality would not be real unless individuals as subjects of communication were understood as being isolated from one another in both their physical and psychic-imaginative lives.[20] The problematization of communication therefore presupposes a specific conception of subjectivity that defines concrete individuals as *essentially* solitary. Solitude and privacy—in short, noncommunication—describe individuals' fundamental mode of being, and the theoretical challenge of communication follows from the difficulty of "transcending or overcoming" what might be called the "egocentric predicament" of monadlike, coexisting individuals: Although individuals' bodies exist within one another's reach, a meeting of their minds remains, unfortunately, out of the question.

As obvious as it sounds, the understanding of human subjectivity as essentially solitary stems from a long tradition in philosophy. In fact, reflections on the solitary subject are as old as the discourse of philosophy itself. One hears talk about the Socratic *cogito* (the person looking to his or her own soul), the Augustinian *cogito* (the "inner" person distinct from the flux of "external" things and "higher" truths), the Kantian *cogito* (the *I think* that accompanies all of my representations), and the existentialist's "man" (whose meaningless, involuntary birth is matched only by an equally absurd and lonely death); recently, there is no lack of discussion about the disappearance of the subject altogether.[21] Regardless of the vicissitudes that cardinal philosophical concepts normally undergo, the truth remains that no reflective philosophy has successfully articulated itself without reinterpreting its predecessors' expressions of the *cogito*.

As noted in chapter 1, the conceptualization of the subject takes a significant turn in Descartes. "By lifting the ego out of its immediate entanglement in the world and by thematizing the subject of thought itself, Descartes establishes the apodictic certainty of self as a result of the clarity and distinctness with which it perceives itself."[22] Through introspection, Descartes puts the self—the ego, the subject—on its own feet, setting it free from all unmediated relation to being. As the means by which consciousness grasps itself in unity, self-reflection marks the human being's rise to the rank of a subject. It makes the human being a subjectivity that has its center in itself, a self-consciousness certain of its own standing. This is the first epochal achievement of the concept of "reflection," and it characterizes modern metaphysics as a metaphysics of subjectivity.

This privileging of the *cogito* by Descartes, as Heidegger argues in "The Age of the World Picture," radically alters the meaning of the notion of "subject," that is, of *subjectum,* or (to use the original Greek word) *hypokeimenon.*[23] Prior to Descartes, the *subjectum,* or *hypokeimenon,* is conceived as a kind of basis or foundation of beings, one that has "no special relation to man and none at all to the I."[24] With Descartes, however, man is first turned into a thinking being, and this thinking being is then turned into "the primary and only real *subjectum*—the relational center of that which is as such."[25] The autonomy of a self-thinking of thought, of the *cogito,* of the subject, is firmly secured. The subject becomes an original, fundamental, and founding agent of itself. *"Liberum est quod causa sui est."* Only the subject that knows itself, and thus finds the center of all certitude in itself, is free. The subject emerges as what is "caught in the first place," the *primum captum* whose truth is freedom as self-regulation. In Cartesian metaphysics, subjectivity becomes the theoretical origin from which objects receive their status of objectivity and in relation to which everything else is inquired about. This is the first decisive moment in the modern philosophy of the subject, whose sway, thanks to three hundred years of cultivation, had become all but impossible to resist at the beginning of this century.

As I pointed out in the previous chapter, this Cartesian subject is pushed to a new height by Husserl. In *Cartesian Meditations,* Husserl introduces his project by lamenting the loss of the radical spirit of Cartesianism and calling for its renewal, a second Cartesian overthrow in response to the "demand for a philosophy aiming at the ultimate conceivable freedom from prejudice, shaping itself with actual autonomy according to ultimate evidences it has itself produced, and therefore absolutely self-responsible."[26] Husserl thus launches a "ritual purification" of Descartes by first demonstrating the prejudices implicit in the Cartesian construction of the unprejudiced and then exorcising those prejudices by installing a disinterested transcendental subject in lieu of Descartes's *res cogitans.* This transcendental, or reduced, ego, argues Husserl, is not like the Cartesian *substantia cogitans,* "a little *tag-end of the world.*" Husserl's ego "is not a piece of the world . . . [and] neither the world nor any worldly object is a piece of [the] ego."[27] This purified, but wakeful, ego-subject is reduced to and hence indistinguishable from pure consciousness itself as a "non-participant on-looker" that always refers to itself in referring to the real. Embracing the "impulse" of Descartes's *Medita-*

tions, but avoiding the "seductive aberrations, into which Descartes and later thinkers strayed," Husserl cuts consciousness free once and for all from the world and posits an unworldly flow of intentionality as an absolute origin of things.[28] Every object, every being becomes a meaning *for* consciousness and, as such, is *relative to* consciousness. "The reduction," writes Ricoeur,

> thus places the Husserlian *cogito* at the heart of the idealist tradition by extend-
> ing the Cartesian *cogito,* the Kantian *cogito,* the Fichtean *cogito.* The *Cartesian
> Meditations* go much further in the direction of the self-sufficiency of con-
> sciousness and move as far as a *radical subjectivism* which no longer allows any
> outcome other than conquering solipsism by its own excesses and deriving
> the other from the originary constitution of the *ego cogito.*[29]

By exorcising Descartes's aberrations, Husserl collapses the polar structure of *cogito-cogitatum* by *subjectivizing* what is supposed to transcend the func-tioning *cogito.* This is the birth of constitutive phenomenology, the moment of idealization in an originally descriptive project, out of which the tran-scendental subject emerges as the "principle of principles," an absolute I who functions as the sole source of exterior plenitude. Subjectivity surfaces as (or rather results in) *subjectivism,* and the prejudice of the self-identical ego is reinscribed by Husserl's transcendentalese as metaphysical truth.

This idealizing subjectivization of reflective consciousness severs the sub-ject irrevocably from the world: The inward spiraling of reflection secretes ideas in the exclusive privacy of the ego, away from others. This is how phenomenology rearticulates the Cartesian I, and in so doing, it also mod-ernizes nineteenth-century idealism's notion of the "subject" by reviving Descartes's epistemological impulse. Unlike Hegel, whose subjective ideal-ism narrates as universal history the story of the mind's coming-to-know-itself through a long march of alienation and misrecognition, Husserl re-jects the historicist perspective and adopts the phenomenological reduction to counteract any speculative dialectic that claims to unify the self and other through sublative mediations. Yet, unlike Søren Kierkegaard's antidialectic of authentic selfhood, which approaches individualization by way of a nega-tion of the undifferentiated identity of self and other, Husserl's reflection is grounded in an epistemologically tested transcendental ego-subject that stays clear of any social determination, any encounter with others. A new meta-physics of interiority is born, an updated apriorism of interiority reaffirm-ing the boundary between reality and illusion drawn long before by Plato.

By grounding metaphysics in epistemic certitude, Husserlian phenome-nology rejuvenates an interest in transcendentalism, providing a veracious finale to the Enlightenment-inspired project of modernity. As such, it functions more or less as the nontranscendable horizon of metaphysical thinking in the twentieth century, representing, as Derrida might say, metaphysics' finest hour as it revamps the stage for various contemporary philosophies of the subject. It is in this intellectual context that the problem of communication assumes its modern formulation by severing its link with the classical study of rhetoric, defined as the practical art of verbal persuasion. Moreover, it is against the backdrop of a modernized transcendentalism that the solitary subject of communication is thematized. Derived from a transcendental subjectivism, the subject of communication cannot but be defined as a unique, isolated—that is, lonely—entity. Characterized by his or her essential aloneness, by his or her detachment from worldly contingencies, the individual communicating subject is conceived on the basis of a knowing, self-conscious mind existing with but irretrievably distanced from other subjects and the social world.

Communication as Mediation: The Postal Principle

I never told you anything, only transferred what I saw or believed I saw.
—*Jacques Derrida*

I need to voice a cautionary note concerning my preceding remarks. I am not suggesting that the communicative subject *is* the phenomenological subject. I *am* suggesting, however, that it is phenomenology, or more exactly, the Husserlian phenomenology through its rearticulation of the Cartesian paradigm, that frames the construction of the communicative subject. The Husserlian ego-subject presents a philosophically tested, and hence conceptually credible, picture of person/mind, according to which communication scholars, consciously or unconsciously, develop their own image of the agent of communication. In other words, modern communication theories borrow from phenomenology a specific image of the I that furnishes the anthropological assumption indispensable for addressing the problem of the transcendence of individuality. Without this image, the central question of communication would not have been "invented"; without this image, the issue of the transcendence of individuality would not have achieved its problem-position.

Having achieved its system-specific problem-position, this image of the I—the subject of communication as an essentially discrete, solitary agent of meaning and action—begins to function as a *primitive* term in the problematic of communication theories. The solitary subject becomes a primitive of the problematic of communication first because it is a necessary constituent of the problematic, and second because the nature of this constituent is determined before its participation in the problematic, prior to the construction of theories. As a pretheoretical given, the conception of the solitary subject renders the sharing of feelings or experiences between individuals problematic, although it remains itself unquestioned. For this very reason, the theoretical challenge of communication is translated as the challenge of privacy—a challenge resulting from the encounter of multiple communicative subjects, each characterized as a disparate realm of private meanings and experiences. The postulation of the solitary communicative subject thus becomes the precondition for theorizing about communication, for it legitimates raising the question of communication to begin with and at the same time anticipates possible answers to it under the condition set by the problematic.[30]

Formulated as the transcendence of subjectivity, of the solipsistic I, the problem of communication can immediately be rewritten as a problem of mediation. That is, given two or more self-enclosed, islandlike monads, what must intervene to break their respective self-enclosure? What must come between those monads to free them from their egocentric predicament? Because precommunicative subjectivity signifies *privacy, singularity,* and *identity,* communication is thought to transcend this privacy, this singularity, this identity and to transform individuals' private being (that is, their solitude) into a different form of cobeing—a new condition of mediated existence in which the difference and distance between individuals, caused by the precommunicative privacy, are superseded.

Translated as the happening of mediation, communication represents the embodiment of an interplay between self and other, between that which stays the same and that which appears to the former as different. It becomes a dialectic of identity and difference in the true sense of the term, for it occasions an adventure, a journey (*ventura*) from the self to (*ad*) the other, through which the self approaches itself *other*-wise; that is, *re*-cognizing itself anew through the mediation of an alien double. True to the Hegelian *Aufhebung,* this process unfolds as a simultaneous overcoming and sustaining of an origin, a progression in which an initial moment gives way to a subsequent condition through sublative syntheses. Such a dialectical happening brings about a transition from individuality to sociality, from private, or lonely, existence to community/commonality. This is the telos of communication as a dialectical becoming. Thanks to the transformation it brings forth, the initial alienation that plagues isolated individuals is overcome, and the I becomes (a member of) the We.

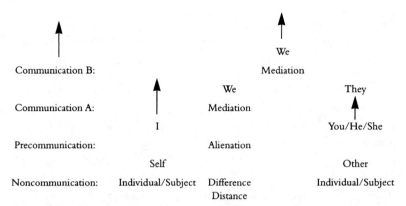

Figure 1. The problematic of communication

We can diagram the problematic of communication as in figure 1, which describes the basic structure of communicative events, according to which the transcendence of precommunicative subjectivity can be plotted as a series of mediations. The confrontation of two given terms (I and you) at one level reaches toward a synthesis (we) at a higher level, only to be unified again with yet another opposing term in an ascending spiral. According to this picture, the change from noncommunication to communication can be seen as the movement of the subject in relation to its other, a movement in which the monadic closure of the self breaks open and precommunicative solitude is transformed into a state of communion as a function of exchange in time. Two minds meet, and this meeting of minds sublates alienation by constituting a new identity for both parties. From this dialectical point of view, despite perspectival differences or contextual variations, all forms of communication can be interpreted as moments within a mediational becoming that moves the participants from one situation to the next, from one kind of relationship to another.

With the notion of mediation, have we arrived at the "question of its questions" underlying communication theories? If, indeed, one can translate the central problem of communication into a question of mediation, is the issue of mediation then the "mother question" raised by the problematic of communication? Why is the problem of communication so readily translatable into an issue of mediation? Is it because the notion of mediation itself is dominated by, or is an instance of, another more general but so far unknown principle that telegraphically governs the inner workings of the problematic as a whole at a more global and deeper level?

As I pointed out earlier, mediation presupposes difference and distance. Yet, as one can also observe from figure 1, the idea of communication as mediation is predicated on two conditions: First, the subject is prepositioned within the theoretical space opened by the problematic; that is, the agents of communication — I, you, and the like — are fixed, predefined terms. Second, the mediation between those agents (that is, when communication succeeds) involves a projected movement toward a new identity as the very transcendence of their premediational difference and distance. Bound by the possibility of a fixed starting point, the process of mediation, as indicated earlier, can only be teleological; it displays a directed, prestructured progression as the overcoming of precommunicative differences.

Given the fixity of subjects' positions in the problematic, communication as mediation can be easily redescribed as the delivery of messages from someone, somewhere (the sender) to someone else, somewhere else (the receiver). To the extent that the solitary subject is posited, that is, as long as the subject of communication is predefined as a self-enclosed, unconnected source of meaning and intention, communication as mediation must be viewed essentially as a sending (*envoi*), an event of *giving* oneself *over*, during which a representative of the subject, something representing or standing for the subject, is dispatched to another party, another subject. To communicate, in this view, is to make happen the event of transmission, to bring about an alteration of one's identity through transmission-based exchange. At the same time, however, since the journey of mediation is predetermined as one of eliminating difference and reducing distance, this delivery or sending of the message turns out to be a return of the message, because the destination of the message, of that which is sent by one signatory, is determined before the sending of that message. Written by a signatory and addressed to a receiver identified beforehand, the message (that is, that which represents the subject) in fact travels inside a closed circuit, inside a homogeneous space; like a letter, it moves from one address to another without ever leaving a premapped territory.

A number of points concerning communication as delivery can be inferred here. First, the notion of communication as the delivery/return of messages presupposes the identity of both the addresser and the addressee. For a message to be delivered, the address(ee) must be accurate and must be known prior to the sending by the addresser. Second, this in turn presupposes the proper function of a delivery apparatus — a "postal system," to borrow an apt metaphor from Derrida.[31] As a system of addresses in which senders and receivers are represented (that is, identified) in terms of their distance from one another, the postal apparatus ensures a regular exchange by which messages can be sent "under proper signature to the proper recipient."[32] In fact, the message can be *freely* delivered precisely because it is *in chain*. Third, the notion of delivery/return also presupposes the identity of the message. Traveling across the post's chain of relays—the post being "nothing but a 'little fold,' a relay to mark that there is nothing but relays"—the message keeps to itself; it remains unaffected by the process of sending.[33] It travels throughout the postal service in good working order; that is, "under the diversity of words from diverse languages, under the diversity of the uses of the same word, under the diversity of contexts or of syntactic systems, the same sense or the same referent, the same representative content would keep its inviolable identity."[34] Having an identity and being able to keep it intact during delivery, the message circulates *as* message but always inside the postal network, whose function is to protect or maintain this property (that is, identity) of the message in transit. Addressed to private citizens and yet depending on a public institution for its service, the messages, to draw on Derrida again, are like postcards; they are both closed and open, private and public at the same time. Although written for one, postcards are nevertheless available to be read by many—"even if in an envelope, they are made to circulate like an open but illegible letter."[35]

My point is that the dialectic of mediation, which articulates the problematic of communication, is itself governed by another more general principle, a principle I call the *postal principle*. As the hidden law regulating sending and receiving in general, the postal principle governs all mediations as exchange in its most generalized sense. In other words, by regulating sending and receiving in general, the postal principle also regulates the dialectic of mediations from the beginning; it regulates mediations as exchange *in principle*. Understood in this way, the postal principle can be viewed as the *medium* of communication as such, the universal mediator that mediates all events of exchange within a given network, *rather than the reverse*. The postal principle becomes *the* law of communication and enjoys an absolute status in relation to events of mediation in that it governs—rather than being governed by—them. The postal principle, qua universal medium, achieves this governance by establishing a system of equivalences, a structure of substitutability, within the given network of postal relays. By providing a universal measure of systemwide substitution, a standard for intrasystemic translations, the postal principle effects the reduction of the different into the same, the domestication of the alien into the customary, and, as urban planners say, the gentrification of the unfit into the acceptable. In so doing, it confers proper "currency" to messages, making them mobile as well as well posted, namely, making possible their movements as *transmissions.*

Representing a principle governing sending and return in general, the postcard is no longer simply a figure, image, or trope of mediation. In fact, just the opposite is true. Exploiting the figurative power of the postcard to counteract the lure of metaphysical reasoning, Derrida writes: "If on the contrary I think the postal and the post card from the side of being, of language, and not the inverse, etc., then the post is no longer a simple metaphor, it is, as locus of all transfers and of all correspondences, the 'proper' possibility of all possible rhetoric."[36] As the locus of all transfers and correspondences, the post mediates every exchange; it mediates all mediations. No longer one metaphor among many, the post must be recognized as the structural principle of metaphorization itself, the most general *perspective* of mediation, which all mediations must observe. In this way, the postal principle unifies the concepts of communication, exchange, and mediation under one rule, namely, its own *rationality* as universal mediation. To the extent that the problematic of communication involves the identity of the addresser, of the addressee, and of the message, and the proper functioning of a delivery mechanism, it is overdetermined by the "postal ideology," by the structural principle of preordained delivery. Although it determines how events of mediation are regulated, the problematic of communication is itself a subordinate structure, determined as it is by the postal principle. In short, it is itself a "determined text" inscribed in the general text of postal tracing and retracing. In fact, the concept of communication can be translated so effortlessly into the concept of mediation because both notions partake in the same economy of the *envoi,* both are governed by the same *postal ideology.* If, as Althusser suggests, a problematic works through a chain of command leading from question to answer, one could say that the postal principle is the sole occupant of the command post within the problematic of communication.

That communication should be construed as a postal affair is not just an ethereal thesis produced by theoretical reflection. It represents a major leitmotif in our cultural imagination, a widely held doxa frequently rehearsed in the venues of modern popular culture. Take, for example, a recent advertisement by the Japanese telecommunications company Hitachi: "Communication is not simply sending a message...it is creating true understanding—swiftly, clearly and precisely."[37] The message from Hitachi seems unambiguous: communication is not a mere sending of messages; it is the creation of true understanding with clarity, precision, and speed, in short, the kind of efficiency that Hitachi promises to deliver. In the tele-postal epoch in which we now find ourselves, messages like this are sent to us all the time by the ever expanding modern-day post offices (from Federal Express and home-shopping networks to the Internet). But is this message as simple, clear, and reasonable as it first appears? Does the sender, Hitachi, really know or mean what it transmits? Can we, the receiver, decide what the message is? Whether or not one agrees with Hitachi's message, whether or not one shares with Hitachi the faith in the coming of a communication utopia, a world made transparent by true understanding among its people(s), one can at least raise the following questions: How could "true understanding" (as opposed to "false understanding," which a mere sending of messages creates) be possible if receiving is not already inscribed in the sending? And how could this "true understanding," if it were possible to "create" it, be communicated "swiftly, clearly and precisely" if the sender and receiver were not already blessed with the kind of delivery system that Hitachi is trying to market? Finally, if we are already in possession of an efficient delivery system, and if true understanding can be achieved through efficient communications, should we not conclude that communication is but mere sending, that communication is *nothing but* "simply sending a message"?

Metaphorics at Large in Communication

Metaphor, then, always carries its death within itself. And this death, surely, is also the death of philosophy. But the genitive is double. — *Jacques Derrida*

The foregoing questions give us reasons to rethink Hitachi's message. More than that, they make us wonder whether a message, or any message like Hitachi's, can ever be as clear, simple, and reasonable as it first appears. Most of all, they make us wonder whether any sender, to the extent that he or she sends a message in the form of "communication *is*...," is not somehow as confused in his or her sending as Hitachi seems to be. In any case, we have reason to be suspicious as to whether any message that states "communication *is*..." can be free from its own postal determination, its own postal metaphorization. In the following, using these questions as leads, I intend to show how, despite their best efforts, theorists' attempts to "define" communication are necessarily frustrated by the same postal metaphorization that is already at work within the problematic as a regulated whole, how seemingly straightforward statements about communication are curved by the same kind of "postal pressure" that converts the question of communication into one of mediation.

To begin, let us imagine the following situation: A student, sufficiently intrigued by Hitachi's advertisement, decides to take a course in communication theory to find out what communication is. As he expected, the instructor begins the class by discussing the word *communication,* offering along the way several working definitions: Communication is the *transmission* of information from a source to a destination; communication is a *negotiation* of meaning among individuals in determinate situations; communication refers to the sequence of interactions through which individuals *coordinate* their behaviors with one another to achieve their respective goals; communication is the *convergence* of individuals' intentions through both verbal and nonverbal activities; and so on. Before the instructor can go on, however, the student raises his hand and asks the instructor to explain these sentences. As it turns out, the student does not know what *transmission*—let alone the more abstract words such as *negotiation, coordination,* and *convergence*—means in its sentential context. Having been in similar situations in the past and fully aware of the danger of abstract talk, the instructor decides to use her tried-and-true method: elaborating the notion of transmission through the example of sending a message from one computer terminal to another over an electronic network; elaborating the notion of coordination through the example of two students moving a refrigerator from the trunk of a car to the third floor of the residence building; elaborating the notion of convergence through the example of two roommates' choosing which video to watch; and so on. The student seems satisfied, and the instructor is reassured of her teaching ability.

For the sake of precision and generalizability, let me break our hypothetical scenario into five segments, summarized as follows:

1. X (the student) wants to know Y (the concept "communication").
2. X goes to Z (the instructor) for help.
3. Z sends X the following messages: *transmission as* sending an E-mail message (M^1); *negotiation as* two people moving a heavy object (M^2); *convergence as* two friends reaching consensus in a decision-making process (M^3).
4. X receives Z's messages.
5. X obtains the desired knowledge by having understood Z's messages that Y = M^1, M^2, M^3.

Looking at the diegetic loop from 1 to 5, one can see that Y is successfully expounded by appealing to three examples, M^1, M^2, and M^3. In other words, episodes of mundane activities, namely, M^1, M^2, M^3, presumably familiar to

X, are strategically chosen to provide the tangible referents for the word *communication* (Y). By referencing these examples, the instructor (Z) succeeds in facilitating the student's comprehension of a signifier in question by anchoring it in concrete signifieds. Various definitions of communication (Y *is* M^1; Y *is* M^2; Y *is* M^3) can then be reintroduced, each invoking one of these preselected examples-signifieds whose familiarity to the student abets the definitions' validity and correctness. As it is not my purpose to catalogue all the possible examples here, it will suffice to note that in each case communication is invariably explicated with reference to certain other events or processes that in one way or another reflect the dialectical journey discussed earlier.

The examples used by the professor (M^1, M^2, M^3) create what can be called "surrogate ideas of communication"—familiar images selected to illuminate communication, to give communication's variable contour a stable visage. Snapshots of everyday events, these images of communication originally are means to an end; they are intended as pedagogical devices— conceptual midwives working as illustrative samples to help the student (that is, anyone with "an eye for resemblances," as Aristotle says) gain insight into something else on the basis of an "archaic (original) trope": communication is *like* a dialogue, communication is *like* the flow of quantifiable information in a cybernetic system, and so on. As we can observe from this scenario, however, because of their critical importance to X's understanding of communication as an abstract concept, these surrogates, despite their pedestrian appearance and origin, quickly overstep their assigned function and stand *in place of* the concept that they are supposed to illustrate. To the student so instructed, seeing two people typing messages to one another across a computer network, for instance, is not *merely seeing* two people punching strings of letters back and forth on the keyboards; it is *seeing that* they are *communicating*. Something beyond perception takes place in this instance; something more than perceptual information is successfully transmitted from Z to X. What happens, in effect, is a usurpation of the abstract by the concrete, a reversal of the signifier (Y) and the signified (M^1, M^2, M^3), where the vehicle overtakes the tenor and the images replace what they are chosen to illuminate (Y = M^1, M^2, M^3). In other words, by supplanting the concept they serve, by standing in its place, these images *of* communication slough off their representational heuristic character and become founding concepts themselves ("Y *as* M" becomes "Y *is* M"). "Concepts need conceptual personae (*personnages conceptuels*) that play a part in their definition," but in this case the conceptual personae have taken the place of the concept they are supposed to help define.[38] As far as the student's understanding of the concept "communication" goes, it is the particular (M^1, M^2, M^3) that constructs the universal (Y), rather than the reverse.

Because of the covert metaphorization (for example, the shift from "Y *as* M^1"to "Y *is* M^1") in the sending of M from Z to X, M^1, M^2, and M^3 have discreetly become *constitutive of* the student's understanding of communication. As this little classroom drama shows, not only do M^1, M^2, and M^3 make Z's lectures explanatory and expressive, thus making possible X's comprehension of Y, but, more important, these surrogate images perform an *epistemic* function in knowledge production, displaying a power beyond their explicative value in directing second-order theoretical acts, acts that rely on the availability of proper "definitions" of communication, for example, constructing "models" of communication. These images, as Lawrence Grossberg notes, "are discursive codes or theoretical vocabularies available as resources for the articulation of communication theories in the present historical-intellectual situation."[39] Effecting a transference between the literal and the figurative, more precisely, reversing the order between the idea and the example, these images are not just innocuous "rhetorical flowers" that wither away after their metaphorical charge is released; rather, they are *enabling images* charged with *"expressing the idea"* of communication, which by itself is perhaps unthinkable except through the "controlled insight" of specific troping.[40]

Clearly, there is no denying the value of metaphor in teaching as well as in learning. Linguistically, metaphor is one of the most cost-effective means of conveying the similarity in difference. As Derrida reminds us, "as an effect of *mimesis,* the manifestation of analogy," metaphor is *"a means of knowledge,* a means that is subordinate, but *certain.*"[41] Metaphor assists in the acquisition of new information by showing resemblance, by linking the known to the unknown. It is rooted in the pleasure of *knowing* as recognition of the same in the apparently different, thereby making possible the expansion of meaning and understanding through an epistemic extension in the mode of "as if." Although metaphorical transfer represents a necessary moment in theory construction, however, an overreliance on fundamental troping to the degree of usurpation described above raises serious questions regarding the validity of explanatory discourses in which the usurpation takes place. For while the use of metaphor is rhetorically effective in concept explication — recall how quickly our student is satisfied by the instructor's explanation — a generalized troping in theory inevitably compromises the theory's logical rigor and coherence.[42] Most of all, it raises questions as to whether theories, particularly communication theories, are nothing but postal constructs, narratives made of rhetorical sentences rather than truth-functional propositions. Before exploring this issue in detail, I wish to take a brief look at what Derrida says of the role of metaphor in philosophy, as his reflection will guide my rereading of the problematic of communication in the following section.

Following Nietzsche's iconoclastic claim that truth is nothing more than "a mobile army of metaphors,"[43] Derrida extends the argument so far as to suggest that philosophical discourses in general, which have traditionally been claimed to be "colorless," are in fact metaphorical through and through; that philosophy, in a word, is "white mythology," after the French idiom *nuit blanche* (white night), which refers to the forgotten events of a sleepless night caused by intoxication, anxiety, or other agitated states. In Derrida's opinion, philosophy is white, not colorless, and mythological, not rational, because the founding concepts of philosophy are irredeemably metaphorical: the metaphor of "sun" for Plato and Aristotle, the metaphor of *lumen naturale* for Descartes — in fact, the whole heliotropic system of metaphors underlying the Western metaphysics *tout court*.[44] For this reason, metaphysicians are, as Derrida quotes Anatole France as having said, "sad poets, they take the colour out of ancient fables, and are no more than collectors of fables. They produce a white mythology."[45] But because of a series of white night–like events, philosophers have lost or forgotten the metaphorical origin of their writings, their mythopoetic condition of possibility buried by memory lapses as if during the long sleepless night of the Occidental Reason:

> *Metaphysic* — the white mythology which reassembles and reflects the culture of the West: the white man takes his own mythology, Indo-European mythology, his own *logos*, that is the *mythos* of his idiom, for the universal form of that he must still wish to call Reason.... Further: *White mythology* — metaphysics has *erased* within itself the *fabulous scene* that has produced it, the scene that nevertheless remains active and stirring, inscribed in white ink, an invisible design covered in the palimpsest.[46]

For Derrida, then, philosophy is (and cannot but be) a culture-specific *tropology*, a *metaphorics* that universalizes itself by claiming to be about reason but that in fact has either forgotten its tropological root or erased — not so innocently — its metaphorical ground.[47] Believing itself to be written in *proper* language, in a language proper to logos, philosophy has not merely denied the voice of its own *nonproper*, namely, metaphorical, subtext; worse still, because of this denial or willful ignorance, it has become powerless to *control* the tropology that empowered it in the first place. Failing to recognize its root "in a higher order of metaphorics (the founding tropes)," the white mythology, imbued with faded metaphors, mistakenly thinks of itself as colorless and rootless; it thus becomes ignorant of or oblivious to the fact that it must use and always has used metaphors—at least one—as the proper concepts within its own constitution.[48] It is this process of metaphorization that produces the "proper" of philosophy that philosophy proper can no longer articulate; it is this double maneuver of forgetting and erasure that pushes philosophy's own condition of possibility outside the domain of its own circumspection of control and surveillance.[49] Indeed, philosophy was born, but this birth was possible only by forgetting "*l'unique thèse de la philosophie,*" its history of pregnancy, its pregnant history. In Derrida's opinion the results are costly, however:

> Philosophy is deprived of what it provides itself. Its instruments belonging to its field, it is incapable of dominating its general *tropology* and *metaphorics.* It could only perceive its metaphorics around a blind spot or central deafness. The concept of metaphor would describe this contour, but it is not even certain that the concept thereby circumscribes an organizing centre; and this *formal law* holds for every philosopheme. . . .
>
> . . . It is therefore enveloped in the field that a general metaphorology of philosophy would seek to dominate. Metaphor has been issued from a network of philosophemes which themselves correspond to tropes or to figures, and these philosophemes are contemporaneous to or in systematic solidarity with these tropes or figures. This stratum of "instituting" tropes, the layer of "primary" philosophemes . . . cannot be dominated. It cannot dominate itself, cannot be dominated by what it has itself engendered, has made to grow on its own soil, supported on its own base.[50]

Born of an (in)voluntary ignorance and forgetfulness, philosophy *always* and *already* has been what it seeks to deny or conceal: *Metaphysics is metaphorics.*

Although it remains an open question whether Derrida's "hermeneutics of suspicion" toward philosophy's origin can be extended beyond philosophical writings, his critical diagnosis of philosophy's nonphilosophical foundation does inspire skepticism toward the foundation of communication theories. Not only does it spawn suspicion of communication theories' epistemic adequacy, it also, at the very least, gives reasons to subject communication theories to a similar diagnostic critique. If philosophy is indeed "mythology," that is, a tropology with its tropological origin erased or forgotten, can the same be said of communication theories that also—at least initially—rely on metaphors? If communication indeed cannot be thought or imagined other than through a set of enabling images, what does this necessity imply for the problematic of communication in general and the theoretical possibilities within that problematic in particular? If theory building in communication inevitably employs and deploys metaphors, however implicitly — that is, if metaphors institute rather than simply represent (or constitute rather than simply decorate) — might it then not be the case that theories of communication are, in reality, rhetorical constructs no different from what are normally described as "literary or fictional" artifacts, since their syntax, like philosophy's, is borrowed from and made possible by an outside language, the language of metaphorics? Furthermore, if communication theories are essentially rhetorical constructs, that is, if they are a *function* of a certain "system of metaphors," what is the discursive logic — what Derrida calls the "formal law" — of this metaphorical space that renders the discourse on communication "incapable of dominating its general *tropology* and *metaphorics*"?

These are not trivial rhetorical questions. They bear directly on the very foundation of communication theories, and to the extent that a theory always presupposes an (implicit) philosophy of its subject matter, the answers one gives to these questions will determine whether or not communication theories succeed in achieving the objective set out for them. If it makes sense at all — as Derrida thinks it does — to proclaim the "end" of metaphysics because of its mythopoetic genesis, can one also speak of the "end" of communication theories if they, too, unfold according to the same structural principle of determination? Without being too dramatic, my question can be stated simply: How much do we learn from reading communication theories if what they offer amounts to nothing more than a mere commutation between one set of concepts and their surrogates? Before one can answer this question, one needs to go back to the problematic of communication, to reexamine the ground in and on which communication theories are constructed.

Rereading the Problematic of Communication

Let us agree that... communication is only possible between two persons used to the same... forms, trained to code and decode meaning by using the same key. — *Michel Serres*

For, as the proverb says, they cannot know each other until they have eaten a requisite amount of salt together. — *Aristotle*

Roland Barthes once cautioned that "those who fail to reread are obliged to read the same story everywhere."[51] To reread something is not simply to go over it one more time. Rereading must resist parrotry; it must constantly be on guard against repeating the old message. To reread the problematic of communication in this sense requires that one perform the double task of "staying within" its parameter and yet remaining "indifferent to" its suggestions. But how does one do that? Because reading is never innocent, never without preconceptions, one needs to be aware of what one is looking for so as not repeat what one wishes to avoid. Perhaps a good way to begin, then, is to ask how the problematic of communication as an active structure of determination is itself *determined*. In what sense is the problematic of communication itself a *determined* structure of determination? Since the problematic of communication is governed, as suggested earlier, by the postal principle, our task is to find out if and how this postal government itself displays the same kind of metaphorical displacement that is displayed in the postal construction of communication.

Now let us pick up the thread we left in mapping the problematic of communication. As suggested earlier, the problem of communication can be redefined as a question of mediation. Mediation, as also suggested earlier, presupposes difference; there must be at least two subjects in an oppositional relation of some sort. (I should add that opposition or antagonism between two parties is not the enemy of communication; indifference is.) The oppositional relation between the two creates a tension that carries them toward a resolution through a sequence of negotiation and coordination. During this process, the participants are forced to exchange their roles. In verbal communication, for example, any utterance must be issued from the other's point of view if the verbal exchange is to continue. Although far less dramatic than the Hegelian scenario of role reversal resulting from participants' "struggle to death," each and every word in the linguistic event "expresses [both speaker and listener] in relation to each other. I give myself verbal shape from another's point of view," and the other must do the same.[52] As the product of a reciprocal relation between speaker and listener, "the word is a two-sided act ... determined by whose word it is and for whom it is meant."[53] Verbal communication is thus always *dialogic* in nature; it requires a minimal level of reciprocity and would not be possible without perspective-taking—what George Herbert Mead calls "taking the role of the other"—on the part of the participants. One enters into conversation only to become an other for the other; in conversation one appears to the other as an other.

In "Platonic Dialogue," Michel Serres attempts to sketch the condition of possibility of dialogue and its relation to what is called the "dialectic" in idealist philosophy.[54] Employing the language of information theory, Serres argues that dialogue always depends on a joint effort by the interlocutors to fight against "noise," against any third party that threatens the reciprocity between the interlocutors. Serres's argument is based on the recognition that, in every communicative event, participants "must unite against the phenomena of interference and confusion, or against individuals with some stake in interrupting communication."[55] Whether it is the casual exchange of greetings, a routine or intimate phone conversation between friends, or the most serious philosophical discourse, such as the *Meditations*, sender and receiver, writer and reader, must join forces to expel the interference, the evil demon, a "third man," namely, any party that may interrupt the sending/receiving of messages. Since the transmission of signals is always in danger of defective channels, hysteresis, espionage, and inadvertent errors of all sorts, a successful communication requires a constant vigilance against impurity and confusion. It requires a struggle, on the one hand, against the irrelevant and ambiguous signals that must be pushed back into the background and, on the other hand, against the cacophony in the signals that the interlocutors address to one another—the regional accents, mispronunciations, inaudible pronunciations, stammerings, coughs, ejaculations, dysphonias, words started and then canceled, and ungrammatical formulations—and the cacography in the graphics. Indeed, it is the dynamic dialogism underlying all forms of linguistic exchange that leads Serres to conclude that to communicate *"is to suppose a third man and to seek to exclude him*; a successful communication is the exclusion of the third man."[56]

According to Serres's neo-Socratic viewpoint, communication is fundamentally an act of exclusion, for it involves a necessary violence to silence and resist the outsider: the barbarian, the intruder, the stranger. Because of their joint effort against a common enemy, interlocuters in action, argues Serres, "are in no way opposed, as in the traditional conception of the dialectical game; on the contrary, they are on the same side, tied together by a mutual interest: they battle together against noise."[57] To communicate in this sense is to form an alliance among coconspirators, to create a *socius secretus* of friends or equals "who are not each Other for each other but all variants of the Same"—in short, to create a *city*, a civilized community composed of rational, reasonable, free individuals bonded together by a common project of holding back the tide of noise or symbolic pollution.[58] It is this bilateral attempt by interlocutors to drive away the alienating other during their linguistic exchange that leads Serres to conclude further that "the most profound dialectical problem is not the problem of the Other, who is only a variety—or a variation—of the Same, it is the problem of the third man."[59] Although mediation involves two opposing terms, the oppositional relation between them rests fundamentally on the principle of cooperation, on a preelected telos of commonality or identity. Although communication appears to involve only two subjects, a successful exchange of messages always presupposes the threatening presence of a third party — what Serres calls "the prosopopeia of noise" — against whom the sender and receiver enact the collective ritual of exorcism.

While no one can deny the importance of perspective-taking and the principle of cooperation in verbal exchange, one crucial question nevertheless remains: How is noise or interference, namely, Serres's third man, to be excluded? What is it that enables interlocutors to identify or detect beforehand the prosopopeia of noise, thus preventing its intrusion and disturbance? On what basis do they unite and fight on the same side at the outset? From where do discoursing residents of the city obtain the "requisite amount of salt," as Aristotle quaintly put it, and how much of it do they have to consume before they can communicate with one another? Simply stated, if communication as mediation is based on a fundamental cooperation, what makes cooperation possible in the first place?

These questions all seem to have an easy answer: language. As long as individuals *speak the same language,* so goes the folk wisdom, communication will not be a problem. Language provides a universal medium that unites the interlocutors and locates them on the same side against cacography, against cacophony, against nonsense, against heresy (*hairesis* [choice]). In a well-known statement on linguistics and poetics, Roman Jakobson presented a rapid survey of the constitutive factors in any act of verbal communication:

> The *addresser* sends a *message* to the *addressee.* To be operative the message requires a *context* referred to . . . a *code* fully, or at least partially, common to the addresser and addressee . . . and, finally, a *contact* . . . enabling both of them to enter and stay in communication.[60]

Obviously, the most critical factor of all in this depiction of communication is the code. *Speaking the same language* means adopting the same code. Code is the key to successful communication in that it provides for communicators a standard of translation, thus allowing the addresser and the addressee to exchange their reciprocal roles, turning the source into reception and reception into source. Controlling all kinds of semiotic traffic within the postal zone, the code establishes the possibility of *commonality* in a world of difference, locking in messages as it locks out the intruder as well as the eavesdroppers. Internally, the code establishes the basis for coordination; externally, it allows those who adopt the code to combat and exclude those who do not.

The code thus enables the communication between two originally solitary and unconnected subjects, for it is the code that mediates the precommunicative difference by opening up a passageway betwixt and between two private worlds: Embodying the measure of equivalence, the code works as the go-between that couples two worlds "according to a given rhythm." But we could push further the question raised earlier and ask exactly how the code does that. What is so special about the code that it is able to help individuals transcend their differences? On what basis does the code provide the key for conversing individuals to establish commonality? The answer lies in the assumption that a code is essentially *intersubjective*. By its very nature as well as in principle, a code is the living and working embodiment of intersubjectivity. Although it must be internalized, the code cannot be the exclusive, private property of any individual. Not only must the code be recognized as binding and functional by those who adopt it, it must also be recognized by code users as efficacious against private meaning, against autism. Since rules can and do change, and since they can be violated deliberately, in accounting for the way the individual's private meaning is transcended, the availability of rules of exchange or cooperation is not as important as the *postulation, ex hypothesi,* of a mediating agent, an *inter*subjective mechanism that intervenes and establishes contact between what stands apart before the moment of its intervention. *Intersubjectivity* is the key term in explaining how individuality is transcended, and the concept of code is but one of its theoretical representatives, one of its manifestations. In fact, the code can guarantee the successful transmission of messages *precisely because it is intersubjective.*

To say codes are intersubjective is to say that they possess the capacity to overcome privacy and supersede solitude; codes translate what is subjective or idiosyncratic into something objective and accessible. Codes break down secrecy and break open autism, securing encoding and decoding by making entry and exit possible. They are the enforcer of the postal principle, the medium that exorcises the demon of the third man, the necessary apparatus that ensures the open circulation of meaning as delivery and return. In short, they signal the death of concealment and silence; they signal the birth of voice, the inauguration of sounds in human, nay, social forms. Derrida asks us to imagine a writing whose code would be so idiomatic as to be established and known, as secret cipher, by only two "subjects." Could we maintain that, following the death of the receiver or even of both partners, the mark left by one of them is still writing? Yes, to the extent that, organized by a code, even an unknown and non-linguistic one, it is constituted in its identity as mark by its iterability, in the absence of such and such a person, and hence ultimately of every empirically determined "subject." This implies that *there is no such thing as a code — organon of iterability, which could be structurally secret.*[61]

In fact, were codes not intersubjective or social in nature, it would not make any sense to talk about *encoding* and *decoding* messages, nor would it be possible or even necessary to distinguish a coded message from (uncoded) noise.

Hence, when one claims that individuals communicate through a common language, a code, or whatever one may choose to call it, what one really means is that different individuals participate in or are assisted by an intersubjective structure of meaning in which their difference, their privacy, collapses into a larger system of commonality and public meaning. Within this structure of intersubjectivity, every word, every expression, is "twiceborn," doubling back and forth between the speaker and listener in a spiral of shared and shareable signs, much like the intimate conversation of lovers. Indeed, communication could well be construed through the image of the reciprocating dialogue between lovers, for having undergone a history of courtship, each one knows what the other desires, and each one knows that the other knows what he/she himself/herself desires. Lovers are those who know the passwords to each other's heart; lovers are protocommunicators. This protocommunication is what happens between Kitty and Levin — that wonderful, but not so rare, exchange of hearts movingly described by Tolstoy in *Anna Karenina*:

> He sat down and wrote out a long sentence [in the code]. She understood it all, and without asking if she was right, took the chalk and wrote the answer at once.... He could not find the words she meant at all; but in her beautiful eyes, radiant with joy, he saw all that he wanted to know. And he wrote down three letters. But before he had finished writing she read it under his hand, finished the sentence herself, and wrote the answer: "yes."[62]

Now what enables Kitty to write that trusting "yes"? What enables her, and for that matter, anyone like her, to penetrate the privacy of thought and uncover the loved one's intention, which words alone fail to express? Is it the "magic" of love, or is it the "requisite amount of salt" they must have consumed together?

What I am suggesting is that the question of communication cannot be answered successfully unless one posits intersubjectivity as the mediating term. That is, to make mediation possible between two subjects, it is *necessary* to bring in a third term, something other than the two subjects — be it a history of romance, or a certain shared amount of salt — that is capable of dissolving their precommunicative differences and of ensuring that mediation happens. The introduction of intersubjectivity meets this demand, serving the crucial function of closing off the circuit of question and answer first opened by the existential enigma of communication. Once intersubjectivity is brought in, it becomes possible to "answer" how individuality is transcended, and this possibility puts an end to the theoretical challenge constituted by the conflict between the natural certainty (that is, that people do communicate) and the reflective puzzle (that is, solipsism). Communication is now possible, its mystery solved, because the outward opposition between privacy and openness caused by the duality of self versus other, individual versus social meaning, can now be resituated into a unifying structure of shared and shareable meaning in which noncommunication or solipsistic existence represents but a transient phase in the dialectic of sociality. Without an intersubjective code as the mediating agent, the gulf between individual subjects would remain open; without intersubjectivity, mediation of difference and privacy could not be explained; without intersubjectivity, lovers' dialogue would appear at best "magical." Serres is only partially right: A "third man" is not the enemy of communication; instead, it is the prerequisite of communication, if only because it is the signs of the "third man," the savage's footprints, that cause interlocutors to unite and to invent the secret passwords. In fact, without a secret code as intermediary, it would be impossible to "exclude" Serres's "third man," just as, without any background noise, it would be impossible for one to hear anything save, as John Cage declared after emerging from a perfectly soundproof room, the rustling, buzzing, and whooshing of one's own muscular twitching and blood flow.

Ignotum per Ignotius; or, Theoretical Ventriloquism

> Their elements are presented in succession. They form a chain.
> —*Jacques Derrida*

The preceding analysis should make it clear that the problematic of communication is fundamentally a triadic structure, consisting of three interrelated concepts: the *subject, mediation,* and *intersubjectivity.* Chained together by the postal principle, these three master signifiers of the problematic make their appearance in a necessary sequence, tracing a loop that determines for communication theories their underlying syntagmatic form. This loop reflects the problematic's structural necessity: Once the first term, the subject, is defined as solitary, the problematic must immediately recruit the third term, intersubjectivity, which it then makes available to the theory to answer the question thematized by way of the second term, mediation. The problematic of communication articulates itself through this looplike structure, and by following through this loop, communication theories in turn reproduce the problematic as a finite economy of sending and return.

As can be inferred from my discussion in the preceding section, the third term of the triad, intersubjectivity, which provides a solution to the problem of mediation, is internally invoked: It is generated from within the problematic in response to the problematic's initial move of postulating a solitary subject. Yet although intersubjectivity serves to close off the ever renewable question of how mediation is possible, the fact that it is internally invoked creates a peculiar problem in that it forecloses the question set up by the problematic. For no sooner is the solitary subject posited and the mother question of communication thematized as mediation, than the initial existential enigma of privacy dissolves itself without having to undergo due critical treatment. The enigma dissolves because intersubjectivity, having been invoked, starts to circulate in the problematic as a universal mediating concept and delivers itself, whenever and wherever needed, to answer the question of how individuality is transcended. In other words, by invoking intersubjectivity internally, the theory finds within its conceptual repertoire a "licensed signifier" to manage the challenge posed by the solitude of subjectivity and, in so doing, effectively blocks any further exploration of the relation between privacy and mediation; ipso facto, the mother question of communication is quickly explained away; more precisely, it is sidestepped: Individuality (that is, egocentricity) is and can be transcended *on the basis of* intersubjectivity.

This controlled chain reaction within the problematic of communication betrays a strategy — what I call, à la Derrida, "the logic of deferral" — that enables communication theories to postpone answering the mother question created by the existential enigma of privacy and solitude. To illustrate how this strategy works, let me draw a quick example from sociology. "Social role" and "interaction" are among the most basic concepts in sociological writings; hardly any sociological explanation can be constructed without them. In standard sociology textbooks, social role is usually defined as aspects of behavior, as the embodiment of norms, as part of some structure or system of interactive relationship, and so forth. "A *role*," as one typical definition goes, "is a patterned sequence of learned *actions* or deeds performed by a person in an *interaction* situation."[63] The notion of interaction, on the other hand, is usually introduced by comparing it to *action*, which is supposed to be a more elementary unit of meaningful behavior than *inter-action*. But how is social action defined? How can this elementary form of human behavior be distinguished from social interaction? When one searches sociology textbooks for an answer, one quickly discovers that, not only are *social action* and *interaction* ultimately indistinguishable, but both concepts are also invariably characterized through the concept of "role embodiment." To quote another typical statement: "Fundamental in the mechanism of symbolic *interaction* is the process of *role taking*."[64] Now it does not take much critical acumen to discern that the definitions of these terms (*action/interaction, social roles*) travel full circle: *Social role* is recognized as a résumé of an individual's interaction-based performances, and conversely, *interaction* is knowable only through the role performances an individual displays in his or her actions. Although both concepts are presented as independent, primitive concepts, it turns out that one is defined or clarified in relation to the other, which itself is illuminated by or receives meaning from the same group of cognates. In this situation—as is the case in all metaphoric transfers—the defining term is already contained in the term(s) to be defined; the *definiendum* is already *operatively implicated* in the *definiens*, and vice versa.

What happens in this example resembles a classic case of begging the question, a fallacy resulting from the circularity in the discussion of a target concept and its surrogates. Predictably, such a circular discussion radically compromises the explanatory utility of the concepts involved. Given this example, if one asks how social interaction is possible or actualized, the typical reply must be that in social life, human beings take on roles that lay out predictable patterns of behavior immediately intelligible for all societal members. But if the question is turned toward social role, that is, if one asks how social role can be identified, one soon realizes that social role is actually an abstraction, a theoretical construct, a *performance imagery*, as one able critic calls it, of significant aspects of the social interactive process; *it has to be embodied*.[65] In the former case, one is left wondering how roles become socially meaningful in the first place; in the latter case, the question as to how interaction can begin at all—without assuming that the subjects (actors) take definite roles—is still left unanswered. Through substitutive reversals, these different species of "social bonds" can be seen to play a game of weight transfer, tilting back and forth without any point of stable reference. When this happens, when the defining term put forward only trades places with the term to be defined, our sociologist-author, not unlike the professor of communication in our earlier example, furtively unburdens him- or herself of the task of noncircularly clarifying what each concept means.

What I am suggesting is that the kind of postal play taking place between social role and interaction also takes place between mediation and intersubjectivity in communication theories, and that this play, when undetected, allows communication theorists to evade addressing the mother question with which communication theories begin. Recall that intersubjectivity is strategically invoked from within the problematic of communication in reaction to the challenge of solipsism. But one should not forget that this "autoproduction of a third term" within the problematic exacts a theoretical toll, trading away the theory's explanatory integrity. Because it is invoked by the problematic, intersubjectivity can be mobilized effectively to *explain* how individuality is transcended; at the same time, however, because it is invoked internally, that is, attributed a priori with the capacity to mediate differences through the problematic's autogenesis, intersubjectivity is itself unexplained and unexplainable. This means two things. First, inasmuch as it is an unexplainable term, that is, since it is positioned *outside* problematization, intersubjectivity is transcendentalized. It functions as a "transcendental signifier" in relation to other concepts within the problematic in the specific sense that it accounts for mediation but is itself unaccounted for. Second, as an unexplained term, that is, as a signifier immune to reflexive critique, intersubjectivity also designates the problematic's own blind spot or "central deafness": It commands the scene of exchange and mediation, but the source of its commanding authority is hidden. This, then, is how the logic of deferral works: By mobilizing intersubjectivity (or any of its representatives, such as codes, rules, or language, each of which performs the *assigned* function of mediation) as an inoculated, universal mediator, the theoretical challenge of solipsism is silenced, and the existential mystery of communication is ostensibly cleared away, precisely by *not* subjecting intersubjectivity to critical interrogation but by installing it as a point of stability and closure that anchors communication theories' postal metaphorics.

The logic of deferral endemic to communication theories reveals that they are founded on a *fundamental analogism,* a principle of substitution between intersubjectivity and mediation, that determines the theories' limited field of vision, their subject-based *oculus mundi.* In these theories, intersubjectivity and mediation work as paired metaphors: Mediation is understood as the concrete manifestation of intersubjectivity. Conversely, intersubjectivity is thought to be materialized in actual mediational events: One cannot be *imag(in)ed* save by reference to the other—the two closely bound in a reversible relationship. It is through these paired metaphors that the problematic of communication delivers its final message. For what unfolds henceforth in theories is the continuation of an oscillation between mediation and intersubjectivity, a recursive nominal displacement in which one slides into the other only to loop back again to its paradigmatic analogue, its conceptual double.

It is through the circular sliding between intersubjectivity and mediation that the problematic of communication as a whole manages to maintain its coherence and unity. Yet because there is a movement of reversal, a nominal exchange between intersubjectivity and mediation, the bilateral movement between these two concepts becomes the only constant of the problematic. Being a constant, this movement keeps open the possibility of theorists' enunciations (such as "communication is X" or "mediation happens because Y"), but being *the* constant, this movement keeps itself from being scrutinized. Hiding its own emptiness through perpetual transference and substitution, the fundamental analogism that sets theorizing in motion is itself never spoken, never announced. It recedes as the *silence* of the problematic, the *unconscious* of all communication theories.

At the same time, because of the nominal reversibility between communication/mediation and intersubjectivity, any theoretical statement containing them will possess no fixed or fixable defining term, as either one of them can act as proxy for the other. As a result, a theory's own condition of possibility is turned upside down, for what is introduced as *explanans* (intersubjectivity) is already contained in the *explanadum* (communication); what is antecedent reemerges as concluding propositions: Communication and intersubjectivity can be understood only *tautologically*. Trapped in a play of equivalence, such a conception of communication, as Paul de Man says of poetic objects, "gives itself the totality which it then claims to define, but it is in fact the tautology of its own position" within a predetermined postal space.[66] Because of the lack of a terminal referent whose meaning does not presuppose prior understanding of the terms within the problematic, any theoretical advance or explanatory account generated by the problematic would necessarily be compromised by that problematic's own postal play. In this regard, theories of communication resemble ventriloquism, and theorists resemble ventriloquists, for what theorists can do now is keep repeating the vacuous statements that communication occurs because it is possible, or that communication is possible because it takes place.

If the aim of a communication theory is to demystify the existential enigma of solitude, this nominal play indicates that it falls far short of its objective, that there is a clear discrepancy between what the theory actually does and what it is often unsuspectingly thought to do. Inasmuch as communication theorists defer transmitting the secret truth to the reader, they resemble incompetent psychoanalysts, and their discourse, repeating the structure it seeks to analyze, "limps and closes badly." Like a bad analyst who re-Oedipalizes the patient through his talking cure, the communication theorist offers us a story about mediation that ends up remystifying intersubjectivity. Although one text claims to analyze and elucidate another, it turns out that the relationship could be inverted; "that the analyzing text is elucidated by the analyzed text, which already contains an implicit account of and reflection upon the analyst's moves."[67] In the final analysis, despite all the good work it does, intersubjectivity explains nothing but must be itself explained.

I should reiterate, however, that although it radically compromises the propositional strength of communication theories, the logic of deferral is not an accidental defect of the problematic; rather, it reflects its "structural necessity." Given the manner in which the problematic of communication is constructed, the act of "reversible substitution" must be committed because it terminates a chain of problematization that otherwise would continue indefinitely. For if one questions the mediating term, intersubjectivity, the same way one questions mediation, or if one questions mediation and intersubjectivity simultaneously, one would perforce face the necessity of bringing in yet another mediating term, and this process could go on ad infinitum. Following the postal command sent by the existential enigma of communication, the logic of deferral merely reflects the subterranean metaphorics of communication theories, and those who fall victim to it are merely abiding by the problematic's own postal regulation. Viewed in this way, the problematic of communication can be regarded as a prison house for communication theorists, a conceptual panopticon that interns ventriloquist-theorists and performs ventriloquist shows upon a highly guarded stage. Simply put, it allows for the generation of communication theories as explanatory accounts for an existential enigma, but it does so only by tacitly prescribing the question in advance, a question whose answers only perpetuate the working of the problematic and leave the preunderstanding of its key concepts unchallenged.

How much do we gain after all? What do we really learn from reading communication theories? If the message from communication theories can only be delivered through metaphors, should we not then read these theories as one more case of *ignotum per ignotius,* if not *ignorabimus,* not infrequent in a science as young as communication theory? If phenomenology's success in bringing about the philosophical turn in communication studies climaxes in tautology, should we not conclude, then, that phenomenology has spent its critical fortune?

3 / The Inaugural Relation: Toward an Ontology of Communication

It is therefore not a priori certain that literature is a reliable source of
information about anything but its own language. — *Paul de Man*

One need only consider oft-neglected rhetoric. — *Mikhail Bakhtin*

One of the things that various contemporary critical theories share is the
contention that language is *fundamentally* and *essentially* rhetorical. "It is not
difficult," as de Man, reiterating Nietzsche, claims confidently,

> to demonstrate that what is called "rhetorical," as the devices of a conscious
> art, is present as a device of unconscious art in language and its development.
> We can go so far as to say that rhetoric is an extension (*Fortbildung*) of the de-
> vices embedded in language at the clear light of reason. No such thing as an
> unrhetorical, "natural" language exists that could be used as a point of refer-
> ence: *language is itself the result of purely rhetorical tricks and devices.*[1]

Behind this celebration of the rhetoricity of language lies the idea that
rhetoric is not mere embellishment, not Hume's "instrument of Error and
Deceit," still less Kant's "art of playing for one's own purpose upon the
weakness of men"; rather, it constitutes the productive logic interior to all
linguistic activities. What one witnesses here is in effect nothing short of "a
full reversal of established priorities which traditionally rooted the authority of the language in its adequation to an extralinguistic referent or meaning, rather than in the intralinguistic resources of figures."[2]

This privileging of the rhetorical within human linguistic practice goes beyond the pedestrian neo-Aristotelian interpretation of rhetoric as the strategic use of language, shaking loose, in its wake, many of our habits of (binary) thinking from their intellectual grooves. Once language is regarded as "the result of purely rhetorical tricks and devices," the Platonist distinction between fiction and truth that has long held a firm grip on philosophies of language loses its assured standing, for reality is acknowledged not merely to be always and already mediated by language but, rather, constituted as such by linguistic signs according to their own reason. Rather than and prior to representing the world for human circumspection, language, through a kind of force unique to itself, establishes the world *as* present. What is highlighted by this new rhetorical consciousness is the constitutive potential of language, a protolinguisticality or metaphoricity that, as Rodolphe Gasché describes it, "is not endowed with those qualities traditionally attributed to metaphor but rather with attributes which in traditional philosophy would be called constituting or transcendental."[3] In the turn and counterturn of language, so goes the current dictum, "the words seem less tools of the will than the will the tool of the words."[4] It makes sense to say that a distinct rhetorical turn has been taken in the checkered journey of modern critical discourses.

This new rhetorical view of language is more than a well-tempered alternative to the long-held referential and instrumental conceptions of language. Although it opposes the belief in the tidy correspondence between words and things, it goes further to suggest that the referential relation between words and things — what Barthes calls "realism" in general — is itself a rhetorical effect, the outcome of a deeper figural play perpetually fueled by "the duplicities of language."[5] According to this new gospel of words, rhetoric is not merely *epistemic* because it extends knowledge; more significant, it is *ontological* in the sense that the very possibility of signification, the very visibility of being, depends on a certain noncoincidence between expression and what is expressed, between the actual sign and what it signifies. "Language," as Barbara Johnson notes, "exists only in the space of its own foreignness to itself."[6] Rhetoric is more than truth-effective; it is inherently truth-evocative and reality-creative, if only because, to quote de Man again, "*unmediated expression is a philosophical impossibility.*"[7]

As is well known, de Man's talk of the impossibility of "unmediated expression," whose echoes are presently abundant, represents a revisionist recuperation of the Sophist doctrine whose radicality is given a new lease on life by Nietzsche. Expanding Nietzsche's notion of rhetoric as a system of tropes, de Man affirms emphatically that "trope is not a derived, marginal, or aberrant form of language but the linguistic paradigm *par excellence.* The figurative structure is not one linguistic mode among others but it characterizes language as such."[8] According to this Nietzschean view of language (of which de Man is one of the staunchest and most rigorous spokesmen of late), it is rhetoric, not grammar (logic), that grounds the referential possibility of language, however aberrant and indecisive its eventual realization. In the textual universe, the figural praxis always precedes metafigural reflection, and the representational or expressive efficacy of language is but an afterthought of those who inhabit that universe.

What I tried to show in chapter 2 with reference to the problematic of communication is that, much like literary works playing out the possibilities given to them by their medium, communication theories also are determined by a specific metaphorical infrastructure. And this rhetorical organization from within frustrates those theories' attempt to explain the existential enigma of communication that generates them. Since they cannot explicate the phenomenon that motivates them other than through substitution, displacement, or delay, these theories are at the mercy of a genetically coded circularity, creating and re-creating within themselves tropical folds that "scientific" discourses wish to avoid. From my perspective, this represents an ironic failure on the part of communication theorists, who, after so much effort, have succeeded only in providing a simulacrum rather than real illumination of the phenomena whose mystery it is their task to solve.

If communication theories inevitably play out a predetermined metaphorical infrastructure, that is, if communication theories are indeed controlled by subtextual metaphorics and their subsequent linguistic devices, what is the role of theorists other than to reproduce more of the same? Is there any "possibility of escaping from the pitfalls of rhetoric by becoming aware of the rhetoricity of language"?[9] Does a critical awareness of the rhetoricity of language not somehow reinvigorate communication theorists to break free from the figural play inherent in their theorizing? If not, would a reversal of the given conceptual dichotomies "restore things to their proper order"?[10] In short, how could theorizing about communication find a way out of the metaphorical orbit preconstituted for it and still respond to the initial existential enigma that brings that theorizing into being? These are certainly not rhetorical questions, and the answers to them can come only from a critical rethinking of the rhetorical mechanism underlying the problematic of communication theories. Needless to say, this rethinking must avoid adding one more trope to a series of earlier reversals or replacing one rhetorical mode with another; what is needed, instead, is to carefully think *through* the discursive circularity engendered by the problematic's own hidden rhetorical subtext. The discursive constriction imposed on communication theories by their problematic's rhetorical plot can be loosened only by *unlinking* the chain of nominal substitution and equivocation between mediation and intersubjectivity that so far has infested the development of those theories. It is to this unlinking that I now turn.

Reading the Circle and the Hermeneutic Return

Beyond a certain point there is no return. This point must be reached.
—*Franz Kafka*

At the end of the preceding chapter, I described communication theories as ventriloquism. I chose this description for two reasons: First, current theorizing about communication involves a preunderstanding of a pair of concepts that are not only unproblematized but also unproblematizable within the theoretical space open to them; second, such a preunderstanding is repeated by communication theories through a chain of metonymic invocations. Unable to say what communication is or how it is possible except by appealing to (various images of) intersubjectivity, communication theories beg the question they purport to answer and become embroiled in the vicissitudes of figural language, exhibiting, as metaphors often do, an unwarranted slide of meaning from analogy to identity. The crux of the problem with communication theories, of its ventriloquism, can therefore be said to reside in a metonymic redundancy that manifests itself in the nominal substitution between intersubjectivity and mediation as two functionally equivalent signifiers.

The circular exchange between mediation and intersubjectivity does not occur by accident; rather, it reflects the rhetorical movement constitutive of communication theories as overdetermined discourses generated by the problematic. Though concealed behind a "coded unfolding," this rhetorical movement reveals the *textuality* of communication theories, and as such provides a vantage point for a metareflection on the problematic as a whole. What I wish to propose, then, is a Heideggerian critique of what might be called the "textual prehistory" of communication theories: Instead of treating this rhetoric-induced to-and-fro movement between two signifiers (i.e., communication and intersubjectivity) as a mere *epistemological* defect, I shall attempt an archaeological reading of this movement to uncover the pretextual mise-en-scène that supports and protracts the double play of the "metaphorical couplet" of mediation and intersubjectivity. My purpose here is twofold: to show how this circular movement caused by that metaphorical couplet results necessarily from an ontological shortsightedness, and to show how an "existential analysis" of this shortsightedness from a Heideggerian perspective may lead to a nontranscendental regrounding of communication theories. By situating the metaphorical play underlying the problematic of communication in the context of Heidegger's *existential analytic,* I shall seek to take apart what rhetoric has persistently tried to force together; and by reading ventriloquism as a symptom of a particular *unthought* in communication theories, I wish to push the phenomenology of communication toward the breaking point of its bipolar economy founded on a metaphysics of the subject. As Heidegger remarks at the end of *Identity and Difference,* "Only when we thoughtfully turn toward (*zuwenden*) what has already been thought will we be turned in readiness (*verwendet*) to what must still be thought."[11]

Before I force a contact between communication theories' rhetorical subtext and Heidegger's fundamental ontology, however, it is helpful to take a look at how the problem of circularity diagnosed above is managed within the phenomenological discourse. By examining how the problem of intersubjectivity is dealt with by post-Husserlian phenomenologists, paying attention at the same time to their rethinking of questions regarding the status of the subject, we shall get a better sense of the possibility and limit of the constitutive-subjectivist paradigm with which, as I will show later, Heidegger's existential analytic constitutes an irreversible break.

You Must Take for Granted the Taken-for-Granted

Man's beliefs at any time are so much experience *funded.* — *William James*

Let us not pretend to doubt in philosophy what we do not doubt in our hearts. — *C. S. Peirce*

In "From Restricted to General Economy: Hegelianism without Reserve," Derrida remarks that phenomenology

> corresponds to a restricted economy: restricted to commercial value . . . , limited to the meaning (*sens*) and the established value of objects, and to their *circulation.* The *circularity* of absolute knowledge could dominate, could comprehend only this circulation, only the *circuit of reproductive consumption.* The absolute production and destruction of value, the exceeding energy as such, the energy which "can only be lost without the slightest aim, consequently without any meaning"—all this escapes phenomenology as restricted economy.[12]

In what way is phenomenology so "restricted" that it can comprehend only the "circulation of meaning"? How does phenomenology restrict the possible "destruction of value" that, according to Derrida, escapes or exceeds its "circuit of reproductive consumption"? Finally, how does phenomenology's restricted economy bear upon the question of intersubjectivity? Because *restriction* means confinement or forced closure, a restricted economy must be one that everywhere governs manifold and heterogeneous phenomena according to laws or principles that repress heterogeneity. How is this repression of multiplicity achieved? How does this totalizing, punitive law of phenomenology enforce itself?

As we saw in chapter 1, Husserlian phenomenology begins by radicalizing the Cartesian understanding of the self. Fundamentally, and by his own admission, Husserl inherits the Cartesian model of reflection. By retracing the route of reflection, radical Cartesianism seeks to push back beyond the Cartesian *cogito* to a fully perspicuous point of origin of all knowledge, the indubitable matrix of all form and content. In this sense, Husserlian phenomenology can be interpreted as a post-Cartesian critique of selfhood. But this Cartesian self with which Husserl begins is not as simple or innocent a point of departure as Husserl seems to think. For although it is "prior in itself," "antecedent," and "continually presupposed," the self is essentially *relative,* because it is *not* self-sufficient, because its "identity is not the simple abstract position of a thing as immediately what it is and only what it is; rather, it actualizes itself as a *grasping of itself* by the unity that I am in myself: an Ego, an irreducible kernel of self-constitution."[13] Whoever says "I" presupposes this self-constituted ego, however attenuated or remote it may be. Derived from a reflexive grasping, the self as subject is congenitally split. It cannot come to be unless it sees itself through a double vision, through a mirror image, in which the self-subject turns back on itself and grasps its own identity with itself, and the object, through the same double vision, emerges as the reflection of the subject, rather than something other than the subject. In the final analysis, the self and the reflection, which represents an internal possibility of the self, are born at the same moment, by the same act. It would be naive and philosophically fallacious to think of the self as a primitive given in ordinary nonphilosophical consciousness.

Since reflection and self are intertwined from the beginning, any inquiry of the latter on the basis of the former faces an intractable difficulty. This difficulty becomes apparent when the question of self-foundation is raised.

That is, if the foundation of philosophy is to be found in the *I think,* could the *thinking* of an *I* be a good judge of the validity of its own thinking? To phrase the question differently, could the *thinking* of the I *think* the "I think" in its entirety and in total transparency?

As early as 1790, Fichte recognized the incoherence of self-reflection because of the problem of "infinite regress":

> You are conscious of yourself, you say; thus you necessarily distinguish your *thinking* I from the I which is *thought* in its thinking. But in order for you to do this, that which thinks in this thinking must be the object of a higher thinking, in order to be an object of consciousness; and you immediately obtain a new *subject,* which is once more conscious of that which was formerly self-consciousness. But I now argue again as before; and once we have begun to proceed in accordance with this law, you can nowhere show me a place where we should stop; we will continue to infinity, needing for each consciousness a new consciousness, whose object the former is, and thus we will never be able to reach the point of assuming an actual consciousness.[14]

In phenomenology's language, this means that in any reflective process, the *cogitatione* (that is, the mental act) of the *ego* unavoidably generates its corresponding *cogitatum* with each act of self-reflection, the result of which is that the tertiary structure of intentional acts (*ego-cogito-cogitatum*) is reproduced throughout the reflective process without any terminal point. Once reflection takes its course, it cannot (and should not) stop, for reflection can always pose its own previous moment as a new object. If the relation of reflection is intended to provide an account of what it is to be a self, any reflection-based inquiry of selfhood can only fail, for two reasons. First, in the very activity of reflection (which in principle can go on ad infinitum), the self is already presupposed, simply because if the subject of the act of reflection were not already the self, the object-self of which it comes to have knowledge could not be identical with it. Second, unless the subject-self is already in some sense acquainted with itself, it would not be able to recognize the object as itself: There is nothing inherent in a reflected image that reveals to the onlooker that it is his or her *own* image, and the subject cannot appeal to any third term for knowledge or verification of identity of the two poles, for this would involve an infinite regress, an interminable spiral of self-mirroring.[15] In both cases, self-reflection proves to be either redundant or for naught, for it only affirms what the self allows it to affirm and consequently does not and cannot provide anything beyond the empty truism that the reflecting self is capable of self-reflection.

Given its starting point *in* the self, reflection, however critical, can never close the gap between that which reflects and that which is at each moment being reflected upon. There is invariably a moment of active reflection, a residue of the "I *think,*" that antedates the formation and positioning of the "I," and that hence escapes reflection's own grasp; there is always an instantaneously invoked and perpetually reproduced inadequation between finite consciousness and its reflective ideal—an inadequation created by an extrareflective blind spot in the reflective act that prevents it from ever "assuming an actual consciousness." Because of this ever renewed residue of the "I think," a kind of "exceeding energy," as Derrida calls it, the self-evidence of the agent of reflection cannot be secured by any reflective effort. Consequently, the claim of reflective philosophy is destined to be defeated by reflection's own steadfast performance.

Husserl's shift from descriptive to transcendental phenomenology can best be understood as a response to this problem of infinite regress, an inevitable obstacle in the journey of reduction. For Husserl, the transcendental turn is necessary because, having committed to the rational absolute, he must install a "firstness of the ego" to halt the reduction; he needs to postulate a moment of absolute knowledge *above* and *beyond* the sphere of infinite regress. Like Kant (and many nineteenth-century German idealists, with whom Husserl engages in an unspoken dialogue), who postulates, perhaps prematurely, a "transcendental unity of apperception" as the condition of possibility for all empirical consciousness, Husserl, too, institutes the transcendental ego as the agency of synthesis that transforms the manifold of intuitions into an objective, coherent world. Transcendental consciousness therefore designates for Husserl a stopping point beyond which reduction cannot go, a moment of self-assurance that supports and justifies all others.[16]

Such stoppage in the form of a transcendental agency independent of reflective processes is a prerequisite to any reflection-based critical philosophy. For if critical philosophy does not wish to give in to skepticism and relativism, it must halt its problematizing at some point and announce a first principle. Critical philosophy, upon whose ideal Husserl models his own inquiry, must reflect an a priori recognition of absolute necessity: that a given state of affairs could not be otherwise, *in principle.* For that reason, Husserl is forced in the end to posit something as origin that, to the extent that it serves the function of closing the loop of recursive reflection, must be thought *transcendentally.* After all, if phenomenology, or any other philosophy for that matter, can in theory problematize *continuously,* it cannot in practice problematize *globally*, for global problematization, if conceivable at all, runs into the same problem as does relativism, and so the integrity of the critical project is undermined.[17] At any rate, unless phenomenology relinquishes its objective as providing a foundation for the sciences, which it cannot, it will have to totalize or "restrict" differences. As far as transcendental phenomenology goes, the moment of (transcendental) constitution ensues inevitably from the impossibility of absolute reduction, after which the empirical ego exists only insofar as it speaks the *father tongue* of the transcendental subject.

In Husserl's system, the closure or totalization is thus achieved by the absoluteness of transcendental consciousness. Located above the conscious world, transcendental consciousness governs all the commerce of intentional activities within a grand constitutive *récit*. It functions as the last guarantor and regulative agent of all the production and consumption of sense (*sens*). Standing at the *end* of reduction, this unifying and unified consciousness also functions as the *beginning* of objective plenitude, in that everything encountered before and during the reduction finds its place in a "circuit of reproductive consumption" that the transcendental subject oversees as an impartial spectator. As an economy of sense and being, Husserlianism is and must be extremely frugal; it saves everything and expends nothing.

As discussed in chapter 1, Husserl's transcendentalism faces many difficulties, not the least of which is the question of intersubjectivity. Approaching reality in terms of constitution according to which others appear only as *sense* correlative to the ego's intending acts, constitutive phenomenology ironically lapses into the solipsism that it has worked diligently to refute. Briefly, the problem can be restated as follows: (1) How is it that the transcendental ego can constitute other (independent, "external") transcendental egos and animate organisms? (2) How can this constitution be done "correctly" by the transcendental ego that is necessarily locked into itself? In other words, given the privileged or private access I have to myself—a condition occasioned by reduction, how can I claim to know how you feel or think, or even whether you feel or think, or whether you exist as a person (or mind) in the same sense that I know I am a person (or mind)? The chasm between the self and other seems decisive and too wide to cross.

To facilitate my following argument, let me briefly recount Husserl's strategy, discussed in chapter 1. In his analysis of Husserl's discussion of transcendental intersubjectivity, Alfred Schutz identifies four stages in Husserl's argument: (1) the isolation of the primordial world of one's peculiar ownness by the epoche; (2) the apperception of the other through pairing; (3) the constitution of objective, intersubjective nature; and (4) the constitution of higher forms of community.[18] Schutz finds insurmountable problems in each stage. In retrospect, it becomes apparent that Husserl's problem starts as early as the first stage, for once the retreat to one's world of ownness is effected, the monadic closure of the ego becomes complete. With this egological closure,

> how can the subjective egological evidence of sense become objective and intersubjective? How can it give rise to an ideal and true object, with all the characteristics that we know it to have: omnitemporal validity, universal normativity, intelligibility for "*everyone*," uprootedness out of all "*here and now*" factuality, and so forth?...How can subjectivity go out of itself in order to encounter or constitute the object?[19]

If reduction were to practice what it preaches, the egological sphere would be cleared up and expurgated of any such "soft datum" as an alien other or essential stranger. Contrary to Husserl's game plan, and despite his complaints that only a handful of faithfuls have understood its significance, the transcendental turn does not deliver to the philosopher the solution to solipsism that reduction promises; instead, it compounds the already massive difficulty of the question of the other by further isolating the ego to a point of no return.

The universal certitude that transcendental idealism proffers is thus purchased at too high a price. Although the transcendental reduction ensures the certainty of my reality, it does so only by eliminating or suppressing the real *differences* that mark the relation between me and the world prior to the reduction. Appropriated by a totalizing consciousness, the radical otherness of the other is mollified qualitatively and absorbed into an artificial — for Husserl, purified — sphere of ownness characterized by homogeneity and singularity: To the I-ego, the other is not an other *as such* but as one of its many *cogitables,* namely, as something consciously intended in me. Inasmuch as the other never achieves apodictic presence, the self remains, to borrow Aristotle's phrase, "a solitary game piece." The reflective self cannot transcend its radical solitude, cannot travel outside its monadic universe, and cannot recognize another face. It can only "reflect on" its confinement, on the unbridgeable gap between itself and the other, between the same and the different. And given this gap, Husserl's subsequent attempts to link egos through bodily transposition is doomed to fail. What his theory of appresentative empathy can generate, as Ortega y Gasset argues, is at most an abstract identification that is irrelevant to human social life: "*Ego,* strictly, is something that I alone am, and if I refer it to an Other, I have to change its meaning. *Alter Ego* has to be understood analogically: there is in the abstract Other *something* that is in him what the *Ego* is in me. The two *Egos,* mine and the analogical one, have in common only certain abstract components, which, being abstract, are unreal."[20]

It would not be difficult to predict how Husserl's followers maneuver their way out of the impasse Husserl himself faces. Now that the transcendental turn causes an insurmountable problem—that is, because intersubjectivity is not a "problem of constitution which can be solved within the transcendental sphere"—the logical alternative is to revert to the mundane world of everyday existence, to where the ego *naturally* is. And this is exactly what existentialist phenomenologists and many phenomenologically inclined social theorists did. From Merleau-Ponty's description of the interpersonal encounter at the prepersonal level of the body-subject, to Heidegger's hermeneutical recovery of *Mitsein* (being-with) as constitutive of personal being, to Sartre's discussion of the "transformative power" of the "look" of the other, and beyond, a whole generation of phenomenologists have refused to embark on Husserl's transcendental reductive flight. Instead of looking inward, they cast their gaze outward on the surrounding world. The existential turn of phenomenology therefore means a return to the life-world as the unfettered context of the natural attitude. In this world of mundane existence, individuals act and react before they reflect. For them there is no question of transcendental intersubjectivity, if by that is meant intersubjectivity of a plurality of transcendental egos. What one finds instead, Husserl's successors suggest, is the concrete practical environment of one's everyday activities, in which consciousness is always busy and in contact with others. As a result of reversing Husserl's ascending movement toward a transcendental "community of monads," intersubjectivity is, as it were, declassified; it reappears as "a datum of the life-world," no more questionable than the existence of things in my phenomenal field, and the question of intersubjectivity, as Schutz rightly argues, should be approached as an "intramundane problem."

What does it mean to say that intersubjectivity is "a datum of the life-world" and "should be approached as an intramundane problem"? Since transcendental reduction traps the ego in an untransferable solitude and can constitute other egos only abstractly, the antitranscendental descent toward the mundane entails that other egos be given in the concrete. From the point of view of existential phenomenology, this means that the natural, routine, everyday world in which the ego finds itself is already a world with others. In other words, before we become aware of ourselves as independent beings, namely, prior to self-reflection, we have already had the basic experience that there are others who are not I, that all humans live in one and the same world, with the result that living means essentially "co-living," *living together*.

The word *already* holds the key here. In this word, in its twofold meaning, one can discern not only the motivation for the existential turn within phenomenology but also the exact meaning of its intramundane reformulation of the question of intersubjectivity. In its original, simple sense, *already* means beforehand, prior to a specified time. Its function is to augment the verb in a sentence, to underline the completion of an action or the temporal precedence of one event in relation to another, as, for example, in "Let's take the suitcases outside, I have *already* called the cab," or "John had *already* gone to bed *before* Mary left home." In this sense, *already* indicates either the temporal pastness of a single event or the sequential order of events that take place at different moments in time. In the context of phenomenology's mundane shift, however, the word *already* signifies something beyond its temporal senses; it takes on the additional meaning of "metaphysical priority." In contrast to *already's* first meaning, which reports the temporal relations between empirically identifiable states of affair, this second meaning states a *relation between concepts,* underlining *not* the chronological order of action(s) but the logical precedence of one concept over another within a given theoretical system. According to this second meaning of *already,* the social world, for example, can be characterized as *already* intersubjective not merely because intersubjectivity is a fact predating any individual's birth, but also in the distinct sense that intersubjectivity enjoys a conceptual precedence over the individual because it answers a specific theoretical demand. In that theoretical system, intersubjectivity precedes individuals *in principle,* as well as *in fact.* What I am suggesting is that, given these two possible senses of the word *already* as applied to the life-world, the turn within phenomenology from the transcendental to the mundane parallels a shift from the first to the second meaning of *already.* In fact, as I shall argue, it is by raising the life-world as what is to be *described phenomenologically* to the status of being a *metaphysical given,* namely, by endowing intersubjectivity with metaphysical priority over the subject, that phenomenology finalizes its reflection on intersubjectivity and settles the problem of solipsism.

Grounding the Life-World: Social Ontology

To set about establishing a fundamental defect here would mean
undermining not only our consciences, but, what is far worse, our feet.
　　　　　　　　　　　　　　　　　　　　　—Franz Kafka

To better understand the life-world's seemingly paradoxical ascent from the
mundane to the metaphysical level, we need first to examine the temporal
aspect of the reversal between the ego and the life-world. In terms of its
temporal dimension, the *alreadiness* of the life-world suggests that before
the ego becomes aware of its solitude, it has "already" lived and interacted
with others. The life of every individual is so intrinsically and irredeemably
affected by others (consider the preverbal interaction between the child
and mother) that one's interiority, one's inmost individuality, is not only
marked by the traces of other human beings but, more significant, is made
possible by one's encounter with them. "As long as we are born and brought
up by mothers," we are condemned to living in a world of others, a world
including our contemporaries, with whom we have to make do, willingly
or not; our successors, whom we cannot possibly experience directly, but
whom we nevertheless consider in our choices; and last, our predecessors,
on whose world we cannot act but whose actions and products are handed
down to us in the form of a tradition we can modify but not completely
reject.[21]

From an existential-phenomenological point of view, the *social* nature of
the world in which we live is an irreducible fact. "The world of my daily
life," says Schutz, "is by no means my private world but is *from the outset* an
intersubjective one, shared by my fellow men, experienced and interpreted
by others; in brief, it is a world *common to* all of us."[22] This common world,
the "paramount reality" on which the vital and practical structures of our
daily affairs are built, is by nature older than I: Not only does it predate my
existence, but it also continues to exist after I disappear. The temporal meaning of phenomenology's worldly turn is therefore clear: Intersubjectivity
precedes individuality in fact, and the reality of the intersubjective world
precedes the possibility of establishing my, or anyone else's, sphere of ownness.

But how is all this possible? Although my prereflective experiences of
others can testify that others exist before me and that my experiential world
cannot be quixotically my own, it is not clear how this common world
comes about. If indeed both "you" and the world are older than I, how is it
that I can participate in your world, and you in mine, while maintaining

separate identities? As Schutz puts it, "How is a common world in terms of common intentionalities possible?" To aver that community preexists its members in time, that I am I only insofar as I join the we, is one thing; to show how that community is established and perpetuated when its members come and go is quite another. The problem of intersubjectivity reemerges in full force as a question regarding the *formation* of the life-world as experientially intersubjective.

This question of the formation of the social world, of the genesis of intersubjective experience, cannot be answered satisfactorily at the level of descriptive phenomenology because this question demands not an explication of the life-world experienced by individuals as intersubjective but, rather, a genetic account capable of establishing the foundation of intersubjectivity and its continual sociohistorical manifestation in and through individuals' lived experiences. At stake here, in other words, is the metaphysical problem of *fundamental-grounding,* of providing a necessary and sufficient reason for the occurrence of intersubjective experiences as they are lived by all of us prereflectively. It is this necessity to "ground intersubjectivity fundamentally" that pushes phenomenology beyond its descriptive assignment and transforms it into a social ontology, and with that grounding the temporal meaning of *alreadiness* begins to be compounded by that of "metaphysical priority."

Despite its centrality to critical philosophy in general and to intersubjective phenomenology in particular, the project of fundamental-grounding is plagued by a peculiar difficulty — an aporia derived from what Karl-Otto Apel calls the "thesis of the impossibility of philosophical fundamental-grounding."[23] Apel argues that fundamental-grounding, as conceived of by the critical-rationalist philosophy, is an impossible project because every attempt to fulfill the claim for a philosophical fundamental-grounding "leads to a situation with three alternatives, all of which appear unacceptable."[24] Basically, Apel's argument is that fundamental-grounding, whatever form it takes, is necessarily undermined by the specter of the following trilemma: (1) an *infinite regress* that is demanded by the necessity of always going further back in search of reasons but that is not practically feasible and therefore yields no solid foundation; (2) a *logical circle* in the deduction resulting from the fact that one is forced in the grounding process to resort to statements that have already shown themselves to be in need of grounding — a process that, because it is logically faulty, likewise leads to no solid foundation; and (3) a *cessation of the process* at a particular point. This cessation is in principle feasible but would involve an arbitrary suspension of the principle of sufficient grounding.

Since intersubjective phenomenology cannot eschew the question of how intersubjectivity itself is founded, it inevitably faces this trilemma. At the same time, however, since a phenomenology of intersubjectivity cannot forgo its self-image as a *foundational* science, it has no choice but to reject the first two terms of the trilemma because of their failure to yield any solid foundation. This leaves only the third alternative. But although stopping the process at a particular point is feasible, this alternative proves to be a limited blessing: The achievability of supposedly apparent and convincing *knowledge-evidence* on which the search for foundation is premised can itself be subject to fundamental doubt, so that any grounding by means of this supposed knowledge-evidence merely amounts to a forced and arbitrary termination in the grounding process — a situation, as Apel points out perceptively, that is "entirely analogous to the suspension of the causal principle through the introduction of a *causa sui*."[25] Consequently, grounding in the sense of the third alternative turns out to be "*grounding by appeal to a dogma,* precipitated not so much by warrant and justification as by will-to-foundation."[26] Nor does "going back to extra-linguistic stages of the process" alter this fact because "with respect to such stages, it is always possible to ask for their grounding. Any thesis for self-grounding of such fundamental stages must, as with the corresponding theses for certain statements, be viewed as a disguise for the resolution to suspend the principle of sufficient grounding in this case."[27] The cessation strategy of fundamental-grounding thus reveals itself to depend on an unjustifiable act of self-fabrication; fundamental-grounding is in truth compulsory grounding.

Should one conclude from this that the quest for foundation is entirely futile? If the quest for foundation cannot shake off elements of obligatory self-fabrication, does that mean that a phenomenology of intersubjectivity must therefore forsake its aspiration to be a presuppositionless science? In any event, how does phenomenology of intersubjectivity deal with this problem? To be sure, fundamental-grounding may involve dogmatizing elements of one's conviction, but this does not mean that all moments of dogmatizing cessation are of equal force and credence. Some cessations may be premature and others may be one-sided, and these will therefore not be convincing. Our crucial task is to detect *at which moment* during the grounding process the act of dogmatizing takes place and to determine the implication of such a cessation for the conceptual system that requires it.

As indicated earlier, post-Husserlian phenomenologies of intersubjectivity can be distinguished by the twin reactions against phenomenology's founding gestures: the rejection of the transcendental point of view and the opposition to the reduction to the sphere of ownness. As a result, existential-phenomenological analysis of intersubjectivity abandons Husserl's aprioristic-constitutive perspective and focuses instead on the everyday world as given through common sense. Reversing Husserl's "unobtrusive" sliding of constitution from explication to creation (*Kreation*), Schutz, for one, tries to restore phenomenological constitutional analysis to its original meaning: the *clarification* of the sense-structure of intersubjectivity and of the world accepted-by-me-as-objective. What happens is a radical redefinition of the phenomenological enterprise, a new proposal for research, unambiguously stated by Schutz and Thomas Luckmann at the opening of *The Structures of the Life-World*:

> The sciences that would explain human action and thought must begin with a description of the foundational structures of what is prescientific, the reality which seems self-evident to man remaining within the natural attitude. This reality is the everyday life-world.... Only in the world of everyday life can a common, communicative, surrounding world be constituted. The world of everyday life is consequently man's fundamental and paramount reality.[28]

How should one read these sentences by Schutz and Luckmann? How should one construe their assertion that the everyday life-world is "man's fundamental and paramount reality"? What kind of commitment is there behind these statements? Above all, how does this passage bear on the problem of fundamental-grounding mentioned above? My suggestion is that this passage should not be read as a mere declarative statement voicing phenomenologists' observation that the life-world is temporally prior to individual existence; nor should it be read, as is often suggested, as some kind of statement of purpose calling for a counterresearch program against the functional-structural sociology with which it competes. Rather, these sentences are *ontological propositions,* and as such they entail an *ontological commitment* that responds to the problem of fundamental-grounding that existential phenomenology is forced to confront.

That the notion of the life-world should be interpreted ontologically can be read off Schutz and Luckmann's next remarks: "By the everyday life-world is to be understood that province of reality which the wide-awake and normal adult simply *takes for granted* in the attitude of common sense. By this taken-for-grantedness, we designate everything which we experience as *unquestionable*; every state of affairs is for us unproblematic until further notice."[29] Schutz and Luckmann's point is clear enough. The taken-for-granted life-world is the irreducible substratum of social life, the bottom floor at which all activities we call "social" are staged. It designates a level of experience and meaning that, at any given moment, is not only undoubted but also undoubtable. Schutz writes: "The taken-for-granted (*das Fraglos-gegeben*) is always that particular level of experience which presents itself as *not in need of further analysis.*"[30] This everyday life-world, so taken for granted, is where social life begins, and for that very reason, it is also where intersubjective phenomenology marks its reflexive point of investigation. Phenomenological reduction lets up here, no sooner, no later.

The twofold meanings of the taken-for-granted, invoked by Schutz and Luckmann, can now be stated precisely. First, it suggests the irreducibility of a certain naive trust in reality, a trust that the world is *such and such* — similar to what Santayana calls the *animal faith*. Second, it suggests the permanence or ever-presence of that faith; that is, it suggests that at any given moment there is always some part of reality that is accepted as valid or unproblematic. However, this naive faith implied by the taken-for-granted — a kind of "idealization" that "I can do it again, and so forth and so on," which shadows every moment of waking consciousness — should not be confused with any context-bound psychological credulity. What *is* taken for granted in the life-world during one's conscious life is not merely this or that situation or experience — subjective feelings vary from moment to moment even when objective conditions remain stable — but, rather, the *impossibility of not taking something for granted*. Although the taken-for-granted is often used to designate convictions that an individual may hold under specific situations (for example, my belief that when I put a letter in the mailbox, it will be delivered to its destination, or that when I enter the main lane of the highway from a ramp, other drivers will react to my signal light and keep their distance), the concept as such refers to the horizonal structure of meaning and action in general and does not correspond to anything mental or psychological in its contextual particularity. Strictly speaking, one does not and cannot live in the life-world as a perennial drifter, for even the most fluxlike journey through life is punctuated by situations whose meaningfulness is guaranteed by a more or less routinized (that is, taken-for-granted) background. As the irreducible substratum of social reality, the taken-for-granted life-world indicates, as Suzanne Bachelard rightly concludes, "the furthest limit to which phenomenological reduction can be carried."[31] This limiting and limited life-world sets the limit of our existence; for that reason, it also functions as a limiting concept for the descriptive inquiry on intersubjectivity.

My point so far is that the concept of the life-world, articulated through the taken-for-granted, signals the moment of cessation in the post-Husserlian phenomenology of intersubjectivity, the point where its search for the foundation of intersubjectivity can be laid to rest. It constitutes a point of *dogmatizing authority* during the course of phenomenological analysis that interrupts and arrests the process of fundamental-grounding. When the life-world is ushered in as the "irreducible" dimension of its object of inquiry, descriptive phenomenology reaches its borderline, and social ontology must take over. The process of fundamental-grounding can stop at this point because intersubjectivity is now supposed to have its ground in the everyday life-world, which, bracketing or reduction notwithstanding, *must* be taken for granted not only in experience but also in theory. Just as transcendental phenomenology grounds intersubjectivity in an absolute transcendental subject, post-Husserlian phenomenology reanchors it in the taken-for-granted everyday life-world. Although the life-world displaces the transcendental ego, it serves the same function on its new theoretical platform as the transcendental ego does in the context of constitutive idealism. This taken-for-granted intersubjective life-world, contrary to the usual interpretations, therefore cannot simply be a *pragmatic* postulate that vouchsafes the possibility of common discourse. Although it begins as a descriptive concept, it ends as an ontological postulate.

Whether Schutz and Luckmann and others following their lead conceive their work as "ontology," I leave to them to decide. My contention is that the difficulty of fundamental-grounding and of the circularity between mediation and intersubjectivity plaguing communication theories cannot be surmounted unless one raises the concept of the life-world, regardless of its original intent and possible interpretations, to the ontological level. Only by ontologizing the life-world, that is, by placing it dogmatically above and hence outside communication theories' rhetorical plot, can one terminate the infinite regress of searching for ground.

Does this strategy of ontologizing exorcise the tropical enfiguration within communication theories? Are communication theories firmly grounded now that any vexing question concerning the circularity of their modus operandi can readily be deferred to phenomenologists? In short, does the hypostatization of an intersubjective life-world suffice to solve the problem of mediation and transcendence? I think not. For although an ontologized life-world delivers what communication theory must assume but cannot provide for itself, the strategy of ontologizing bypasses one important question: the question concerning the relation between the subject and the world. The strategy of ontologizing is essentially a strategy of prioritization; by prioritizing the world over the subject, such a strategy simply suppresses one term within a dichotomous order while leaving the underlying dualist metaphysics intact. To *assert* that social experience is irreducibly communal without a complimentary critique of solitude sidesteps necessary reflections on the ontological meaning of communality; and to highlight the experience of "growing old together" as defining evidence for sociality without a parallel critique of mundane subjectivity leaves unexplored the ontological structure of "togetherness" that ensconces itself behind the momentary merging of two or more streams of "biographical consciousness." As long as the subject is still couched in egological terms, the transcendence of subjectivity will persist as a problem; and to the extent that transcendence of subjectivity remains problematic, the question of mediation and related issues pertaining to intersubjectivity cannot be said to have been solved. The transcendental regrounding of communication that we have been pursuing so far cannot rest content with a phenomenological metaphysics of the life-world; it also needs to incorporate "fundamental ontology" as a critique of subjectivity underscrutinized in post-Husserlian social phenomenologies. It is here that one encounters the second threshold in the return journey toward the ontological foundation of communication. And it is at this point, too, that our return journey needs to make a "Heideggerian turn." Just as descriptive phenomenology was forced earlier to submit to metaphysics, the phenomenology of the life-world must now give way to a fundamental ontology that responds to the hermeneutic complexity of existence—mundane or otherwise. By juxtaposing being and communication against the backdrop of Heidegger's hermeneutics of *Dasein,* I shall follow this second threshold for yet another round of grounding-breaking in the theorizing about communication.

Fundamental Ontology: *Quo Vadis?*

We shall always return to metaphysics as to a beloved one with whom we have had a quarrel. — *Immanuel Kant*

Kant thought it was a "scandal of philosophy" that no one had yet succeeded in proving the existence of objects in the external world. In *Being and Time,* Heidegger turns Kant's conception of the scandal of philosophy on its head. What is scandalous, says Heidegger, "is not that this proof has yet to be given, but that *such proofs are expected and attempted again and again.*"[32] The real scandal of philosophy, in other words, is the unquestioned central- ity and sovereignty of epistemology implied in Kant's chagrin. To Heideg- ger, the epistemological demand for *proving* the external world makes sense only against a background of uncritical assumptions about the nature of our ordinary epistemic situations and about the conditions for making our every- day activities fully intelligible. The seemingly innocent request for proof is in fact buttressed by the sizable operation of a sophisticated — but nonetheless misguided — metaphysical stage setting that is completed well before the skeptic ever makes his appearance. Both the narrow puzzle of skepticism and the attempt at "overcoming metaphysics" through epistemology in the broad sense are metaphysical at their core. "'Epistemology' and what goes under that name," contends Heidegger, "is at bottom metaphysics and ontology which is based on truth as the certainty of guaranteed representation."[33]

It is against representational metaphysics that Heidegger launches his rev- olutionary project of fundamental ontology. *Being and Time* signals the be- ginning of Heidegger's diachronic rethinking of the question of Being (*Seins- frage*). By breaking with the prevailing epistemological orientation of the nineteenth century, *Being and Time* reinitiates a "return to metaphysics." This return, however, is meant to be different from previous attempts. Truly archae- ological in that it avoids "free-floating constructions" and tradition-bound epistemological posits, *Being and Time* undertakes to dislodge the subject- object model and the rationalist presuppositions of the Cartesian paradigm in order to bring to light the plain sources of intelligibility already implicit in our everyday existence. This search for existential intelligibility based on an interpretation of man's worldly being disengages philosophical reflection from the Cartesian quest for certainty and, in so doing, puts an end to the kind of foundationalism promised by Husserl's all-powerful ego.

Although *Being and Time* is dedicated to Husserl, the rupture with Husserl- ianism is unmistakable. As Heidegger sees it, Husserl's project of phenome- nology as a strict and universal science is a circular enterprise; that is, phe- nomenology as a rigorous science is possible only insofar as one couches the subject matter of its research in concepts that already presuppose cen- tral phenomenological tenets. This is because "Husserl's primary question is simply not concerned with the character of the being of consciousness. Rather, he is guided by the following concern: *how can consciousness become the possible object of an absolute science?* The primary concern which guides him is the *idea of an absolute science.*"[34] In Heidegger's reading, Husserl's attempt to construct phenomenology as an absolute science involves a prejudgment—predicated, as it is, on a *postulated,* not revealed, distinction between the subject and object. This prejudgment opens the possibility of phenomenology as a specular science, a science that feeds on the presumed distance between the seeing and the seen. The central role that reduction plays in phenomenological reflection must be understood against this prejudgment, against the specular distance that reduction creates between consciousness and its object. Given this prefigured distance, phenomenologists' itinerary becomes predictable; their exploration turns out to be a guided tour: The natural attitude (as the subject) posits a world (as the object), and the transcendental consciousness (as the subject of all subjects) further disentangles itself from the natural attitude and turns the latter—together with the posited world—into a pure phenomenon (that is, an object).[35] The key to the whole phenomenological enterprise thus revolves around a certain interpretation of the natural attitude, an interpretation that remains implicit throughout phenomenology's critical progression. It is only because the relation between the natural attitude and the world is conceptualized as "positing a world as real" that Husserl's project succeeds.

Critical of Husserl's prejudgment, Heidegger finds Husserl's characterization of the natural attitude unjustifiable and states that the so-called natural attitude in Husserl

> is an experience which is totally *un*natural. For it includes a well-defined theoretical position in which every entity is taken a priori as a lawfully regulated flow of occurrences in the spatio-temporal exteriority of the world.... Man's natural manner of experience, by contrast, cannot be called an attitude.[36]

According to Heidegger, what Husserl thinks of as "natural"—that which subsequently poses itself as the object of phenomenological reduction—is in fact a manufactured result, a fiction-reality contrived by a certain "well-defined theoretical" exercise that distorts actual experiences. This distortion reaches its full magnitude when transcendental reduction is implemented alongside eidetic reduction. This latter reduction, in aiming for the essence of the object, rules out the Being and existence of the object in question. Moreover, Heidegger continues,

> in the consideration and elaboration of pure consciousness, merely the *what-content* is brought to the fore, without any inquiry into the being of the acts in the sense of their existence. Not only is this question not raised in the reduction, the transcendental as well as the eidetic; it *gets lost precisely through them.*[37]

Heidegger's point is as clear as it is forceful: An ontological clarification of the Being of the natural attitude cannot be based on a systematic variation and a comparison between different (possible) worlds, because the original experience of a human being—phenomenologists' experiences notwithstanding—is that of being bound to just one world. When analyzing an entity *"whose what is precisely to be and nothing but to be,"* the "ideative regard" of such an entity cast by Husserl, warns Heidegger, would lead only to a most fundamental misunderstanding.[38] Instead of latching onto the thesis of a manifold of possible worlds, phenomenologists should restrict themselves to *one* world, to the *phenomenal* world.

Retrieving the original Greek meaning of *phenomenon,* which was clouded by Husserl's intentionalist appropriation, *Being and Time* closes off the transcendental-constitutive vector of phenomenology as the master science of consciousness and introduces a hermeneutic inquiry of Dasein as preliminary to a more immediate illumination of Being as such.[39] Heidegger's preference for the technical term *Dasein* to Husserl's term *consciousness* or Dilthey's term *life* is deliberate. By renaming human existence "Dasein" (being-there), Heidegger tries to steer his fundamental ontology clear of the connotations of psychologism or naturalistic empirical anthropology on the one hand and the epistemological orientation underlying the Husserlian and neo-Kantian rationalism on the other. From Heidegger's standpoint, the concept of the "knowing subject," trapped within its "veil of ideas" and constituting its world out of meaningless "hyletic data," is a highly specialized and abstract way of understanding humanity that originates essentially from idealistic interests and has no real counterpart in individuals' actual lives. True to phenomenology's call to return to things themselves, fundamental ontology begins by returning to where man always and already *is.* Rather than plunging into the mind's inner chamber, *existential analytic* focuses on man's factical being-in-the-world: the situatedness and inalienable fact of having-been-in an environing world (*Umwelt*). The neologism *Dasein* is designed to capture the fact that one is always and already "thrown" into a world of cultural and historical (that is, sedimented) meanings that make up the untranscendable horizon in which things become intelligible to Dasein but that cannot itself be grounded by something beyond that horizon. "Dasein," as Heidegger says, "never comes back behind its thrownness."[40]

Within the framework of existential inquiry, man's factical being-there, namely, his "originary rootedness" in existence, takes priority over abstract and abstractive knowledge; consequently, the method of existential analytic — the regional metaphysics of Dasein prefatory to the explication of Being qua Being—consists not in the kind of purposive reflection and predicative reasoning characteristic of scientific research but, rather, in an interpretive clarification of Dasein's facticity—a hermeneutics of man as essentially being-in-the-world (*in-der-Welt-sein*) "more primordial, as over against the ontical inquiry of the positive sciences."[41] In this way, the methodological doctrine of hermeneutics formulated earlier by Dilthey is transformed by Heidegger into a hermeneutics of facticity, bringing about a fundamental reorientation of the phenomenological stance that involves a retrospective questioning not only of historicism and of Dilthey but also of the essentialism that links Husserl with Plato. In a more contemporary and graphic language, we can say that phenomenology, which aspires to be a "universal grammar" of cognition, is displaced by fundamental ontology as a "textual analysis" of Being's original petroglyphic structure (*compositio*).

In a 1928 lecture, Heidegger defined the objective of fundamental ontology:

> By "fundamental ontology" we understand the foundation of ontology in general (*die Grundlegung der Ontologie überhaupt*). To this belong: (1) the demonstrative grounding of the inner possibility of the question of Being as the basic problem of metaphysics—the interpretation of Dasein as temporality (*Zeitlichkeit*); (2) the laying out of the basic problems encompassed by the question of Being—the temporal (*temporale*) exposition of the problem of Being; (3) the development of the self-understanding of this problematic, its task and limits—the overturn (*Umschlag*).[42]

For Heidegger, fundamental ontology does not "limp along after" the sciences, trying to tidy their methods and concepts. Rather, it has the responsibility of both demonstrating and acting as the "productive logic" that first discloses an area of Being for a science and makes its structures transparent. The task of fundamental ontology, in other words, is to provide a *metaphysica generalis*—a science *of Being as such*—and to do so by offering a "genealogy of the different possible ways of Being."[43] As the science of sciences, fundamental ontology precedes *metaphysica specialis*, which lays out the condition for the possibility of specific ontic disciplines. In addressing the question of Being as such, fundamental ontology aims at "ascertaining the *a priori* conditions not only for the possibility of the sciences which examine entities of such and such a type... but also for the possibility of those ontologies themselves which are prior to the ontical sciences and which provide their foundation."[44] The ultimate goal of *Being and Time* is to stake out such an ontology as a basis for all regional ontologies by working out the question of Being in general.

But the fundamental ontology that Heidegger has in mind, as pointed out earlier, is critically different from a traditional metaphysics based on a representational relation between subject and object. In order to see better how Heidegger's approach differs from traditional perspectives, which he believes would only lead metaphysics into an abyss, it is helpful to take a look at his reading of Kant, who for Heidegger was perhaps the greatest metaphysician before Nietzsche. In *Kant and the Problem of Metaphysics,* Heidegger praises Kant for having made metaphysics a problem again. Metaphysics asks about beings as such and in totality. It seeks to ground the manifestation of being—the ontic truth—in the disclosedness of being's constitution of Being, of its ontological truth. The question about the possibility of ontic knowledge is attributed to the question about the possibility of that which enables ontic knowledge, namely, to the question about the possibility of ontological knowledge. In Heidegger's reading, the significance of Kant's "Copernican revolution" consists in its leading the question about the possibility of ontic knowledge back to the question concerning the possibility of ontology itself. In Kant, metaphysics becomes problematic once again.

In redressing the abuses of reason by both empiricism and idealism (Berkeley and Descartes), Kant's first *Critique* proposes the famed formal-transcendental approach that, by demarcating the bound of reason, is supposed to put metaphysics on a firm footing again. According to Heidegger, for Kant knowledge is transcendental when it concerns itself not just with beings, with objects, "but rather with our mode of knowledge of objects insofar as this is to be possible *a priori.*"[45] Transcendental knowledge is ontological knowledge (a priori synthesis, according to Kant); similarly, ontology "is called transcendental philosophy because it contains the conditions and first elements of *knowledge a priori.*"[46] Because it deals exclusively with knowledge a priori,

> transcendental knowledge does not investigate beings themselves, but rather the possibility of the precedent understanding of Being, which means at the same time the ontological constitution of beings. It concerns the going-beyond (transcendence) of pure reason toward beings so that experience can now first of all take the measure of them as possible objects. To make the possibility of ontology problematic means to ask about the possibility, that is, about the essence of this transcendence belonging to the understanding of Being, to philosophize transcendentally.[47]

To the extent that (1) "pure reason" knows the principles a priori, that (2) ontological knowledge, or a priori synthesis, is but judging about these principles, and that (3) pure reason must be delimited in its essence and separated from its misuse, transcendental philosophy as the question about the possibility of ontology is none other than the critique of pure reason.

As is well known, Kant's gallant reconstructive critique of rationality is motivated by an anxiety over what he perceives to be a collapse of epistemological certainty during the eighteenth century, a problem made all the more intolerable in view of the marvelous advancement in the empirical sciences such as chemistry and mechanics. But his attempt to ground metaphysics through transcendental critique contains a blindness of its own, a bias traceable to Descartes. This bias is readily discernible in a number of tensions besetting not only Kant's conception of Being but also the conformity theory of truth concomitant with it, for example, the tension between the "here-below" and the "thingliest of things" beyond all experience, and between the *ob-jectum* "out-there" and the *sub-jectum* "in here" that somehow must go out of itself to enfold and possess the former, its object. The resolution of these tensions proves to be one of Kant's major challenges. But since Kant's project begins as a struggle with an epistemological issue, its guiding question being "whether the real can be independent 'of consciousness' or whether there can be a transcendence of consciousness to the 'sphere' of the real," Kant's thinking remains circumvented within a binomial problematic of a Cartesian kind.[48] This in part is why he feels the need to prove the existence of the external world. What Kant inherits from Descartes, as Heidegger points out, is the idea that the basic condition of knowing is the ego as "I-think." For Kant, as well as for Descartes, the ego exists as a permanent, abiding principle of thinking and judging; as such it cannot be a representation or a represented object; rather, it is the ground of the possibility of all representing, all perceiving, hence of all the perceivedness of beings and thus the ground of all being. As original synthetic unity of apperception, the ego in Kant's schematism functions as the fundamental ontological foundation of being, "the vehicle of all concepts of understanding," and this is so not only because it makes possible the basic a priori ontological concepts, but also in the more important and determinate sense that the ego combines, or "agglutinates," everything passing through the "categories," which reflect nothing but the possible forms of unity in a predetermined correspondence to all the possible modes of knowing.

Comprehended on the basis of the highest principle of the ego, the Being of all entities in the Kantian universe is determined in advance. That is, inasmuch as the ego is the self-grounding ground of all grounds, the moment the ego is enthroned as *subjectum,* things that are not the I "are essentially such as stand as something else in relation to a 'subject,' [and they] lie over against it as *objectum.* The things themselves become 'objects.' "[49] This is the "I-principle" underlying modern representational metaphysics, according to which the Being of all entities is determined by their relation to the subject. Endowed with a capacity to combine, that is, to file things, as it were, in Idea's well-organized archive, the ego becomes "the subject for itself... All entities are therefore either objects of the subject or the subject of the subject."[50] This is dualism at its modern metaphysical height. When the thinking of a subject is made the basic principle of all metaphysics, entities come to be grounded in the "re-presenting" (*vorstellen* [placing before]) of the subject. Entities are encountered as "standing against" (*gegenständige*) the representing of the I. "The Being of things is now seen to be grounded in the possibility of experience," and "the search for 'Being' is now directed not toward a 'reality in itself' but toward the subjective roots of the transcendental consciousness."[51] As a result, the subject becomes "what can and believes it can offer itself representations"; correlatively, "in representation, the present, the presentation of what is presented, comes back, returns as a double effigy, an image, a copy, an idea as a picture of the thing henceforth at hand, in the absence of the thing, available, disposed and put forward for, by and in the subject."[52] Variable interpretations notwithstanding, metaphysics is at bottom representationism. In Heidegger's view, Kant's "Copernican revolution" was already a fait accompli in the rise of modern science.

Heidegger repeatedly suggests that the root of the problem with Kant's representationism is that it fails to grasp the transcendental I as factical, essentially temporal existence, that it fails to recognize that the I of the "I am" is always and already *somewhere* and *at some point in time* — in short, that "I am" means "I am *here* and *for a while.*" Although it is not to be thought of as "substance," the I for Kant (and for Husserl, too) is nonetheless thought of as "substantial," that is, as something abiding, unchanging, and constant, as something "which has always been present at hand."[53] Kant's failure to give a "*yes* to time," argues Heidegger, blinds him to "the phenomenon of the world," thereby causing him to forget that transcendence is *being-already alongside things.* Because of this atemporal bias or blindness, the pure I is reified "in accordance with the generally dominant interpretation set over against all temporality and all time," the result of which is that presence is deprived of its thoroughgoing temporal character.[54] Kant thus makes the same fundamental omission as did Descartes, who did not explain the sense of Being of the *sum* of the *cogito sum* in primordial fashion but, rather, interpreted it in terms of "the Cartesian approach of an isolated, present subject." Kant thereby concurs with the failure of ancient ontology, which, by expounding the temporal as object of intuition, was incapable of thinking about time in its primordiality. A "monumental ambiguity" ensues, for, failing to recognize "the place where being comes to be in time, it becomes impossible to know whether Being is only the creation of the human will or an Absolute that dips down into time through the medium of the human subject."[55] Ultimately, "the transcendental illusion" to which Kant thinks previous metaphysicians fall victim creeps back and ensnares him in yet another round in the "tournament with metaphysics."[56]

The *There* of Being

The existential proposition, "Dasein *is* its disclosedness," means at the same time that the Being which is an issue for this entity in its very Being is to be its "there." —*Martin Heidegger*

Heidegger's reading of Kant shows that the latter's thinking, as far as the question of Being goes, does not travel far enough. In fact, Heidegger thinks that Kant's transcendental critique of knowledge is performed in the face of a false dilemma: If the categories of human understanding cannot be found in the transcendent world of nature, then they must be sought in the immanent sphere of transcendental consciousness. Although Kant recognizes the necessity of finite existence and its importance to the principles of intelligibility from which a priori knowledge obtains its foundation, the critical idealism he arrives at subordinates (transcendent) object to (immanent) subject, leading ironically to "a high degree of ontological indeterminacy," for the simple reason that, as Frederick Olafson points out, "it becomes unclear what entity *in* the world can be identified with that subject, even though some such identity continues to be presupposed."[57] One of Heidegger's purposes in *Kant and the Problem of Metaphysics* is to correct this mistake by wresting—violently, to be sure—from Kant what he "intended to say" but "recoiled from."

Heidegger's judgment that in Kant there is something that is left unsaid but that deserves to be developed confirms Kant's contribution, but the same judgment also implies that Kant's reconstruction of metaphysics is ultimately a failed project that only fundamental ontology can salvage. Anticipating conservatives' resistance to his proposal, namely, fundamental ontology, Heidegger highlights the vulnerability of traditional ontologies: "Ontology, whether transcendental or precritical, is subject to criticism not because it thinks the Being of beings and thereby subjugates Being to a concept, but because it does not think the truth of Being and so fails to realize the fact that *there is a kind of thought more rigorous than the conceptual*."[58] Understandably, fundamental ontology, in contradistinction to traditional metaphysics, gives itself the task of capturing and reflecting that "rigorous thought." But ontology as a most general science will be possible only if it is guided in advance by a grasp of what we mean by the word *Being*. For although "ontological inquiry is indeed more primordial, as over against the ontical inquiry of the positive sciences," it will remain, argues Heidegger, "naive and opaque if in its researches into the Being of entities it fails to discuss the *meaning* of Being in general."[59] In other words, since fundamental ontology has to do with the *meaning* of Being, of what it means to be, it must first deal with "the problem of the internal possibility of the *understanding* of Being, from which all specific questions relative to Being arise."[60] In fact, "the question of the meaning of Being becomes possible at all only if there *is* something like an understanding of Being," and "to lay bare the horizon within which something like Being in general becomes *understandable* is," according to Heidegger, "tantamount to clarifying the possibility of having any understanding of Being at all."[61]

Because any interrogation implies a questioner and something that is being questioned, the interrogation of Being and the subsequent working-out (*Ausarbeitung*) of fundamental ontology become a two-pronged task. It involves, on the one hand, the question of the topos of being (that is, where is this "internal possibility of the *understanding* of Being" to be found?) and, on the other hand, the question of *interpreting* that understanding once that topos of possibility is located. Fundamental ontology is by necessity a *hermeneutic topology* of Being.

As noted earlier, any question about Being, as seeking, must be guided by what is sought. The meaning of Being, as that which is sought in the questioning, must already, in some way, be available to those who, to the extent that they are seeking, always already have a vague, average understanding of Being but are nonetheless perplexed by it. "We do not *know* what 'Being' means. But if we ask, 'What *is* "Being"?,' we already hold ourselves within an understanding of the 'is,' without being able to fix conceptually what the 'is' signifies."[62] The very asking of the question about Being, even in that almost empty form in which it is ordinarily formulated, testifies to that vague, average understanding of Being that is already granted to the inquirer in some fashion. Being, in other words, is in every case preunderstood as "that which determines beings as beings," as that which must always and already be available, that which must always be understood in advance, in order for beings to be accessible as such.[63] Insofar as Being determines beings in their character as being, beings can be grasped in such character only within the compass of a prior grasp of Being. The ontological clarification of Being therefore must proceed from its preontological understanding, from its ontic perspicuousness. In fact, Being can be appropriately asked about in the questioning only if it is asked about in a way that accords with the preunderstanding of it as determining beings as beings.

Since Being, as that which is asked about, requires its own way of being exhibited, in contradistinction to the ways proper to beings, fundamental ontology, likewise, requires its own conceptuality, its own proper starting point. This means that "insofar as Being constitutes what is asked about, and Being means Being of beings, *beings themselves* turn out to be *what is questioned in the question of Being.*"[64] Beings themselves are to be made directly subject to interrogation, and the questioning is to occupy itself with beings in such a way as to question them about Being. But exactly where should the questioner begin? Although the questioner has been led all along by an average, vague preunderstanding of Being, that is, although an implicit comprehension of Being remains a "fact," there is no guarantee that he or she will be able to enter the hermeneutical circle of this preunderstanding in a manner adequate to the task at hand. The crucial questions at this juncture are, *which beings are to be questioned and from which beings are we able to learn the meaning of Being*—that is, from which Beings can we read off (*ablesen*) Being? Which beings provide the place where existential analytic, dedicated to the question of the meaning of Being, can appropriately begin?[65]

Before giving the answer, Heidegger directs readers' attention to a related issue: The questioning of Being through beings must consider the proper strategy for working out this questioning. If the ontological must be sought in the ontic, how could the former be canvassed in adequate clarity on the basis of the latter? How is the grasp of Being to be carried through "in complete transparency to itself" against a certain preontological vagueness?[66] Because questioning about Being is a mode of Being proper to the questioner, the questioning is itself a mode of what is asked about in that very questioning. That is to say, because questioning about Being belongs to Being, a questioning about Being is *immediately* a questioning about questioning. Thus, questioning about Being immediately yields a questioning about questioning—that is, the question of Being is *immediately reflexive.*[67] To work out this question, to carry it through "in complete transparency to itself," means to *let the questioning be reflexive.* It means, in other words, to join to the questioning of Being a questioning of the questioning and of the questioner, to join to the thematic dimension of the question a reflexive dimension.[68] A topology of Being and a reflexive hermeneutic converge as one in fundamental ontology. Heidegger sums it up:

> Thus, to work out the question of Being means: to make a being—the questioner—transparent in his Being. The asking of the question, as a mode of *Being* of a being, is itself essentially determined by that which is asked about in it—by Being. . . . The explicit and transparent posing of the question about the meaning of Being demands a suitable prior explication of a Being (Dasein) with regard to its Being.[69]

It is at precisely this point that Heidegger introduces the term *Dasein* as "this being, which we ourselves are and which has questioning as one of its possibilities of Being."[70] Dasein designates the topos wherein interrogation of Being through beings can properly begin. Because an understanding of Being belongs *essentially* to Dasein's being, that is, because Dasein is essentially reflexive—being both the subject and the object of reflection—Dasein's existence makes available a pertinent region of inquiry in which "the further course of working out of the problem of fundamental ontology" can be initiated. As a special reflexive entity (*ein Seiende*) that has the question of being as its ultimate concern, Dasein constitutes an existential opening in the form of a temporal, historical, and mortal organization where being first becomes apparent and approachable. It signals the very occurrence of the question of being as the creation of metaphysics. This entity, Dasein, is the "there, by whose Being the disclosive breakthrough into the realm of beings occurs."[71] It is with this breakthrough that the being that man himself is, as well as the being that he is not, becomes manifest.

It is through a hermeneutic topology of Dasein that both Dasein's need of Being, which lies in oblivion, and the hidden meaning of this needfulness, which lies in preontological obscurity, are exposed. This exposure defines the business of the fundamental ontology, and this exposure promises the overcoming of representational metaphysics. *Exposure* is the key word here. Exposure means making manifest or laying bare; it involves the manipulation of the source of illumination; and, ultimately, it means giving things their proper place in being, their taking-place in visibility. To expose metaphysics as representationism in this sense means to subject its *compositio* to a different action of light than transcendental luminosity; it means destroying the overgrowth of metaphysics by "reexposing" the path to the prephilosophical "profundity of experience" that predates the birth of metaphysics. It must be remarked immediately that this destruction through lighting is not and cannot be a global annihilation; total destruction, if possible at all, is a meaningless project and deserves no effort. In fact, this destruction through exposure can only be a partial, discriminatory destruction that, as Heidegger maintains, "is far from having the *negative* sense of shaking off the ontological tradition. We must, on the contrary, stake out the positive possibilities of that tradition, and this always means keeping it within its *limits*; these in turn are given factically in the way the question is formulated at the time, and in the way the possible field for investigation is thus bound off."[72] The destruction of metaphysics through exposure therefore means setting the limits of traditional metaphysics and keeping it within that limit. It involves a confrontation of ontology with ontology so as to make possible a redefinition of transcendentalism, whereby the ontological tradition can be properly delimited by a tracing back to ontology's own origin. This overcoming of traditional metaphysics, as Reiner Schürmann describes it,

> does not put an end to the transcendental method as such. To question the "there" that we are instead of the I, and to disengage from being-there the structures of its performance in the world instead of the I's a priori structures of objective knowledge, is still to seek the origin of phenomena. The starting point, to be sure, is no longer sought in perception and knowledge but rather in our being's involvement with things and with others. The origin as epistemological demands an analytic of the understanding, and the origin as existential demands an analytic of being-in-the-world. The shift from one to the other discloses "the originary meaning" of the transcendental, so that even the Kantian critique is now exposed in "its proper tendency, possibly still hidden from Kant." The proper tendency of transcendentalism becomes apparent when the a priori is recognized no longer in the acts by which the understanding gives itself totalities, but in the possibility of totalization proper to our being.[73]

Being-in-the-world (*Da-Sein*) is this originary basis of metaphysics. Because Dasein is (at) the foundation of metaphysics, and because the disclosure of the constitution of its Being is ontology, the analytic of Dasein can properly be called *fundamental ontology*.

The mutation of transcendentalism from Husserl to Heidegger thus has to do with the role of man, of that creature whose remoteness from Being brings about the ironic closeness of a radical questioning of Being that makes fundamental ontology possible. In this fundamental-ontological inquiry, the condition of our knowing and experiencing is no longer sought purely in human terms, but in our relation to the being of entities in their totality. In defiance of Husserl's creeds, Heidegger's existential analytic does not "fill in" a posteriori the formal concept of the transcendental I; on the contrary, it designates the a priori stratum that makes possible any philosophy of the I, of the subject's consciousness. Through its ontological essence, "being-there" is an origin more originary than consciousness. And the explication of this origin cannot be sought in the formal structures of consciousness, but in the ontological structures through which the entity we are is said to belong to Being as such. The published parts of *Being and Time* represent the first step toward that goal.

Being as Relational Totality

Any entity can be accentuated as an emblem of Being.
—*Maurice Merleau-Ponty*

There was a time when I saw,
I saw... figures of relations between things, and not
things themselves.

—*Paul Valéry*

For Husserl, phenomenology remains, from start to finish, an eidetic-noetic science whose progress is measured by idealities and the degree of their formal organization. Eidetic-noetic investigations reflect a quest for Being of the type that is transcendentally guaranteed to be available, that is, to be present in principle to essential intuition. Clarity, distinctness, and apodicticity are its necessary characteristics, which make it translucent and masterable by the subject grasping itself in absolute self-reflection. For all its attempts to found a new science, phenomenology does not see or offer anything new, carrying on as it does the ocularcentricity of Greek and, to a greater extent, Cartesian metaphysics, which conceives Being in terms of presence or self-presence.[74]

In this context, one can justifiably interpret Dasein as a critical extension of Husserl's understanding of what constitutes adequate phenomenological "evidence." As Stephen Watson critically observes, "if the phenomenological principle of principles had in fact incontestably raised the question of the *Evidenz* of what got 'presented,' it never fundamentally questioned the nature of *presence* as such"; that is, "if phenomenological intuitionism disclosed an *Evidenz, that Evidenz* itself was always based on a presence taken-for-granted."[75] Although the reduction helps suspend faith in the appearance of things, the eidetic intuitionism upon which transcendental clarity is based does not really risk (rather, it strategically omits) questioning the phenomena themselves. Overconfident in a transcendental optics that often blurs the distinction between the given and its appearance, between *Erscheinung* and its *Schein,* phenomenology in its Husserlian mode is able to proceed only if it overlooks the necessity of "interpretation" embedded in the very event of *phenomenalization.*

Heidegger thus finds in Husserl's phenomenology a hermeneutic shortcoming, a lack of critical awareness regarding its own limitations as phenomenology. To amend this deficiency, Heidegger believes that Husserl's conception of "transcendence," which is always understood *immanently,* that is, located inside (or derived from) the subject, must be radicalized:

> For why can I let a pure thing of the world be encountered at all in bodily presence? Only because the world is already there in thus letting it be encountered, because letting-it-be encountered is but a particular mode of my being-in-the-world and because world means nothing other than what is always present for the entity in it. I can see a natural thing in its bodily presence only on the basis of this being-in-the-world.[76]

Being-in-the-world emerges as the ever receding but never disappearing horizon of presence, a horizon always in excess of the subject's ideations. It exists as the constitutive antecedence of the subject's reflective possibilities, an enabling gestalt that the pure phenomenological intuition does not heed, but without which the present could not be. Unless Husserl completely gives up the claim of rigor that supports his vision of a presuppositionless science, the pure "seeing" of phenomenology must be extended ex post facto to include this anterior ground of being-in-the-world; it must recognize the fact that "to make present is always to encounter presence on the ground of an event already past and the specificity of an already presupposed referential context."[77]

Although Dasein can be interpreted as a revisionary concept that maintains continuity with phenomenology's more familiar terms (*person, spirit, self, consciousness, subject, I,* and the like), its true significance lies in the degree to which it destroys the representational metaphysics that perpetuates a dualist economy by privileging the subject over the object. The English translation of Dasein, being-in-the-world, conveys the idea quite well. This hyphenated, somewhat awkward translation nevertheless makes explicit the idea that man and the world, although distinct, are essentially related. To be is always to be *there* in the world: "Dasein, in so far as it *is,* has always submitted itself already to a 'world' which it encounters, and this *submission* belongs essentially to its Being."[78] Conversely, the presence of the world immediately signifies Dasein's *ek-sistence* as being-absorbed-in-its-possibilities (*Beiseinem-Möglichkeiten-seins*) that constantly projects (that is, transcends) itself out of itself into the world. One being an essential, integral part of the other, man and the world must be considered to be mutually constitutive;

they are *equiprimordial* in a joint coming-to-be that is being-in-the-world. Viewed in this way, Dasein can no longer be understood as a substantial I with specifiable content in its consciousness; it is not a thing with properties or a self-contained field of mental workings but, rather, *a way of being* whose essence is its relation with the world and its possibilities thereof. Heidegger contrasts markedly with Husserl:

> One's own Dasein becomes something that it can itself proximally "come across" only when it looks away from "experience" and the "center of its action," or does not as yet "see" them at all. Dasein finds "itself" proximally in what it does, uses, expects, avoids — in those things environmentally ready-to-hand with which it is proximally concerned.[79]

By necessity rather than by choice, Dasein is precognitively "involved with," "fascinated by," and "absorbed in" the world, so much so that when it "directs itself toward something and grasps it, it does not somehow first get out of an inner sphere in which it has been proximally encapsulated, but its primary kind of being is such that it is always 'outside' alongside entities which it encounters and which belong to the world already discovered."[80] One will not understand the truth of existence if one does not let go of Husserl's constructionist theory of knowledge that substantializes the knower as the origin of the known.

This antisubstantial, antidualist understanding of Dasein results directly from Heidegger's conception of existence as "openness" or "disclosure," informed by his "transformative reading" of the Greek philosophers. According to Heidegger, the Greeks were the first to experience entities (*To on, ta onta*) as *phainomena,* as something that of themselves show themselves or appear.[81] In appearing, an entity appears *as* something meaningful: as a sword that the warrior can wield or as the ship that he can launch or as the god that he can revere or challenge. This "as" character bespeaks the advent of meaning among entities, the irruption of significance and spirit that occurs only with the arrival of man. The uniqueness of Dasein as "the living being that has *logos*" is that one's essence is the locus of meaning and that one has access to entities only in terms of their appearance-as or being-as in logos. Unlike any other entities that simply occupy space and persist through time, Dasein *ek-sists*; it *ek-sists* in the special sense that it always stands *ahead of* itself, that is, open to its own possibilities as transcendence.

Since "it is essential to the basic constitution of Dasein that there is *constantly something to be settled,*" Dasein has no essence, if by essence is meant any fixed qualities or features an entity possesses.[82] Constantly standing ahead of itself, that is, remaining unsettled all the time, Dasein cannot be anything but its very own openness. "The particle *Da* refers to this essential openness. By reason of this openness, this be-ing (*Dasein*), together with the 'being there' of the world, is 'there' for itself."[83] This existential-ontological structure of the human be-ing, namely, that it is in such a way as to be its own *Da* (openness), can be expressed by saying that Dasein is a *lumen naturale*, a "natural light" in the expanse of being. Thrown into being and without settlement, Dasein is singularly "enlightened"; as being-in-the-world, that is, abandoned to the world, it is "lighted" in itself in such a way that it is itself a "place of light." Things that are "merely present" can come to full light only through a be-ing that is itself "lighted."[84] In existence, Dasein does not "proceed from some inside to some outside; rather, the nature of *ek-sistence* is out-standing standing-within the essential sunderance of the clearing of beings."[85] Heidegger discusses Dasein's openness to Being as follows:

> Dasein in its Being alongside things brings along with it something like a range of openness. Dasein as Being-there in and through its Being-alongside... things lets be something like a "there" for the first time, something like a *there,* that is, a range of openness with which entities can make themselves manifest for the first time. The "there" is not a place distinct from "over there" (*Dort*). To be there (*Da sein*) is not "to be hither and thither" (*hier und dort sein*) but to be that very entity which first of all brings with it the possibility and the making possible of something which can be oriented here and there. *The there is the space broken open in itself* (*aufgebrochen*). And insofar as existence belongs to Dasein, it is a break through (*Einbruch*) into space, i.e., such that the spatiality (*Räumhaftigkeit*) of space first of all becomes manifest in itself.[86]

Dasein is this happening of the opening, of giving openness, of breaking through into space. *Dasein is disclosedness,* the letting-be of light, of visibility itself. Letting-be presupposes the concept of openness, a range of openness that is opened up in the letting-be and that belongs to letting-be. This range of openness, coextensive with Dasein's being-there, of course, is not a formal concept of Being reached through abstraction. Being-in for Heidegger does not mean spatially contained in (as water is in a cup) or next to (as a chair is beside a table). Being-in means *being-alongside* (*sein-bei*); that is, being-open-for. As soon as it exists, Dasein is always already open for something. Unlike entities that passively endure nature's sundry encumbrances, Dasein finds itself in a range of openness that it has opened up with its own existence.

Qualified by its *Da,* the being of Dasein must be understood as "situated disclosure." This situated disclosure points to the mutual presence of Dasein and the world; it characterizes the coming into presence of the *average every-day world* as a structure of *significance* into which Dasein is thrown and according to whose relations Dasein exists as historic being. This significance-world of Dasein's is revealed through what Heidegger calls the "state of mind" or "mood" (*Befindlichkeit*) that binds Dasein affectively to a particular situation, to its place in the world and to its moment in history. As the inescapable environment of Dasein's existence, the significance-world announces through temporal unfolding a disclosive region of Dasein's action and making-do, a field laid out in terms of roles, goals, and equipment for achieving those goals, which involves Dasein toward realizing its possibilities as being-in-the-world. This significance-world, in other words, *relates* Dasein *to* its surroundings, which simultaneously appear to Dasein as the gathering of its "relatives," of recognizable faces:

> In its familiarity with these relationships, Dasein "signifies" to itself: in a primordial manner it gives itself both its Being and its potentiality-for-Being as something which it is to understand with regard to its Being-in-the-world. The "for-the-sake-of-which" signifies an "in-order-to"; this in turn, a "toward this"; the latter, an "in-which" of letting something be involved; and that in turn, the "with-which" of an involvement. These relationships are bound up with one another as a primordial totality; they are what they are as this signifying in which Dasein gives itself beforehand its Being-in-the-world as something to be understood. The *relational totality* of this signifying we call "significance." This is what makes up the structure of the world—the structure of that wherein Dasein as such already is.[87]

Heidegger thus gives the screw of phenomenological description a sharp hermeneutic turn. Consequently, "the 'as' of the phenomenological appeal to the evidence of the 'meant as meant' . . . differs from Husserl to Heidegger, becoming inextricably contextual and *hermeneutic* in the recognition that truth is as much a matter of producing (*Herstellen*) as it is of proving."[88] Revealed *as* "involvement," our relationship to the world, our being in it, is hermeneutical through and through precisely because the world is not something strange that we struggle to grasp conceptually as an object in order to make sense of it; quite the contrary, it is always a familiar, understood world in which, as Dilthey says, "we are at home everywhere." In contrast to the credo of orthodox phenomenology, existential analysis makes it clear that our relationship to the world is one of practical concern and situated entanglement rather than one of theoretical interest and dispassionate observation. In this world, we know how to get on, in a practical way, with everything around us—that is, with what is "ready-to-hand"; this is so because we do not intuit what is ready-to-hand as an object of cognition; rather, we take it in, in terms of its "in-order-to," in terms of its prereflective relevance to the situation in which we find ourselves.[89] Because of this prereflective involvement, the already meaningfulness of the world is not a result of intentionality imposing meaning on the subject-dependent object. On the contrary, consciousness arches toward the sense-object precisely because Dasein as openness has already submitted to a "primordial totality" saturated with "significance."

Toward an Ontology of Communication

Really, universally, relations stop nowhere. — *Henry James*

Nothing is itself alone. Things are because of interrelations or interactions. — *Wallace Stevens*

I do not believe in things, I believe in relationships. — *Georges Braque*

How does one rethink Being in the wake of Heidegger's existential analytic? Should we start "meditating poetically," as Heidegger seems to suggest? If the existential-hermeneutic articulation of Dasein destructures representational metaphysics and decenters the Cartesian-Kantian subject, is it not then possible to bring about a restructuring at a deeper level and from a different angle? If so, what does this deep structure of Being—both hidden and revealed in Dasein, simultaneously carried on and destroyed by Dasein—look like? To bring the question closer to home, how does Heidegger's existential interpretation of Dasein bear upon the theorization of communication that always assumes a centered and centralizing subject?

These are difficult questions, and I do not pretend to be able to answer them all. My purpose in raising these questions is to establish a proper Heideggerian framework in which I shall seek to address the last of these questions. As pointed out earlier, one of the most valuable insights into existence provided by existential analysis is that Dasein and the world are *equiprimordial*. By interpreting the basic structures of man's Being, delineated in the compound expression "being-in-the-world," Heidegger is able to show that the world must be conceived as the existential dimension of man through which is predisclosed the matrix of all possible relationships, a range of openness within which Dasein encounters beings first of all through "concernful circumspection" (*Umsicht*). This dimension of intelligibility, of "total meaningfulness," is projected by Dasein as that within which Dasein lives and works and encounters other beings. "It is by means of man's being-in-the-world that the World as such becomes luminous, insofar as man — by virtue of his understanding 'ek-sistence' — makes manifest the Being of beings. So intimate is the *correlation* between World and man, who as Dasein makes possible the World's illumination, that only insofar as Dasein is, 'is there' Being."[90] Mutatis mutandis, Being is to be understood as "the luminosity of World" brought about by man, who as Dasein is always and already in it.

Although the expression *intimate correlation* accurately conveys the essential connectedness between man and world, I think Heidegger's point can be put in stronger terms. For correlation, however intimate, presupposes separation and difference between two entities, between two planes of visibility, while the meaning of being-in-the-world consists precisely in the radical inseparability of man and world: Man is essentially worldly and the worldliness of the world signifies at once the thereness of man. The relation between them is essential and internal rather than accidental and external. When interpreted properly, being-in-the-world means that man and world, though ontically distinct, are *ontologically the same,* in that they belong essentially together in the event of opening that defines being-in-the-world as *care*-ful *ek-sistence.* Seen from this perspective, *ek-sistence* could arguably be described as an *intertext* of man and world, that is, as a constitutive structure of in-between, a nexus, manifesting itself in Dasein's factical configuration of worldly situatedness on the one hand and the world's meaningful embodiment in Dasein's temporal existence on the other. Being-in-the-world is intertextual not only because "Dasein," as Charles Scott notes, "is a world-relational occurrence in which things are manifest" but also, more pointedly, because each of its structural constituents necessarily refers to the others and requires them for its own proper identity.[91] The proper place of Dasein is always beside itself, in the world, just as the proper place of the world is beside its four corners, in Dasein. For the simple truth is that without man there would be no world, and, by the same token, in the absence of the world, man could not be. Man and world make simultaneous presence in *ek-static* unity — each one being an internal dimension of the other. Through their mutual dependence, their essential relatedness, man and world expropriate one another, thus coming to be what they are. Inasmuch as the world can be read as the human text-analogue, the meaning of human existence in turn becomes readable only in the "nascent logos of the lived world." Lest the meaning of the expression "the equiprimordiality of man and world" be reduced to triviality, one must hold fast to the notion of "ontological sameness" that has always escaped the gaze of representational metaphysics.

What is suggested here, I must point out, is not some kind of anthropomorphic monism inspired by the oft-voiced, New Age–like objection to the artificial separation of humankind from its natural environment. By suggesting that being-in-the-world be read as an intertext, I mean to bring into relief what I propose to call the *relational ontology* predicated on Heidegger's insight that being-in-the-world is a structural whole, that being as *ek-sistence* is a relational totality that precedes any ontic differentiation. This I take to be one major contribution of *Being and Time.* According to this relational ontology, man (the subject) is neither prior nor posterior to the world (the object); man and world are but two aspects of one unified ontological occurrence. Being aspects of one and the same event, man and world should be regarded as *relata* within one constitutive relation that precedes their transformation into antithetical opposites. Ontologically, the Being-horizon antecedes the encounter of man with beings that takes place within it, in much the same way that logicians speak of the principle that condition always antecedes the conditioned. The Being-horizon as a relational totality is an abiding presence (*Anwesenheit*) that makes it possible for the beings that are to become manifest, to become present as themselves. It is in this horizon of presence that the world assumes its specific shape and individuals take on recognizable faces as they encounter the former. Inasmuch as Dasein is itself manifest in the manifestness of things, the disclosive region of things' manifestness also unconceals Dasein's world-relational presence.

This ontological sameness of man and world reveals the structural nature of being as presence. Because man and world are ontologically inseparable — that is, because being-in-the-world constitutes a relational totality in which objects make their presence as worldly beings — it follows that the presence of an object depends as much on its singular being-there as on the relational network that forms the background of its illumination. This essential membership of an object, its essential belongingness to a whole, negates that object's independence, for its identifiable presence takes shape only against a preexisting totality and is achieved or achievable only through the difference between itself and its relational other within that totality. Simply put, it is the unarticulated whole that determines the parts belonging to it: A part makes its presence as a part only insofar as it is differentially articulated through contrastive associations to other coexisting parts within the same pregiven whole. Heidegger clearly demonstrates this protostructuralist idea in his discussion of the notion of "equipment": "Taken strictly, there 'is' no such thing as *an* equipment. To the being of any equipment there always belongs a totality of equipment, in which it can be this equipment that it is."[92] A piece of equipment, like any other object in our environment, is not a separate, independent particular; it is what it is only insofar as it fits in a certain way into an "equipmental totality." What a piece of equipment *is*, is entirely dependent on how it is incorporated into the total equipmental context.

Within the relational field of presence, then, a thing is no-thing apart from the internal relation to difference, for its very identity depends on a reference-to-other and presupposes its own thoroughgoing situatedness within a diacritically articulated web. What is most "proper to" a thing, in other words, is its substitutability, its being in any case in the place of the other. As Mark Taylor puts it, "there is (nothing) no thing-in-itself, for self-relation is always mediated by relation-to-other."[93] In the clearing of Being, "everything," as Plato says in *Cratylus*, "like ceramic pots, leaks."[94] It is through this leaking, through a structural crossing over among all the parts within a whole, that the whole and the parts assume their respective appearances, and these appearances, to the extent that they are relatively and differentially articulated, are always conditioned by that relational totality. Despite its speculative bent, Hegel's discussion on the relation between the same and the different appears pertinent and is worth quoting in full:

> Thus something *through its own nature* relates itself to the other, because otherness is posited in it as its own moment; its being-within-self includes the negation within it, by means of which alone it now has its affirmative determinate being. But the other is also qualitatively distinguished from this and is thus posited outside the something. The negation of its other is now the quality of the something, for it is in this sublating of its other that it is something. It is only in this sublating that the other is really opposed to another determinate being; the other is only externally opposed to the *first* something, or rather, since in fact they are *directly* connected, . . . their connection is this, that determinate being has *passed over* into otherness, something into other, and something is just as much an other as the other itself is. Now in so far as the being-with-self is the non-being of the otherness which is contained in it but which at the same time has a distinct being of its own, the something is itself the negation, *the ceasing of an other in it*; it is posited as relating itself negatively to the other and in so doing preserving itself; this other, the being-within-self of the something as negation of the negation, is its *in-itself*, and at the same time this sublation is *present in it* as a simple negation, namely as its negation of the other something external to it.[95]

To the extent that determinate entities are co-relative, otherness ceases to be merely other and difference is no longer indifferent. And to the extent that identity is achieved and achievable only through the detour of difference, relation-to-other constitutes the reality of self-relation. "Though overlooked (or repressed) by common sense, *difference from* other is at the same time *relation to* other."[96] In fact, "we can evoke an actual or real identity only by embodying difference, a real and actual difference, a difference making identity manifest, and making it manifest as itself. Only the presence of difference calls identity forth, and it calls it forth in its difference from itself, in its difference from an identity which is internally the same."[97] That which "is equal to itself and is for-itself is such only in its absolute difference from every other. And this difference implies a relation with other things, a relation that is the cessation of its being-for-itself."[98] In this light, being-for-itself and being-for-others are both the same and different: the same because they reflect into one another, different because their reciprocal reflection sustains at every moment a difference that establishes the condition of their respective selfsameness. There can be no identity without difference any more than there can be difference apart from identity: "each *is, only in so far as the other is*; it is what it is through the other, through its own non-being"; for the same reason, "each is, *in so far* as the other is not; it is what it is through the non-being of the other; it is *reflection-into-self.*"[99] Because all things are *radically* related, everything is exhaustively relative as exteriority folds into interiority and interiority unfolds into exteriority. Herein lies the central theme of relational ontology: Being itself is relational because (the total field of) presence itself is structured relationally. Structured relationally—that is, being same and different at once—Being is both multiple and singular. Being is multiple because its presence is not limited to any single entity, any single being. "All being is in Being"; Being transcends singularity.[100] On the other hand, Being's transcendence of singularity does not mean that Being should be viewed as the total sum of present beings. For Being is not an additive concept, nor a supercategory subsuming multifarious members; in making things present, Being keeps its *ek-static* unity in which multiplicity becomes manifest as such within one and the same region of disclosure. The elusive truth of Being, then, does not hide behind some beguiling veil of appearance, nor is it ensconced in the recess of consciousness's interiority. Rather, it is stretched out—literally—in the *lateral depth* of interrelated beings, of beings' thoroughgoing interrelatedness. "Being excludes all alterity. It can leave nothing outside and cannot remain outside... The being of beings is the light in which all things are in relationship."[101] The poetic wisdom of Wallace Stevens and Henry James contains an ontological truth: Beings *are* because of their interrelations; beings *are* where relations *are*. Taylor puts it best when he states that "*relation is ontologically constitutive—to be is to be related.*"[102]

Relation is not a silent concept any more. It communicates; its sending can now be received. The sending is this: It is the relational structure of Being at the ontological level that establishes the possibility of communication as mediation between subjects at the ontic level. It is the ontological relatedness among all the things present that makes possible the ontic event of communication as transcendence of their difference and distance. In short, ontological relatedness founds communicability, which, not unlike a deep structure or a genetic code, determines the surface (that is, grounded) varieties of intersubjective phenomena and enables them to proliferate. What I am suggesting is this: From the standpoint of relational ontology, human existence is already structured *communicatively,* that is, as a "referential totality" (*eine Verweisungsganzheit*) that puts man and world in perpetual communication and, on that basis, grounds each and every local interreference within that world as man's lived environment. Ontologically, man and world communicate, each participating in the presence of the other within one continuous event of opening, of taking-place, that constitutes the absolute horizon of being as a region of precommunicative plenitude. *Ontologically, communication has always and already occurred.* Communication precedes existence—*to be is to communicate.* This, I think, is the actual meaning buried under the apparent truism of such notorious sayings as "Communication is the *conditio sine qua non* of human life and social order" or "You cannot not communicate." "You cannot not communicate" does not simply mean that whatever one does carries meaning or that one's action (including nonaction) will always be interpreted by (and hence mean something to) others. Rather, it voices the deeper ontological truth that one's very existence *is communication* between self and others, between self and world. Ontologically speaking, communication communicates; ontic exchanges of meaning between subjects, of information between machines, and so on are mere alibis of the event, the *taking-place,* of communication.

What conclusion can be drawn from this ontological articulation of communication? What implication is there for the problematic of communication that predisposes inquirers' reflection always in terms of the ontic givenness of the subject? First, inasmuch as communication can be interpreted as a constitutive structure that grounds the presence of man and world through an intertextual opening of being, it follows that communication constitutes the worldly individual as subject. The solitary *cogito,* that idealized agent who transmits and receives information on its own, is no longer the irreducible, self-sufficient foundation of communication. As a worldly being, the communicative subject does not and cannot exist apart from the relational structure of existence that constitutes it as the vehicle of mediation in the first place. As Sartre put it, "individuals do not exist first, in order to then communicate, but communication constitutes them in their very being."[103] Subjectivity is the effect of communication, not the other way around. From a relational point of view, barring God, a subject in itself is an unobtainable and unintelligible construct: Relatively constituted, the subject is always double, other-dependent, or, to resurrect a worn-out expression, internally split. For the same reason, a noncommunicative, totally autistic subject is equally unobtainable and illusory. "Pure solitude," as Derrida rightly points out, "is absolute nonsolitude, whether it cuts off all relation to the other or whether it relates to all that is other (*tout-autre*), which is also not relating at all."[104] Solitude presupposes the existence of others, and the experience of solitude presupposes a prior experience of being-with. No matter who, no matter where, no matter when, man is condemned to communicate. Philippe Sollers is perhaps closest to the truth when he says: "Neither the 'normal man' nor the 'madman' actually communicates: they are, more precisely, *communicated*... (from without and from within)."[105]

Second, because communication is *prior to* the reflective construction of subjectivity, that is, because subjectivity presupposes the relational opening of Being from which it receives the possibility of its ontic concretion, the subject-centered problematic of communication sketched in the last chapter needs to be overturned. Such an overturning entails inverting the conceptual hierarchy that posits and valorizes the subject as an unmediated source of meaning (see figure 2). What is taken in the old problematic as pregiven and primitive at the moment of communication must now be reconstructed as derivative from and secondary to the event of communication itself, to the universal dissolution of indifference that signifies the truth of beings and presence. According to the new conceptual order, communication is the ground (*Grund*); it is the ontological foundation from which various intersubjective exchanges receive the possibility of expressing their spatial and temporal multiplicity.[106]

Heidegger could well have been talking about communication when he wrote of the bridge:

It does not just connect banks that are already there. The banks emerge as banks only as the bridge crosses the stream. The bridge designedly causes them to lie across from each other. One side is set off against the other by the bridge. Nor do the banks stretch along the stream as indifferent border strips of dry

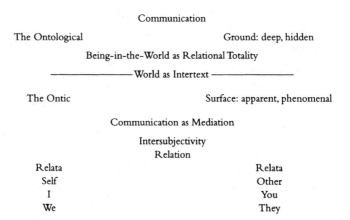

Figure 2. The ontological structure of communication

land. With the banks, the bridge brings to the stream the one and the other expanse of the landscape lying behind them. It brings stream and bank and land into each other's neighborhood.[107]

To exist is to cross bridges, one after another. To exist is to gather and be gathered by what lies in one's neighborhood. Communication is bridge-crossing. Just as each bridge joins two banks previously distant from and unconnected to one another, each event of communication actualizes the possibility of transcendence held out for those who dare to travel into a distant land. If communication between individuals strikes one as miraculous or mysterious, if one still feels the need to ask how communication is possible, it is because one has yet to acknowledge the facticity of one's bridge-like existence. On the other hand, if one never questions the possibility of intersubjective transaction, that is, if one is blessed with constant certainty of the reality of communication, it is because a bridge has already been built *before* the journey of transcendence is taken.

Part II

The Economy of Difference

4 / The In-Difference of Being

To ridicule philosophy is really to philosophize. — *Blaise Pascal*

Heidegger's fundamental ontology begins by revisiting the question posed to him by his early reading of Franz Brentano's treatise on Aristotle: What is the unified meaning of the manifold sense of Being? Around the time of the publication of *Being and Time,* Heidegger thought that the question of the truth of Being is not a matter of correspondence, of adequation between finite consciousness and transcendent reality but that, instead, the truth of Being means the discoveredness of beings. The discovering of beings that become discovered and thus become "true" occurs primordially within the environment's relations of meaning and significance. The truth of Being, in this early stage of Heidegger's thinking, is bound to the disclosedness of Dasein, where the discovering activity of Dasein measures up to the discoveredness of beings by virtue of Dasein's concernful rootedness in the world.

Heidegger's early notion of truth as disclosedness, however, undergoes a subtle and significant shift in his later works. The shift can be observed when Heidegger dispenses with the word *Wahrheit,* with truth as preserving (*verwahren*), and begins to think the sheer happening or event of *a-letheia,* according to which there appears only the successive unfoldings of the multiple events of Being, the multiple sendings of the epochs. At this point, Heidegger's thinking, when pushed to its extreme, is no longer concerned with the meaning or the truth of Being as illuminating disclosure but, rather, with the giving or granting of meaning and truth as such. Placed in the context

115

of Heidegger's overall development, the later Heidegger can be read as an answer to his early question by saying that there is (*es gibt*) only the manifold sense, the many senses, the endless unfolding of sense after sense, truth after truth, of Being in a process that he ultimately describes as a groundless play, a Heraclitean play without origin and without why.

Heidegger's path of thinking, his "way toward the neighborhood of Being," has been interpreted and pursued differently. In his reflection on the encounter between Gadamer and Derrida, John Caputo observes that there have been two types of reactions to Heidegger's calling, the right wing and left wing.[1] Gadamer is the leading representative of right-wing Heideggerianism. Gadamer is characterized as right wing because, attracted to the conservative side of Heidegger, he "is always more interested in the gift of the presence—the 'present' which tradition makes to us—than in the giving itself, the *es gibt*."[2] In Gadamer there lingers the ghost of Hegel, of German Romanticism, and of a metaphysics of monologic soul inspired by Plato, which causes him to genuflect to past teachings, to the deep truth and wisdom of the classic, in short, to an *onto-logic* that links the modern to the ancient. Caputo maintains that, although critical of the Hegelian teleologism and its hierarchical proclivity, Gadamer's philosophical hermeneutics remains in the end essentialist and traditionalist, manifesting "a certain retreat into the classical idea of *Wesen* as deep essence, *essentia*, . . . and in an unmistakable resistance to Heidegger's attempt to think *Wesen* verbally, as the sheer coming to presence (*An-wesen*) and passing away (*Ab-wesen*) of the epochs of presence."[3]

Derrida's thinking, in contrast to Gadamer's halfhearted appropriation of Heidegger's critique of metaphysics, represents for Caputo the more radical, left-wing development of the Heideggerian project. More in tune with the later Heidegger and against Gadamer's faith that tradition will deliver the goods, Derrida's deconstruction of logocentrism begins by doubting the wisdom handed down to us by tradition. Like any good left-winger, Derrida does not believe there is a deep ontology inscribed in the *Muttersprache*, a matriarchal ontology that eventually submits to patriarchal dictates. For Derrida, language, tradition, mind, truth, transcendence, and Being itself are merely more or less stable—hence more or less unstable—unities of meaning, relatively frail textual concoctions held together in part by violence, in part by inertia, and in part by their usefulness in life.[4] Instead of seeking origin and restoring the past to support the legitimacy of the present, Derrida tries to show that various discourses on Being, Heidegger's own included, are themselves caused by an irretrievable loss of that origin. Effect, truth as effect, Being as effect, meaning as effect—this is the battle cry of the left-wing Heideggerian.

Clearly, the right-wing and left-wing reactions to Heidegger result from two very different interpretations of Heidegger's overall project, particularly his reflection on language and its relation to Being. Whereas Gadamer puts more emphasis on the early Heidegger, thus presenting Heideggerianism as a philosophy of meaning—of the preservation, cultivation, and recommencement of meaning—Derrida revitalizes the skeptical and allegorical side of the later Heidegger to refute the possibility of any final grasp of Being as such. Whereas Gadamer thinks that there are deep deposits of meaning in the tradition into which we have been fortunately placed, and that the task of hermeneutics is to learn how to mine that wealth and make it available to the less fortunate, Derrida, taking the spirit of Heidegger's overcoming of metaphysics closer to heart, engages actively in a pitiless critique of essentialism, of any deep structure or hidden message. Finally, while the right wing cultivates faith and trust—trust in logos, trust in reading, faith in the good will of conversation—the left-wing deconstructionist casts a suspicious eye on everything the right wing deems to be trustworthy. In contrast to the right-wing aerial development of Heidegger's ontology, deconstruction practices a writing from below, a parodying writing that shows that classic writers, despite their best efforts, cannot save themselves from a fall into the inscrutable depth (*profondeur*), the immeasurable earthly volume (*la terre lourde, grave, et dure*) of their own medium.[5] Doubting that one can ever gain access to things themselves except by the mazelike markings of cold print, the left-wing deconstructionist has no appetite or use for ontology.

Given the right-wing and left-wing developments of Heidegger, how do I position the interpretation of Heidegger I developed in chapter 3? Does my relationalist reading of Heidegger impose a premature closure on *Seinsfrage*? In light of the left-wing interpretation of Heidegger, is my attempt at an ontology of communication reactionary or logocentric? In this chapter, I wish to address these questions by examining the argument of the left-wing Heideggerian, as exemplified by Derrida. By explicating the critical procedures of Derrida's deconstruction of logocentrism, my objective is to lay the groundwork for what can be called an *aneconomic* perspective, from which the problem of communication can be rethought in a noncircular, that is, nonexchangelike, way.

Like a Novel Commodity: What Is Deconstruction?

If a word which I use is to have any meaning, I must "commit myself" by its use. If you commit yourself, there are consequences.
                                                                    —*Ludwig Wittgenstein*

Like a novel commodity brought to the public for the first time, deconstruction means different things to different people. To some, deconstruction represents one of the better things that has happened to Western thought recently, promising at long last a true liberation from the conceptual status quo by undermining its metaphysical repression; to others deconstruction is sheer bad news, not proffering emancipation but merely reflecting, if not exacerbating, the already serious cultural ills one has come to identify by oft-heard diagnostic phrases like "apocalyptic irrationalism," "cognitive atheism," "moral nihilism," and "dogmatic relativism." While one can freely surmise why deconstruction is capable of simultaneously provoking intense aversion and anxiety in some and reverent following and adulation in others — a question quite interesting in its own right — I think it is more productive and intellectually responsible to at least try to understand why deconstruction does what it does and how it reaches its conclusion.

Presumably, one should go to the "father(s)" of deconstruction for a quick answer. The complication, however, is that Derrida himself rarely uses the term *deconstruction,* and when he does, this term is so entangled with other equally difficult concepts that a clear picture always eludes one's focus.[6] At his silence — which is by no means innocent — it falls on those who practice it to spell out what deconstruction is. For a start, let us sample several well-known descriptions offered by deconstruction's major proponents:

JONATHAN CULLER: Deconstruction does not elucidate texts in the traditional sense of attempting to grasp a unifying content or theme; it investigates the work of metaphysical oppositions in their argument and the way in which textual figures and relations ... produce a double, aporetic logic.

PAUL DE MAN: The deconstruction is not something we have added to the text but it constitutes the text in the first place. A literary text simultaneously asserts and denies the authority of its own rhetorical mode, and by reading the text as we did we were only trying to come closer to being as rigorous a reader as the author had to be in order to write the sentence in the first place.

BARBARA JOHNSON: Deconstruction is not a form of textual vandalism designed to prove that meaning is impossible. In fact, the word "deconstruction" is closely related not to the word "destruction" but to the word "analysis," which etymologically means "to undo" — a virtual synonym for "to de-construct." The deconstruction of a text does not proceed by random doubt or generalized skepticism, but by the careful teasing out of warring forces of signification *within the text itself*. If anything is destroyed in a deconstructive reading, it is not meaning but the claim to unequivocal domination of one mode of signifying over another.

J. HILLIS MILLER: Deconstruction is not a dismantling of the structure of a text but a demonstration that it has already dismantled itself. Its apparently solid ground is no rock but thin air.

CHRISTOPHER NORRIS: Deconstruction is the vigilant seeking-out of those "aporias," blind spots or moments of self-contradiction where a text involuntarily betrays the tension between rhetoric and logic, between what it manifestly *means to say* and what it is nonetheless *constrained to mean*.[7]

What is deconstruction after all? If the lesson of deconstruction is to distrust any authorial voice, how do we interpret these passages? Would Derrida agree with these descriptions? Does it matter if he agrees or disagrees? Do these definitions, to the extent that they manage to say something, fall victim to the irony "between what they mean to say and what they are nonetheless constrained to mean?"

Despite our authors' use of the third-person indicative form, "S is P," in their descriptions of deconstruction, we must note that deconstruction cannot be adequately understood in the abstract, that any attempt to grasp it in terms of an essentialist, rigid definition is more than likely to miss the point. To give deconstruction too precise a formulation runs the risk not only of pulling it back into the orbit of metaphysical nebulosity from which it tries to free itself but also of brushing over the nuanced and specific activity of deconstruction in favor of a generalized, hence problematic, idea of that activity, which, as an idea, tends to lose sight of all the differences it makes in local applications. What we ought to do, when trying to understand what deconstruction is all about, is to focus on the actual operation of deconstruction, on what happens when deconstruction takes place. In this spirit, I propose to juxtapose Heidegger and Derrida. If deconstruction, as the authors just cited emphatically insist, has always and already taken place in the text, that is, if self-deconstruction has always and already happened in the target text, which is then restaged post facto in critical writings, composing this double text of Heidegger and Derrida should yield good results. By investigating the relation between Heidegger and Derrida and examining how the former deconstructs himself in the eyes of the latter, we might take hold of something about deconstruction that inherently resists discovery otherwise.

The Odd Couple *Aujourd'hui*: Heidegger and Derrida

Say what you choose, so long as it does not prevent you from seeing the
facts. (And when you see them, there is a good deal that you'll not say.)
—*Ludwig Wittgenstein*

It is a truism that anything is similar to, and also different from,
everything else. — *Thomas Kuhn*

These two quotes set up a nice point of departure for our comparative inquiry.
What is the relation between Derrida and Heidegger? How are they different from and similar to each other—in light of the philosophical problematics
within which they operate? What we face is the question of difference, a difference perhaps infinitesimal but radical, as Derrida would say, between two
philosophers, two philosophies, or, rather, two kinds of writing. But difference
can be articulated only if those that are compared and contrasted bear sufficient
resemblance to each other. Difference may in fact be something that, for various reasons, is not shared but is not in principle unshareable, and similarity
may be difference that is simply ignored or held in temporary abeyance.

Following Wittgenstein's aphorism, I will say what I choose to say about
Heidegger and Derrida. The choices always have to be made, some deliberately and some out of necessity. In what follows, first I compare and contrast *destruction* with *deconstruction* in reference to *ontological difference,* which,
for Heidegger, constitutes the central theme of any worthy ontological reflection. Why and how is Heidegger's reading of the Western metaphysics
not deconstructive? Why and how is Derrida's critique of phenomenology
and transcendental philosophy in general not (that is, more than and/or less
than) destructive? As is well known, at stake is the notion of "presence."
How do these two philosophers understand it differently, and on what basis
do they differ? What would happen to ontology if presence were deconstructed? After discussing these issues, I will try to demonstrate how a deconstructive understanding of Heidegger's *Seinsfrage* displaces the very project
of fundamental ontology, and how that displacement dissolves any "Heideggerian hope" and transforms philosophy into a kind of writing.

Deconstruction and the Ontological Difference

To show...the very age and body of the time his form and pressure.
—*William Shakespeare*

Heidegger's destruction of Western metaphysics is motivated by a longing
for its origin (*arche*) and a desire for its restoration. This desire, its object being the true meaning of Being, is evidenced by Heidegger's sustained proj-

ect of fundamental ontology that unifies his reflections on Being. The elaboration of such a fundamental ontology, as discussed in chapter 3, involves a twofold task. It requires, on the one hand, a detailed existential analytic (*Analytik des Dasein*) and, on the other hand, a diachronic analysis of the already existing ontologies (*Destruktion der bisherigen Ontologie*). The existential analytic sets into operation an interpretation of Being insofar as Being is *there,* of the *Sein* that is *da,* that offers itself whenever a concrete human being actualizes its own being temporally in-the-world. This interpretation yields a set of "existentials" that lay bare the essential structure of Dasein's factical existence and its ontological constitution. The analysis of the existing ontologies, in contrast, takes the form of a radical critique of the history of Western metaphysics. Because philosophy for Heidegger is always a construction (*Konstruktion*), any meaningful critique of philosophy must necessarily be a historical destruction (*Destruktion*) of the conceptual quarry from which philosophical constructions draw their building materials:

> These three basic components of phenomenological method — reduction, construction, destruction — belong together in their content and must receive grounding in their mutual pertinence. Construction in philosophy is necessarily destruction, that is to say, a deconstructing of traditional concepts carried out in a historical recursion to the tradition.[8]

Destruction in the Heideggerian sense therefore should be understood as "critical reappropriation" of a universal tendency of philosophical thinking to which belong the equally essential moments of reduction and construction.

Conceived as a "recursion to the tradition," the pathway (*methodos*) of Heidegger's destruction is properly genealogical, for to destroy metaphysics now means to retrace metaphysics to its root, to the unthought (*das Ungedachte*) and the unsaid that keep afloat traditional metaphysical thinkings and sayings. This can be done, of course, only by scrupulously peeling off the sedimented layers of transcriptions until what remains concealed in the horizon of comprehension of the determination of Being is fully exposed. To achieve this exposure, destruction needs to work on two fronts simultaneously. First, it needs to attend to the thematized expressions of existing ontologies so as to uncover the internal structure and the constitutive elements that make those expressions possible. Second, and more radical, it needs to think beneath and through the silent problematic of the traditional ontologies toward the very ground of metaphysics, the hiding place, the home (*oikos*) of an (un)thought that not only has not been thought but that also resists being completely mastered by thought and from which thought receives room to issue and abide in its essence.

Not to be confused with a childlike act of dismantling, Heidegger's de-struction is a historically informed de-construction (*Abbau*) aimed specifi-cally at certain ontological motifs prevailing from ancient Greece. Bound by and working within the tradition it attempts to unravel, it is at once a philosophical and historical cognition that works as a positive appropria-tion (*positiv Aneignung*) of a grand legacy from its forgotten and concealed sources. Not to do away with, but out of a profound respect for, the history of philosophy, destruction essays toward what Heidegger later calls the true *overcoming* (*Überwindung*) of that history by effecting an intense and genuine dialogue with the past.

There is no question that destruction is a violent act; it conjures up the images of darkness, chaos, and suffering. But Heidegger's destruction as *Abbau* does not destroy for the sake of destroying; instead, it counteracts the already repressive violence that metaphysics has exercised over thinking. *Abbau* is a kind of recuperative and memorative violence necessary to counterbalance metaphysicians' brutal force. This violence is recuperative because its ulti-mate purpose is to construct a true science of Being in terms of an original and originary experience of Being; it is memorative because it amounts to a receptive approximation toward the fresh self-presentation of Being.

Behind this violent step back (*Schritt zurück*) "out of metaphysics into the issuant and abiding essence of metaphysics," that is, under the disguise of a memorial recuperation, lingers Heidegger's aspiration for homecoming.[9] This genuine homecoming of Dasein, as *Being and Time* sets out to show, is the roundabout journey in the thankful remembrance of Being, a return at long last to the arche, to the topos, the whereabouts, of Being. It represents a response to Being's insistent calling, and it requires a piety on the part of the thinking respondent. "To think 'Being,' " writes Heidegger,

> means to respond to the appeal of its presencing. The response stems from the appeal and releases itself toward that appeal. The responding is a giving way before the appeal and in this way an entering into its speech. But to the appeal of Being there also belongs the early uncovered has-been (*aletheia, logos, phusis*) as well as the veiled advent of what announces itself in the possible turnabout of the oblivion of Being (in the keeping of its nature). The responding must take into account all of this, on the strength of long concentration and in con-stant testing of this hearing, if it is to hear the appeal of being... [This think-ing] is rooted in the essential destiny of Being, though itself never compelling as a proposition. On the contrary, it is only a possible occasion to follow the path of responding, and indeed to follow it in the complete concentration of care and caution toward Being that language has *already* come to.[10]

In responding to an "early uncovered has-been," this thinking can be nothing but an attempt at remembering. In this way, it *"renounces* the claim to binding cultural achievement or a deed of the spirit...Everything depends on the *step back* fraught with *error* into the thoughtful reflection that attends the *turnabout of the oblivion of Being.*"[11]

Stepping back so that it can move forward, that is, progressing by regressing, fundamental ontology turns out to be a topology of Being. The topology of Being, Otto Pöggeler once remarked, "materializes" Heidegger's fundamental ontology.[12] As a topology, fundamental ontology maps, charts, draws lines, and establishes signposts in the amorphous field of presence outlined by the ever receding and ever expanding horizon of thinking. Through this destructive cartography, fundamental ontology reorients thinking about Being by rearticulating its logos against historical errors, against cultural blindness, against discursive dereliction. By virtue of this topological destruction/ construction, "those primordial experiences" of Being — manifested, for example, in the profound simplicity of the fragments of the works of pre-Socratic thinkers — can be identified and located, and the first dispatch from Being can be brought to view again.

The necessity for destruction/construction in fundamental ontology has yet another source: Heidegger's macroscopic diagnosis of the history of metaphysics. According to this diagnosis, Western metaphysics represents a progressive *ekleipsis,* a chronic failure. The reason for this failure lies in what Heidegger calls the "oblivion of the distinction between Being and being," namely, the oblivion or effacement of the ontological difference. This effacement inducts Being as a universal singular, reducing beings to one master signifier, to one singular name, Being. "Whatever the name that metaphysics gives to the Being of beings," as Michel Haar observes, "it seems that metaphysics is summed up in the project of assigning an exclusive and unique name to Being. The moment it is 'identified,' Being is lost as Being, reduced to a being, for to name Being is to say *what* it is...to affirm, Being is this, and nothing else."[13] This exclusive naming posits Being in full domination and, in so doing, represses through a nominal singularity the "many manners" in which Being appears as beings. It allows metaphysicians to give a fetishized concept the semblance of positivity, the form of totality and systematic representation, whose result is that this concept, this singular name "Being," is regarded as the sole cause of ordinary beings. Because of this obliteration of the ontic-ontological distinction, that is, because Being begins to play God, Heidegger writes, "the history of the Western world comes to be borne out. It is the event of metaphysics. What now is stands in the shadow of the already foregone destiny of Being's oblivion."[14]

The moment of the *ekleipsis* of Being signals the moment of beginning, but it is also the beginning of darkness, whose development and continuation are determined by a fateful indistinction. The time of darkness is the time when things are not seen clearly; it is the time of not being able to see, of invisibility or, at best, of shadows. The consequence of such a beginning and of the thinking that comes afterward is, according to Heidegger, that

> the very relation between presencing and what is present remains unthought. From early on it seems as though presencing and what is present were each something for itself. Presencing itself unnoticeably becomes something present. Represented in the manner of something present, it is elevated above whatever else is present and so becomes the highest being present. As soon as presencing is named, it is represented as some present being. Ultimately, presencing as such is not distinguished from what is present; it is taken merely as the most universal or the highest of present being, thereby becoming one among such beings. The essence of presencing, and with it the distinction between presencing and what is present, remains forgotten. The oblivion of Being is oblivion of the distinction between Being and beings.[15]

As the result of this indiscretion, philosophical thinking is lost to itself, becoming blind to its proper object and ignorant of the source that provoked it to begin with.

This blindness to the critical distinction between Being and beings, however, does not result from an inadvertent blunder made by philosophers, nor is it the result of metaphysicians' temporary myopia that could have been corrected had they kept up their self-examination. The oblivion of the ontological difference, Heidegger reminds us,

> is by no means the consequence of a forgetfulness of thinking. Oblivion of Being belongs to the self-veiling essence of Being. It belongs so essentially to the destiny of Being that the dawn of this destiny rises as the unveiling of what is present in its presencing... since Being—together with its essence, its distinction from beings—keeps to itself.[16]

What Heidegger is suggesting, aside from his somewhat formidable invocation of the "destiny of Being," is that the oblivion of the ontological difference contains a double-edged indication concerning the unique relation between Being and beings in general and the self-eclipsing nature of Being in particular. It refers, on the one hand, to Dasein's fateful inattention to the difference between Being and beings, a forgetful indifference that determines the direction of and the interpretations reached in Western ontology — a groundless ontology that, by treating Being as a being, is henceforward ever at a distance from its intended object. On the other hand, this notion also brings to the fore the essentially and intrinsically elusive nature of Being. It indicates the peculiar evasiveness of Being's presencing as an instantaneous interplay of presence and absence.

This instantaneous interplay of presence and absence, this simultaneous self-veiling and self-unveiling of Being as such, Heidegger calls the "self-spectacle of presencing" (*Ereignis*). *Ereignis*, usually translated as "appropriation" or the "event of appropriation," refers to the very "eventing" of all events, the "happening" of all happenings, the "occurring" of all occurrences.[17] It designates the appropriative process of Being's coming-to-be, a happening in which the fourfold (*Geviert*) — that is, heaven, earth, mortal, and divine — brings itself into relief according to the equiprimordial disclosure of its constitutive moments. Heidegger forewarns us that, as the genesis of beings pure and simple, *Ereignis* is essentially equivocal (more precisely, secretive), bearing within itself a lateral sliding that necessarily cancels its own working in its self-presentation. In accord with its own happening, its own *taking-place*, *Ereignis* comes forth as the illumination of the present; at the same time, however, as the present comes to be (in and through presencing), *Ereignis* as presencing immediately erases itself and withdraws into an absence. *Ereignis* in any case gives nothing to see, for its coming forth is (the same as) its stepping back. This stepping back characterizes Being's proper disclosure, its gift to beings; it properly characterizes *Ereignis*. "Reconcealment, withdrawal," writes Heidegger, "is the way in which Being 'endures' as Being, in which it dispenses itself, that is, gives itself out."[18] Disclosure and reconcealment, presence and absence, therefore constitute an internal dimension within each other in the event of Be-ing; each exists nonpresently within the other as Be-ing.

The lateral interplay between presence and absence as two coaspectual dimensions of a single event of presencing characterizes the mobile, fluid structure of the truth of existence as *aletheia*, a sending-out (*Geschick*) of and a letting-be (*Gelassenheit*) by Being that clears and regions a world by lighting it up. In this primordial worlding of the world, the difference between Being and beings is constantly at play and yet remains the same in each and every event of presencing, for the two, though never identical, belong to each other *essentially*. The history of the world, the continuous existence of all worldly beings, therefore can be seen to stand in the wake of a constant iteration and reiteration of a primitive difference, an in-difference that, for all of its self-effacing attempts, is always busy at work in Being's coming to be, in Being's becoming present. Through *Ereignis,* presence bodies forth as the present, in whatever it is, but never without the absencing of its presencing that is nothing but presence's own self-erasure. Conversely, through self-erasure, Being makes room for beings — allowing the present to stand in place of its own self-erasure. For this reason, the presencing is present only in its absence, that is, by virtue of the difference that persists always and already in the midst of beings, between the present and the absent. Just as the visibility of things is the same as the invisibility of the thingness of things, so the visibility of beings is the same as the invisibility of the beingness of beings. The logic of presencing manifests itself as a highly vertiginous dynamic of events' coming-to-be, rooted in an instant and simultaneous cancellation of eventing as such.

The self-veiling character of Being, the self-withdrawal of *Ereignis,* makes it clear that Being as Being does not leave its point of origin. In letting things be, and in unveiling itself for thinking, Being nevertheless maintains its own integrity, keeps itself intact, while at the same time supervening and thereby providing the illuminative clearing wherein the entities can arise and be the things they are. Being prevails, but only as an ecstatic unity, and because it is ecstatically unitary through and through, it prevents itself from being seen. Being cannot be seen because it has always and already withdrawn itself behind beings that are present, thus becoming a difference that it is not; Being cannot be seized essentially because it carries off the property of itself the moment thinking begins to apprehend it. What can be grasped in the event of *Ereignis* is only the trace it left behind, the trace of its becoming other, namely, the difference between the unseeable Being and the seeable beings. When this difference differentiates, that is, when it unfolds into things present, they arise in full color and multiplicity. The full color and multiplicity of things present henceforth saturate the field of presence — for within the field of presence as the "world," nothing is absent: The world lacks nothing. But, in this event, the self-spectacle of Being imperceptibly recedes behind the present and maintains itself by withdrawing into nonpresence. Always appearing indirectly because it never makes itself known except through the detour of difference, Being is present in and through absence, or, rather, it is nonpresently present in the present; by the same token, beings are always present and cannot but be present through Being's secretive absencing.

Given this double sense of the ontological difference, it becomes possible to see that the ontological difference not only constitutes the condition of ontology but also becomes its object. By linking the ontic and the ontological as difference, the ontological difference marks a fundamental heterogeneity in the realm of knowledge; it constitutes a lack, a lack for the elucidation of Being, which ontology must address. At the same time, inasmuch as the difference between Being and beings evokes the ontological inquiry, this difference itself becomes the first and primary object of ontological reflection. As the science of the general, ontology has no place to start except with thinking the very difference between Being and beings that poses a constant challenge to the reflection on the *onto.* The ontological difference functions as a difference that anticipates the proper transcendence of that difference.

As I pointed out in chapter 3, in order for transcendence to be possible, in order for the ontological inquiry to be able to take its first step, Dasein must in some sense exist both within and outside the ontological clearing. In the language of *Being and Time,* one can say that Dasein must be both authentic and inauthentic. Defined by its preontological comprehension of Being, Dasein embodies the between with open passages toward both Being and beings. This betweenness of Dasein is precisely what makes the transcendence of existence possible; it is what grounds Dasein's comportment toward the world and, as Heidegger takes great pains to show in *Being and Time,* is ultimately rooted in the temporality of Dasein. The transcendence of Dasein thus constitutes the liaison between Being and beings, which, according to Dasein's own truth, takes the form of a temporal unfolding. This is one of the central themes in Heidegger, a theme to which he returns time and again:

> As ecstatic-horizonal unity of temporalizing, temporality is the condition of possibility of transcendence.... Because temporality constitutes the basic constitution of the being we call the Dasein, to which entity the understanding of beings belongs as determination of its existence, and because time constitutes the original self-projection pure and simple, being is already always unveiled—hence beings are either disclosed or uncovered—in every factical Dasein, since it exists....
>
> ...The distinction between being and beings is there (*ist da*), latent in the Dasein and its existence, even if not in explicit awareness. The distinction is *there, ist da* [i.e., exists]; that is to say, it has the mode of being of the Dasein: it belongs to existence. Existence means, as it were, "to be in the performance of this distinction..." *This distinction between being and beings is temporalized in the temporalizing of temporality.*[19]

What Heidegger means is that the factical existence of Dasein as a temporal being-in-the-world (that is, Dasein's existence as a being that takes time and is in time) manifests the ontological difference; that the temporal existence of Dasein is the very embodiment of the ontological difference. Dasein's being-there is the *same* as the "performance of this distinction"; in fact, Dasein is what it is precisely by "performing" this (in)distinction. To the extent that Dasein is there, to the extent that it *is* in the world, Dasein exists across two realms, the ontic and the ontological, and its transcendent, self-projective nature anticipates the traversal from the ontic to the ontological by first living through its ontic ambiguity. In Dasein's existence, in its existential performance that cuts across the ontological difference, one finds not only the oblivion to that difference but also the possibility of overcoming that oblivion, as Dasein's preontological cognizance of that difference develops into "an explicitly understood difference."[20]

The notion of "ontological difference" provides an opening into the gallery of Heidegger's thoughtful approximations toward Being, ranging from his interpretations of Aristotle, Kant, Hegel, Nietzsche, and others to his later meditative essays that inch their way toward the essence of language and art. It indicates the "one thought" that Heidegger confesses to have been thinking throughout his life; it indicates the "primal scene" of thinking that Heidegger, following Hölderlin and Trakl, keeps revisiting. The fact that "The Anaximander Fragment" is the final essay in *Holzwege* signifies at once a historical beginning and a philosophical conclusion.[21] By going back to Anaximander, by returning to a textual event that commences a destiny, Heidegger completes the circle of thinking. It is in Heidegger's continual returning to "the unitary ground of Being" that one witnesses again, and yet for the first time, the exchange of gifts between Being and beings; it is in this same return to a point of origin, to the thinking that precedes the obfuscating wiles of rationality and discursive representations, that one catches the cadence of Heidegger's thinking, the rhythm of fundamental ontology — "at the end to arrive at early Greek thinking."[22]

From Destruction to Deconstruction: Homecoming versus Nomadism

> Then thinking would be coming-into-the-nearness of distance.
> — *Martin Heidegger*

> Philosophy is properly nostalgia — the aspiration to be *at home everywhere.*
> — *Novalis [Friedrich von Hardenberg]*

If, as I said at the opening of the preceding section, Heidegger's destruction of Western metaphysics is motivated by a longing for its origin and a desire for its restoration, Derrida's left-wing Heideggerianism, or more exactly, his *post-meta-anti*-philosophical thinking or "abnormal philosophy" (if we are still allowed to use the word *philosophy*) represents a radical denial of any such possibility.[23] It is a resolute rejection of any "Heideggerian hope." If a Heideggerian can be described as a nostalgic traveler on the way home to the house of Being, a Derridean is a true nomad. A nomad makes a home everywhere but is never truly at home anywhere; for a nomad, there is no home; no-where *is* home.

Fundamental ontology is a topology of Being; in order for thinking beings to orient themselves in the clearing of Being, a topological destruction has to be effected. This destructive topography is a second clearing that, after the ambivalent clearing of Being, clears a new path on top of the old one so that the way back to the abode of Being, to the "native country of thought," can be embarked upon again. For a nomad, however, destruction as clearing the way is utterly meaningless. Clearing is discrimination; it implies a sense of direction and purpose, of relative positions that mark a separation of one place from another. For a nomad, however, the difference of space makes no difference; for the nomad there are only "different" places that, for all practical purposes, are simply the same.

But nomads, chasing water and grass, may wander — often purposefully — into the land of the settlement, into the land *propre*, for wander they must. With each stride the boundary is immediately crossed and redrawn, and the boundary constantly crossed and redrawn is no boundary at all. Nomads travel the boundless because they are homeless and rootless. A boundary is a self-limitation of those who are earth-bound, the homesteaders or city dwellers. As Orientalists are fond of saying, "Genghis Khan did not understand the phenomenon of the city."[24] But they are wrong; Genghis Khan understood it only too well, as history has shown. Never once did he fail to enter a city at will. Even the Great Wall could not keep out the great northern horseman, could not prevent him from marrying Emperor Han Wu's daughter.

With the nomad as the living embodiment of the rootless, the homeless, and the boundless comes a perpetual displacement — if not elimination — of a series of conceptual couples (such as inside/outside, central/peripheral) that traditionally demarcate and define our social space. Embodying the boundless, the nomad disregards lines that insist on separating space, that predefine and hence foreclose the original open. Within the boundless space, each point is just as central (and for that matter, just as peripheral) as any other point.

But the boundlessness of the space in which the nomad roams also affects his experience of and relation to time. The boundlessness of space makes the nomad a perpetual traveler, and perpetual traveling can only mean the nonexistence of final destination. Without destination, the nomad can afford to be oblivious of time. The nomad does not have to be on time. This, in fact, is the nomad's only luxury, which comes from rock-bottom poverty or, from a different point of view, from total freedom, of going-no-where.

Moving on so that he may return to where he comes from, the Heideggerian conceives of himself as the destructionist/constructionist. Moving on because he must and because he is disoriented or nonorientable with reference to social geography and the domestic calendar, a Derridean is poised to be a de-constructionist. Deconstruction is nomadic thinking in action and practice. Nomadism is live deconstruction. Before I elaborate on deconstruction, however, let me stop to examine more closely some points of difference between Heidegger and Derrida that substantiate my analogy of nomadism and homecoming.

In one of his later works, *On Time and Being*, Heidegger writes that "to think Being without beings means: to think Being without regard to metaphysics. Yet a disregard for metaphysics still prevails even in the intention to overcome metaphysics. Therefore, our task is to cease all overcoming, and leave metaphysics to itself."[25] This determination to "cease all overcoming, and leave metaphysics to itself" reveals Heidegger's recognition that even though the past is past, its ghost may well still be with us, that the very idea of "thinking through" tradition and replacing a disoriented metaphysics with a fundamental ontology is itself guided by tradition. But this critical awareness does not stop Heidegger from pursuing the issue of *Seinsfrage*. In fact, his persistent inquiry toward a true understanding of Being has led him to "trace Being to its own from Appropriation."[26] Appropriation, as said earlier, is the presencing pure and simple; it is the "it gives" (*es gibt*) pure and simple. This "it gives," Heidegger now believes, is what must be thought:

> In the sending of the destiny of Being, in the extending of time, there becomes manifest a dedication, a delivering over into what is their own, namely of Being as presence and of time as the realm of the open. What determines both, time and Being, in their own, that is, in their belonging together, we shall call *Ereignis,* the event of Appropriation...that "event" is not simply an occurrence, but that which makes any occurrence possible. What this word names can be thought now only in the light of what becomes manifest in our looking ahead toward Being and toward time as destiny and an extending, to which time and Being belong.... Accordingly, the It that gives in "It gives Being," "It gives time," proves to be Appropriation.[27]

Some pages later, Heidegger continues:

> The thinking that begins with *Being and Time* is thus, on the one hand, an awakening from the oblivion of Being — an awakening which must be understood as a recollection of something which has never been thought — but on the other hand, as this awakening, not an extinguishing of the oblivion of Being, but placing oneself in it and standing within it. Thus the awakening from the oblivion of Being to the oblivion of Being is the awakening into *Ereignis*.[28]

Although Heidegger tries to maintain a certain continuity with *Being and Time*, his thinking, as reflected in these passages, has clearly entered into a new phase, indicating a *Kehre* in his career as the fundamental ontologist. Rather than displaying the structure of Dasein, the ultimate task of *Seinsfrage* now concerns "that thinking that explicitly enters Appropriation in order to say It in terms of It about It."[29] The kind of thinking that directly thinks Being, that does not treat Being as beings but enters Appropriation, will have to think "Being as the event of Appropriation."[30] That is,

> [if we] think Being in the sense of presencing and allowing-to-presence that are there in destiny — which in turn lies in the extending of true time which opens and conceals — then Being belongs into Appropriating. Giving and its gift receive their determination from Appropriating. In that case, Being would be a *species* of Appropriation, and not the other way around.[31]

Appropriation now becomes the origin of Being, for time and space receive their determination from it as extending and as the realm of the open. More general and more primitive than Being, Appropriation is that which binds all thinking, "providing thinking submits to the call of what must be thought."[32] It appears as the centripetal, self-standing source from which disseminates everything that is, and to which thinking, once awakened to the gift of Being, must ultimately return.

In Heidegger's reading, Being as Appropriation, as *Ereignis*, is what the Greek experiences. It fathered metaphysics, begetting a history of thinking that (mis)takes the sent (the present) for the sending (the giving, *es gibt*). In his usual direct manner, Heidegger writes: "Metaphysics is the history of the way Being is stamped (*Seinsprägungen*), that is, seen from the *Ereignis*, the history of the withdrawing of the *sender* in favor of the dispatches (*Schickungen, envois*) which were sent along, of the current letting-presence of the present."[33] At long last, it is now time to retrieve this hitherto unthought sender, to receive its sending. And to "enter into thinking this unthought (*Ereignis*) means: to pursue more originally what the Greeks have thought, to see it in the source of its reality. To see it so is in its own way Greek, and yet in respect of what it sees is no longer Greek, is never again, Greek."[34]

It is precisely this intention to out-Greek the Greek by harking back to an original master term, to supersede (*hebt auf*) the oblivion of Being by way of an originary experience called *Ereignis,* that makes Heidegger appear to be a bit too homesick in Derrida's eyes. For Derrida, Being, let alone Appropriation, is possibly nothing more than a metalinguistic notion that results from a transcendental deduction based on the need for something to which language could refer. As a metalinguistic entity, it is empty; worse yet, it turns out in the last analysis to be a morphological trick that language plays on us. Whether as Appropriation/Expropriation or as presencing/absencing, Being institutes itself as the highest "transcendental signified," a master referent that in reality is but one signifier with a capital *B,* a morpheme, a paper Being, dislocated from the self-referentiality of language as something outside the play of differences by the blind faith of the metaphysics of presence. The trouble with the "question of Being," with *Seinsfrage,* then, is that it never lets go of the attempt to think Being in terms of self-presencing, believing that it can be done without *representation.* Unfortunately, this attempt to track Being to its root in full presence will not work, for, as Derrida explains,

> the fact remains that Being which is nothing, which is not a being, cannot be said, cannot say itself, except *in the ontic metaphor*... And if Heidegger radically deconstructed the authority of the *present* over metaphysics, it was in order to lead us to think the presence of the present. But the thought of this presence only metaphorizes, by a profound necessity which cannot be escaped by a simple decision, the language it deconstructs.[35]

To speak about Being is at once to speak about the failure of this speaking — a profound need of ontology that is at the same time its need to rely on ontic metaphors. As Heidegger's later meditations on *Ereignis,* the gift (*Gabe*), and the giving of the "it gives" begin to overtake his earlier talk about Dasein, "he invariably ends up in a movement beyond Being, ground, presence, and truth, landing in an abyss (*Ab-grund*) of dis-appropriation (*Ent-eignis*)":[36]

> Truth, unveiling, illumination are no longer decided in the appropriation of the truth of Being, but are cast into its bottomless abyss as non-truth, veiling, dissimulation. The history of Being becomes a history in which no being, no thing, happens except *Ereignis'* unfathomable process. The proper-ty of the abyss (*das Eigentum des Abgrundes*) is necessarily the abyss of proper-ty, the violence of an event which befalls without Being.[37]

There may be more than the misfortune of truth being clouded by non-truth; there may also be, as Caputo keenly observes, the problem of a lack of style on the part of metaphysics: The fashion of onto-hermeneutics' paternal language pales sorrily before the unfathomable style of *Ereignis*.[38]

To be sure, this abyssal emptiness of Being, this difficulty (or rather, impossibility) of talking about it "without mutilation," is already implicitly present in Heidegger's own discussion. At the end of "Time and Being," Heidegger concludes: "Appropriation neither *is*, nor *is* Appropriation *there*... What remains to be said? Only this: Appropriation appropriates."[39] Such tautological expression is most revealing for Derrida. It betrays not only the shaky future of the project of *Seinsfrage* because it metaphorizes and hence metamorphoses Being, but it also suggests that the notion of Being itself may be nothing more than an "effect," an "imaginary tail" of onto-hermeneutics' own wishful soliloquy.

Derridean Doubt and the Metaphysics of Presence

What is the good of passing from one untenable position to another, of seeking justification always on the same plane? — *Samuel Beckett*

Just a few days before his death, Heidegger ended a letter to a friend with this sentence: "For there is need to deliberate whether and how, in the age of technologized homogeneous world-civilization, there can still be a homeland (*Heimat*)."[40] That the word *homeland* should stand at the end of Heidegger's last writing is no mere accident. It concludes a lifework, a work of a lifetime of thinking. Homeland is where all journeys begin and where they all come to rest. The question of the "homeland" is the question of origin, of coming and going, of permanent address, of the side/site chosen, of the lot divided, of the destiny commanded; philosophically speaking, it is the question of Being. Indeed, it is with the figure of the "homeland" that Heidegger's *Seinsfrage* becomes an urgent question; it is also in this figure that fundamental ontology becomes an Odyssean story, a story about homesickness or nostalgia narrated as a provisional exile leading to restful reappropriation.

Derrida is not homesick; he follows no Odyssean path. Never looking homeward, he deconstructs. As a nomadic practice, deconstruction does not aspire to bring an end to metaphysics and to inaugurate some kind of post-philosophical thinking.[41] From a deconstructive point of view, apocalyptic pronouncements of any sort — be they talk of end or beginning, death or rebirth — remain complicitous with the postal principle of presence and cannot be considered as anything other than metaphysical in the traditional Platonic sense. Although Derrida and Heidegger share the view that the different themes and theories of philosophy are versions of a single system, they part company in terms of their readings of and reactions toward the tradition from which they both come. Whereas Heidegger understands metaphysical thinking as "fall" or "errancy," as departing from "what is present in its presence and thus re-represents it in terms of its ground as something grounded," Derrida reads the history of metaphysics (the work of Heidegger himself included) as a "repetition" of the groundlessness of ground, as a "repetition" of the illusion of there being a ground.[42] According to Derrida, the "single system" in which the search for ground represses its own frustration by instituting a hierarchy of philosophemes is centered on the notion of "presence." This single system, for Derrida,

> is the determination of being as *presence* in all the senses of the word. It would be possible to show that all the terms related to fundamentals, to principles, or the center have always designated the constant of presence — *eidos, telos, arche, energeia, ousia* (essence, existence, substance, subject), *aletheia*, transcendentality, consciousness or conscience, God, man, and so forth.[43]

Presence for Derrida comprehends the history of metaphysics; it designates a fundamental *value* shared by and exchangeable within ostensibly different metaphysical systems, giving these systems an underlying unity, their intelligible and identifiable form. It is this "single system of presence" that deconstruction seeks to confront and to unsettle.

In the process of identifying the "unthought," the "other," or the "unconsciousness," repressed by the "single system" of Western metaphysics, Derrida performs a double reading on a variety of texts — Rousseau, Saussure, Plato, Genet, Hegel, Mallarmé, Husserl, Lévi-Strauss, Austin, Kant, Condillac — in order to show that these texts are woven from different and competing strands that, unbeknownst to and despite the intention of their authors, can never result in a cogent synthesis; rather, they displace each other in a continual textual wandering.

In *Speech and Phenomena,* for example, Derrida takes issue with Husserl's theory of the sign and proceeds to deconstruct the logocentric position on which Husserl's crucial but ultimately untenable distinction of "expression" and "indication" is founded.[44] The power of Derrida's critique here, as well as in numerous other cases, derives from the fact that his deconstructive reading operates consistently within Husserl's home site, within the problematic of Husserlian phenomenology, rather than launching objections from an external point of view. Drawing on Husserl's own account of internal time consciousness, Derrida demonstrates that meaning (which for Husserl is an ideal transparency of conscious intention present to consciousness itself at the moment of utterance) is not, as Husserl wishes, a simple presence, something given in and of itself in the interior clarity of consciousness, but is always and already part of a system of "traces" and contrasts that exceeds the boundary of any present instant. The ideality of meaning, crucial to the coherence of Husserl's transcendental residence, turns out to depend on the possibility of "re-iteration," but this possibility of reiteration in turn causes Husserl's own conceptualization of the ideality of meaning to boomerang. As a result, not only does the absolute distinction between expression and indication collapse, but the expressive sign, which is privileged by Husserl's phonocentrism as primary, pure, and original, is also unmasked as being dependent upon indicative signification. A self-contradiction is forced into the open, signaling a crisis at the root of Husserl's theory, an immanent crisis that even Husserl's arboreal complexity cannot control. As Derrida comments, "Husserl's premises should sanction our saying exactly the contrary."[45]

What Derrida does with reference to Husserl accords well with Johnson's description of deconstruction as "teasing out the warring forces of signification" within Husserl's text.[46] By way of an ultraclose reading, this teasing out utilizes the very logic of Husserl's own argument to show how it "undoes" itself; that is, it shows how Husserl's phenomenology of the sign involves a central paradox or aporia and how that theory is made possible only by repressing that aporia, which, curiously enough, functions from the outset as the constitutive dichotomy mobilizing Husserl's reflection on signs. This is not philosophical criticism in the normal sense, for what Derrida (rather, what his reading) does to Husserl is not so much *criticizing* Husserl as *demonstrating* how his text functions against its own explicit (metaphysical) assertions, and this is done not by creating ambiguity but by uncovering a systematic "other message" in and through what is being said.

Although the issue taken up in *Speech and Phenomena* is local, the implication of its analysis reaches far beyond the purview of a phenomenology of the sign. It anticipates the wider and deeper problematization of the notion of "presence" in such a way that even Heidegger's global reconstruction of the science of Being has to be rethought. But before I discuss Derrida's problematization (and going beyond) of Heidegger, it is helpful to examine and elaborate in more detail the strategy of deconstruction that I previously characterized as "nomadic thinking."

Deconstruction I: Strategic Seduction and Seductive Strategy

in naming have we divided what
unnaming will not undivide.
                    —*A. R. Ammons*

To know what deconstruction is, one must see how it works and what it does when it works. In its most general sense, Derrida's deconstruction can be recapitulated in one simple phrase: *d'une certaine manière* (in a certain way). As pre-texts for the following discussion, I select two quotations from Derrida:

> What I want to emphasize is simply that the passage beyond philosophy does not consist in turning the page of philosophy (which usually amounts to philosophizing badly), but in continuing to read philosophers *in a certain way*.[47]

> The movements of deconstruction do not destroy structures from the outside. They are not possible and effective, nor can they take accurate aim, except by inhabiting those structures. Inhabiting them *in a certain way*, because one always inhabits, and all the more when one does not suspect it. Operating necessarily from the inside, borrowing all the strategies and economic resources of subversion from the old structures, borrowing them structurally, that is to say without being able to isolate their elements and atoms, the enterprise of deconstruction always *in a certain way* falls prey to its own work.[48]

The first quotation introduces deconstruction as a way of "reading," a way of rereading philosophers' passages that encourages the readers to go beyond the philosophers' passages in print. But what exactly is this certain way of reading? How does it proceed? What makes this rereading of philosophy deconstructive? The second quotation gives us a clue. Deconstruction, Derrida tells us, does not "destroy structures from the outside"; instead it works from within the text it chooses to work on. Now we know this much: Deconstructive reading requires that we stop turning the page of philosophy and begin to inhabit the pages of its texts. It means that we must take up residence within the two covers of a philosopher's writing, refusing to go on as the eyes might wish, strolling the borderline between pages, between lines, between words, between footnotes, or if we like, stopping right in front of the title.

Once we forgo the luxury of turning Derrida's page too quickly and read it carefully, we realize that deconstruction hinges on the special way it inhabits the text. It is as much reading as it is living. Inhabitation is our natural mode of existence; we always and already inhabit some place — in the city or in the forest, in our native country or in a foreign land, in a friendly neighborhood or in a hostile environment. Except for the inside and the outside, there is no other place to live, no other living space. But to live/ read deconstructively, one must inhabit the text differently. Deconstructive inhabitation is an inhabitation *in a certain way*; it is an alert and suspicious kind of inhabitation that transforms deconstruction into a particular kind of textual operation that I will describe as strategic, parasitic, nomadic, partisan, and seductive.

To the extent that deconstruction seeks to bring about a subversion of the old structures, it must wage war against them. To bring down old philosophies, there must occur a war of reading, a paper war, whose outcome can be decided only by warring readings. In this war over words, over knowledge, over warring philosophies, method is all important: It becomes strategy. Each move of deconstruction needs to be executed according to a carefully calculated stratagem that fits into an overall war plan.[49] The stratagem one adopts to fight this paper war, however, cannot be carried out by some new weaponry. Rather, as Derrida informs us, deconstruction must borrow "all the strategies and economic resources of subversion from the old structure, borrowing them structurally," that is, borrowing them wholesale. In its paper war against philosophy, deconstruction has "no language — no syntax and no lexicon — which is foreign to" the enemy.[50] Not unlike a judo master who exploits the strength of the opponent, a deconstructionist turns the aporiastic forces in philosophical texts against themselves, thus flooring their authors by deception, chicanery, and if necessary, dirty tricks.

Deconstruction's strategic planning of textual warfare calculates the gains and losses, the advances and retreats, whose sole purpose is to maneuver the enemy into desired positions, to trap and immobilize that enemy on ground where he or she is susceptible to ambush. To that end, the deconstructionist has to play the imposter and work as a double agent, as Derrida did when he dressed up as a Husserlian to betray the master code of Husserl's logo-phono-centric deployment. The deconstructive double agent feigns alliance and conducts clandestine operations behind the enemy's line. The feigned alliance enables him to move freely across the war zone. Freely crossing the war zone, the deconstructive mole traverses the lines separating the self from the other, friend from foe; he becomes a wartime nomad. By carrying one identity over another, a wartime nomad is capable of living sometimes here, sometimes there, as the situation of war demands. At the same time, because of the double identity he assumes, the nomadic double agent has the advantage of feeding in both camps. Like a parasite, he establishes stations within both the host and rival, winning by juggling information with multiple patrons. This is what deconstructive inhabitation means: never peaceful coexistence but intricate and deceitful cohabitation that eventually leads to the defeat of the seemingly stronger one. "The structure of the area in which we are operating," Derrida concludes, "calls for a strategy that is complex and tortuous, involuted and full of artifice: for example, exploiting the target against itself by discovering it at times to be the 'basis' of an operation directed against it, or even discovering 'in it' the cryptic reserve of something utterly different."[51]

Cohabitation of heterogeneous bodies has always been an ideal rather than a historical reality. When the war is over, boundaries are immediately negotiated and established, and double agents are quickly eliminated, for double agents are useful only in war and their existence signals the white heat of war. As double agents die accidentally in war and are eliminated necessarily after the war, "the enterprise of deconstruction always in a certain way falls prey to its own work."[52] Deconstruction implies self-destruction; deconstruction necessarily exhibits, through a kind of catastrophic reversal, its own demise, its own deconstruction, because from the very beginning it has had a double identity and has pledged a double loyalty. In the deconstructive war game, nothing succeeds like a failure; in the deconstructive battle, *qui perd gagne* (who loses, wins).

Although the deconstructive parasite turns the host's nutrient into its own energy and thereby explodes the host's orderly organization, as the preceding characterization suggests, a well-rounded deconstruction does not merely work from within the text it reads. Deconstruction conducts outside attacks as well. Besides infesting the "founding concepts" of metaphysics by remaining inside its "original problematic," an effective deconstruction must also project a change of terrain so as to attack philosophy's strongholds "in a discontinuous and irruptive fashion, by brutally placing [the deconstructionist] outside":[53]

> To "deconstruct" philosophy, thus, would be to think — in a most faithful, interior way — the structured genealogy of philosophy's concepts, but at the same time to determine — *from a certain exterior* that is unqualifiable or unnameable by philosophy — what this history has been able to dissimulate or forbid, making itself into a history by means of this somewhere motivated repression. By means of this simultaneous faithful and violent circulation between the inside and the outside of philosophy — that is of the West — there is produced a certain textual work that gives great pleasure.[54]

Deconstruction works both within and without. It is not only parasitic but also seductive. Whereas a parasite takes up residence inside someone else's body, the seducer often lives next door. Seduction always comes from outside the household. Like a seductress, the deconstructionist enchants philosophers to loosen their defense mechanisms, rekindles their repressed desires, and thus reanimates the infinite possibility of their textual aberrations. Deconstruction seduces philosophers for a certain pleasure, luring them only to strip them naked, patronizing their texts only to unweave the threads of phono-logo-centric philosophemes, "to make them slide — without mistreating them — to the point of their nonpertinence, their exhaustion, their closure."[55]

Deconstruction II: The Double Science

> ... the theatre was changed
> To something else.
>   *—Wallace Stevens*

Seduction is a scintillating endeavor. Seducing philosophers so that their high-sounding discourse gives itself away as corrupt and vain is not only liberating but fun:

> To laugh at philosophy... such, in effect, is the form of the awakening [which] henceforth calls for an entire "discipline," an entire "method of meditation" that acknowledges the philosopher's byways, understands his techniques, makes use of his ruses, manipulates his cards, lets him deploy his strategy, appropriates his texts. Then, thanks to this work... but quickly, furtively, and unforeseeably breaking with it, as betrayal or detachment, drily,... a certain burst of laughter exceeds it and destroys its sense.[56]

To laugh at philosophy, to destroy its sense by excessive laughter — such is the pleasurable labor of deconstruction's strategic seduction; such, when it happens, is the deconstructionist's reward for fighting the paper war against philosophy.

Writing after the Laughter

Deconstruction's deceleration of metaphysics, however, does not stop with a burst of laughter. Awakening is hardly a laughing matter, and deconstruction, contrary to popular conceptions, is definitely not just a sporadic frolicking with sacred texts. After seducing the text, the deconstructionist faces the demanding task of preserving his results, of keeping his reason for laughing at philosophy from decay. This requires a "discipline," a new "method of meditation," in essence, a new writing. Lest his reading be pulled back into the orbit of logocentrism and become an object of self-ridicule, the deconstructionist must invent a new syntax, a disciplined dialect proper to the nonsite (*non-lieu*) in which old topics in the philosophical space can continue to be discussed in some other way. While the deconstructionist begins by *reading* philosophy in a certain way, his mission will not be accomplished until he starts *writing* in a certain way.

How does the deconstructionist achieve that? How does he keep his feet in the nonsite while making an infectious contact with that which in principle falls within the territory of reason (for example, the laws of identity, of noncontradiction, of the excluded middle)? How does the deconstructionist's new dialect work *around* the limit of our logical precepts without totally sacrificing sense-making? How does it cross over the narrow, anguishing passage (*angoisse, angustia*) between meaning and nonmeaning? The answer, in a word, is that the deconstructionist plays "a *double scene* upon a double stage"; that he rewrites according to a new textual (a)logic of the "neither . . . nor," something "undecidable," something "unqualifiable and unnameable by philosophy."[57] More than being a seductive reading, deconstruction is also a double science. Only by doing a double science can the deconstructionist interrogate philosophy *nonphilosophically*; only by enacting a double writing can he finish his job.

What, then, is this double writing? How is it actually performed? Early in "The Double Session," in the course of discussing the possible Hegelian or Platonic overtones of the word *idea* in Mallarmé's writing, Derrida gives the reader a warning: "But a reading here should no longer be carried out as a simple table of concepts or words, as static or statistical sort of punctuation. *One must reconstitute a chain in motion, the effects of a network and the play of a syntax.*"[58]

Although Derrida is discussing reading, the principle advocated in this passage applies equally well to writing. According to this prescription, deconstructive writing "must reconstitute a chain in motion" that activates the "play of a syntax" against the stasis of logos. To write in this way, to set free the play of a syntax, however, does not mean the renunciation of all syntactic organizations. Rather, it means to rewrite, to rewrite *in a certain way*. This rewriting, as Maurice Blanchot explains it,

> does not refer to any preliminary writing, no more than to an anteriority of language or presence or signification. Rewriting—a doubling that always precedes or suspends unity while demarking it: to rewrite holds itself apart from all productive initiative and pretends to produce *nothing*, not even the past or the future or the present of writing. To rewrite by repeating that which

has no place, will have no place, has had no place, inscribes itself in a nonuni-
fied system of relations that cross without any point of intersection affirming
their coincidence, inscribing themselves under the exigency of the return by
which we are torn away from the modes of temporality that are always measured by a unity of presence.[59]

Pretending to produce nothing, this rewriting "is to mine the *movement* of
desire rather than its fulfillment, refusing to stop and totalize itself, or doing
so only by feint."[60] It is a kind of writing that both employs and subverts
the language of the text at hand, a writing that exploits the devices of a
negative dialectic of composition, decomposition, and recomposition of both
old and new terms in philosophy. It is, in other words, a writing in the ex-
hibitive rather than in the logical mode, a writing that is triggered by a self-
consuming sliding of the signifiers in which old signifieds as well as the oppositions to which they are attached are reinscribed, only to be rendered
functionless. Finally, one can say that it is an antihermeneutical, antisublative
writing that writes the vanishing of the vanishing mediators, a graphematic
writing that "desituates" presence by outrunning any "contextual" determination and galvanizes an explosion of remotivated signifiers by foreground-
ing the materiality of that writing itself.

To write *differently,* to communicate ideas against conventional protocols
and decorum, deconstruction's double writing, as suggested earlier, takes effect through a change of syntax, through a variation of form. It produces
new narratives by refashioning the old memories; it weaves new patterns
on top of the old fabric. In the process, deconstructive (re-)writing inevitably traverses multiple semiotic planes. So in Derrida's *Glas,* for example, one finds the "masculine" text of philosophy (Hegel) juxtaposed with
the "feminine" writing of literature (Genet) — two texts, two columns of
words, suspended in a kind of pas de deux.[61] Cultivating the semantic reserve and sonorous repercussions of the text's recurrent vocabularies (for
example, *glace*/glass/gel, *aigle*/Hegel, air/*terre*), and placing them in alien
contexts, a new split text is created — a medium of floating indetermination "in which opposites are opposed, the movement and the play that links
them among themselves, reverses them or makes one side cross over into
the other."[62] This split writing thwarts the demand of clarity and linear argumentation by forcing the textual fragments it contains into a proximity
normally prohibited. It multiplies references and voices; it fades in and out,
binding grammars, themes, and letters without the unity of presence.

This double writing pretends to say nothing. Constantly doubling and
hence continuously doubled, it occupies a strategic position to disturb the

scene of writing by meting out its textual wealth through "theft or brico-lage of the logos." This disturbance, this theft, says Geoffrey Hartman,

> redistributes the logos by a new principle of equity, as unreferable to laws of property, boundary, etc. (Roman, capitalistic, paternal, national) as the volatile seed of flowers. Property, even in the form of the *nom propre*, is *non-propre*, and writing is an act of crossing the line of the text, of making it indeterminate, or revealing the *midi* as the *mit-dit*. "La force rare du texte, c'est que vous ne puissiez pas le surprendre (et donc limiter) à dire: *ceci est cela*." (*Glas*, p. 222).[63]

Ceci est cela—one becomes the other; *ceci est cela*—neither one nor the other. In this instance, "what has been excluded is allowed to cross the line, or to be present even when absent, like a horizon."[64] To write in this way is to (re-)compose an other through the same, by muddling the text's margins, by crossing genres, by blurring the "what" and the "how" — "an ellipsis both of form and content: neither full speech nor a perfect circle. More or less, neither more nor less. Perhaps an entirely other question."[65] It is perhaps an entirely other question because what is being (re-)composed does not belong to the old regime of discourse, because what is being (re-)composed remains an aleatory composition. Whereas, in normal writing, chance always takes the fall at the hand of causal determination, in deconstructive writing, the pen gleefully toils against the pressure of necessity.

Writing with Old Names

Structurally, deconstructive double writing is composed of two activities that complete the circle of its engagement with philosophers' texts. The first is the *overturning*, a reversal of philosophy's binarism and hierarchy that have hitherto worked to guarantee a certain readability of its statements. The second can be called *reinscription*, a strategy that consists in prolonging the reversed opposition momentarily achieved along a grammatological continuum ad infinitum. This strategy of prolonging resists the ever present desire to reestablish a new hierarchy, and it manages to do so by nothing other than further prolonging the prolonging itself, that is, by a constant displacing of the displacement of the opposition at hand.

In an interview with Jean-Louis Houdebine and Guy Scarpetta, Derrida talks about the "general strategy of deconstruction," the first phase of which, he tells us, is

> to avoid both simply *neutralizing* the binary opposition of metaphysics and simply *residing* within the closed field of these oppositions, thus confirming it.
>
> Therefore we must proceed using a double gesture, according to a unity that is both systematic and in and of itself divided, a double writing, that is, a

writing that is in and of itself multiple, what I called in "*La Double Séance*," a double science. On the other hand, we must traverse a phase of overturning (*renversement*). I insist constantly and strongly on the necessity of this phase of overturning. To deconstruct the opposition, first of all, is to overturn the hierarchy at a given moment... The necessity of this phase is structural; it is the necessity of an interminable analysis.[66]

The necessity of this overturning results directly from Derrida's by now widely accepted observation that "in a classical opposition we are not dealing with a peaceful coexistence of a *vis-à-vis,* but rather with a violent hierarchy. One of the two terms governs the other (axiologically, logically, etc.), or has the upper hand."[67] The purpose of overturning is to weaken the upper hand, to enfeeble philosophy's violent hierarchization by reversing the hidden asymmetry that *is* the ideology of the logos. As a necessary moment in an interminable analysis, this overturning must be continuous; it must be performed with each reading. In this regard, deconstruction exemplifies in concrete practice the critical spirit of phenomenological enterprise as "perennial beginning."

Following this diligent overturning comes the second act, *reinscription.* To keep both the old and new hierarchies off balance, an operation beyond overturning must be performed, an operation that not only reverses the given hierarchies in philosophy but also "puts in writing" an arrangement in which the new relationship of the metaphysical couple can be maintained. Derrida describes the necessity of reinscription as follows:

> That being said—and on the other hand—to remain in this (first) phase is still to operate on the terrain of and from within the deconstructed system. By means of this double, and precisely stratified, dislodged and dislodging, writing, we must also *mark the interval* between inversion, which brings low what was high, and the eruptive emergence of a new "concept," a concept that can no longer be, and never could be, included in the previous regime.[68]

To flesh out this marking of the interval and "the eruptive emergence of a new concept," Derrida uses—changingly and interchangeably—a number of words, derived from his reading of various historical figures (the *pharmakon* of Plato, the *supplément* of Rousseau, the *hymen* of Mallarmé, to name a few), which intimate what he, *by analogy,* calls the "undecidables." These undecidables need to be examined closely, for they play a central role in the activities of reinscription.

The first thing that can be said about these undecidables—which are neither signifier nor signified because they are empty signifiers to begin with and which, in another context, Derrida refers to as *monstrosities*—is that they cannot be named. They cannot be named because "these words admit into their game contradiction and noncontradiction (and the contradiction and noncontradiction between contradiction and noncontradiction)."[69] Embodying contradictions, these words reject any appellation. They become nominally unfixed and unfixable because, like the disseminating seme(n), they are at different places all at once. Multiple and illegitimate in that they have no proper belonging except intrusive embodiments, these "biogenetic" morphemes are always in disguise and are possible and conceivable only in disguise, "even if these are separated by a veil, which is both transcended, intersected (*entr'ouvert*).[70] Speaking of *hymen*, Derrida writes:

> "Undecidability" is not caused here by some enigmatic equivocality, or some inexhaustible ambivalence of a word in a "natural" language, and still less by some "*Gegensinn der Urworte*" (Abel). In dealing here with *hymen*, it is not a matter of repeating what Hegel undertook to do with German words like *Aufhebung, Urteil, Meinen, Beispiel*, etc., marveling over that lucky accident that installs a natural language within the elements of speculative dialectics. What counts here is not the lexical richness, the semantic infiniteness of a word or concept, its depth or breadth, the sedimentation that has produced inside it two contradictory layers of signification (continuity and discontinuity, inside and outside, identity and difference, etc.). What counts here is the formal syntactical *praxis* that composes and decomposes it.[71]

Evidently, Derrida's undecidables are very different from "logical paradoxes" in philosophy. They are called *undecidables* because they magnify the impossibility of reading, because, that is, they "suspend the decidable opposition between what is true and false and put all the concepts that belong to the philosophical system of decidability into brackets."[72] The unreadability of these undecidables, as Derrida insists, does not result simply from a central ambiguity or choice, a simple semantic puzzle. Far from it: Their unreadability follows from the manner in which the values or meanings of these terms both urge choice and prevent that choice from being made. Residing in the text, these undecidables generate assertions that radically exclude each other. They produce meaning by inviting choice "while destroying the foundation of any choice."[73] Derrida continues:

> What holds for "hymen" also holds, *mutatis mutandis,* for all other signs which, like *pharmakon, supplément, différance,* and others, have a double, contradictory, undecidable value that always derives from their syntax, whether the latter is in a sense "internal," articulating and combining under the same yoke, *huph-'hen,* two incompatible meanings, or "external," dependent on the code in which the word is made to function. But the syntactical composition and de-

composition of a sign renders this alternative between internal and external inoperative. One is simply dealing with greater or lesser syntactical units at work, and with economic differences in condensation.[74]

Like subatomic particles whose flickerings at the border between the real and the immaterial somehow constitute the physical universe, these undecidables, signifying the "between" that at the same time is its two poles, the "void" that at the same time is full of matter, constitute what Gasché, also by analogy, calls the "infrastructure" of the textual universe.[75] *Infra-structural,* that is, creating suspense "due only to the placement and not the content," these undecidables mark the "points of indefinite pivoting" within the text "that can never be mediated, mastered, sublated, or dialecticized through any *Erinnerung* or *Aufhebung*."[76] Because of their irreducible excess of form over content, these undecidables signify spacing and articulation; they have as their meaning the possibility of syntax. Resembling what is known to grammarians as "syncategoremata" — lexemes such as *and, or, if, some, only, but, in between,* which cannot be used by themselves but only in conjunction with other terms — these undecidables order the play of meaning and organize the articulation of difference by making available a "fund" from which dialectics draws its currencies of thetic oppositions.[77] "*Neither purely syntactic nor purely semantic,*" these words nevertheless mark the "articulated opening" of signification, an opening that is the space of writing, the space of signs' double articulation.[78] Thanks to them, writing as usual becomes possible; from them, double writing receives the order, "Go."

It is from within the between, around the void, that the double writing proceeds to write, or more precisely, reinscribe itself. "Everything is played out, everything and all the rest — that is to say, the game — is played out in the *entre,*" the limen, the juncture, the threshold.[79] This game of double science attempts an interminable articulation of "unities of simulacrum," repeats "false" verbal properties, vacillating between two poles of the opposition *without ever constituting a third term.*[80] Such an experimental practice of inscription cannot but transgress the norm of morphology, semantics, syntax, and the normal mode of delivery, approximating in effect an "impossible" writing, impossible in that it is the very process of everlasting marginalizing, of becoming "other" that by its very nature can never be completed.

Impossible as it is, the double writing has to be written. To write it, the deconstructionist resorts to "old names." Paradoxically, and yet necessarily, deconstruction "evolves" into a science of old names: *paleonymy* or *paleonymics.* Paleonymy works under the understanding that the old names can be read, but now they *must be* read *sous rature* (under erasure). This means that the old conceptual or metaphysical oppositions survive on the paper, retain appearance, but are no longer operative, no longer functional. Physically marked or crossed out as soon as they are inscribed (for example, the sign ✖ that ill-named ~~thing~~), the appearance of the crossed-out terms communicates at exactly the same instant their death, their silence, their dubious usefulness:

> What, then, is the "strategic" necessity that requires the occasional maintenance of an *old name* in order to launch a new concept? With all the reservations imposed by this classical distinction between the name and the concept, one might begin to describe this operation. Taking into account the fact that a name does not name the punctual simplicity of a concept, but rather a system of predicates defining a concept, a conceptual structure *centered* on a given predicate, we proceed: (1) to the extraction (*prélèvement*, setting-apart) of a reduced predicative trait that is held in reserve, limited in a given conceptual structure (limited for motivations and relations of force to be analyzed), *named X*; (2) to the de-limitation, the grafting and regulated extension of the extracted (set-apart) predicate, the name X being maintained as a kind of *lever of intervention,* in order to maintain a grasp on the previous organization, which is to be transformed effectively. Therefore, extraction (setting-apart), graft, extension: you know that this is what I call, according to the process I have just described, *writing*.[81]

This mixing of old names and their instantaneous erasures constitutes (the process of) *l'écriture,* the double writing as interminable reinscription. In this interminable reinscription, the old names name the new game, the game of grafting, of new branches, for it is the science of the old that breaks open the possibilities for new growth, and it is the memory of the old names that recalls the "lever of intervention," the lever that renders effective the intervention that deconstruction brings into play.

By way of seduction and by writing a palimpsest where the surface text and the shadow text take turns dethroning each other, deconstruction communicates to us the problematic nature of communication. While an Archie Bunker can only be exasperated by a certain Edith's sublime response to his question "What difference does it make?" the Archie-debunker acknowledges with foresight the importance/impotence of communication.[82] Here the double writing becomes strategic again, the stratagem being paleonymy. Here, too, we may conclude, at least for the time being, as Derrida does, by saying

> despite the general displacement of the classical, "philosophical," occidental concept of writing, it seems necessary to retain, provisionally and strategically, *the old names*. This entails an entire logic of *paleonymics*....Deconstruction cannot be restricted or immediately pass to a neutralization; it must...put

into practice a *reversal* of the classical opposition *and* a general displacement of the system. It is on that condition alone that deconstruction will provide the means of *intervening.* . . . Deconstruction does not consist in moving from one concept to another, but in reversing and displacing a conceptual order as well as the non-conceptual order with which it is articulated. . . . To leave to this new concept the old name of writing is tantamount to maintaining the structure of *graft,* the transition and indispensible adherence to an effective *intervention* in the constituted historical field. It is to give to everything at stake in the operations of deconstruction the chance and the force, the power of *communication.*[83]

Strategic, parasitic, and seductive, deconstruction is apparently nihilistic, but, at root, it is affirmative — without, however, being *thetic.* It begins by affirming or recognizing, in the diplomatic sense, the otherness of the text, and it ends by affirming the necessity of communication for strategic intervention that avoids, in an equally diplomatic manner, the danger of reaffirming the old structure of the names it disrupts.

Being and Its Void

Being itself is distress. — *Martin Heidegger*

How do we intervene and inhabit in a certain way Heidegger's discourse on Being? How do we "double read" Heidegger's presentations on presence, to read them, that is, *counterintuitively?* Mindful of the importance of "maintaining the structure of *graft,* " of the possibility of "branching" in the growth of knowledge, we will have to proceed slowly and nonlinearly; we will have to unlearn some lessons and forgo some habits. Not only do we have to resist the seduction of Heidegger's call, the seduction of its meaning and presence, we also need to seduce Heidegger's text passive-aggressively, to hear his message *with another ear,* and to set loose the "force" that surges out of bounds, that metamorphoses into surplus meaning behind its proper signification.

Drawing on Derrida's "logic of the *supplément,* " I shall seek to set in motion a little tremor (*ébranlement*) to Heidegger's "house of Being" by trekking a particular byway obliquely marked in Heidegger's topology of Being. By rereading a certain Heideggerian "passage," the passage from beings to nothing, I intend to demonstrate that the apparent plenitude of Being is in fact made possible by, or, rather, centers around, an atrium of "nothingness," of the nonfullness of Being, that Being requires as its condition of illumination and intelligibility the moment of nonbeing, the moment of opacity that ultimately blurs the boundary between the two sides that any "passage" must assume. After simulating this little tremor, I will then emulate Derrida's "logic of paleonymy," retaining the old name, Being, so as to bring into sharp relief the working of *différance* as "a certain trembling, a certain decentering that is not the position of another center, and that, not a center, ultimately decenters Being."[84]

As can be inferred from previous discussions, the "logic of the *supplément*" articulates the parasitism of texts. "To supplement" means "to provide for, to supply." But something needs provision and can be supplemented only if it is not complete in and of itself, only if it lacks something that must be provided for from outside itself. To the extent that this something needs supplement, to the extent that something else can be added to it, the nature of this something will remain unfixed until the outside provides the necessary addition. Understood in this way, the supplement is no longer an element of accidental intrusion. In fact, through its function as a constant reminder of the self-insufficiency of the host, it designates the source, the *other*-location, from which what is initially regarded as the outside reemerges as the inside according to the principle of "necessary return."

Capitalizing on the supplement's essential mobility, its inherent atopicality, Derrida tries to underline the fact that any fixed order of priority within a text (inside/outside, cause/effect, nature/culture, fiction/reality), the author's intention and effort notwithstanding, is never fixed or fixable, that no text, as long as it involves more than a single verb *to be,* can be said to have a "pure" meaning, a thetic core uncontaminated or unimpregnable by external elements. Take Rousseau's *Confessions,* for example. If one reads it, as Derrida does, with the kind of attention it deserves, one would not fail to discern certain logical twists and roundabout locutions that Rousseau is forced to make, not only in passages of a more "personal" nature but also in his generalized reflections on language, music, sexual morality, and the politics of culture. In each case, one finds the conscientious confessor wanting to say one thing but ending up saying quite another, or effectively bending the projectile of his express argument. The cumulative effect of these textual slippages, evidenced periphrastically in Rousseau's shuttling movement between past, pluperfect, and future-perfect tenses, is that the careful reader is left wondering, among other things, whether this good author is really *confessing,* or just narrativizing a fiction that pretends to be confessional.[85]

This intractable textual event of the *supplément,* however, is not an isolated incidence; it is most certainly not the outcome of the writer's own doing. Instead, it signals the *happening* of the text, a happening that takes place when *l'écriture* takes place. In fact, "once alerted to it," Jonathan Culler assures us, we can find it at work in the most diverse contexts. We are dealing with a logic of the supplement when something characterized as marginal with respect to a plenitude—as writing is marginal to the activity of speech or perversion to normal sexuality—is identified as a substitute for that plenitude or as something which can supplement or complete it. It then becomes possible to show that what were conceived as the distinguishing characteristics of the marginal are in fact the defining qualities of the central object of consideration.[86]

That the turning of the center depends on the return of the marginal characterizes the way in which writing, as long as it involves more than a single verb *to be*, constructs its argument, its thetic appearance as text. Using this as our guide, we can define our task of reading Heidegger more precisely: to show how the plenitude of Being, the turning point of Heidegger's reflections, is inhabited from the outset and in an essential way by a hollowness of Being, a nothingness that is *at* the center but *is not* a center, that is both a division and deferral of that plenitude, and that, finally, reveals beings as beings. Our task, in other words, is to demonstrate how what is initially regarded in Heidegger's texts as the outside actually and unexpectedly inhabits the inside, what is initially excluded as unessential grounds the very possibility of exclusion, and finally, how the contamination of the purity of Being by the lack of being is what illuminates Being as pure presence in the first place.

In the preface to *The Essence of Reasons* (1928), Heidegger states: "Nothingness is the NOT of being and thus is Being experienced from the point of being."[87] This passage suggests that being is, at least experientially, more primordial than its NOT, nothingness, which can only be experienced "from the point of being." The experience of nothingness is an experience through negation, through the nihilation of beings, and hence is secondary or derivative with respect to beings that are always and already copresent with Dasein.

In an important essay, "What Is Metaphysics?" written one year after *The Essence of Reasons,* one can find confirmation for our interpretation: "The nothing is the complete negation of the totality of beings. The totality of beings must be given in advance so as to be able to fall prey straightaway to negation—in which the nothing itself could be manifest."[88] But this "definition" of nothing as the negation of the totality of beings, Heidegger warns us, is not the nothing as such. For negation is always an act of the intellect, an exercise in logic, and the result of this is that nothing is treated as something, as a being, such that we obtain only a formal concept of the imagined nothing but never the nothing itself. The nothing that really *nothings,* according to Heidegger, can be achieved only on the basis of the fundamental experience of the nothing. In fact, the nothing is revealed, becomes present, Heidegger continues, only through Dasein's direct—if rare—"projection into nothing" (*Sichhineingehalten in das Nichts*), namely, Dasein's fundamental experience of anxiety (*Angst*). By bringing Dasein face to face with its irrepressible *thereness,* by forcing it to face its facticity as being-in-the-world, anxiety collects Dasein—through trembling and nausea—into an inimitable unique singularity. In so doing, it delivers nothingness to Dasein (or it delivers Dasein into nothingness, which amounts to saying the same) by communicating to it its aloneness in presence through a total dissipation of the things present:

> Anxiety reveals the nothing.
> We "hover" in anxiety. More precisely, anxiety leaves us hanging because it induces the slipping away of beings as a whole. This implies that we ourselves—we men who are in being—in the midst of beings slip from ourselves. At bottom therefore it is not as though "you" or "I" feel ill at ease; rather it is this way for some "one." In the altogether unsettling experience of this hovering where there is nothing to hold onto, pure Da-sein is all that is still there.[89]

Before the subject-object dichotomy takes hold of our thinking, the "pure Da-sein" encounters the nothing in anxiety. "In the lucid vision sustained by fresh remembrances we must say that that in the face of which and for which we are 'anxious' was 'really'—nothing. Indeed: the nothing itself—as such—was there."[90] The nothing was there, beforehand, out of which the *thereness* of Dasein is. In this way, "Da-sein" can only mean, as Heidegger concludes, "being held out into the nothing."[91] Nothing, therefore, awaits Dasein, for it must have already taken its place whereby Dasein confronts its thrownness into the world, its situated facticity as a being that is *there.* In fact, "only on the ground of the original revelation of the nothing can human existence approach and penetrate beings."[92]

What is the principle behind Heidegger's thinking regarding Being and nothingness? What is the role of "nothing" as it relates a being, Dasein, to beings? Above all, how is the nothing revealed in anxiety? How is it presented in relation to beings that are present and that it negates? For Heidegger, one thing is certain: the nothing is not revealed as a being, "just as little is it given as an object."[93] "Rather," he says, "in anxiety the nothing is encountered *at one with beings* as a whole . . . the nothing makes itself known *with beings* and *in beings* expressly as a slipping away of the whole."[94] If the nothing is encountered *at one with beings,* if it "makes itself known *with*

beings and *in beings,*" what is the "difference," we might ask, between the
nothing and beings by whose slipping away as a whole the nothing becomes known? Is the nothing experienced from the point of view of beings? Or are beings experienced on the basis of the original opening of the
nothing within whose abode Dasein exists and matures to be capable of
experiencing *Angst*? Is it possible to decide? Is it, perhaps, undecidable?

The following passage seems to capture the argument of "What Is Metaphysics?":

> In the clear night of the nothing of anxiety the original openness of beings as
> such arises: that they are beings — and not nothing.... The essence of the
> originally nihilating nothing lies in this, that it brings Dasein for the first time
> before beings as such. Only on the ground of the original revelation of the
> nothing can human existence approach and penetrate beings.[95]

It would not be inaccurate to say that "the nothing of anxiety" constitutes
the condition of possibility of beings, that this nothing "is constitutive of
the pure essence in which any being can be and manifest as a being, as such
and such."[96] In accord with its nihilating essence, "the nothing directs us precisely toward Being."[97] Through this nothing, this *nonobject* of anxiety, beings as a whole, as not nothing, become present; they make their presence,
that is, before individuation and without differentiation. But it would be a
mistake to infer that the nothing is more primordial than beings. For the
anxiety that reveals the nothing as such and brings forth beings to disclosure
is born of an objectless "state of mind," the uncanny mood of *Angst* that
overtakes Dasein when it finds itself most immersed in beings, so immersed
that the overabundance of beings overwhelms its existence, its singular being-
there, by outstripping this or that particular being. "Anxiety is indeed anxiety in the face of... but not in the face of this or that thing. Anxiety in the
face of... is always anxiety for..., but not for this or that."[98] In other
words, "the indeterminateness of that in the face of which and for which
we become anxious is no mere lack of determination but rather the essential impossibility of determining it."[99] The preponderance of beings defies
determination and particularization on the part of Dasein. It announces itself as "the nothing," a nothing that, paradoxically, is fullest in its beguiling
emptiness. Using the language of record keeping, of identification, we may
say that it is the initial of all initials, an original faceless voice or a voiceless
face that gives beings their identifiable appearances. This is why, as Heidegger maintains, the nothing is not *nihil negativum*; rather, it is the fullest expression of beings' presence as a whole, so full that the presence as this or that

particular being slips into absence, into the ground that *in-forms* the figure of the nothing.

Is the nothing full or empty? Is it a wellspring or a void? Does it have a face or not? Does it exist "before," "behind," or "after" beings? Is it the ground or the figure? Is it absent or present? Is it primary or secondary, an original or a simulacrum? Is it essential to Being's illumination or a mere accidental company to beings' undifferentiated appearances? Could the nothing—whether as the ontological foundation behind negation or as the logical or conceptual opposite of beings—"nothing" itself? If it could, is this nothing really nothing? If it could not, what kind of thing is this nothing? Finally, is it possible, given the mutual implication of the terms Heidegger uses in discussing the nothing and beings, to give any definite answer?

No, for no certainty is in sight. Disclosed *at one with beings,* the nothing trails its own negation, thus recurring on the positive side of presence and visibility. Trailing beings because it is "nothing," and yet trailing beings *as* nothing because it is that which provides for beings what they must already have had, namely, their presence; this nothing *is;* it *ek-sists.* As the negation of beings, the nothing slips away, but as "the nothing of anxiety," it comes back—reemerging, that is, as the *supplément* of beings, just as beings supplement the nothing so as to make themselves slip away as a whole. The nothing and beings therefore must be said to cohabit in one and the same event of presencing, each inhabiting or entrapping the other as its own essential constitutive element. Neither is earlier or later; they appear *equiprimordially.* No thing can exclude the nothing; for the same reason, the nothing always includes all the things that it, as the nothing, cannot exclude. There is no absolute point zero—there is always more than one, always less than one. There is no pure punctual moment of genesis or division—there is always internal and original complication by an other. There is either the situation of "*both... and*" or an event of "*neither... nor,*" as the "logic of the *supplément*" dictates.

Loose Play: *Différance*

Yes, even then, when already all was fading... there could be no things
but nameless things, no names but thingless names. — *Samuel Beckett*

It is to Heraclitus that I refer myself in the last analysis. — *Jacques Derrida*

The logic of the supplement does not mean that there is no difference between beings and nothing, between presence and absence, between the inside and the outside, between the central and the marginal. It does mean, however, that the self-identity of any of those terms depends as much on its own "indifferent" prioritization as on the supplementary relations that differ and defer it from other related and contrastive terms, their binary relatives systematically suppressed by the movement of writing as it seeks to make "good sense." More broadly speaking, it means that philosophical writing, as long as it involves more than a single verb *to be,* is not only a dangerous business because it can be accused of falsification, but that it is also an irredeemably dirty activity because the divisions it creates are never clearcut, because the categories it deploys are never pure, because, in a word, the *parergon* always and already insinuates itself in the *ergon.* By showing the predicament of nonchoice in philosophers' writing careers, by revealing their unrecognized victimization by the double scheme of *suppléer* (meaning both "to fill a deficiency" ["to complete"] and "to take the place of" ["to replace"]), the logic of supplementarity forces aspiring philosophers to recognize the differential and relational movement that vibrates beneath the foundation of any philosophical system — an amorphous root complex that nowhere constitutes a center or touches ground in a transcendental instance that would itself be without radicles or ancestors.

Once the supplement is exposed and its effects are acknowledged, the end of innocence begins (or should begin), for there takes place (or should take place) the dissolution of a bad faith in metaphysics, in its underlying utopian confidence in a final solution. The supplement ungrounds grounding, be it transcendental, psychoanalytic, or hermeneutico-existential; it denies the possibility of any ground. "Ground" implies a stopping point, a definite and nonmoving *topos,* a "would-be authority," as Gilles Deleuze and Félix Guattari call it.[100] What the logic of the supplement makes plain, however, is an open-ended process of grounding, a process propelled by a force of internal strife and indecision so that it has no choice but to indefinitely postpone any final closure or determination. What philosophy tries to achieve in each instance, and consequently what we observe in each of its attempts, is an ongoing act (make-believe) of grounding; however, a ceaseless grounding in effect is no different than an inane affair of ungrounding, in that it never reaches any solid ground. To borrow a term from seismologists, the ground turns out to be a "float sheet" atop molten lava, and, as a float sheet, it shifts without warning, like a mirage appearing and disappearing in reaction to the endless dislocation of ground-searching. This *utopia* (that is, nowhere) of ground does not result from the fact that humans are finite or that thinking is limited; rather, it follows from the *supplément's* broadcasting that nothing, not even a thing, is originally founded on a self-sufficient or self-identical moment or instance. One thing is itself only insofar as it differs from other things either present or absent with it: Identity must be defined through the detour of difference, and because of that, the foundation philosophers dream of always turns out differently than what they hope for.

This ungrounding difference designates one of Derrida's most celebrated undecidables, *différance*. By deliberately misspelling one letter, a fragile letter that can be easily misprinted and that therefore appears to be a good birthplace for a revolution in print, Derrida brings about a change in and by writing: The epsilon is gone, long live the alpha. Although the distinguishing *a* makes no difference phonetically, it leaves a visible mark graphically. A new word thus appears on the page, but because its change is unpronounced, this alphabetic revolution remains silent. It occasions a change that from one point of view makes no difference, yet from another point of view produces minute but persistent shock effects because of its violation of the basic spelling of the word. Different or not, the distinguishing *a* insists on being written and becomes present sharply in writing. Derrida thus constructed something unheard of, a neologism,

> which is not a name, which is not a pure nominal unity, and continually breaks up in a chain of different substitutions. . . . What we do know. . . is that there never has been and never will be a unique word, a master name. This is why thinking about the letter *a* of differance is not the primary prescription, nor is it the prophetic announcement of some imminent and still unheard-of-designation. There is nothing kerygmatic about this "word" so long as we can perceive its reduction to a lower-case letter.[101]

Connoting both "differing" and "deferring," *différance* is often characterized as "spacing." But as an undecidable operating in a double register that presents no synthesis and thus provides leverage for "undoing" the unifying presumption of any text or thought entity, the "spacing" also contains in itself the element of "temporalizing." Although confined to the "silent tomb," the *a* in *différance* nevertheless causes an "interminable disquietude of thought," a disquietude that disorganizes philosophy's appointments by confusing their dates and places.[102] In the *writing* of philosophy, in its attempt to become timeless, time is often misplaced, and place is as often timed incorrectly. We do not need theorists of relativity to instruct us in what a lower-case *a* can do. After all, how can I defer, that is, delay (*de* [off] + [*laier*] leave) or carry away (*dis* [away] + [*ferre*] carry), anything if I have no room left, and how could I differ from you if there is no time for disagreement?

Destabilizing any category (such as the space and time that coordinate experiences, the form and content that organize objects, or the analytic and synthetic that classify propositions), *différance* underlies the asymmetrical undercurrent of a kind of "textual instantiation" in which one term folds, or, rather, transforms, without friction and without any warning into another at exactly the moment it unfolds itself into presence and vice versa. It is differing and deferring everywhere and all at once. Meditating on the equivocal meaning of "to differ," Derrida writes:

> We do know that the verb "to differ" (*différer*) ... has two seemingly quite distinct meanings ... namely, the action of postponing until later, of taking into account, the taking account of time and forces in an operation that implies an economic reckoning, a detour, a respite, a delay, a reserve, a representation. ... "To differ" in this sense is to temporalize, to resort, consciously or unconsciously, to the temporal and temporalizing mediation of a detour that suspends the accomplishment of fulfillment of "desire" or "will," or carries desire or will out in a way that annuls or tempers their effect. ... this temporalizing is also a temporalization and spacing, is space's becoming-temporal and time's becoming-spatial.[103]

Going beyond the order of hearing and voicing, the neographism of *différance* procures something that difference cannot generate. By causing a minimal change (the substitution of *a* for *e*), it creates maximal effect (the transformation of space into time and time into space) — a creation that, because of the transformative confusion it causes, ensures the survivability of its effects. *Différance* thus effects a new complex of meaning — "it is immediately and irreducibly multivalent."[104]

In the following, instead of attempting an apology for *différance*, I shall limit myself to the notion of "differing" and "deferring" as constituting the basic thrust of *différance*'s essentially equivocal sense in order to show how it grounds what Derrida calls the *text*. I will then compare and contrast Derrida's "text" with Heidegger's "Being" to display, first, how the former differs from and displaces the latter, and second, how this displacement calls into question the classical activity of "philosophizing" in its dominant mode.

The undecidable and instantaneous self-transformation of space into time and time into space embodied in *différance* can be interpreted as deriving from collapsing two insights of Derrida's father figures, Saussure and Husserl, into one. Grafting Saussure's conception of the diacritical difference as the foundation of sign function (that is, to differ) to a phenomenological understanding of time consciousness as a multilayered structuring of the past, present, and future (that is, to defer), Derrida radicalizes both terms through the logic of the supplement that implants one deeply within the other. The radicalization of Saussure's semiotic difference, the systemic and relational difference that links a part, the phoneme /a/, for example, to a whole, namely, to the ever expandable but regulated sound universe of English, consists in temporalizing its spatial or synchronic character, whereas the radicalization of phenomenological temporality lies in transforming the lineal — albeit over-laying — progression of sedimented moments of time into a vertical, para-digmatic decentered matrix of attention, protension, and retention where the "living present," a now-point, can never be pinpointed except as the trace-effect along an errant trajectory of the present, past, and future, each of which is itself nothing but the trace-effect of yet another equivalent trajectory.

Differing and deferring, *différance* dissolves the idea of presence, mani-fested as ageless essence or self-identical substance, into traces and echoes. The "presence" of meaning, of identity, the "presence" as essence, as origin, and the present as a kind of temporal simplicity of the living now — none of these can ever be a fulfilled ideal; rather, they are constantly constituted and reconstituted as an "effect," a simulacrum-effect within a system of dif-ferences and sliding substitutes. Active, forceful, *différance* designates, in Der-rida's words, the "productive and primordial constituting causality, the process of scission and division whose differings and differences would be products or constituted effects."[105] In other words, "what we note as *différance*," Der-rida continues,

> will thus be the *movement of the play* that "produces" (and not by something that is simply an activity) these differences, these effects of difference. This does not mean that the difference which produces differences is before them in a simple and in itself unmodified and indifferent present. Differance is the non-full, non-simple "origin"; it is the structured and differing origin of differences.
>
> Since language (which Saussure says is a classification) has not fallen from the sky, it is clear that the differences have been produced; they are the effects produced, but effects that do not have as their cause a subject or substance, a thing in general, or a being that is somewhere present and itself escapes the play of difference. If such a presence were implied (quite classically) in the gen-eral concept of cause, we would therefore have to talk about an effect without a cause, something that would very quickly lead to no longer talking about ef-fects. I have tried to indicate a way out of the closure imposed by this system, namely, by means of the "trace." No more an effect than a cause, the "trace" cannot of itself, taken outside its context, suffice to bring about the required transgression.[106]

As can easily be seen from this passage, the idea of presence as effect means that presence is produced by a *play* of differences, that it accomplishes ap-pearance only as or at the juncture within a system where differential forces intersect and where traces (are forced to) invest themselves in aggregates in reaction to the system's equifinalistic tendency toward closure and stasis. What might not be so easily understood, however, is Derrida's insistence that the presence-effect does not and could not have any cause — except as "trace" in a highly contextualized sense, and in that case this contextualized trace refers only to further traces without ever reaching any original cause.

To grasp Derrida's reasoning, two points must be understood with adequate precision. *Différance,* Derrida says, is the "movement of the *play* that 'produces'" differences. "To play" means "to act, to perform"; it means to move or operate within a bounded space, as machine parts do. But parts can move and perform their specific functions only if there is a certain *looseness* in the system, only if there is a congenital "undecidability," a freedom *within* the system *from* the system's totalistic determination, that causes or agitates the parts within it to move and perform, that is, to combine, to permutate, and to substitute. It is this looseness, these chance irregularities (*écarts*) within a regulated whole — what Derrida elsewhere calls the *in-fini,* something that is neither finite nor infinite, but literally, the finite *within* the infinite — that makes it impossible for the system not to play.[107] It is this looseness as the structural instability of the system — call it "excess," or "lack," which amounts to the same thing — that generates the energy that the system needs to exist. Because of its function, this looseness, this structural freedom from determination, can be regarded as the center of the system in that it commands and limits the play of the system which it inhabits. At the same time, however, since this looseness, either as "excess" or as "lack," is free from the system's determination, this center is in truth an "impossible" center — impossible in the sense that it remains *extrinsic to* the system because it does not itself enter into the functional processes of combination and substitution. It is in this sense, and in this sense only, that we can say that the "movement of *play*" has no origin. Having no origin, that is, functioning without identifiable intrasystemic cause, *différance* also has no essence and cannot be the object of even the most refined form of essential intuition (*Wesensschau*). Like *pharmakon* or *hymen,* *différance* escapes both perceptual and conceptual grasping: "Not only can it not allow itself to be taken up into the *as such* of its name or its appearing, but it threatens the authority of the *as such* in general, the thing's presence in its essence."[108] In short, *différance* cannot, "in classical affirmation, be affirmed without being negated."[109]

The second reason why *différance* cannot be ontologized classically is that *différance* is meant as pure *alterity.* Irreducibly other, alterity designates that which is absolutely *antipunctual.* The antipunctual is that which constitutes no phenomenality. That is to say, being antipunctual, *différance* can never be said to arrive or appear because its appearance or arrival, if appearance or arrival could ever be mentioned, is either too early or too late. Indeed, what is radically other never appears as such, but only appears *parasitically*, that is, *in* the other and *as* an other. "As the movement that structures any dissociation," *différance*, Gasché argues, "functions *infrastructurally*, and not *foundationally*."[110] That is, "as an originary synthesis not preceded by any absolute simplicity," *différance* is before all the determination of a particular difference, "the *pure* movement which produces difference."[111] Perpetually in motion, *différance* differences; constantly differencing from itself, from its own difference, *différance* is always already (*toujours déjà*) *other* without constituting any positivity. Consequently, difference can never be registered in any essential way. Because of this lack of positivity, and provided that one does not confuse *différance* with the differends it constitutes, the qualification *essence* simply cannot be bestowed on it. If *différance is* anything at all, it can only be the *becoming trace of the trace itself*, the *arche-trace*. Yet since the arche-trace is a trace of which the trace is only a trace, that is, "since the trace can only imprint itself by referring to the other, to another trace ('the trace of its reflection'), by letting itself be upstaged and forgotten, its force of production stands in necessary relation to the energy of its own erasure."[112] Because of the close proximity between tracing and effacing, because of the *sameness* and *simultaneity* of its birth and demise, the arche-trace can never be presented *as such* outside the differences through which it traces the appearance of others.

Residing *infrastructurally* in its own traces as a self-effacing trace, the arche-trace has no theater of its own. It cannot show itself because it has no place to show itself, because for it to be itself is for it to become a trace of itself, to become its own trace. Responding to the question of whether the trace is a *philosophical* concept, Derrida puts it straightforwardly:

> you cannot say that the trace is philosophical or not philosophical. *The trace is nothing.* . . . The trace is something you cannot experience *as such*. But if for the moment we speak easily of the experience of the trace, then what I said in my remarks is that in the experience of the trace *as such,* the experience *as such* of the trace *as such* — precisely the *as such* does not work any more. The experience is not philosophical as such; the philosophy comes afterward.[113]

The trace is nothing because the trace absences. Its *coming,* as it were, is always beleaguered by the "threat or anguish of its immediate disappearance, of the disappearance of its disappearance."[114] Coming by going, arriving by departing, the arche-trace *is* not; it is always and already another trace in that it has always and already dispersed itself (by its own erasure) into its own simulacra:

The trace, where the relationship with the other is marked, articulates its possibility in the entire field of the entity (*étant*), which metaphysics has defined as the being-present starting from the occulted movement of the trace. The trace must be thought before the entity. But the movement of the trace is necessarily occulted, it produces itself as self-occultation. When the other announces itself as such, it presents itself in the dissimulation of itself.[115]

That being the case, the question of what the arche-trace is cannot be asked, because the question implies that it could appear, come into view, in its essence. To ask what the arche-trace is not only presupposes a difference that the arche-trace is intended to explain but also repeats metaphysics' mistake in substantializing what is perpetually a pure and unmotivated movement, thereby reinstating as the principle of principles that which undermines the very possibility of having such a principle. Indeed, if the trace *is* only in relation to another trace in self-effacement, then this trace has nothing that could be called its own or that could, as its proper essence, be made to body forth as such.

This reinterpretation of presence as trace puts into question a number of cardinal philosophical concepts. Take (almost at random) "origin," for example.[116] "Origin" signifies a beginning point; it implies the existence of a "first time." The idea of trace, however, suggests that the beginning must have already begun and that the putative first time of the beginning is not really first after all, because if the "first time" were the only time, if it were to last as the first time all the time, it would not be the origin of anything at all. For the first time to be the first time, to be prior to all other moments, there must be a second time, a latecomer. (Incidentally, we should not forget to ask: If the first time is *truly original,* how can it be known or recognized?) From this moment on, the first time is doubled; it must necessarily keep this second time close to itself; it must exist in an unalterable and unadulterated proximity to its second time. Through an ironic twist of relation, this second time now takes on a priority in the very constitution of the first time, because it is this second time that makes the first time the first and not the other way around. A remarkable consequence follows: Since the first time now depends essentially on its second time to appear as the origin, the first time, for all its claim to chronological priority or nonderivativeness, turns out to be *not* the first time but, rather, a third time.[117] For it now exists in essential relation to both the second time and the supposedly pure first time that anchors the whole temporal sequence.

Like Nietzsche's deconstruction of causality, "the concept of origin," as Derrida writes, "is nothing but the myth of addition, of supplementarity annulled by being purely additive. It is the myth of the effacement of the trace, that is to say, of an originary differance that is neither absence nor presence, neither negative nor positive. Originary differance is supplementarity as *structure*."[118] The idea of the trace thus de-reifies the originality of origin by unveiling its duplicitous, retroactive constitution. Trace intervenes into everything as an originary delay; origin is always delayed, a delayed origin, a nonoriginary origin.

If the deconstruction of origin proves to be unsettling to philosophy, it is not merely because it reveals one of metaphysics' most cherished concepts to be a case of *metalepsis*, based, that is, on a reversal of the actual order of temporal priority, "a putting of the earlier later and the later earlier and so creating a false appearance of a necessary sequence."[119] More disquieting in this regard is the indication that other representatives of the metaphysics of presence, to the extent that they are all dispatched in one way or another on the principle of decidable priority, could likewise be deconstructed. Take (again, almost at random) the notion of "perception," for example. As a philosophical concept, perception has always enjoyed a privileged status compared to other modes of consciousness. It signifies immediacy by delivering to consciousness a unique, *radiant* quality of the object as the living present. For this reason, perception offers an ideal beginning point for philosophy, constituted and reconstituted *via negativum* as the venue from which epistemic corrigibility is to be transcended. However, just as it disarticulated "origin," the trace nature of *différance* fundamentally de-idealizes perception. As a primitive mode of an outward-bound conscious act, perception always tends toward particularization; it is always directed at "this" or "that"— either this or that—as the focus of its action. In its intending, perception must suppress the horizonal differences that greet it; it must fight off the ambiguity or opaqueness of the visible. Perception survives in presence, for it always perceives "something," at least as something, in the "pure actuality of the now." This primitive grasp or comprehension of something as something by the perceptual act, based on its noematic predisposition for clarity regarding the perceived object, entails a corresponding oblivion to the difference, to the retentional-protensional frame and the unavoidable background unclarity constituted by the heterogeneous colors and shapes that open up and saturate the perceptual field in which the object under focus takes on identity and integrity only in contradistinction to an inarticulate other that embodies the invisible. Perception rides over its *plus ultra*, but in so doing, it not only forgets its own birth as representation but also overlooks the possibility that the thing under focus itself can always escape its gaze. It is against this oblivion to the difference, to the shadows and traces exceeding the horizon of a lighted object, that Derrida makes his astounding confession that he does not believe in perception.[120]

Being and/or Text

There is no longer concealed Being but the very being of this
concealment: dissimulation itself. — *Maurice Blanchot*

Distrusting perception, Derrida excavates behind presence something "older than" Being, something that takes place before Being, something whose coming, because of its age, is always delayed, something whose arrival, because of its belatedness, is delay itself. The delayed arrival of this something, its belated appearance, keeps itself out of our reach and prevents us from traveling back in time to witness its occurrence. All we can come to know about it at any given moment are the traces left behind by it; all we can perceive in each instance is constituted by the *trait/retrait* of its traces as traces.[121] Not even the eidetic vision of the phenomenologist could pierce through the phenomenal opacity woven by its traces, for each seeing, however phenomenologically reductive, only causes further deflections in the labyrinth of traces and creates more fake images in a house of mirrors. There is no presentation; there are only representations that barely retain the difference between themselves and their source. "Nothing," says Derrida, "neither among the elements nor within the system, is anywhere ever simply present or absent. There are only, everywhere, differences and traces of traces."[122] This *trait/retrait* of traces unveils what Derrida calls the "play of difference"; something made of both "chance and necessity in an endless calculus." And this play of difference in turn constitutes what Derrida calls the "*text,*" the "*proto-writing,*" or the "*arche-writing.*"

One of the most inflated terms in contemporary critical vocabulary, the word *text* has been used to refer to a wide variety of objects, ranging from things as particular as a menu in a restaurant, episodes (or part of an episode) of a television comedy, or cultural artifacts of various sorts to phenomena as broad and vague as religion or even culture in its entirety. What do these objects have in common? If the concept of the text applies to all of them, what is it that permits and encourages such a generous application? If, as Derrida argues, there is nothing outside the text ("Il n'y a pas de hors-texte"), what is that "textual interior" so imperialist as to permit nothing to fall outside it? More specifically, what does Derrida mean by the *text*?

On several occasions, Derrida stresses that the generalization of the concept of the text sanctioned by deconstruction does not imply a "theology of the Text" and should not lead to a new "idealism" of the text.[123] Derrida's "general text" must be sharply distinguished from "writings on the page," from what we normally call the *book*. In its traditional determination — whether empirical, idealist, or dialectical — the book is always defined as a totality: "It always implies a closure upon itself with a clear inside and outside, whether it is the empirical closure of a corpus, the intelligibility of a work, or the dialectical totality of its formal or thematic meanings."[124] In contrast to the book, whose ostensible beginning and end create an impression of unity, the general text, because it defies totalization and hence is not a totality, has no outside or inside, nor can it be said to begin or end at any particular point. As Derrida takes great pains to show in "Living On," the general text is, rather, the *border* between the inside and outside, that undecidable seam or fold crossing over between words, between pages, from which the assignment of insides and outsides takes place and at which this distinction ultimately collapses.[125]

Functioning as the fold that binds words in proper order within the margin, the general text breathes life into those words — enabling them to mean and to become readable. In this light, the text in Derrida can be understood in the Saussurean sense as the "unmotivated production" of signs, as semiotic *productivity* itself. Oswald Ducrot and Tzvetan Todorov explain:

> Defining the text as productivity amounts to saying — to bring ourselves... to the ultimately *theoretical* implications of such a definition — that the text has always functioned as a *transgressive* field with regard to the system according to which our perception, our grammar, our metaphysics, and even our scientific knowledge are organized, a system according to which a subject, situated in the center of a world that provides it with something like a horizon, learns to decipher the *supposedly prior meaning* of this world, a meaning that is indeed understood to be originary with regard to the subject's experience of the world, a system that can only be, indissolubly, that of the *sign*.[126]

The productivity of the general text designates the possibility of signification that predates not only the construction of the text's thematic unity and semantic plenitude but also the constitution of the subject as the consumer of the textual product. It refers to the signifying *force* preceding the *structure* or *form* of utterances that pushes the frontier of the text's readability by making its medium work. Ducrot and Todorov continue:

> The text "makes work of language" by *going back to what precedes it*; or better, ... it opens a gap between, on the one hand, the "natural" language of everyday

usage, destined for representation and comprehension, a structured surface that we expect to reflect the structure of an outside and to express a subjectivity (individual or collective), and, on the other hand, the underlying volume of signifying practices, "where the meaning and its subject sprout" at every moment, where signification germinates "from within the language and its very materiality," according to models and in a play of combinations (those of a practice within the signifier) that are radically "foreign" to the language of communication.[127]

It is this prerepresentational, precommunicative, signifying volume that Derrida explores. It is this (nonoriginary) combinatory play of presignifying differences that the Derridean concept of the "text" aims to highlight. And finally, it is the irreducibility of this pretextual play of the sign that leads Derrida to say, "There is nothing outside the text."

Texts for Derrida occur only in writing. A text is a *happening*, a *taking place* of writing; each text is a living memory of writing as written. Properly understood, the general text for Derrida registers what must have already been written in the structure of the sign, an arche-writing that prewrites itself all over the place and before actual writing takes place:

> *There is* such a general text everywhere that (that is, everywhere) this discourse and its order (essence, sense, truth, meaning, consciousness, ideality, etc.) are *overflowed,* that is, everywhere that their authority is put back into the position of a *mark* in a chain that this authority intrinsically and illusorily believes it wishes to, and does in fact, govern. This general text is not limited, of course, as will (or would) be quickly understood, to writings on the page. The writing of this text, moreover, has the exterior limit only of a certain *re-mark*. Writing on the page, and then "literature," are determined types of this re-mark.[128]

Different writings on the page are "determined types" of arche-writing, which is *there* before the author and reader alike. Everything is already re-marked; everything (that is, every *meaningful* thing) is already textualized. "There is nothing outside the text" does not mean that all is language, or that the world is like a big manuscript composed by some divine scribe. Derrida could just as well have said that *there is nothing inside the text,* either. One could no longer talk of either the inside or the outside of the text because this very distinction (in fact, the whole of referentiality or mimesis) presupposes clear-cut borderlines within what is perpetually drifting.

This, I think, is what the *productivity* of the text means. It is *différance* in action as the differential articulation/conjunction of restricted and free motions, an unhampered and yet controlled dancing of traces/effects (a *jouer* that is also a *nouer*) that institutes the pretextual opening-up of a textual web in which each "textual instance" concretizes writing that signifies by "repeating" the trails and traces that the textual web already marked down. Generated by *différance* — provided we remember that this generation has always and already been generated — which constitutes itself by dynamically dividing itself, Derrida's general text is necessarily and internally split. Every text is inescapably a double text; "there are always two texts in one."[129] "Two texts, two hands, two kinds of looking, two kinds of listening. At once together and separate."[130] Any text for Derrida, then, is by nature a palimpsest, doubly written and in principle open for double reading.

Unfortunately, in the normal practice of writing and reading, this is hardly understood adequately. The palimpsest is rarely recognized and read as such. The more apparent stratum (that is, the surface) of the text is always read as the whole text; and the subsequent reading, as a surface reading, only reconfirms the reading it achieved at first. In fact, philosophy (and all meaning-centered communication theories, too) have all along promoted and safeguarded the surface reading of the text and have relegated the shadow text to "unreason" or "irrationality." As Vincent Descombes explains:

> Only the first of these "two texts in one" is preserved by classical interpretation; it is written under the aegis of presence, favoring meaning, reason and truth.... The second text — other and yet the same — is that which the classical reading never deciphers. The first text, however, the one which it is prepared to read, contains fissures or traces which give indication of the second. Now comes the vital point: between the two texts no synthesis is possible, no fusing into one, for the second is not the *opposite* of the first (which might be reconciled with it by a "surmounting" of their "differences"), but rather its *counterpart, slightly phased*. A reading of the general text therefore requires a *double science* rendering apparent the duplicity of any text.[131]

Although philosophy has preached all along that the text is one, that it is a unity, the general text for Derrida is always the text of "two texts in one," composed of "one text of presence and one text of non-presence," one text composed of "one manifest and therefore dominant text and one latent and therefore subordinate text."[132] Each text is (like) a *hymen*, both virginity and copulation; every text is (like) a *pharmakon*, both poison and remedy. In contrast to a book, which embodies a totality and which appears as a whole by having a front and back, Derrida's text *is* itself as other, and every inscription, every sentence, being double, is its own simulacrum. "Between the text by Plato and itself, or the text by Hegel and itself," and we might add, the text by Heidegger and itself, "there passes a 'scarcely perceptible veil,' separating Platonism from itself, Hegelianism from itself," and Heideggerianism from itself.[133] Every (textual) product of *différance* is intrinsically defective; every text is potentially self-deconstructive. A slight displacement, a slight change of the habit of reading, a little frivolity or playfulness is all that is needed to turn the text against itself, to inflect the shadow text against the surface text, and to rewrite the wisdom of the former into the tragicomedy of the latter. Duplicity, equivocality, undecidability — only they reflect the nature of meaning's untamed economy; only they could alert us to the impending "return of the repressed."

In what way is Heidegger's text separated from itself? How does Heidegger's meditation on Being fail to coincide with Being? How is Heidegger's fundamental ontology internally split, that is, doubly written and thus open for double reading? Finally, is Being itself not a "double text," and ontology a "double writing" incognito? In "The Anaximander Fragment," Heidegger writes:

> The point of Being (*die Sache des Seins*) is to be the Being of beings. The linguistic form of this enigmatic and multivalent genetive designates a genesis (*Genesis*), a provenance (*Herkunft*) of the present from the presence (*des Anwesenden aus dem Anwesen*). But with the unfolding of these two, the essence (*Wesen*) of this provenance remains hidden (*verborgen*).[134]

Two messages can be extracted from this passage. First, because Being is the being of beings, ontology must start from beings, from the beingness of beings. Second, because the difference between presence and the present is hidden, ontology must broach itself by thinking that difference as difference. As pointed out earlier, the idea of "ontological difference" in Heidegger plays an ambivalent double role. It designates a relation between two realms of thought, between two kinds of presence, that are both continuous and discontinuous. The discontinuity between Being and beings diagnoses the problem of traditional metaphysics, the problem that Being is thought of as a being without realizing the radical heterogeneity between the two. However, by thinking seriously and for the first time about the ontological difference, Heidegger's reflection implies that Being, though concealed by the difference, can nevertheless be brought from behind the present into presence; the ontological difference, in a roundabout way, points to the topos of Being. Although Being as such is absent in the disclosure of beings, it is nonetheless absently present in beings to the extent that its own effacement in and through beings accords well with its essence. Beings for Heidegger are therefore not mere simulacra but, rather, honorable aliases of Being; though named differently from Being, beings are "the same as" — which is not to say "identical with" — Being. As Heidegger himself acknowledges:

The difference between Being and beings, however, can in turn be experienced as something forgotten only if it is already discovered with the presence of the present (*mit dem Anwesen des Anwesenden*) and if it is thus sealed in a trace (*so eine Spur gepräge hat*) that remains preserved (*gewährt bleibt*) in the language which Being appropriates.[135]

This passage recapitulates what was earlier dubbed the "Heideggerian faith in the belonging-together of Being and Truth": that mortal Dasein, as seeker of truth, is in its ontological constitution responsive and responding to the call of Being. This is one of the consistent themes in Heidegger, made clear as early as *Being and Time*:

Why must we presuppose that there is truth? What is "presupposing"? What do we have in mind with the "must" and the "we"? What does it mean to say "there is truth" ("*es gibt Wahrheit*")? "We" presuppose truth because "we," being in the kind of Being which Dasein possesses, *are* "in the truth." ... It is not we who presuppose "truth"; but it is "*truth*" that makes it possible ontologically for us to be able to *be* such that we "presuppose" anything at all. Truth is what first *makes possible* anything like presupposing.[136]

Although forgetful, Dasein, being what it is (amidst beings), stands nonetheless close to Being, thanks to the latter's illumination, irrespective of the distance created by the ontological difference. Dasein's being is the very passage of truth to Truth through beings.

If Being and beings indeed bear such a hermeneutical relation to each other, if one indeed dwells in the other as a trace (or, rather, inhabits it like a parasite), can Being completely separate itself from beings? Since Being, in its appearing, always recedes into silence, how could it break its mutism unless it were to delegate beings as its spokespersons, its medium? How could Being be heard without resorting to the speech of beings, a language it does not and cannot speak? If self-effacement, the becoming trace of Being into beings, accords naturally to the essence of Being, isn't it more the case that beings first bring Being into its absencing presence than the other way around, isn't it the case that beings first reveal Being, revealing it, that is, before ontology retrospectively understands that it is Being that lights up the region of beings?

Struggling against "logic" and "representational thinking," the later Heidegger seeks the ground (*Grund*), the self-hiding topos of Being. The search stops when Heidegger arrives at an abyss, a point beyond representation where thinking can no longer orient itself forward and where the hermeneutico-phenomenological excavation reaches rock bottom. This abyss is the abyssal origin of *Ereignis*, the original ground of Being that is without ground, without address. Heidegger writes: "Being as grounding has no ground; it plays as non-ground of every game which dispenses Being and ground to us."[137] Having no ground and without origin, Being can be understood only as *autoproduction* par excellence, an originary genesis, a coming forth (*Herkunft*) that nevertheless keeps to itself. It grounds beings but is not itself grounded. Being, therefore, can only be "abandoned Being," for it must leave itself, effacing its own appearance by speaking in multiple voices and thus coming back to its own emptiness in excess. Adopting the acoustic images that the later Heidegger trades on, we can say that it is the "pure speech," the speech before any speaking, that *translates* sound into voice and voice into sound but does not make itself heard. Drawing on a fragment of Heraclitus, Heidegger compares the groundlessness of Being to child's play: "The child plays because he plays. The 'because' sinks into play; there is no 'why': ... There is only the game itself ... but this 'only' is everything, the One, the Unique."[138] Being as *Ereignis,* Truth as *aletheia,* has no motivation and cannot be approached in terms of the ratiocination characteristic of the representational economy. Being's appropriation is expropriation, and its expropriation is appropriation. Speaking of Being's expropriation of itself as self-ensconcement, Derrida reiterates this abyssal nature of Being sighted by Heidegger:

> Finally, then, once the question of production, doing, machination, the question of the event (which is one meaning of *Ereignis*) has been uprooted from ontology, the proper-ty or propriation is named as exactly that which is proper to nothing and no one.... Perhaps truth's abyss as non-truth, propriation as appropriation/a-ppropriation, the declaration become parodying dissimulation.[139]

Parodying itself or not, Being is Being because *it is*; it is its own *isness* — no more and no less, self-sufficient and self-evident. Entangled in a "process of propriation," the *giving* and the *gift* in the *es gibt Sein* dissimulate one another: "The *giving* and the *gift* can be construed neither in the boundaries of Being's horizon nor from the vantage point of its truth, its meaning. Just as there is no such thing then as a Being ... there is also no such thing as an essence of the *es gibt* in the *es gibt Sein,* that is, of Being's giving and gift."[140] Being and ground : the same = Being : abyss (groundless).

This disquieting abyss (*Abgrund*) deserves to be thought through seriously. And one can push this mystery of Being a little further by asking how this *isness* of Being is presented. To say that it presents itself as presencing, or that an abyss is abyssal, is hardly more than exchanging one ambiguous expression for another, or to use Richard Rorty's words, "a movement from one ineffable to another."[141] Let us not forget that Being is always the being of beings. Being must "make sense," and its sense is made by the presence of beings. To speak itself, Being must *quote* beings, must inscribe itself in what is close to itself, and must leave a trail of its unconcealment in what is thus unconcealed by itself. To present itself, to make itself known, Being needs the "body" of beings, even though this "body" can only be its parodying dissimulation. Since veiling and unveiling are intertwined, since illumination and dissimulation become indistinguishable in the abysslike event of Being, since, that is, "the proper-ty of the abyss is necessarily the abyss of proper-ty" in Being's dissimulative appropriation, ontology, as *the* discourse of the *propre*, unwarily but necessarily becomes a kind of indirect discourse on Being: It becomes a proleptic and analeptic telling and retelling of what is distanced by space and time, always citational, that is, *textual*. The ontological difference should not and cannot be transcended; rather, it should and will be kept as the difference through which Dasein as a hermeneutical possibility enters into the play of Being. Without this difference, Dasein would lack the point of entrance; without it, ontology could not be.

At the same time, because of the *necessary* intervention of the ontological difference in the thinking of Being, there inevitably exists a chasm, a gap, a parallel, or rather, a chiastic doubling (of Being) in the order of Being. Being and beings signify each other in the sense that each, being different from the other, refers to the other as its signified through an unwanted mediation, namely, the groundless play of difference between the two. Each constitutes a trace, a signature, for and within the other. Being and beings are the same, in that they belong together, but the two are not identical because there is a fundamental difference between them. Belonging together and yet different from each other, Being and beings *ex*-press each other. The sameness, not the identity, of the two makes the thinking about Being not only endless and infinite, that is, metonymic, but also metaphorical. To think Being as Be-ing, the ontological difference must be constantly entertained, for to stop thinking that difference amounts to losing sight of the difference as difference and evokes the false identity of Being and beings. The ontological difference therefore effects a contiguity, a syntagmatic relation of Being and beings that sustains a metonymic extension along which thinking approaches Being, but never without sustaining a distance between thinking and what is being thought. By the same token, the sameness of Being and beings constitutes a similarity, a paradigmatic relation of the present to the presence, that engenders the thinking of Being as presence, but never without reproducing a difference between the thought of Being and Being as such. Thinking about Being therefore resembles writing about Being, and writing about Being points to the way in which Being can be thought; each doubles the other because of the abyss that each has to face but does not always recognize. As long as they make sense, as long as they can be thought, Being and beings are subject to the same logic of signification, the logic of *writing*, the logic of *différance*, that is, the logic of differing and deferring.

Within the thinking/writing of Being, Being is both the signifier and the signified. The bar between the two persists but is not uncrossable. Yet with a bar in between, the expressions of Being become unavoidably oxymoronic. Being is *and* is not what it appears to be. It appropriates the language of someone else; it speaks in the voice of an other. It is and is not what it says. There are two voices in one, slightly out of sync. "There will be no unique name, not even the name Being."[142] No master term, no transcendental signified should terminate the thinking/writing of/about Being. Being is an (oxymoronic) metaphor; philosophy is a kind of writing. Being : Metaphor = Philosophy : writing. Always a difference, always at a distance, either too early or too late.

Beginning Ends?

This question we leave to thinking as a task. — *Martin Heidegger*

Heidegger was a serious thinker and a skillful storyteller. Taking advantage of one of modernity's most ambitious narratives—phenomenology—he renarrated for us moderns a story of a "second coming," an eschatology built upon the myth of the Greek as a great beginning, an exciting moment of radiant gods and gleaming temples.[143] Recently we have been hearing a different message, a different story telling us that gods have never existed and that temples have always been empty. Now that the end of onto-theology is upon us, could we be as hopeful as Heidegger? For Heidegger hoped to be more Greek than the Greeks themselves, "to pursue more originally what the Greeks have thought, to see it in the source of its reality. To see it so is in its own way Greek, and yet in respect of what it sees is no longer Greek, is never again, Greek."[144] Has the history of metaphysics really brought us closer to that unique happening before history, the Greek happening that became our destiny? Has Heidegger's fundamental ontology succeeded in closing the book on Occidental metaphysics?

Isn't it this security of nearness that is being disturbed today, this belonging together and this reciprocal appropriation of the name of man and the name of being, such as dwells and dwells on itself in the language of the Occident, in its *oikonomia,* embedded in it, inscribed according to the gospel of metaphysics and forgotten; and also such as is awakened by the destruction of ontotheology? But this disturbance—which can come only from a certain outside—was already necessitated in the very structure which it solicits. The extremity (*marge*) of this structure was already branded (*marquée*) into its ownmost living flesh (*corps propre*). In the thinking and the language of being the end of man has been prescribed from all time, and this prescription has done nothing but modulate the equivocity of the *end,* in the play between *telos* and death. In the reading of this play one can, in every sense of the word, *entendre* the following sequence: the end of man is the end of the thinking of being; man is the end of the thinking of being; the end of man is the end of the thinking of being. Man is from all time his ownmost (*propre*) end, that is to say, the end of his belonging (*son propre*). Being is from all time its ownmost end, that is to say, the end of its belonging.[145]

Being's end begins at the exact moment when its beginning begins to end. Being's end begins at the exact moment when beings are thought as the beginning of Being. Since the belonging-together of Being and thinking represents an indispensable relationship, human thinking about Being shall remain for all time an unfinished project. This, we now realize, is the historic consequence of the *in-difference* of Being.

What is the difference between Heidegger and Derrida after all? And what is their similarity? Both Heidegger and Derrida know that phonemes matter, but Derrida realizes that Heidegger's litany of Being is just Heidegger's, not Being's or Europe's.[146] Is Derrida's thought a continuous radicalization of Heidegger's, or is it, as Gayatri Spivak suggests, a modest prying open of the Heideggerian text?[147] Does it make any difference anymore to know the difference? Something cannot be different from another without, in some respect, being similar to it. Deconstruction is different and yet similar to destruction. *Différance* is different from and yet similar to *Ereignis* or *presencing.* What is the exact difference? If that question can still be raised, the answer has to be deferred—perhaps until the next season of dehiscence.

5 / Deconstructing Communication: Derrida and the (Im)Possibility of Communication

The rule of the undetermined is itself undetermined. — *Aristotle*

Metaphysics is concerned with laying the groundwork for philosophical constructions. It is an *archi*tectural business of sketching a Being/beings blueprint, of drawing a Being/beings grid, whose purpose is to frame things, the multiple, according to a unifying vision, the universal. As made abundantly clear in *Being and Time*, Heidegger's project is subtly different: Heidegger is not interested in offering a rival proposal of his own in the bidding for metaphysical construction; nor is he interested in marketing yet another new and improved "printer" capable of graphing the discursive despotism of "reason," "spirit," "self-consciousness," or whatever one chooses to call it, by means of its discriminatory stylus of exclusion and reduction. Heidegger's objective is to *question beyond* metaphysics, to return to the arche of metaphysics' system building by critically examining what actually takes place *in* all such undertakings.[1]

In Heidegger's view, the problem with the history of metaphysics is not that there has been a lack of discussion of Being. Rather, the problem lies in the fact that metaphysical reflections so far have not been radical enough: They have yet to take the necessary two steps back, from beings to Being and from Being to the "upon-which" of its projection.[2] This archaeological step back is necessary because all ontical experience of entities...is based upon projections of the Being of the corresponding entities—projections which in every case are more or less transparent. *But in these projections there lies hidden the "upon which" of the projection, and on this, as it were, the understanding of Being nourishes itself.*[3]

If fundamental ontology is to succeed in questioning beyond metaphysics, it must work its way through Being's projections in beings—to track Being's ontic traces against their transparency until it reaches their source, the hidden upon-which where the understanding of Being nourishes itself in repose. This hidden upon-which is the ground of metaphysics; this hidden upon-which is what sustains (*halt*) and maintains in subsistence (*nährt*) all metaphysical thinking, and because of that, this upon-which constitutes the object of fundamental ontological reflections, marking a terrain of thinking where the line, the slash, between Being/beings can be properly crossed.

As I suggested in the beginning of chapter 4, there have been two developments concerning how and whether the line or slash between Being/beings can be crossed. The right-wing Heideggerian (such as Gadamer) responds to Heidegger's calling with faith and embarks on the journey toward Being on the serene assumption that there is sufficient light shed from beings to find Being. The left-wing Heideggerian (such as Derrida), in contrast, sees no such illuminated passage and maintains instead that the crossing from the ontic to the ontological is always and everywhere obstructed by the delay structure of writing. Whereas Gadamer waits patiently for the message/passage from Being to beings, Derrida, with more nerve and "ready for anxiety," relinquishes any hope for such delivery and deliverance. For Derrida, Being's sending is always postponed, addressed amiss; Hermes cannot find his way out of the *abîme,* the dark and silent abyss, circumscribed by a play of traces that plays without why, without beginning, and without end.

In this chapter, following the lead of the left Heideggerian, I intend to push the phenomenology of communication beyond its Heideggerian horizon by submitting it to a Derridean critique. Specifically, I wish to investigate how and to what extent the Derridean blockage of the crossing between Being/beings challenges the onto-hermeneutical understanding of communication as destined delivery. By focusing on Derrida's overturning of the speech/writing binary, my purpose is to demonstrate, first, how Derrida's deconstruction of logocentrism reveals an uncontrollable "asemantic drifting" within the exchange of messages, and second, how this asemantic drifting of the message undermines the possibility of any phenomenologically based theory of communication by tangling up the orderly relation presumed to exist between sending, receiving, and the context in which they take place.

What Is the Message? *Positivity* as the Critical Dogmatics of Communication

But deconstruction is not a critical operation, the critical is its object;
deconstruction always bears, at one moment or another, on the
confidence invested in the critical, critico-theoretical, that is to say,
deciding authority, the ultimate possibility of the decidable;
deconstruction is deconstruction of critical dogmatics. —*Jacques Derrida*

What is the "critical dogmatics" of communication theories? What constitutes the "deciding authority" in communication theories so that it determines uncontestedly the critico-theoretical orientation of an entire discipline? Since "words and concepts receive meaning only in sequences of differences, one can justify one's language, and one's choice of terms, only within a topic (an orientation in space) and a historical strategy. The justification can therefore never be absolute and definitive. It corresponds to a condition of forces and translates a historical calculation."[4] What is the "condition of forces" that opens the topic, the topical space, of communication theories and gives them the structure of decidability? And what is the historical calculation or strategy that establishes for communication theorists what Erving Goffman calls the "working consensus," a system of predicates and instructions designed to give their activities the appearance of working toward a common goal, a unified science of communication?

In "Communication: A Semiotic of Misunderstanding," João Natali argues that communication theory is "saturated with positivity"—a positivity "founded on a desire for universality and thus resistant to approaches which are able to contradict it."[5] Spoken by an outsider, that is, from a perspective synthesizing three positions generally disregarded within mainline communication theories (that is, Marxism, psychoanalysis, and structuralism), Natali's indictment deserves a serious hearing—all the more so when one considers its sociopolitical implications. It is clear that Natali's intent in his essay is more than polemical. By revealing a certain blind spot in communication theory and the conceptual limitation that blindness entails, Natali seeks not only to reenergize the sclerotic state of communication theory but also to redefine its future—a task that can be achieved, as he rightly believes, only by rigorously contesting communication theory's hidden ideological underpinnings. It is with this objective in mind that Natali sets up his metacritical shop, where the first-order "critical operations" of communication theory can themselves be critiqued in toto. Before addressing the theoretical significance of Natali's criticism, I wish to examine briefly the argument underlying his oppositional stance.

According to Natali, communication theory, by its selective attention to certain social relationships as paradigmatic of communication, has systematically deflected attention from others. This selective attention in practice solidifies communication theorists' unspoken decision to exclude a group of phenomena that therefore by default do not qualify as proper objects of inquiry. Chief among the excluded is the phenomenon of "misunderstanding." Premised on a functionalist conception of the subject-language (or sender-medium) relation according to which the former, conceived as a self-determining and hence self-responsible agent of action, uses the latter as an instrument to convey his or her thoughts to others, communication theory in Natali's view has all but lost sight of the intricate interrelationship between itself, ideology, and the relative influence of the unconscious on the individual's communicative acts. This blindness to the complex interaction among language (the medium), the message, the subject (sender/receiver), and their sociosemiotic environment (the context), a blindness that is by no means uncritical, causes communication theorists to reify *understanding* as the *ideal,* the *telos,* and the *norm* of communicative activities. Under this view, to communicate is — principally — to achieve understanding, and instances of misunderstanding, of equivocation, of ambiguity, of nonsense, can be viewed only negatively, that is, as lack, aberration, or dysfunction. This normative principle, a "deciding authority" founded, as it were, on the "ultimate possibility of the decidable," dictates an a priori determination of communication as regulated exchange, yielding in its wake an axiomatic of inquiry that approaches communication either in the image of an act of delivery or as a network of relays that carries out that act, both of which, as if in lockstep, reinforce the preconception of communication as the reduction of difference. As a result, actual communicative events, many of which divagate from the rule of reciprocity, are economized in a prescriptive fashion, economized, that is, by what I called earlier the "postal principle," an idea(l) based on sending and receiving, according to which the unity of sender and addressee is supported or justified by the working of a tele(o)-system, an apparatus of delivery that transports messages — letters, *logoi,* dispatches, *envois, Schickungen* — across the line, from end to end, from person to person, from one computer terminal to another, from station to station, from epoch to epoch.[6]

One can thus find in communication theory a certain *hermeneutic ideology,* an implicit value judgment anchored in the primacy of understanding that, by exercising its prescriptive authority, valorizes certain objects or relations (such as the conscious intention, consensus) to the suppression of others (such as the unconscious, desire, conflict, uncertainty, dispute, ambiguity). Postulating understanding as the norm, as the paradigmatic ideal, and categorizing any failure of understanding as incidental and anomalous (the prime example being Claude Shannon and Warren Weaver's mathematical model of information flow in which "noise," an always possible anti-information in a communication network, is given a negative sign in its equation of transmission, stipulating that it should be subtracted from the message emitted from the source to the destination), communication theory willy-nilly promotes social cooperation at the expense of social difference and conflicting interests. By repressing what remains singular and noneconomic in the process of transmission, that is, by silencing all the "noises," all the troublemaking signals that compete with the official message, such a theory not only ignores the reality of concrete social struggle but also overlooks the constancy of "semiotic crisis" at the heart of each historical sign, thereby helping to legitimate the sociopolitical status quo that countenances, a posteriori, the theory's normative, a priori, basis. Constructed from the vantage point that excludes "disorder" at its originary moment, communication theory, contends Natali, plays right into the hands of the capitalistic social system by supporting the one-way, center-to-periphery structure of its media institutions and ancillary agencies. "Communication theory," as Natali writes, "has definitely an effective source of legitimation, within the discursive tide where capitalist social formations fish for proofs of their legitimacy."[7]

Let me return to the theoretical import of Natali's essay. If positivity characterizes the underlying dogmatics of communication theories, a deconstruction of these theories must begin with a critical analysis of this positivity. But what is "positivity"? What does Natali mean by it? Why are communication theories overburdened with it? How does this positivity universalize itself as *the* order of theorizing in communication? In what way is this positivity complicit with the commission of an act that legitimates the paradigmatic representation of communication as hermeneutical transmission?

Since Natali argues that communication theory begins by excluding misunderstanding, his notion of "positivity" can best be understood with reference to this exclusion — to communication theory's significant initial gesture that culminates in an orientation against entropy, against anything that jeopardizes the act of delivery or obstructs the pathway of the postal network. As an initial clarification, positivity can be taken to mean the postulation and consequent reification of identifiable components that constitute a communicative process. It stems, on the one hand, from a forced fragmentation of a unified object, an "arbitrary punctuation" of totality (for example, a verbal exchange), into a finite number of combinative parts (such as sender, message, receiver) whose relationship reflects a predetermined analytic operation. On the other hand, it designates the fixation of those artificially separated elements and the subsequent construction of a theoretical syntax that arrays those elements in a particular pattern and reinforces their fixed positioning. Positivity in communication theory results from this double operation, an operation that confirms the validity of its own representation of communication by insisting on performing that operation. In other words, by decomposing a whole into parts and recomposing the parts into a whole, this double operation not only anatomizes communication as the transport of message/ information according to a self-validating part-whole organization, but it also reimposes this import/export image of information transfer on reality, on actual events, thus universalizing it as the general truth of communication. It is against this universalizing representation, against the imposition on reality of an economic representation created by an arbitrary punctuation, that Natali accuses communication theory of being "saturated with positivity." In the following, rather than pursuing Natali's far-reaching critical impulse, I shall identify two interconnected assumptions coded by communication theories in their discussions about the transmission and exchange of meaning. A close analysis of these assumptions will help bring into relief the pertinence of a deconstruction of the positivity envisioned by Natali.

Jakobson's model of communication is perhaps the single most quoted source in modern communication theory.[8] Since this model is proposed as a universal representation of communication, I will use it here as a test case. Jakobson's model involves six components: addresser, context, message, contact, code, and addressee. These six components correspond to six functions: the emotive, the referential, the poetic, the phatic, the metalingual, and the conative. In any actual communicative event, Jakobson tells us, one of these six functions is always dominant to a greater or lesser extent over the others, depending on the point of view of the observer. So, for example, when I hear a technician say "testing, testing, one, two..." while checking a loudspeaker or telephone line, I can safely conclude that the function of that utterance is phatic, for the technician's primary purpose in making that utterance is to find out whether the loudspeaker or telephone line is working—despite the fact that the same utterance can also be made to refer to existing objects (loudspeaker, telephone line, tools, and the like) in the surroundings. Alternatively, if I hear you saying "Look!" "Listen!" or "Now see here . . ." to your partner, I can justifiably infer that the conative (or vocative, or imperative) function now dominates the structure of the speech event as a whole, since your messages, so uttered in that context, are clearly angled toward your partner, the addressee. At any rate, the central point of Jakobson's model is that the so-called message of an exchange does not and cannot supply all of the meaning of the verbal event in question, for what is communicated in each instance depends to a large extent on the context, the code, the means of contact, and the combinations thereof. The meaning of a message, in other words, resides in the *total* act of communication, a situation in which the grammatical elements of the message often play a limited part and are easily overshadowed by a myriad of extralinguistic factors. By identifying and then hierarchically organizing the different functions that verbal communication comes to serve, Jakobson's model, true to the formalist-functionalist commitment of its Prague school background, brings a semblance of order to a wide variety of human symbolic practices — giving a unity, as Jakobson says, to the "diversity of linguistic genres" hitherto treated in isolation by different disciplines.

What has Jakobson's model achieved? What is the real significance of such a model of communication? Is this model true to life? Is it possible to model the same phenomena differently? Most important, on what basis is this model constructed? If one examines Jakobson's model carefully, paying close attention to its components and the relationships among them, two characteristics can be discerned. First, the model is made up of a finite number of distinct and separate parts that, according to Jakobson, constitute a total communicative event. The model, in other words, presupposes the *decomposability* or *divisibility* of what is in reality continuous and dynamic into discrete and static constitutive units, units supposedly identifiable across situations. Second, the constitutive units of the model stand in a *linear-sequential* relation to one another. The model implies a telos inscribed in a unidirectional movement, a telos that links parts of a whole as marked points within a series, points whose positions, one will do well to remember, are pre-fixed by the model's original act of punctuation. By punctuating a totality into finite parts that can be recombined only by following the original rule of division when the need to reconstitute the original totality arises, the model represents communication, more precisely, the verbal event, by serializing it into a concatenation of multiple subevents. According to this representation, communication begins with the addresser and ends with the addressee, forming a procession with all its participants lined up in sequence. Once this serialization is completed, once the procession is off, the fate of each member is sealed; that is, it is determined by its placement in the sequential order that the model implies. Take the moment of "message," for example. Not only is it positioned between the addresser and the addressee, but it also follows a definite trajectory: It must flow, in principle, from the addresser, the beginning, to the addressee, the end, despite the periodic pull exerted on it by context. In fact, the destiny of the message is already written into the very positioning of the addresser/sender and the addressee/receiver from the outset, given the former's need to encode the message and the echolike retro-translation, that is, decoding, that must be performed by the latter to complete the process. A linear logic thus orchestrates the procession; it governs the model as a structural whole. Indeed, no matter how hard one tries to qualify the one-way relationship between the addresser (who initiates the transmission) and the addressee (who terminates the transmission) — invoking, for example, such additional variables as feedback — the initial punctuation performed by the model makes it impossible to alter the relational movement between them as parts within a whole. In fact, given its linear-logical construction, the model would be pointless without predefining the truth of communication as the movement of a message from one end of the line to the other. Moreover, if one asks if linearity and decomposability have anything in common, it becomes clear that a "spatial bias" is embedded in the model. With the addresser and addressee separated and then coupled through some kind of "contact," Jakobson's model demands that communication be represented as the extension of the message in space. It reflects a rhetoric of mastery as a semiotics of spatial control that prefers points and lines and their connections to nonlinear patterns that register the irregularity of the informational traffic.[9]

A model is a representation; it implies an organization of the real. By organizing the real, the model projects itself as *realistic*. By appearing realistic, the model often succeeds in substituting for the real, depending on the purpose for which it is constructed. At any rate, the more the model appears realistic, the better its chance to become a substitute for the real. This much appears incontrovertible — until one recognizes the following: Like any act of representation, the construction of a model presupposes two conditions — first, a distance between itself and that which it represents, and second, an active point of view, a centralizing perspective through which the distant object is brought within view, into proper focus. Because of the distance between itself and the represented object, a model can never fully capture the real object, no matter how credible its representation appears. Since it cannot fully capture the real, since its referent always maintains a certain degree of otherness by keeping its distance, the model cannot succeed fully in substituting for the real, for it is not and can never be its real referent. Similarly, to the extent that the model's construction depends on an active vision, it is governed by the organizing perspective that it assumes. The model is never more than a perspectival construct, based, as it is, on a partial vision or limited re-view. Seen in this light, a model must be understood as a "coded representation," a kind of representation whose verisimilitude (the reality-effect that all models, to the extent that they intend to appear realistic, seek to achieve) consists precisely in disguising its coded nature, its representational character.

If a model as representation is always coded, then what is the code, if any, that governs Jakobson's model as a whole? What is the underlying code of which the model's linearity diagnosed earlier represents a local symptom, and about which our clinical reading of that model presents only a partial analysis? As briefly mentioned in the earlier discussion of Natali, there is a hidden complicity between (or a common bias shared by) Jakobson's model and certain theories of signification and media practice. Constructed on the basis of conservation, of transmission against distortion or loss, of understanding against misunderstanding, the model is not merely abstract and reductive; more significant, it betrays a covert idealist fallacy, detectable in a specific "metaphysics of the sign" that Jakobson shares with both formalism and certain one-dimensional Marxist theories of symbolic practice such as the early Frankfurt school, Hans Magnus Enzensberger, and others.[10]

To explicate this "master code" of idealism, let me focus on one of its most pronounced symptoms in communication and media theories: the postulation of the communicative subjects (the addresser/sender, the encoder/decoder, the addressee/receiver) as pregiven entities, that is, as self-determining agents logically and chronologically anterior to their participation in various interactive processes.[11] Derived from the Cartesian self-transparent ego, this conception of the communicative subject makes two mistakes by sliding over a whole process of complex psychosocial determinations in the formation of the subject. First, by positing the addresser/sender as a self-determining intentional I, this Cartesian view overlooks the unique and essential role that language plays in transforming the individual into a subject. Insofar as verbal exchange is concerned, it fails to recognize that it is language, or more exactly, the first-person pronoun, that provides, before everything else, the possibility for the speaker to posit him- or herself first as the subject of a sentence and subsequently as the *en-gendered* agent of socially meaningful action. The subject as I therefore cannot come about without language, for the possibility of the I depends on what might be called the "transformative hospitality" of language, a symbolic reception hosted by language on behalf of the social structure that inducts anyone capable of saying "I" as the subject. "It is in and through language," as Emile Benveniste argues, "that man constitutes himself as a *subject,* because language alone establishes the concept of 'ego' in reality."[12] The I exists in and by means of *saying* I; the I is not a pregiven *subjectum,* a preexisting substance, that decides to speak; the I emerges as a result of being spoken and exists thereafter only as a *spoken* subject. The subject, in other words, is the subject of its own living discourse, posited in and by means of it. The "basis of subjectivity," to use Benveniste's expression, is not something underlying the subject's action; it *is* an action, the action of speaking.

Second, by ignoring the psycholinguistic constitution of the I, the Cartesian-based communicative subject also overlooks the determination of the sociocultural milieu (for example, family, community, ethnic and religious background) that exerts pressure on one's subjectivity-in-process (*sujet en procès*), not only through its linguistic reality but also through its heterogeneous and often contradictory gender- and class-specific moral, political, and economic demands. The I, as we know it, is no more than an unstable body unit, wrapped by permeable skin and constantly reworked by external elements. Taking advantage of the vocabulary of grammar, we may say that the I is really a me in the "accusative" case, not only because it can be referred to only by an indefinite one (*on* in French) referring to itself from the outside, but also because its unity, its indexical cohesiveness, is from start to finish swayed by outside pressures. Contrary to the abstract image of the addresser depicted in Jakobson's model, the I who speaks and responds is not some kind of Chomskyan "competent" speaker; the speaking I is at the same time always a *sexed, socialized,* and *politicized* subject whose speech is inextricably tied to social, historical, and political conditions at the moment of the utterance that reach far beyond what a variable such as "context" can capture.

These two mistakes reflect a fundamental error of the Cartesian perspective that modern communication theory inherits. Essentially, the error consists of a failure to recognize the effect of the other in the constitution of subjectivity. Overcoming the evil demon and the diabolical world through "rational doubt," the Cartesian ego believes itself to be above illusion and (self-)deception. Such an image of the self leaves no room for the unconscious any more than it grants any place for social institutions and their signifying practices, both of which preexist the possibility of enunciation and interpersonal interactions. Borrowing too readily from this Cartesian heritage, traditional communication theory cannot help turning a deaf ear to culture and history, thus re-creating a subject that is gender-blind, culturally absolutist, and historically frozen. Such an understanding of the communicative subject is unavoidably idealist, for divorced from culture and history, it corresponds not to any concrete reality but to a theoretical fiction yielded by introspection and abstraction.

One of the more obvious problems resulting from this idealist construction of the communicative subject is a certain confusion regarding the order of priority in the conceptual structure underpinning modern communication theories. Paying insufficient attention to the fact that communication *imposes* structure on the individual, determinately constraining the encoding and decoding of those involved in the process, this Cartesian-based subject gets the picture upside down; it misses the fact that individuals are *constituted* as functioning communicators only insofar as they participate in communication, only insofar as they are *positioned* as sender or receiver differentially according to the *medium* and the *context* of a particular communicative event.[13] Before the addresser can function as an addresser, it must have already been *addressed*; before the addresser is able to establish any "contextual contact" with its addressee, the addresser must have been an addressee itself.

In "Requiem for the Media," Jean Baudrillard similarly criticizes Jakobson's "simulational model of communication." Baudrillard argues that, from its inception, the model

> excludes the reciprocity and antagonism of interlocutors, and the ambivalence of their exchange. What really circulates is information, a semantic content that is assumed to be legible and univocal. The agency of the code guarantees this univocality, and by the same token the respective positions of encoder and decoder... the formula has a formal coherence that assures it as the only *possible* schema of communication. But as soon as one posits ambivalent relations, it all collapses. There is no code for ambivalence; and without a code, no more encoder, no more decoder: the extras flee the stage. Even a message becomes impossible, since it would, after all, have to be defined as "emitted" and "received." It is as if the entire formalization exists only to avert this catastrophe. And therein resides its "scientific" status. What it underpins, in fact, is the terrorism of the code.[14]

According to Baudrillard, Jakobson's "scientific" modeling of communication is made possible by making the "code" central. In Jakobson's guiding schema,

the code becomes the only agency that speaks, that exchanges itself and repro-
duces through the dissociation of the two terms and the univocality (or equivocality, or multivocality—it hardly matters—through the non-ambivalence)
of the message.... So, this basic communication succeeds in giving us, as a reduced model, a perfect epitome of social exchange *such as it is*—such as, at
any rate, the abstraction of the code, the forced rationality and terrorism of
separation regulate it. So much for scientific objectivity.[15]

By making paramount the code that functions as the mechanism safe-
guarding the univocality of the message, Jakobson succeeds in creating a
metastable representation of events or phenomena that in reality harbor multivalent elements and are in constant flux. This metastable representation is
constructed at the expense of (by repressing) the heterogeneity and contradictions that invariably inhabit actual processes of social communication. As
a result,

> each communication process is thus vectorized into a single meaning, from
> the transmitter to the receiver; the latter can become transmitter in its turn,
> and the same schema is reproduced.... This structure is given as objective and
> scientific, since it follows the methodological rule of decomposing its object
> into simple elements. In fact, it is satisfied with an empirical given, an abstrac-
> tion from lived experience and reality; that is, the ideological categories that
> express a certain type of social relation.[16]

A wishing-away, so to speak, of social antagonism and interpersonal ambivalence is inherent in Jakobson's transmission model, an "ideological matrix" that, using "code" that is essentially a structure of *repetition* to asphyxiate
living, nonrepeatable "events," creates an algorithm-like schema to mimic
reality in which teleology and linear causality cannot always be found.

This, I think, is why Baudrillard describes Jakobson's model as "terrorist": The model becomes terrorist not because it destroys order but because
it creates false unity by domesticating disorder, by imposing order on disorder. In fact, it is for this very reason that one observes that the positivity of
the code goes hand in hand with the positivity of the message and that of
the subject (the addresser/addressee) as well. For it is out of the same idealist ideology that the model *objectivizes* the "content of communication" as a
univocal dose of information, just as it *subjectivizes* the addresser/addressee
as unconditioned, nonrelative discoursing subjects.

Positivity results from the violence of discourse that imposes patterns on
what in reality might resist orderly representation. It betrays the need for
any field of study to constitute itself *as* a field, with its own limits, identity,
and above all, an effective organizing principle to support the coherence of

its statements. This "positivity fallacy" is not limited to communication theories, and Jakobson should not be blamed for everything his model has been accused of. In "The Order of Discourse," Michel Foucault observes that the image of communication as infinite, free exchange of discourse represents one of the "great myths of European culture."[17] Through these myths, the European Man narrates for himself his "imaginary" but "truth-*full*" past, present, and future. Equipped with a device that facilitates broader Eurocentric appropriations, white men make themselves comfortable in a world they painfully recognize to be increasingly invaded by "others." Trapped in a historically determined "order of things" like everyone else, Jakobson, too, is at the mercy of the same terrorism of the code and cannot but retell the same great myth. The only problem is that an increasing number of critics, losing faith elsewhere, began to question that myth as well — not because they do not believe in anything any more but because myths, once seen as myths, do not seem to retain their "magical power" like they used to.

Two Roads Diverge after Positivity: The Material and the Textual

Un système est une espèce de damnation
qui nous pousse à une abjuration perpétuelle;
il en faut toujours inventer
un autre, et cette fatigue est un cruel
châtiment.
—*Charles Baudelaire*

In his celebrated *Keywords*, Raymond Williams points out that the word *communication* has an unresolved double valence to it.[18] Reacting to shifting sociocultural contexts and the changes in both the means and modes of transporting information, *communication,* from the seventeenth century onward, has developed an unstable semantic field, suggesting at once both *one-way transmission* and *mutual sharing.* This semantic bivalence or instability of the word *communication* puts communication theorists in an interesting situation, turning them into unwilling bifocal scholars as they set out to investigate two incompatible phenomena of inquiry. In consequence, what happens historically in theorizing about communication is that, at any given point, one or the other of the contradictory meanings has been allowed to dominate or repress the other. Models and theories of communication, as Cary Nelson rightly suggests, are "designed to give us the illusion of controlling (or at least) structuring this uncertainty."[19]

For Williams, the split meanings of communication represent a natural outgrowth of the dialectical interaction between the sense and the use of linguistic signs, a process characteristic of the production/consumption of meaning and its carriers in society at large. It eloquently illustrates the effect of not-so-harmonious undercurrents that propel linguistic change, making evident the need to analyze social semiosis from a perspective that is different from both the referential view of language, which anchors the meaning of linguistic signs in the referent, and the intentional view of language, which equates meaning with the speaker's mental state animating the utterance. That one word might take on multiple or even contradictory meanings reveals the fact that language, like many symbolic objects in society, is a *conjunctural* product. A word is not just a morphological entity existing between the covers of a dictionary; rather, like a living creature caught in the process of evolution, it reacts and adjusts to the environment and thus embodies in highly compact form the interactions among the diverse social forces that have an impact on it. Every linguistic sign is thus a microcosm of cultural history, reflecting the ebb and flow of the social life at large and the vicissitude of the collective attitude that symbol users take toward their medium. Seen in this light, a sign is at once particular and general — particular in that it represents a nodal point in a discursive geography that delineates a temporary conclusion of historical changes; general in that it represents a map that is nothing but a momentary spatialization of the social history of meaning as use. The semantic field of a lexicon, therefore, is best understood as a site of both discursive and nondiscursive contestations behind which unfolds an untold and troubled history of struggles over meaning across many layers of the social body. As recent theories of discourse make clear, within any given language the words used and the meanings of the words used change from one discourse to another and from one moment to the next, and this change occurs not simply because of the linguistic variability of the language in question but also because of the material contradictions within the social field in which various discourses take shape and coexist.[20] As Deleuze and Guattari summarize:

> There is no language in itself, nor any universality of language, but a concourse of dialects, patois, slangs, special languages. There exists no ideal "competent" speaker-hearer of language, any more than there exists a homogeneous linguistic community.... There is no mother tongue, but a seizure of power by a dominant tongue within a political multiplicity.[21]

Conflicts are inevitable among discourses, and meanings are always at stake in "a political multiplicity." To mean what one says and to say what one means therefore become a struggle for those who use a language but use it in different ways.

To view language as a "conjunctural product" means to link linguistic signs to the material reality, to the "prose of the everyday life," that affects them and that they in turn affect. It means to disperse the official language's semblance of unity to its local and vernacular variations and to see that unity as a reconstruction by the exercise of nonlinguistic forces such as power, prestige, taste, or capital; differently stated, it means to treat language as "cultural expressions" that reflect the uneven developments in other areas within society, and to see how those expressions rearticulate this developmental unevenness and difference through a kind of diasporalike symbolic revolt. Viewing language in this way demands that we never lose sight of the quotidian *eventness* of language, that we treat language always as living occurrences in the "prosaics of the ordinary," in short, that we never approach language without collapsing the two axes of diachrony (history) and synchrony (system) into one point, into the singular event of *making meaning* defined by its "unfinalizability."[22]

What the preceding critical perspective suggests, as evidenced in Williams's pioneering works, is that communication needs to be approached *materially*. To approach communication materially does not mean to focus solely on media technologies or on the economic factors influencing the way society generates and distributes information. It means to take seriously the claim that "people communicate but always under conditions not of their own making"; and it means to translate this understanding into practice by bringing culture and history back into one's analytic framework so that there is no confusing the "logic of things" with the "things of logic." Two inferences can be drawn from this. First, in contrast to the positivist's notion of communication as a romantic exchange of meaning or intention between disembodied subjects, the critico-material approach conceives of communication as one dimension within a differentially orchestrated complex that regulates the production, reproduction, and consumption of both material and symbolic goods. Like other social productive activities, communication, too, must be viewed as a process of making things, as a distinct form of *signifying practice* that produces signs or meanings and distributes cultural capital under determinate historical and socioeconomic conditions. Such is the principle of the material approach, an antitheoreticist perspective that replaces the search for covering laws by reintroducing communication into the web of social productive processes, of which signification represents one thread.

Second, following the reinsertion of the communicative into the social, the critico-material approach links various communicative practices to individuals' everyday experience as they engage in those practices. To bring back culture and history into one's analysis thus means to combine semiotics with social phenomenology, to link objective structures with lived experiences by mapping in detail the complex relationship between individuals' communicative activities and the social differences that are reproduced, inflected, and negotiated through those activities. This, as I understand it, is the guiding principle of cultural materialism, a dialectical inquiry aimed at discovering "the logic of things" rather than hammering phenomena to fit the "things of logic." And it is in paying close attention to the concrete reality, to a "reality one cannot not know," to its structures of experience, feelings, and affects, that one finds a corrective to the positivity fallacy described above.

By inserting the communicative into the social, the preceding cultural-materialist approach clears the decks for a historicizing critique of the positivity plaguing communication theory, an approach I will call the *exteriorizing deconstruction*. I call this type of historicizing critique exteriorizing deconstruction because it is achieved by dispersing the isolated moment of understanding as a hermeneutical affair into the conflict-ridden ensemble of social heteroglosia, thereby exploding the nodal unity of communication into the interdiscursive practices constitutive of the social structuration in general. Like a chain reaction in nuclear fission, in which a minuscule initial disturbance creates a systemic collapse, this exteriorizing deconstruction defuses the "terrorism of the code" by dissipating the smooth flow of information into a multidimensional compound of voices, countervoices, messages, feedbacks, and counterfeedbacks, in short, into the social fabric woven through strands of competition and appropriation rather than harmonious exchange. Unity is broken down, universality discreated, totality fragmented, transmission rerouted, flow disrupted, gift unreturned—all these not so much because of any alien invasion as because of a putting into practice of the materialist litany "Historicize, historicize."

To derail communication from its teleological track, to exteriorize the microevent of communication to its macrostructure of determination, however, is not the only alternative to positivity. Derrida has presented a different account explaining why people communicate but under conditions beyond their control. Bringing his critique of classical metaphysics to bear on theories of meaning, Derrida puts forward the argument that any exchange of meaning through linguistic means is necessarily disrupted by the very structure of writing, by an endless sending of confused signals without sure origin or definite destination, a postal play of the third kind, one might say, that draws the speaker/writer and the listener/reader alike into the strange sphere of *destinerrance,* of messages running awry. Instead of exploding communication into the broader sociopolitical whole, Derrida moves right into the very interior of the communicative, of communicability itself; and instead of complicating the process of communication by adding to it extratextual factors of determination, Derrida unveils within the structure of communicability itself a fold, a seam, a *pli,* that causes the breakdown of communication by dislocating and jamming all the channels of transmission and exchange among its participants. In contrast to the materialist, exteriorizing approach, Derrida's can be described as an *interiorizing* deconstruction that, nonhistorical and apolitical as it may seem, ends up dismantling any forced closure or totality with as much wit as irony, this time not by dint of social contradiction but by the vertiginous *écriture* marking the limit of the language that we naively think we control. Focusing on language and exploiting its reflexivity to a degree never reached before, Derrida develops a textual strategy that implodes the structure of communicability — an implosion of the infrastructure of meaning transfer brought about not by historical and material conflicts but by the indifference of the medium without which the exchange of meaning cannot take place. While the cause of meaning's instability for Williams is primarily historical, ideological, and cultural, Derrida would argue that the instability belongs intrinsically to the linguistic sign itself; and while Williams reads communication as a constant negotiation and renegotiation among various social dialects, Derrida redescribes communication as an unbridled play of differences, substitutions, and displacements taking place at the limit of signification. If we are often unsure whether we are the beneficiaries or victims of communication — because it means simultaneously both happy intersubjectivity (mutual sharing) and the possibility of alienation or domination (one-way transmission) — Derrida would assure us that our sense of uncertainty comes naturally and inevitably from the very nature of our linguistic being, that we are always and already at the mercy of peripatetic signs.

Loud Voice versus Quiet Writing

One starts things moving without a thought of how to stop them. In order to speak. One starts speaking as if it were possible to stop at will.
— *Samuel Beckett*

Hush! Caution! Echoland! — *James Joyce*

Rorty once described Derrida, somewhat disapprovingly, as a hypertextualist.[23] This is easily understandable, especially when one considers some of the reasons behind the extravagant popularity enjoyed by Derrida's declaration "There is nothing outside the text." To both friends and foes of deconstruction, and even to the less informed bystanders, Derrida's astounding statement comes in handy: it provides them, each according to his or her needs, with something simultaneously manageable (because its meaning seems clear) and resoundingly Derridean (because it runs counter to our normal way of thinking and philosophical sobriety). As a result, the statement "There is no outside to the text," which Derrida admits is the "axial proposition" of his theory, means either that there is literally nothing (existing) outside the text — an apparently pompous assertion that, when read in the absence of its conceptual radicality, is quite simply false (chairs, fruit flies, uranium, the Gobi desert, migrating birds, my blood cells, and millions of other things in the universe are certainly *not* inside the text); or, a little more sophisticatedly, that there is nothing outside the text in that for any thing to exist at all, it must be meaningful in some sense and hence textual, provided one interprets the term *textual* generously.

These two interpretations explain in large measure why the serious subversiveness of Derrida's (abnormal anti-)philosophy is either easily domesticated or uncritically exalted: Because of its mildly exotic allure, for many of its readers it is reminiscent of Parisian *haute couture*. But we can ignore the first interpretation in good conscience for its unacceptable simple-mindedness or sheer lack of intelligence. And the second, somewhat more sophisticated reading fares little better, because almost a century after the "phenomenological movement," it would be at best banal or trivial for Derrida to reaffirm that *to be* is intimately related to *to be meaningful*. Even if everyone agrees that Derrida is indeed a hypertextualist, the question still remains as to exactly what he means by *text* and to what degree his stance is "hyper."

As suggested in chapter 4, Derrida's concept of the text — as well as those scriptural oddities closely associated with it: *hymen, différance, supplément,* archewriting — develops out of a radical critique of the fundamental tenets of structuralism and phenomenology. In deconstructing Saussure and Husserl, to name but two, certain hierarchically organized binary oppositions, foundational not only to structuralism and phenomenology but also to all Western philosophies since Plato, are subject to an intensive textual surgery and finally overturned. One of the better known of these binaries is that of speech and writing, a binary based on the domination of the living voice over physical inscription.

According to Derrida, the working of the speech/writing binary has dominated philosophers' thinking on communication since antiquity.[24] By privileging the voice over inscription, *logos* over *graphos,* theorists of communication, from the Sophists to the present-day grand narrators like Jürgen Habermas, have always approached communication logocentrically, that is, in terms of the immediacy and presence of meaning to consciousness. Like the first term in such binaries as Husserl's expression/indication or Rousseau's and Lévi-Strauss's nature/culture, voice stands on the side of presence. Created by vibrations inside the body, voice signals self-communion, a living proof of the soul's autoaffection, manifested as the standing-forth of meaning on its own origin. Because of the closeness of voice to its source, inner speech represents for philosophers communication in its purest form, an ideal state of the postal operation in which silent breath realizes the delivery of message as immediate, trouble-free self-address. In this conception, the more the self retreats into the silent dialogue with the inner voice, the more certain becomes the self of its own presence and of the effectiveness of its communicative activities. The notions of "self," "voice," and "communication" can thus be seen to constitute a metaphysical triad, according to which the presence of the last (communication) affirms the autonomy of the first (self) through the workings of the second (voice). Because the speech/ writing binary embodies the same metaphysical principle underlying the positivity of communication, I shall examine Derrida's analysis of it before discussing its more general implications.

When meditating on the nature of language, philosophers throughout the ages have always operated under the principle that speech precedes writing, both *logically* and *temporally*; that writing, being a sign or representation of speech that is itself a sign or representation of the mind's idea, is at least two steps removed from what gives rise to it and hence can never capture the idea in its pristine authenticity. Compared to speech, writing appears to be "breathless" in both senses of the term: Ungraced by the living voice animating speech, written words are brain-dead, vegetablelike; moreover, as a graphic representation of speech, written words are condemned to chase strenuously, though without ever catching up, their autoaffected original, the soulful inner voice. Thus, according to Derrida, writing becomes "the supplement *par excellence* since it marks the point where the supplement proposes itself as supplement of supplement, sign of sign, *taking the place* of a speech already significant."[25]

Such is the classical definition of writing spelled out by Aristotle in his *De Interpretatione* and upheld by Rousseau, Locke, Hegel, Husserl, and the present-day speech-act philosophers.[26] According to this tradition, spoken words are the signs people adopt to communicate thoughts or ideas; written words are the secondary symbols that stand in for speech and so — at one further remove — assist in the process of communication. Whereas speech facilitates the mind's expression of itself in a relatively direct fashion, writing can only hope to facilitate speech, thus, because of its lack of immediacy to the mind, the home of *phono*-consciousness, becoming the facilitator of a primary facilitator. Here one unmistakably finds the outline of a hierarchy, a descending order of priority in which writing ranks a very poor third on account of its irrevocable distance or exile from origin, truth, and self-present meaning.[27]

The chief reason writing is ranked so poorly by the philosophers is that writing, as a secondary form of another secondary form, alienates the writer and reader from the origin of meaning; writing leads one astray from the truth of the living utterance defined as self-presence. Speech, in contrast, flows directly from the soul; it is valorized because in speech, so those philosophers think, the meaning of the spoken words and their physical embodiment in the voice stay in so close a proximity to the speaker that the meaning of the utterance becomes almost self-transparent to itself in the interior clarity of the speaking consciousness, as in the case of soliloquy. The voice, in other words, speaks to itself and for itself as voice, free of the burden of transmission, of any possible delay; alterity-free and authentically animated, it manifests the soul where the inhaling and exhaling of air blow away the distinction between form and content. Derrida traces the genesis of phonocentrism, of the power of the voice to "make present" objects to consciousness:

> The ideality of the object, which is only its being-for a nonempirical consciousness, can only be expressed in an element whose phenomenality does not have worldly form. The *name of this element is the voice. The voice is heard.* Phonic signs ("acoustic images" in Saussure's sense, or the phenomenological voice) are heard [*entendus* = "heard" plus "understood"] by the subject who proffers them in the absolute proximity of their present. The subject does not have to pass forth beyond himself to be immediately affected by his expressive activity. My words are "alive" because they seem not to leave me: not to fall outside me, outside my breath, at a visible distance; not to cease to belong to me, to be at my disposition "without further props." In any case, the phenomenon of speech, the phenomenological voice, *gives itself out* in this manner.[28]

Voice is regarded as the ideal medium of meaning, a medium that "does not impair the presence and self-presence of the acts that aim at it, a medium which both preserves the *presence of the object* before intuition and *self-pres-*

ence, the absolute proximity of the acts to themselves."[29] A root supposition can be seen at work in the philosophers' thinking: Although the sound (that is, breath excited by the body) is deemed natural, the labor of the hand (that is, inscription) is thought to denaturalize or distort the soul's natural movement, whose chance of achieving maximal self-coincidence comes only from the possibility of speaking. For only in spoken language—or in a writing that respects the natural priority of speech, namely, the phonetic-alphabetic writing unaffected by hieroglyphic or ideographic anamorphosis—does this apparently ideal coincidence of meaning and expressive intent occur.

The intuitive logic of this natural attitude to speech, which Derrida refers to obliquely in the passage just quoted, is nicely captured by the French phrase, *s'entendre-parler.*[30] "*Entendre*" means both "to hear" and "to understand," with the suasive implication that hearing is in some way a superior or uniquely authentic form of understanding. *S'entendre-parler* could thus be translated as "hearing oneself speak and immediately grasping the sense of one's own utterance." This idea has the force, the persuasive power of a primordial intuition. Hearing/understanding oneself speak represents a de facto truth in our experience of language that appears so massively self-evident that philosophers, normally distrusting and critical of common sense, have not bothered to question it. It is because spoken words are thought of as symbolizing ideas "directly"—without the detourlike passage through the supplementary medium of the written sign—that speech can be safely maintained within the province of a privileged relation to truth and immediacy. Measured against this idea, writing appears at best to be derivative, adventitious, appendagelike, even though a medium somehow necessary to "gain the most space and time by means of the most convenient abbreviation."[31] Coming from an "unknown," "unidentifiable," or "dead" source, writing "displaces the *proper place* of the sentence, the unique time of the sentence pronounced *hic et nunc* by an irreplaceable subject, and in return enervates the voice."[32] Although occasionally necessary for "storing" or "preserving" what speech brings forth beforehand, writing remains the "nonphonetic moment" that lurks within language to create all sorts of dangerous and disruptive effects by skipping over the vital link between articulate sound and intelligible sense. Writing thus seems to be a demeaned species of communication, begetting a representation of yet another representation (that is, speech) closer to an "idea" or a perceived thing. Compared to the sonorous representation of speech, in which the ear "listens to the inner vibration of the body," writing is forever condemned to play a losing game of catch-up; it becomes the inferior term of the binary, the term marked by its exclusion from the immediate circuit of exchange set up between ideas and their voiced representatives.[33]

The Logocentric Scandal of Speech

What would a mark be that one could not cite? And where origin could not be lost on the way? — *Jacques Derrida*

. . . if the whole stole stale mis betold. — *James Joyce*

Is this intuitive logic of speech tenable? If the primacy of speech over writing were indeed as self-evident and indisputable as philosophers think, that is, if philosophers were indeed convinced of writing's secondary status compared to speech, why would they go to such length to repeat a self-evident truth, why would they bother to rebroadcast their established conviction? Take, for example, the oft-heard allegation that writing is the culprit behind the loss of community, of social authenticity. If writing is indeed manifestly the lamentable cause of modernity's evils, be it experienced in Plato's Greek polis, in Rousseau's eighteenth-century European metropolis, or in Lévi-Strauss's modern-day rain forest, whence comes philosophers' indefatigable energy in denigrating the already convicted? Why do philosophers lose their professional cool by belaboring a point that can only be described as something on which they all agree? More to the point, if writing is indeed an artificial and hence incredible means of representation, why do philosophers spend so much time and energy discrediting it *in writing,* an activity they seem to relish? Do they overreact? Do they contradict themselves? Are they being ironic? And why? Does not their anxiety over the danger of writing — an anxiety curiously shared by philosophers who in other respects seem to have little in common — indicate a deep ambivalence, an indication that their "inner ear" hears something that they, as guardians of truth, cannot openly admit? Could the dangerous writing be what makes its own condemnation possible; a *positive* threat turned into a blessing by a "return of the repressed" whose acknowledgment must be disavowed if the *spirit* of philosophy is not to be contaminated by the *letter?* Could one help being suspicious? In any case, there seems to be enough reason for Derrida to examine the issue *deconstructively.*

As he does to any binary opposition he confronts, Derrida starts by pushing this speech/writing couplet to its logical extreme, all the while abiding by the logocentric principle of respecting what has hitherto been privileged. Following an identifiable procedure of "overturning," Derrida begins by asking a simple question: What is it that causes writing to appear the way it does in relation to speech? What is it that renders writing inferior to speech, thus consigning writing to a lowly status as a means of representation and communication? In short, what is (in) the character of the written character that inculpates it, that disqualifies it as a vehicle capable of securing the immediate return of intended meaning to the intending consciousness? It takes little effort to realize that one of the major differences between writing and speech is that a written passage is structured by a certain absence, namely the absence of the addresser, of the addressee, and of the original context in which it takes place. Positively stated, writing survives its origin by securing meaning in physical marks impervious to changes of space and time. But this survival of the mark, it must be noted, is not without its cost; it signals the expiration of speech, of living breath. *Graphos* enters the stage only after *logos* has left the body; rather, graphos lives on only by asphyxiating logos, by disengaging the phono-consciousness that animates the voice from its material embodiment. As a reminder of speech's expiration, writing recalls an absence, a vacancy, a blank upon which graphemes can stake out their claim. For this reason, writing is linked to death, as it concludes the fading away of the spirit, a despiritualization whereby nous, "exiled to the exteriority of the body," indurates in a corporeal extension.

How is the absence characteristic of writing to be understood? How does this absence, the blank scene of writing, figure into the economy of meaning, where voice is thought to coalesce with the speaker's "wanting-to-say" (*vouloir-dire*)? Furthermore, how is this absence parlayed by the logocentric prejudice into a metaphysical principle according to which "absence" as well as its couriers are always viewed negatively? Through the meticulous reading of selected philosophers (Plato, Hegel, Husserl, Rousseau, Austin, to name but a few), Derrida discovers that the absence involved in writing as conceived by those philosophers is of a highly determined kind. In its most classical fashion, this absence is regarded as "a continuous modification, a progressive extenuation of presence. Representation regularly *supplements* presence."[34] The conception of writing as the "extenuation of presence," as supplemental, implies a negative judgment about writing—a judgment that can be made only by positing speaking as the standard or paradigm. According to this standard, writing (as absence) can justifiably be debased because it represents a lack; and writing, by the same reasoning, is considered to be lacking precisely because speech is characterized as fullness, as the presence of consciousness to itself in a closed circle of immanence. Like the pyramid in a sea of sand, writing makes itself available to inquisitive travelers as a monument of alien inscriptions, whose meaning, mediated by lithic numbness, can only be deciphered but can never be restored to a state of original, pristine intelligibility.[35] Such a notion of writing's absence as supplementary or non-essential, argues Derrida, corroborates the law of logocentrism in that writing is *not* conceived as a *break* in presence "but rather as a reparation and a continuous, homogeneous modification of presence in representation."[36] Viewed in this way, writing is not merely *different* from speech; it is determinably and measurably *inferior to* speech.

To save face for writing, to defend the character of the written character, Derrida challenges the legitimacy of the standard adopted by philosophers. What if, Derrida asks, we change the standard? What if those of the East, the Egyptian, and the Chinese, in short, those who have not been blessed with alphabets, were given the jurisdiction over this matter? What if, that is, the absence structuring writing were *of a very different kind*? Since every sign "supposes a certain absence (to be determined)," Derrida continues, would this not be the result of the fact that "the absence in the field of writing is of an *original* kind if any specificity whatsoever of the written sign is to be acknowledged?"[37] Derrida then bends the logocentric dogma closer to its breaking point:

> If, perchance, the predicate thus assumed to characterize the absence proper to writing were itself found to suit every species of sign and communication, there would follow a general displacement: writing no longer would be a species of communication, and all the concepts to whose generality writing was subordinated . . . would appear as noncritical, ill-formed concepts, or rather as concepts destined to ensure the authority and force of a certain historic discourse.[38]

By raising issues and asking questions that philosophers do not raise and cannot ask themselves, Derrida is increasing the pressure on the stress point of the logic of *s'entendre-parler*. If the characteristics by which writing is judged deficient and inferior turn out to be what grant the universal criterion of that judgment, would this not be sufficient to bring about the dehiscence of logo-phono-centrism? If absence is indeed *necessary* to writing, is this "necessity of absence" not what constitutes writing's very condition of possibility rather than a lack or nonfulfillment that destroys it? Is it not possible, in other words, that the logic of speech can be overturned to work as an accomplice in its own eventual defeat? By raising these questions, Derrida is inviting us to witness the para-logic of secondarity in action — the becoming first of the second, the early arrival of the late comer, the ascending of the descent, the delayed dominance of a prior repression, namely, the twisted logic of retroactive memory captured with all its subtlety by Freud's *Nachträglichkeit*. Derrida's response is worth quoting at length:

> A written sign is proffered in the absence of the addressee. . . . But is not this absence only a presence that is distant, delayed, or, in one form or another, idealized in its representation? It does not seem so, or at very least this distance, division, delay, *différance* must be capable of being brought to a certain absolute degree of absence for the structure of writing, supposing that writing exists, to be constituted. . . . My "written communication" must, if you will, remain legible despite the absolute disappearance of every determined addressee in general for it to function as writing, that is, for it to be legible. It must be repeatable — iterable — in the absolute absence of the addressee or of the empirically determinable set of addressees. This iterability (*iter*, once again, comes from *itara, other* in Sanskrit, and everything that follows may be read as the exploitation of the logic which links repetition to alterity), structures the mark of writing itself, and does so moreover for no matter what type of writing . . . A writing that was not structurally legible — iterable — beyond the death of the addressee would not be writing.[39]

That writing requires "iterability" to be possible, as Derrida seeks to argue, is precisely what is repressed by logocentrism's self-assured ethos of *s'entendre-parler*. Yet it is not until the Archi(e)-debunker's critical outcry that this understanding is developed to its rightful but unforeseen conclusion, that writing's absence "is not a continuous modification of presence"; instead, it is a break, a rupture, in presence — the possibility of the "death" of the addresser and the addressee — inscribed in the structure of the mark.[40]

Obviously, the notion of iterability is crucial to the overturning of the speech/writing binary, for it tilts in the opposite direction the one-sided scale of meaning and truth hitherto weighted toward speaking. According to the principle of iterability, what makes writing possible and by extension, makes meaning to be objectively decipherable, is not so much the presence of intention to the consciousness of those who communicate as the repeatability or reiterability of the form that the communicators adopt. Rather than recording or imitating speech, rather than being an ignoble parasite of spoken language and finally, rather than *working for* speech, the repeatability of written signs constitutes the unity of the signifying form of the spoken words and permits their actual repetition and recognition. This is because for any sign, spoken or written, to be a sign at all, it must be identifiable as that sign across empirical variations; signs and meanings must have identity. And this identity is made possible by writing's structural principle of repeatability/reiterability, *not* by speech's phonic similarity or acoustic resemblance. It will be instructive to examine the concept of iterability more closely.

Derrida introduces his notion of iterability through his stringent critique of Austin. According to Derrida, despite all the advances he makes in freeing language from a tradition that links linguistic success directly to the criteria of truth, Austin regrettably falls back into the trap of logocentric metaphysics. Specifically, Austin fails to realize that the condition for making an expression meaningful is that it be determined by the language what will count as a *repetition* of that expression within that language.[41] The meaning of my utterance, for example, cannot be decided once and for all by what I am now saying until it is determined what will count as a *saying of the same thing* at another time and under a different circumstance. That is, to be meaningful, my expression must be capable of functioning *as the same expression,* with the same meaning, in situations other than the present one and from which I as speaker and you as listener may be absent. For this reason, it is not an accidental feature of language that an expression may carry meaning in the absence of the addresser and of the intended addressee. Quite the contrary: The possibility of *not* having the speaker and the listener around functions as the "necessary condition for the constitution of linguistic meaning" in general. A linguistic expression is by necessity such as to be capable of breaking free of the speaker's context, and capable, while remaining the same expression, of being inserted into and functioning within contexts that the speaker cannot have command over through the mastery of the inner states immediately present to him or her. If it were not determined what would count, in times other than the present one, as a saying *again* of what I am now saying, then no stable meaning would have been constituted, and there would be no language that I could be properly said to be speaking.

To see how the principle of iterability works and to draw out its implication for linguistic communication, let us turn to an example suggested by Derrida himself: "Let us consider the extreme case of a 'statement about perception.' Let us suppose that it is produced at the very moment of the perceptual intuition. I say: 'I can see a particular person through the window while I really do see him.' "[42] If we agree that the *meaning* of this sentence is what will have been understood in hearing or reading it, provided only that we understand English, we shall have to admit that the apprehension of its meaning depends on neither a perception nor a perceptual anticipation or representation. "Whoever hears this proposition," Derrida continues, "whether he is next to me or infinitely removed in space and time, should, by right, understand what I mean to say."[43] Derrida's point here is quite straightforward: The meaning of the statement in the example is in no way affected by the phenomenal absence of the state of affairs to which the statement refers. When I say to you that I saw someone through the window, my statement will mean what it says regardless of whether you have a perceptual intuition of that someone or not—in fact, you may be blind, or you may be looking not through the window but at the wall; moreover, my statement will continue to mean what it says even if you are absent from the scene of speaking and cannot constitute a representation of the situation in question. Although the statement about perception states the presence of something, its *meaning* cannot be said to derive from the perceptual fulfillment or the context of utterance that may or may not accompany the act of perception. The statement about perception, as Descombes observes, already states not only presence but also absence.[44] This, according to Derrida, has to be the case because, when I say something meaningful,

> my non-perception, my non-intuition, my absence *hic et nunc* are expressed by that very thing that I say, by *that* which I say and *because* I say it. . . . The absence of intuition—and therefore of the subject of the intuition—is not only *tolerated* by speech, it is *required* by the general structure of signification, when considered *in itself*. It is radically required: the total absence of the subject and object of a statement—the death of the writer and/or the disappearance of the objects he was able to describe—does not prevent a text from "meaning" something.[45]

Derrida's discussion would lead one to say "that subject and object can disappear. It would even say that subject and object, inasmuch as they are only stated as such, have already disappeared (or perhaps have never appeared)."[46] Derrida turns to the first personal pronoun *I* as a further example:

> Just as I need not perceive in order to understand a statement about perception, so there is no need to intuit the object *I* in order to understand the word *I*. . . And just as the import of a statement about perception did not depend on there being actual or even possible perception, so also the signifying function of the *I* does not depend on the life of the speaking subject. . . . My death is structurally necessary to the pronouncing of the *I*. That I am also "alive" and certain about it figures as something that comes over and above the appearance of the meaning. And this structure is operative, it retains its original efficiency, even when I say "I am alive" at the very moment when, if such a thing is possible, I have a full and actual intuition of it. . . . the statement "I am alive" is accompanied by my being dead, and its possibility requires the possibility that I be dead; and conversely. This is not an extraordinary tale by Poe but the ordinary story of language. . . . The anonymity of the written *I*, the impropriety of the *I am writing*, is . . . the "normal situation."[47]

The disappearance of the object, the absence of intuition or representation, the death of the speaker/author and the listener/reader, the loss of the context, all these remain wholly indifferent absences; none of them imperils the "original efficiency" of meaning. For what guarantees the speaker's "possibility of meaning" in the end is not the presence of the meant object or the intention that motivates the speaking but, rather, the availability of some signifying form, a structure of repeatability independent of the speaking and listening consciousness. Derrida recasts basically the same idea:

> this unity of the signifying form is constituted only by its iterability, by the possibility of being repeated in the absence not only of its referent, which goes without saying, but of a determined signified or current intention of signification, as of every present intention of communication. This structural possibility of being severed from its referent or signified (therefore from communication and its context) seems to me to make of every mark, even if oral, a grapheme in general, that is, ... the nonpresence *remaining* [*restance*] of a differential mark cut off from its alleged "production" or origin.[48]

Contrary to Austin, who locates the origin of meaning in the intention of the speaker and in the fixability of the context of the given speech act that secures the listeners' proper uptake, Derrida relocates it in the structural principle of writing's open-ended citability. This citability/repeatability/iterability characteristic of writing is infinite because even to repeat a sign once already means that it can be repeated again and again. Moreover, even if one grants the speaker a privileged access to his or her inner mental states at the moment of utterance, it does not follow that the *meaning* of the utterance could be *reduced* to that intention.[49] For what a speaker's utterance means *now* depends in an essential way not only on future contexts that this present expression may appear in but also on how the practices that function in those future contexts will determine what will count as a repetition of what the speaker is now saying.

Someone might object to this argument by saying that the context of an utterance (call it CX) does determine — in most cases — the meaning of that utterance (call it MX). This is a reasonable proposition and deserves a close analysis. To start, it must be recognized that the validity of this proposition depends on the fulfillment of a prior condition: In order for CX to determine MX, CX must itself be determined. All the talk about the "contextual determination of meaning" will be good for nothing if the "context" itself proves to be indeterminable: Everything here hinges on the determinability of the *con-text*. But what does *context* mean — in this context? Specifically, how does one determine CX? What constitutes CX? How does one locate CX properly? Given everything that happens around CX, what is to be included and what is to be excluded? In other words, how does one determine what is relevant or proper to CX and what is not? Is there any rule one can follow to make the determination? Is this rule of determination itself subject to contextual determination? We seem to be facing more than just an empirical difficulty in delimiting context; we are facing the theoretical impossibility of ever locating it properly. By definition, context is transcontextual. The transcontextual nature of context means that any context always overflows its momentary temporal and spatial location, that by necessity it outruns any empirical capture. In fact, it is the essential nature of context that it be mobile and variable, that it always remain a con/com to other, to its host text. Because of its mobility, because of its variable attachment to and detachment from its host texts, context can be fixed only by reference to an other; that is, it cannot be fixed in and of itself. Irene Harvey's preemptive explication of this issue is particularly illustrative:

> Where does a context begin or end? Derrida will say always—in context. Quite simply, the notion of *context as such* cannot and indeed does not exist. There is no such thing as a context-in-general, by definition. Yet the term exists as such. So one must define context as such always according to context.[50]

There is no context as such; there is no context-in-general, because context dissolves itself, dissolving itself into an empty term, a signifier whose signified is nothing but its own self-dissolution. This perpetual disappearance of any referential anchor for context by itself thus characterizes the *law of contextuality,* and this law can only mean that context always gets lost, that one always loses one's context not only in fact but in principle. Since this law, as law, must have already been enforced before the little rules of contextual determination become applicable, context is no different from text. To put it straightforwardly, context is just more text: It includes not only all the actual situations that are at present indeterminate, but also all the future possible situations that by definition can never be determined, no matter how much information one might acquire concerning the speaker's present situation. Seen in this light, the distinction between text and context is purely nominal, incapable of sustaining any real distinction. This must be the case because in order to read a text "out of context," one must already be in its context; that is, before one can demand that the text be put back in its context, one must be able to separate the text from the context, which can only mean that one must have already taken the text out of its original context. The context of a sentence, spoken or written, Derrida contends against Austin and Searle, is thus never certain, saturated, or saturable; and this is not merely because every sign, linguistic or nonlinguistic, spoken or written, can be *cited,* put between quotation marks, but more important, because there are only contexts, an infinite number of contexts, without any center of absolute anchoring.[51]

Without exhausting all the implications of Derrida's argument, let me offer the following observations. First, the preceding discussion should help us understand why philosophers are so disgusted by writing and yet feel quite attached to it. Writing is reviled by philosophers because it takes away the autonomy and determination of meaning, and it is philosophers' self-endowed mission to control that autonomy and determination. Writing, in other words, displays too much freedom and initiative not to be received by philosophers as contemptuous of their own independence or autonomy. "It is," as Derrida writes, "because writing is *inaugural,* in a fresh sense of the term, that it is dangerous and anguishing."[52] Nevertheless, writing is attractive to philosophers because it offers them a rare means of expressing their thoughts unfettered by the finitude and contingency of their historical existence. Although it compromises the purity of thinking, writing has the advantage of *materializing* thought, of keeping thought visible after the breath expires. As wise men of ancient China used to tell their disciples: Next to conquering vast lands or purifying one's somatic airflow, carving one's thought in stone is the best way to achieve immortality.

Second, Derrida's reflections on writing should enable us to see more clearly where logocentric semiotics goes wrong. Based on the intuitive logic of speech, a logocentric theory of language confuses the de facto "natural" attitude (the logic of *s'entendre-parler*) with a de jure system of regulative concepts that claims to dictate the very nature and limits of rational thought. To be sure, we are "naturally" disposed to accept the priority of speech over writing (that is, people speak before they learn to write; there are far more people who speak than there are people who can read and write) and the idea that writing is de facto confined to a "supplementary" role in linguistic exchange. This intuitive response, however, should not be confused with the de jure argument that would take this kind of factual self-evidence as a basis for claims about the logical *necessity* of thinking as we do.[53] Although our experience is shaped by the assumption that speech precedes writing, it does not justify raising an entire metaphysics—a generalized theory of meaning and truth—on the basis of that experience. The temporal and experiential priority of speech must be clearly separated from the ontological priority of writing. While writing may be historically later, its ontological import precedes speech. "Writing," says Derrida,

> can never be totally inhabited by the voice. The non-phonetic function, the operative silences of alphabetic writing, are not factual accidents or waste products one might hope to reduce.... The *fact* of which we have just spoken is not only an empirical fact, it is the example of an essential law that irreducibly limits the achievement of a teleological ideal.[54]

Finally, we can develop a less context-bound grasp of what Derrida means by text or textuality. A text is the product of writing, a moment, an instance, a passage, a juncture, an effect in the context-free proliferation of dead letters. In fact, it is because letters are dead that the living can use them in any way they want. Since the activity of (ab)using dead characters for the purpose of living is essential to what we call the symbolic and the social, the text can properly be understood as the *breaching* (*frayage*) of nature, the breaking open of a path — *becoming a route* (*rupta, via rupta*) — in nameless matter (*hyle*) that establishes the scene of inscription as culture.[55] Impervious to the "death" of the writer and reader and to the context in which it is written, the text generates "meaning by enregistering it, by entrusting it to an engraving, a groove, a relief to a surface whose essential characteristic is to be infinitely transmissible."[56] "To write," continues Derrida "is to produce a mark that will constitute a kind of machine that is in turn productive, that my future disappearance in principle will not prevent from functioning and from yielding, and yielding itself to, reading and writing."[57] In this way, writing immortalizes itself, ever renewing its own performances by producing more of the same, and, in doing so, it renders irrelevant the propriety and genealogy of the scribes. No empirical inscription can halt the unstoppable drift of graphematic traces, for they are always and already internally differed and deferred and, for the very same reason, futurably in excess. Always in excess, that is, decontextualizing itself before it can be recontextualized by others, text destabilizes its "before" and "after." Since the proper context of the text, which is the only means to thwart writing's auto-mobility, cannot be located, the written text cannot but postpone its wanting-to-say (*vouloir-dire*) by delaying what it means; similarly, since its proper context can only be found in its future possibilities, a text can only mean what it will have said at the moment whose time is always yet to come — its interpretation remains forever open; its meaning forever hostage to the future. This is what text as free play means; this is also why Derrida characterizes texts as orphans of arche-writing, as fatherless figures most "athletic" in the field of textual movement.

The Logocentric Scandal of Communication: Is It Possible?

(Stoop) if you are abcdeminded, to this claybook,
what curios of signs (please stoop), in this allaphbed!
Can you rede (since We and Thou had it out already) its world?
—*James Joyce*

The sign is, if you like, without recourse. —*Jean Baudrillard*

It should not be surprising that Derrida's writing creates a crisis for philosophy and, in particular, for hermeneutics. It unsettles philosophical reason by showing that many of the beliefs by which philosophers define their mission (for example, the availability of some ultimate nonrelational truth; the dismissal of deviant, that is, literary or nonserious, discourse from proper philosophical arguments) are dreamlike—ambiguous and wishful. In an essay on Paul Valéry, a deconstructionist *avant la lettre,* Derrida leaves no doubt about his position on this matter. Derrida cites Valéry approvingly: "We can easily observe that philosophy as defined by its product, which is *in writing,* is objectively a particular branch of literature.... we are forced to assign it a place not far from poetry."[58] Produced by writing, philosophical statements are no more authentic or truth-bearing than are literary expressions, and literary expressions are no more pseudo than are philosophical dicta; they both fall victim to (or rather take advantage of) the figurality of language, its uncontrolled semantic slippage and syntactic leaps and bounds. In fact, the more one believes one can stay clear of or break free from the sign's dictate, the deeper one is likely to sink into the ever widening semiotic quicksand. Derrida quotes Valéry again: "The strongest of them [philosophers] have worn themselves out in the effort to *make their thought speak....* Whatever the words may be—Idea or Being or Noumenon or Cogito or Ego—they are all *ciphers,* the meaning of which is determined solely by the context."[59] Written on paper, carved in stone, or breathed into the ear through air, philosophy is *unthinkable* outside the textual domain; it must reckon with form, its own formal instance, and would not achieve its argumentative force without the rhetorical propulsion that only language can generate. Philosophy, as Christopher Norris keenly observes, "cannot be conducted at full self-critical strength without the kind of disciplined awareness that poets bring to language."[60]

If philosophy is indeed a kind of writing, that is, if the logocentric domination of philosophy (truth) over literature (fiction) is overturned by deconstruction's estranging antidialectic of *secondarity,* then it follows that the *essential* difference hitherto held to exist between an original text and its commentary must be abandoned as well. Just as there is no longer any meaningful difference between literature and criticism, the hierarchy that places philosophy over and beyond its interpretations can no longer be maintained either. "Departed then," claims Derrida, "are . . . the archaeologists, philosophers, hermeneuts, semioticians, semanticians, psychoanalysts, rhetoricians, poeticians, even perhaps all those who still believe, in literature or anything else."[61] With the departure of "absolute knowledge" enters a "textual infinite, an interminable web of texts or interpretations."[62]

Writings are all we have, and to continue to write is all we can do. Poets, philosophers, and theorists as well are in the same self-sustaining interminable business, interminable because writing *"exhibits* the movement of *différance* and hence *changes* when repeated; that is, re-read, for instance."[63] Inasmuch as writing is interminable, the meaning of a text also becomes interminable. And if the meaning of the text is interminable, there is no longer the question of "hermeneutical recuperation," and one is left to savor what Nietzsche calls the "deepest pathos of aesthetic play." There is, then, Derrida writes,

> the Nietzschean *affirmation,* that is the joyous affirmation of the play of the world and of the innocence of becoming, the affirmation of a world of signs without fault, without truth, and without origin which is offered to an active interpretation. *This affirmation then determines the noncenter otherwise than as loss of the center.* And it plays without security. For there is a *sure* play: that which is limited to the *substitution* of *given* and *existing, present,* pieces. In absolute chance, affirmation also surrenders itself to *genetic* indetermination, to the *seminal* adventure of the trace.[64]

To surrender oneself to the seminal adventure of the trace, however, does not mean to indulge in a kind of anarchistic interpretive hedonism. The purport of Derrida's "free play" of the sign is not "Everything goes." Derrida's hypertextualism does not sanction textual orgy any more than it endorses a universal abandonment of interpretive standards. Far from it: Behind this Nietzschean celebration of the innocence of becoming lies Derrida's serious argument for the *undecidability of meaning.* The radical nature of this notion is not always fully acknowledged. The undecidability of meaning does not mean that a word or a text may be ambiguous or interpretable in different ways. By *undecidability* Derrida does not mean to suggest the common sociolinguistic truth that linguistic signs are differently accented in terms of ideology, class, geography, or history. Nor is he repeating the familiar Gadamerian thesis that the meaning of the text is never exhausted through explication, or that the "fusion of horizon" in reading always gives birth to new understandings because of the changing context of "tradition," in which all hermeneutical acts take place. More than the ambiguity or multiplicity of meaning, Derrida's radical undecidability suggests that meaning is *essentially indeterminable,* no matter what. And this is "because writing is *inaugural,* in the primal sense of the word...It does not know where it is going, no knowledge can keep it from the essential precipitation toward the meaning it constitutes, and that is, *primarily, its future.*"[65] In decisive opposition to the thesis that the multiplicity or equivocality of meaning could somehow be reduced to its basal clarity if only one could reconstitute its original context, Derrida's undecidability of meaning would never grant the possibility of recontextualization, not only because recontextualization can go on *ad infinitum* but also because recontextualization is itself an act of *reading.* Context is just more text. Signs do not impose context on themselves in any absolute manner. Context is never given once and for all; it is always *proposed, re-created,* or *invented*—in context. The undecidability of meaning discards any last court of appeal in interpretive disputes. In the case of writing, there is no Court of First Instance.

This radical notion of undecidability of meaning is more than simply disturbing to hermeneutics. It problematizes the foundation of a project that not long ago proudly claimed to have grounded the human sciences anew. Not to be equated with the simple "indeterminacy of meaning" familiar to critics since New Criticism, Derrida's undecidability of meaning causes hermeneutics to adjust itself beyond its conceptual breaking point. In contrast to the impression given by some of his interpreters, Derrida himself takes great care to distinguish his thought from even the most radical of hermeneutical positions. In Derrida's view, however insistently Gadamer and other post-Heideggerian hermeneutic thinkers may emphasize the fundamental unclosability of the horizon of meaning, their thinking still maintains that interpretation must take place within a horizon and be guided by what Gadamer calls "transcendental expectations of meaning"—expectations that are an essential condition for hermeneutic activity—and by an anticipation of coherence that is implicit in the ideal of truth.[66] Derrida, however, repudiates this assumption of an inevitable orientation toward meaning, which, despite its conservative appeal, is tethered to the doxa that the endlessness of interpretation is due to an inexhaustible semantic wealth of the text. Caused by "the dissemination of asemic elements within the text," the undecidability of meaning to which Derrida refers is not something that can be "classed in the categories of *richness, intentionality,* or a *horizon*"; instead, it results from a *structural* necessity marked in the text; it is a function, says Derrida, of "a tropological *structure* that circulates infinitely around itself through the incessant supplement of an extra turn," of "a so on without end."[67] Thus in "The Double Session," Derrida argues that "summation is impossible, without however being exceeded by the infinite richness of a content of sense or meaning; the perspective functions as far as the eye can see, without having the depth of a horizon before or into which we will never have ceased to advance."[68] In contrast to the hermeneutic position, Derrida's view is not that meaning is inexhaustible or that it changes in response to varying contexts but, rather, that any specification of meaning can only function as a self-defeating attempt to stabilize and restrain what he terms the *dissemination* of the text. Meaning, we are advised, is not retrieved from apparent unmeaning but, rather, consists in the repression of unmeaning.[69] As Derrida puts it, "if one cannot summarize dissemination, this is because the force and form of its disruption *burst* the semantic horizon."[70] The hermeneutic stress on multiple, or even infinite, meanings does not face up to this rupture and does not confront the radicality of this aneconomic disruptive burst.

Derrida's *nonpresence* of meaning, then, is very different from hermeneutics' *loss* and subsequent *retrieval* of meaning. Unlike Gadamer and the neo-Grammarians, Derrida is not out to recuperate a lost presence or to preserve the "original strangeness" of the text; for him, there is never anything to lose to begin with and hence nothing to preserve. In the encounter with language, one is "indefinitely referred to a concatenation without basis, without end, and the indefinitely articulated retreat of the forbidden beginning as well as of the hermeneutic archaeology, eschatology or teleology."[71] There is no going *before* or *after* the language, no escaping the unstoppable mediations of signs by other signs. Nothing is really lost, and nothing is therefore ever regained. Affirmative free play is the name of the game; gone is the saddened, negative, guilty, Rousseauian nostalgia for some kind of pre-Fall Oneness. Derrida is often portrayed as merely suggesting that meaning is far more insecure or elusive than philosophers have previously imagined, but the logical consequence of his argument, as Peter Dews indicates, "is not just the volatilization of meaning, but its *destruction*. The infinite regress of meaning—the logic of supplementarity, if it were to be coherent—not only defers meaning to a later moment but *ruins* the very possibility of presence and meaning by deferring them *infinitely*."[72]

Clearly, the threat to hermeneutics from Derrida's writing is not an accident. It follows directly from Derrida's overturning of the speech/writing binarism, which dovetails with his general critique of the metaphysics of presence. As discussed earlier, philosophy traditionally conceived of writing as a deformed species of "general communication," whose model was *conversation* as an event in which living voices transport each other's thoughts back and forth happily. In contrast to the happy exchange of thoughts by living voices, writing appears as a degenerate species of this general communication, a species tarnished by a certain absence, a lack, or a dis-appointment. What Derrida's analysis demonstrates, to philosophers' dismay, is that this absence, this lack or dis-appointment of intentional fulfillment and adequation, turns out to constitute the condition of possibility for the production of meaning in general. Speech, as it were, becomes possible because of the general economy of *écriture*, rather than the other way around. The consequence is remarkable: If *écriture* is what enables written and spoken signs to function as such, this primordial productivity of *écriture* cannot but displace the supposed primordial authenticity accorded to speech, an ingrained phonocentric presumption upon which hermeneutics envisions itself as an approach toward the unsaid or the textually hidden. It is precisely this overturning of the speech/writing couplet that forces hermeneutics to bend itself beyond its means and beyond its conceptual elasticity. As if by a "return of the repressed," *écriture* comes back and says "no" to every interpreter, and laughs at the simplehearted confidence in the possibility of "making it *clear* what you mean."

But if the overturning of phonocentrism problematizes the conceptual foundation of hermeneutics, the undecidability of meaning undermines it. *Écriture* unveils a wild economy of infinite semiosis, an undercurrent of semiotic "dissemination" previously unseen because it is logocentrically repressed. This dissemination unleashes tremendous signifying energy from within each sign and explodes every dialogical situation where the textual drift may hesitate momentarily, that is, for historical or ultratextual reasons. It is this dissemination that renders meaning ultimately undecidable.

As discussed in the previous chapter, *dissemination* designates one of the mainstays of Derrida's "pharmacy," which fights against the spread of the logocentric malady. The radical character of dissemination goes beyond what is usually associated with notions such as "polysemia," "pluravocity," and the like. Without embarking on an extended exegesis of this notion, it will suffice to recall that dissemination is syntactical, unlike polysemia, which is basically a semantic issue. Dissemination is syntactical in the strict sense that the meaning of signs disseminates because of signs' insertability into ever-renewable syntagmatic environments. Dissemination is inseparable from the logic of reiterability and supplementarity, but Derrida adds another dimension to it. As signs circulate through space and time, both their signifying form and their semantic stuff get linked onto numerous "interlocking chains" made up of other signs and become semiotically denser and denser. Dissemination behaves in a spongelike fashion, allowing swimming signs to absorb meanings cumulatively. Dissemination is the sign's self-willing generative diaspora—it goes on, *ceci est cela*—the text lives on (*sur-vit*): *Pharmakon* means both poison and remedy; *hymen* means both virginity and the consummation of sexual contract. Here one sees the force of radical becoming, a persistent adding or joining that is indifferent to opposites, to performative contradictions—more or less, more and less.

How does this (a)logic of dissemination and undecidability bear on communication? In light of the Derridean overturning, what happens to the general communication to which writing belongs, even if as a sorry species? By uncovering the productive primordiality of *écriture*, Derrida demonstrates that *écriture* is the ground of both writing and speaking, although this ground will remain permanently ungrounded because of the self-ensconcement of its grounding effectivity. Now if *écriture* constitutes the structural condition of possibility for speech, which was previously privileged and functioned as a model of communication, it follows that, given the overturning of the speech/writing binary, it is the *écriture* that grounds communication in the first place. Writing as *écriture* is not a bastardized imitation of speech any more; writing is no longer an ignoble or inferior species of communication. Quite the contrary, *communication is a species of écriture. Ecriture* opens up the possibility of semiosis as the most general production of meaning in which messages can be transmitted thanks to the "code," and in which "understanding" occurs when signs are "recognized" by consciousness(es) as a result of their repeatability. *Ecriture* becomes the enabling condition of communication because it is "prior to" both writing and speaking and outlasts the temporal existence of both the sender and receiver. By *virtualizing* dialogue, *écriture* creates an "autonomous transcendental field" unencumbered by the absence of mediate or immediate address; "it is, so to speak, communication become virtual."[73]

At the same time, however, since *écriture* also suggests a primitive, untamed productivity of signs, this infinite dissemination of *écriture* threatens communication at its very root. Driven by the drift of traces, one can only mis-interpret or mis-understand signs. To the extent that mis-understanding is the rule, mis-communication becomes inevitable. The inevitability of mis-communication, however, does not mean that meanings become incapable of being transmitted or disseminated; it does not mean that channels of communication are defective and fail to deliver the messages to their destinations. Quite the opposite: It reflects an uncontrollable inflation of signs that overloads the channel; it means an overdissemination of meanings that leads to meanings' own demise, a total disruption of the proper generation and exchange of meaning as a result of a self-destructive explosion of additions, allusions, translations, associations, displacements, condensations, and alliterations. As the picture on the cover of *The Post Card* illustrates, there is always someone speaking behind one's back; there is always more than one voice speaking at the same time, so that one can no longer be sure what the message is or who is speaking to whom. Signs grow, rhizomelike, ultrafast, like cancer threatening the life of the body in which it grows. Such a cancerous proliferation of signs, traces, delayed associations, and supplementary meanings would eventually destroy any sign's claim to any fixed meaning, because a sign can never be meaning-*full*. This nonfulfillment is, of course, the outcome of an unchecked and uncheckable dissemination, a nonfulfillment created by excess and surplus.

Commenting on the "mad or delirious" production of meaning (*délire*) as it surfaces in extraordinary texts by extraordinary writers such as Antonin Artaud and Louis Wolfson, Jean-Jacques Lecercle makes an important point about the necessity of implanting discontinuity in the flow of signs if they were to be communicative:

> Instead of one, we have a multitude of coined words: left to its own devices, language proliferates. The use of language for the purpose of communication implies a certain restraint, a capacity to discern and differentiate, that is, *not to say things, an ability to stop when one's meaning has been expressed*. But language on its own does not express, conveys no meaning, certainly not somebody's meaning.[74]

For an utterance to be communicative, its meaning cannot be infinitely open. A being who could not renounce saying everything would be incapable of meaning anything. One must leave some things unsaid in order to be able to say others. Just as the flux of sounds must be punctuated before one can hear any meaningful words, so the flow of meaning must be stopped, albeit temporarily, in order for sense to emerge. For one sign, as a part within a whole, cannot be meaningful or make sense until it is confronted by another sign that works against it. To say something, a frontier of the non-sayable must be established; to mean (*vouloir dire*) something, a limit of non-meaning must be set up beforehand and acknowledged. Effective language must be founded, as Lecercle rightly suggests, "on the impossibility of saying *everything* (the grammatical implies the existence of the non-grammatical, and the linguistic structure is based on exclusion: 'one cannot say this')."[75] Dissemination, however, transgresses this rule profoundly. Take any alphabetic language as an example: the alphabet has its order; it has its alpha and its beta, its psi and its omega. But the ordering of the letters in the alphabet does not constitute any sense; on the contrary, to make any sense at all the originally senseless alphabetic syntagm must be torn apart and recoupled; in short, it must be properly *coded*. However, once the original syntagm is unchained and its elements recombined, it is always possible *not* to stop. There one sees the seed of dissemination bearing fruit, perhaps not in diehard, letter-blind philosophers, but certainly in Joyce, Artaud, and Philippe Sollers. In an infinite dissemination of meaning, nothing in principle need be left unsaid or unconnected: Hegel, *aigle*, eagle; *Glas*, glass, *glace*, angle, gala... Why not? Why cannot Hegel be (an) eagle, and why cannot the eagle be caught in a glass? Doesn't Hegel fly like an eagle? Doesn't Hegel look into a glass?

> His name is so strange. From the eagle it draws imperial or historic power. Those who will pronounce his name like the French (there are some) are ludicrous only up to a point: the restitution (semantically infallible for those who have read him a little — but only a little) of magisterial coldness and imperturbable seriousness, the eagle caught in ice and frost, glass and gel.[76]

Communication becomes impossible here not because "privacy" (for example, an idiolect) causes the breakdown of intersubjectivity, but its reverse: "Open" textuality renders the processes and mechanisms of mediation futile. This authorless compulsion to mean, this unstoppable will-to-say, is nothing but dissemination in action.

Dissemination undermines the possibility of communication; dissemination underwrites the impossibility of communication. Here one faces the Derridean paradox of communication: Writing/*écriture* makes communication possible because it grounds the general possibility of meaning, but writing/*écriture* also makes communication impossible because the meaning it engenders disseminates endlessly, making impossible any closure of meaning, any chance of "knowing" what you mean. Writing/*écriture* is both the condition of the possibility and the condition of the impossibility of communication.

Some clarification ought to be made at this point. I am *not* suggesting that understanding does not occur during actual communicative events. It does, *experientially*. There is no denying the fact that when someone sitting next to me at the dinner table says "Could you pass the salt," I respond appropriately because I understand what he or she means. Nor am I denying the fact that when I read, say, a classified advertisement in the newspaper, I understand what that note (or the seller) says. In most of our normal day-to-day communication, hermeneutical suspicion hardly arises — and when it does, it quickly abates — because there is no need to question our *experience* of understanding and being understood, because our pragmatic presumption that "I fully understand what the other means to say providing he says what he means" serves all the practical purposes one possibly needs. But the observation that communicators always manage to interpret each other's messages properly by (re-)contextualizing them or by supplying missing information reflects an *empirical* fact about the psychology of reader-response, about the internal — and mostly unconscious — disposition of the communicators; it does *not* reflect any kind of logical guarantee that understanding must indeed have taken place.[77] The kind of psychological certainty one experiences regarding the encoding/decoding of intention does not and cannot prove that an exchange of meaning has come to pass objectively. Nor will it work to appeal to the kind of practical, enthymematic reasoning that ethnomethodologists uncover when they analyze episodes of routine social interactions. Both beg precisely the questions concerning the nature and functioning of language that are at issue here. In any case, the identification of the condition of possibility of communication does not and cannot rely on introspective certainty or on descriptive data, however strongly they seem to be supported by experience or common sense. In fact, as Derrida points out, any general *theory* of communication will have to be able to proceed in the long run "without in itself implying either that I fully understand what the other says, writes, meant to say or write, or even that he intended to say or write *in full* what remains to be read, or above all that any adequation need obtain between what he consciously intended, what he did, and what I do while 'reading.' "[78]

Signing Off: Signature, Communication, and the Postal Paradox

The signature keeps nothing of all it signs. —*Jacques Derrida*

No value is to be accorded *arche* simply because of its inaugural value.
—*Denis Hollier*

Is it possible to speak of Derrida's message, his message about sending a message? If, as I said earlier, messages are always mis-communicated, that is, if one can no longer be certain whether what one hears is what the other says, it seems pointless to argue over whether one gets the "correct" message or not. It will suffice if one hears something; it will suffice if something can be heard. Now what does one hear from Derrida? What is the message that can be (over-)heard in his communication? Instead of speaking of Derrida's message as such directly, it is perhaps more helpful to look at Derrida's analysis of the sending of a unique message, a history-making event of public communication that founded this nation two hundred years ago.

Invited in 1976 by the University of Virginia to speak on the Declaration of Independence at its bicentennial, Derrida began his talk — after a courteous apology — by raising a curious question: "*Who signs, and with what so-called proper name, the declarative act which founds an institution?*"[79] It was not long before one realized that Derrida was not going to give a conventional textual analysis of this document. His interest was in what might be called the "paradox of the signature."

By focusing on the question of the signature, on the condition under which the Founding Fathers of this nation put their names — in the name of the People — to the Declaration of Independence, Derrida pulled together a number of themes (act, performative/constative, the "present," representing, meaning and enunciation, "I" and "we"), all of which affect and are in turn affected by this act of signing, an act of origination that links writing, broadcast, and the establishment of an institution, the founding of the United States of America. How could signatures represent a people? How could signatures — the writing down of proper names — found a nation? From where does the signature (*firma*) receive its affirmative authority, its rightful capacity of affirming the permanence of its momentary enactment? In its simplest form, Derrida's question is this: *Who* signed the Declaration of Independence and *what* gave them the right to do so? Is not Jefferson a signer? Why should one pause before such an obvious fact? To be sure, the name Jefferson appears on the document, but, as Derrida forewarned his audience, Jefferson does not really sign it; "*by right,* he writes but he does not sign."[80] In fact, he was not even responsible for *writing,* in the productive or initiating sense of the term, but only for *drafting* the document. Are we to say, then, that the collective body of the Continental Congress, the "Representatives of the United States of America, in General Congress, Assembled," is the true signer? That does not seem to be the case. Those representatives, argues Derrida, did not sign either, because in principle at least, the right involved in this case is *divided*. By lending their names to the Declaration, the representatives present at the General Congress signed not only for themselves but also "for" others. They did so because "they have been delegated the proxies, the power of attorney, by the people for signing (Ils ont délégation ou procuration de signature)."[81] They spoke, "declared" themselves, and signed "in the name" of, that is, on behalf of those who in absentia granted them the authority. *By right* then, the signer should be the people, the "good people" represented by their well-meaning and trustworthy representatives. It is the "good people" who declared themselves free and independent by the relay of their representatives and of their representatives of representatives. Have we now identified the true signer? Have we not singled out the true voice of the Declaration, that single legitimating and legitimated voice that, because of practical constraint, must resort to speaking through so many representatives? If the people embody the true voice and legitimate the Declaration, from where does their right come? Do they bestow the right upon themselves by themselves? If so, could such a self-bestowal be rightful? Here one sees the question of the signature deeply intertwined with the question of origin, of right, of representation, in short, of original rightful representation. Following this logic, one can go on to suggest that it is also a question of communication, that is, of communicating, through the writing and signing of a certain document, a group of people's intention of independence and freedom to the world, to all its actual or possible, present or future, addressees.

In any case, here are the "good people" who engaged themselves by engaging their representatives in signing, in having their own declaration signed. The "we" of the Declaration thus speaks "in the name... of the good people." Now did the "good people" really sign? Could we know for sure? Could we decide? Skeptical but not equivocal, Derrida answered: "One cannot decide — and that is the interesting thing, the force of the coup of force of such a declarative act — whether independence is *stated* or *produced by* this utterance."[82] One cannot decide because the People, as the rightful signatory of the Declaration, did not exist *before* the signing; one cannot decide because, however closely one studies the document, it is impossible to tell whether it was the People who *declared* their independence or whether it was the Declaration that gathered the people as an independent signing entity.

There is an undecidability; this is the paradox. The Declaration was not established law in the same sense that the Constitution was later. The signers of the Declaration claimed to be "representatives" of "the good people" of the "free and independent States." However, the legitimating body for the signing of the Declaration, an entity that later in the Constitution could identify itself as "We the People," did not really exist until *after* the signing of the Declaration. So the representatives who represented the People before the signing cannot be properly or rightfully called their representatives, because the People *as such* did not exist until after the signing. In fact, only after the fact did the signatories obtain the right and the power to do what they had already done. The original act could not have been done when it was done, but only after it was done, that is, *après coup*. The original act of signing "seems in some way to have already happened, to have happened before happening, to be always in a past, in advance of the event."[83] The "primal scene" of signing, in other words, did not exist when the signing took place, for it came into existence only when one (re)visited the stage *afterward for the first time.* The act of signing thus exhibits the temporal structure of the future anterior tense, that is, "it will have been."[84] Doing what it will have done, this time-bound original signing simultaneously *asserted* and *undermined* the authority that it is supposed to transcend in its inaugural context. If the act of signing signifies anything, it is that its signification implodes into the act itself; its message is fully absorbed into the signing's own anterior dissolution. The nature of temporal precedence, of causality, is therefore problematized, for neither the act nor the sense it constitutes has absolute priority.

A number of Derrida's philosophical themes that were discussed earlier are played out again here. First, the paradox of the signature is rooted in the trace-structure of signing, which by *merging act* and *inscription* generates an undecidability of authorship. The original act of signing is a deferring act; it defers itself until later. The ensuing paradox is that we cannot decide, and the text cannot decide, whether it is *constating* that the People already are independent or whether it is *performing* the act that then makes the people independent.[85] The text of the Declaration depends upon this undecidability for its effect, on a differing and deferring structure internal to the act of signing as inaugural. Every act of signing is claiming to be at once the act of both stating who one is and making oneself into what one is. The originary act therefore involves a *fable,* a *fabulous performance* staged to conceal the confusion of its own fictioning. If one were already what one claimed to be, why would there be any need for one to make oneself into what one has already been?

The second point concerns Derrida's interest in the connection and the underlying similarity between the problem of representation (of reality) and the associated question of political representation. Those individuals who put their names on the Declaration of Independence on the occasion were *not yet* real representatives of a People. And they did not become representatives until they created the reality, namely the general populace of the land, that they claimed to represent. The gathering of the delegates at the signing of the Declaration was supposed to express and represent a collective will and carry out an assignment as the mere writing down of the voice of the people that had already spoken out. But, at the same time, the delegates' fabulous act of signing was bringing into being the political reality it claimed to be only derivatively representing: It *constitutes* that reality for the first time. The signing, then, created the world it represented, or at least made the creation of the world it represented possible, rather than confirming an already existing state. For the civic-political reality is that unless the document was broadcast, read, and recognized, unless its claim to the independence of its people was confirmed by some decisive victory, the world and the people it envisioned would not come to be:

> The signature invents the signer. This signer can only authorize him- or herself to sign once he or she has come to the end (*parvenu au bout*), if one can say this, of his or her own signature, in a sort of fabulous retroactivity. . . . I have the right to sign, *in truth I will already have had it since I was able to give it to myself.* . . . There was no signer, by right, before the text of the Declaration, which itself remains the producer and guarantor of its own signature. By this fabulous event, by this fable which implies the structure of the trace and is only in truth possible thanks to (*par*) the inadequation to itself of a present, a signature gives itself a name. It opens for *itself* a line of credit, *its* own credit, for itself *to* itself. The *self* surges up here in all cases (nominative, dative, accusative) as soon as a signature gives or extends credit to itself, in a single coup of force, which is also a coup of writing, as the right to write. The coup of force makes right, founds right or the law, gives right, *brings the law to the light of day, gives both birth and day to the law (donner le jour à la loi).*[86]

The founding of the United States depends on this fable, and the signature of every American citizen on his or her passport (that is, as a political subject), on his or her marriage license, promises, checks (that is, as a civic subject) — all these depend on this fabulous coup of force.

Third, and following from the previous two, there is the familiar Derridean theme of the inversion of the relationship between the text and the author, and by extension, between the message and the sender/receiver. Instead of the text being authored, and authorized, by its author or signatory, the text authors, and authorizes, the author. It is usually assumed that there could not be a text without an author, but now we see that unless there is a text, we cannot speak of its author; by the same token, unless there is an event of telecommunication, one cannot speak of the sender or receiver as the source and destiny of messages. It is the text that authorizes its writer to sign, rather than the writer authorizing the work through his or her signature. "The 'subject' of writing does not exist if we mean by that some sovereign solitude of the author."[87] There is the scene of signature, a fabulous stage of signing. "Within that scene, on that stage, the punctual simplicity of the classical subject is not to be found."[88] Just as the sign, as Baudrillard says, is without recourse, so is the signature. And just as the signature is without recourse, the signing author does not exist apart from the event/act of signing.

It is clear that Derrida's purpose in his analysis of the Declaration of Independence is to problematize the *proper-ty* of the law.[89] Using the unstable distinction between the constative and the performative statement as a lever, Derrida seeks to pry loose our uncritical belief in the legal *propriety* by demonstrating that the discursive acts (signing, declaring, broadcasting, and the like) that institute the law always involve a moment of undecidability in their origin, a moment of violence that establishes the law's efficacy and legitimacy but that itself cannot be accounted for or justified by the legal procedures or operations. The very instituting of the law, therefore, can never be *proper* to itself because the original and originary moment of the law is always *before* the law, that is, because the founding act of the law must have taken place *prior to* and *outside* the realm of legality. The first call for order, in other words, is not itself ordered, for it always takes place before the order and is thus necessarily outside any ordering, out of order. Is it a surprise any longer that "justice" must always be *divine,* that justices, as Chinese folklore says, are celestial stars incarnate?

Despite the unique nature of the document and the specificity of its context, Derrida's analysis of the signing of the Declaration of Independence can nevertheless be extended to communicative phenomena in general, insofar as both signing and communication are predicated on the same fundamental postal principle. As Derrida goes to great length to show in *The Post Card,* the post, the *envoi,* represents the principle of (tele-)communication *as* the principle of positionality and identity of both the message and the addresser/addressee. Within any network of exchange, the addresser and the addressee must be prepositioned, and their respective prepositionings are then joined together by the dispatch that circulates teleologically within the network. "For the placing of posts," as Peter Brunette and David Wills write, "the possible and necessary marking of points or positions in a system of relay, is the condition of possibility of the postal, of any system of addressing and sending."[90] Like the sending of messages, signing, too, presupposes separate identities of both the signer and the person to whom the signature is supposed to be addressed. That is, to the extent that signing presupposes the identity of the signer, the representing validity or authenticity of the signature, and the prepositioning of the addressee, the act of signing displays the same fundamental postal structure of communication. Just as the signature bears and authenticates the intention of the senders, all messages in transit within a communication system are signaturelike, and vice versa.

Now where is the paradox? Why and in what respect is a simple sending of a message paradoxical? The paradox, as Derrida argues emphatically in "*Envois*," comes from the fact that "a letter can always not arrive at its destination. Its 'materiality' and 'topology' imply the permanent possibility of its divisibility, of its partition. It can always be fragmented and lost forever."[91] The message, the letter, can simply *not arrive*. It comes, it is sent; it keeps coming, it keeps being sent; but it never comes to be. Not only are there any number of examples of letters, signs, messages, or senses going astray, but that possibility, that threat of nonarrival, accompanies the delivery every step of the way. "It is not that the letter never arrives at its destination, but it belongs to the structure of the letter to be capable, always, of not arriving. And without that threat... the journey of the letter will not even have begun. But with that threat, it may never arrive."[92] Derrida's point is that if the letter can *not arrive*, then, quite simply, it *cannot* arrive. This is because the possibility of deferral, of drifting, exists at every point from the conception of departure to the confirmation of arrival.

Because both delivery and signing are haunted by the same structural threat of the message's nonarrival or *a*destination, the paradox of the signature also invades communication. Communication occurs only insofar as the delivery of the message *may* fail; that is, communication takes place only to the extent that there is a separation between the sender and receiver, and this separation, this distance, this *spacing*, creates the possibility for the message *not* to arrive. For the simple fact is that the event of sending and addressing can *in no way* guarantee arrival; only arrival itself guarantees arrival because "the message does not constitute itself as message in the sense of communicated message until it arrives at its destination; and as long as that destination cannot be assured by the sender, the message cannot be constituted as such by the sender."[93] And this is because the event of sending is divided, in its constitution, by its other event, that of nonarrival. "This possibility-of-never-arriving divides the structure of the letter from the outset. Because... there would be neither postal relay nor analytic movement if the place of the letter were not divisible and if a letter always arrived at its destination."[94] This divisibility is the arche of delivering that, as divided, blocks the return to itself as the moment of punctual origin just as it does the forward movement to a target as predestinate transmission.

As the material embodiment of *différance* and *spacing* in the movement of the message, the postcard, then, is not just a figure of speech. Quite the reverse: Communication by speech — saying/writing something to someone — becomes a figure of the post, which establishes and at the same time undermines the saying/writing of the addresser. The postcard does transmit a message (Greetings! I am well; Wish you were here; and so on), but at the same time, its very form of transmission also produces a series of countereffects, countermessages. The message may be elliptic, fragmentary, anecdotal, significant, or insignificant. Moreover, by virtue of its being open, the postcard also unsettles the frame, the limits, of the traditional carrier of messages. As Wills points out,

> With a postcard one can never be sure what is most important, the image or the text; the legend, the message, or the address. In this sense it has no distinct outside, and it is usually turned inside out in order to be pinned to the wall. But on the other hand, more than other texts, it has neatly prescribed borders, limits to what it can contain. Similar paradoxes occur with respect to a postcard's readability. Because it can be read by anyone, it adopts various devices and varying degrees of illegibility. It inevitably becomes the apology and the substitute, a sign of deferral, for the letter one never gets to write, being entrusted with the task of informing its addressee that one is still alive, conveyed in French by the vaguest of phrases which marks the limit of signification and the beginning of adestination: *faire signe,* to make a sign.[95]

Not only can the postcard mean something it does not say or say something it does not mean, but by being either apocryphal or perfunctory, it upsets even the most sincere "hermeneutical promise" that understanding can and must take place.[96]

This, I think, is the message of Derrida to which we have been trying to listen: "The possibility of posts is always already there, in its very retreat (*retrait*). As soon as *there is,* as soon as it gives (*es gibt*), it destines, it tends... To post is to send by 'counting' with a halt, a relay or a delay involving suspense, the place of a mailman, the possibility of going astray or being forgotten (not of repression, which is a moment of keeping, but of forgetting)."[97] The delivery depends on the postal carrier, on his or her service, but, not being the one who initiates the correspondence but simply the one who transports it, he or she can always breach the contract of service, betray the secret of the letter, lose or mishandle, deliberately or not, the mailbag, thus subverting the link between sending and receiving, and prolonging infinitely one's anticipation of hearing from loved ones.

> As soon as there is, there is *différance* (and this does not await language, especially human language... only the mark and the divisible trait), and there is postal maneuvering, relays, delay, anticipation, destination, telecommunicating network, the possibility, and therefore the *fatal necessity of going astray,* etc. There is strophe (there is strophe in every sense, apostrophe and catastrophe, address in turning the address)... for a post card is never but a piece of a letter, a letter that puts itself, at the very second of the pickup, *into pieces.*[98]

The apostrophe reverses the order of transmission: the postcard can always end up in places other than its presumed single address, and it can always be sent back, according to the return address, to someone who has no idea about such a sending. There is an undecidability of delivery, of the order of generation or sequence of inheritance — the fatal inheritance of multi- or counterfinality. The postcard struggles against delay, but in this struggle, it turns into delay itself. This delay messes up the day's schedule, overturning everything into delay. "In any event, it allegorizes the catastrophic unknown of the order. Finally, one begins to no longer understand what is meant by coming, coming before, coming after, warning, coming back — and the difference between the generations, as well as inheriting, writing one's will, dictating, speaking, being dictated, etc."[99] This is the message that Derrida manages to receive when looking at Matthew Paris's postcard for sale at the Bodleian Library: The son (Plato) dictates to the father (Socrates) what he will have said. This is also where we see Plato facing the presumed origin of his writing; but sitting behind Socrates, Plato sees only the back of Socrates who, one should not forget, never wrote a thing: "There is only the *back,* seen from the back, in what is written, such is the final word. Everything is played out in *retro* and *a tergo.*"[100] This is the retroactive nature of our knowledge, of how we come to know. Socrates' work, the beginning of Western philosophy, exists only as hearsay or anecdote in Plato's writings. The presumed, proper origin is lacking in the beginning, if only because the so-called author or source of writing is sealed forever in a secret pact set up by the son between the father and himself, a plot "by this pair of plotters, the one who scratches and pretends to write in the place of the other who writes and pretends to scratch."[101] Legend is hearsay, and hearsay is truth. No more is post a metaphor.

To return to our example, the signing of the Declaration of Independence sought to establish what the message intended to establish. But by merging act and inscription, the signing created a division within itself; it brought about a not-yet-arrival of the addressee, the People, in the very constitution of itself. Inasmuch as the act of signing involved a fabulous performance that concealed the confusion of its own fiction, the understanding of communication as the transferring of messages from one to the other can be sustained only if one represses the same fabulous performative character of the delivery, only if one forgets that mail, electronic or hand-written, including mail addressed to the loved ones at home, has failed to reach home. Derrida's story about the Declaration of Independence can therefore be read as an allegory of communication. It is an allegory of paradox, an allegory about the intrinsic difficulty of deciding who is speaking to whom, of deciding exactly what is being said or sent in the act of saying or sending it. Such difficulty is not limited to fictive discourse; in fact, as the preceding analysis suggests, it is *promised* by the very structure of delivery, a promise coming from within the movement of the letters at a time when one least expects it.

This (im)possibility of signing, of officially communicating a message to both oneself and others, represents one of the many paradoxes generated by Derrida's deconstruction. These paradoxes emerge because Derrida's deconstruction of traditional philosophemes discloses the *impurity* of those philosophemes; that is, it discloses that a certain *alterity* parasitically inhabits the core of many cardinal philosophical concepts. And these paradoxes can always be made to reveal themselves as such if one knows how to read them "against the grain." The paradox of communication is not alone. Deconstruction embarrasses many philosophers and many philosophies. Paradox has always been there, coexisting with the "guardians of the letter." It can be found in the relationship between Socrates and Plato, "their signing of a pact and forming of a private company with a monopoly over Western thinking"; it can be found in the traffic between conscious and unconscious, between primary and secondary processes, in Freud's work; and it can also be found in the relationship between private individual letter writers and the government-sponsored army of letter carriers.[102] Paradoxes abound: The condition of the possibility of truth is at the same time the condition of truth's impossibility; the condition of the possibility of presence is at the same time the condition of the impossibility of full presence; the condition of proper meaning is the condition of the undecidability of meaning's property; the condition of the possibility of reason is the condition of reason's unfailing failure to be rational.

Paradox is always a disgrace to philosophy, for it harbors contradiction of meaning intolerable to *logos*. At the turn of the century, Husserl made it his life's project to save the European sciences from an impending "crisis." He thought the only way to save Europe and, presumably, the whole of humanity was to reground philosophy on an apodictic foundation. Crisis must be dealt with, and only standing knowledge on an absolutely certain footing could accomplish that task. In fact, each of Husserl's works can be read as an attempt to do just that. With Heidegger's work, this crisis management took a different turn: We started to hear about the "end of philosophy."[103] Something else is needed; only something other than philosophy, something truly "poetic," can save us. Derrida can be read to have continued this project, but with much more modesty or cynicism than his predecessors. The sudden explosion, or rather the celebration, of paradoxes in philosophy and literature during this century, I think, can be read as anticipatory notes to the "monstrosity" that Derrida invokes but never dares to describe.[104]

Some years ago, as if facing up to the difficult predicament of philosophy, Derrida spoke about the apocalyptic tone in philosophy.[105] Apocalyptic or not, such may be Derrida's retelling of Heidegger's story of the mystery of Being, of the changing epochs of Being's elusive presence, a retelling that aims to make it clear once and for all that nothing creates or is capable of creating a "crisis" in philosophy or elsewhere, that a crisis is *always* and *already* at the root of philosophy's foundation and elsewhere. Philosophy is crisis-ridden; politics is crisis-ridden; the economy is crisis-ridden; technology is crisis-ridden; representation is crisis-ridden; inauguration is crisis-ridden; signing is crisis-ridden; writing is crisis-ridden; translation is crisis-ridden; understanding is crisis-ridden; the postal service is crisis-ridden; life in general is crisis-ridden; theory is crisis-ridden; and one must now add, communication is crisis-ridden. How can they not be so? How can they be otherwise? Crisis is chronic, for it *happens* all the time — the normality *before* the event. Crisis is the *happening* of the event, the event (seen) as *happening,* the *eventing* (seen) as such. Real events are always crisis-events; only crises exist as real events. In any event, signs (of crises) are out there; signs (of crises) are already off. It is up to theorists to heed the message.

Conclusion

Till human voices wake us, and we drown. — *T.S. Eliot*

Don't start from the good old things, but the bad new ones.
—*Bertolt Brecht*

Imagine three situations:

1. Someone came and said something to me. I understood her, I knew what she wanted, and I responded. We talked for a while until we both had to leave. A few days later, I had forgotten about the incident. I did not remember who she was, and I did not remember what we talked about. I know incidents like this have happened before, and I know similar events will happen again. Looking back at it now, I cannot say that I know anything about it—I have forgotten about *that* incident.

2. Someone dropped by my office to say hello. Glad to see him, I invited him in. We chatted about the weather and the news, all the while sipping tea. Hours later, he left, and I went back to my work. This has happened before, though not as frequently as I would like. But right now, that is not something I worry about; in fact, after he left, I did not think much about our visit—except that I vaguely remember that we both enjoyed it.

3. Someone came and said something to me. This time, something strange happened. I did not understand what she was saying, and I

221

did not know how to respond. I was puzzled, and I am still puzzled. An incident like this, as far as I can recollect, has never happened to me before, and I would hate to experience it again. But right now, I cannot help thinking about it; I cannot help wondering what has happened or why it happened, although I still do not have the vaguest idea what she said, and I do not think I would know how to respond if it were to happen again. I felt stupid then, and I feel stupid now. Perhaps it was my fault; perhaps...

In each of these situations, something happened: Someone came to me and said something. Silence was broken; utterances were made; as a result, life's flow was interrupted, momentarily. In the first and second situations, not only did the visitor say something to me, but I also responded in kind. What ensued could only be described as a conversation, a free exchange in which meaningful sounds replaced the silence that characterized our individual existence before the encounter. In that exchange, information — significant or trivial — was shared; questions — intelligent or foolish — were asked and answered; issues — pressing or irrelevant — were discussed; mutual concerns — sincere or pretended — were expressed. Because of this exchange, we understood one another a little better; because of this exchange, we, as Schutz might say, grew a little older together — aging through time spent talking to one another. Despite the semantic mobility of the word *communication,* we can justifiably conclude that there was a situation of communication: There took place (an event of) communication, an event that occurred as the happening of mutual understanding.

Not all conversations are equally memorable; every conversation does not impact on our lives equally. In fact, most of the conversations we have, save perhaps a few precious ones, are forgotten shortly after the event. Life goes on, as the cliché goes, irrespective of the little interruptions that talk might create. As in the first situation, the conversation that occupied me for a while soon evaporated after the fact, receding into nothingness, becoming irretrievable. Looking back now, I do not remember a thing. It is as if nothing happened.

That most conversations soon recede into nothingness after the fact can occur for a reason other than either our forgetfulness or the lack of clarity of what was talked about. A different kind of "nothingness" can take over our communication, weakening its force, depleting its significance, until the event leaves no vestige of itself and becomes indistinguishable from the first kind of nothingness. This is what happened in the second situation: Someone visited me, and we had a pleasant conversation. But it was a conversation about nothing, about nothing in particular, for no sooner did the conversation begin than it slipped into utter triviality, into the vapidity of a quotidian act whose purpose, despite the momentary pleasure it afforded, was, as we say, to kill time. Although the utterances exchanged between my visitor and me were neither garbled nor indecipherable nor meaningless, the conversation as a whole did not *mean* anything; it was limited, as it were, to the *there* and *then* and was quickly swamped by the mindless routine of life, becoming shapeless, faded, and finally, gone. What we said to one another has become, for all its clarity at the moment, an idle vehicle, a vehicle without content, a vehicle in which "nothing" was said. What happened in this case can only be called "chatter" or "idle talk"—a kind of communication in which nothing of consequence is communicated except the act of communicating itself, its ritualistic insignificant repetitions. In this situation, "the vehicles of communication," as Peter Fenves puts it, "carry nothing of *weight*. Communication continues to take place, and its pace may very well accelerate, but everything is still somehow idle. In such non-movement—or incessant movement at a standstill—empty and idle talk finds its point of departure: the vehicle of communication, language as structure and act, remains in operation, but it no longer *works,* for whatever it carries is somehow 'nothing.' "[1] In a way similar to what happened in the first situation, a comparable nothingness also took over the communication between me and my second visitor.

That even the most enjoyable of all our conversations can deflate into "idle chatter," spiraling down to "nothingness," reflects the fact that, as existentialists are never tired of saying, we live for the most part *inauthentically.* To the extent that *inauthenticity,* which, one should note, does not connote any moral or ethical deficiency, characterizes our ordinary mode of being, idle chatter, its about-nothingness, will never cease to haunt the episodes of our conversing acts without which what is called the social would not even be able to ascend above its epiphenomenal threshold. In view of the two kinds of nothingness that routinely annihilate our communication, the third situation becomes singularly interesting—not merely because it poses an intellectual problem or practical exigency, but because it creates an uncanny dislocation in me, an existential crisis that no experience and no wisdom can alleviate.

In contrast to what took place in the first two situations, something profoundly strange happened in the third one. Someone came and said something to me, but instead of responding, I became speechless. In fact, I was at a complete loss, unable to make any sense of what was happening. Silence was broken, but it soon resumed. I heard something, but frustration or a sense of my own stupidity was my only response, a silent response that only widened the gap of nonrecognition between her and me. I had every reason to believe that she must have said and meant something, but her message, as it were, remained null, incapable of reaching me. Her message, if it carried what she intended it to mean, appeared too "proper to" her to be communicative, too pure to mean anything to me, that is, too idio(t)lectic not to lapse into sheer noise, into a string of disturbing sounds that remind me of, among other things, my stupidity or ineptitude. This idiolectic message formed a rift between us by forming a void in me. Consequently, there was no exchange, no understanding, and we can only conclude, no communication.

Yes, there was an event; yes, an event began, barely, when she began to say something. But this event did not come to fruition, for nothing, nothing really, happened — except a sudden defamiliarization of my world, an unforeseen estrangement brought about by the least violent of all acts — the mere emitting of sounds — that toppled the sense-structure of my life world. After she breached my silent existence, silence returned, devouring both of us again by expropriating my ability to respond. So nothing, nothing really, happened. But this nothing, compared to "idle chatter" and the "forgetfulness" of an ordinary conversation, was much more dramatic. It produced in me an effect like no other. Considering what happened, or rather, what failed to take place, I must confess that I was profoundly affected by it. In fact, I am still living that event through the unique nothingness brought home to me by the incident, suffering from it, agonizing over it as an event that keeps returning as a nonevent. In any case, the undeniable fact is that there *was* an event, there *took place* a situation that, although nothing, nothing really, happened in it, is still happening now. It was like a traumatic "primal scene," forever gone but constantly coming back.

It is not difficult to see that, contrary to the current widespread ideology, the only communication worth its name takes place in situations like the third one. These situations, despite their variable forms and contents, display the possibility, in a much more powerful fashion than do the first two, of demonstrating the criteria by which we determine whether an event is truly communicative or not. "Something is communicated to me in a strong sense, or *there is* an event of communication," as Geoffrey Bennington remarks, "only when I do not have available to me the means to decode a transparent message. This implies that there is communication only when there is a moment, however minimal, of non-understanding, of *stupidity* with respect to what is said."² *Communication thus implies noncomprehension,* for I am most firmly placed in a situation of communication with the other only when I recognize that someone has come to me but do not understand why and do not quite understand what he, she, or it says. Was there even an utterance? Was that utterance, if there was one, directed toward me? If so, why? It is this sense of apprehension or uncertainty about what is to unfold and the subsequent noncomprehension of what is unfolding that open the space of communication from which it is always too late for one to retreat. As Bennington concludes: "Communication takes place, if at all, in a fundamental and irreducible uncertainty as to the very fact and possibility of communication."³

The truth of communication thus shows itself to be duplicitous: Communication can actually take place when it *appears not to* take place, and it can appear to take place when actually it fails to even begin. This possible failure of communication, the "irreducible uncertainty" implied in the very fact of communication, as reflected in my stupid noncomprehension vis-à-vis my visitor, is constitutive of communication in the same way that silence is constitutive of sounds, or that noise is constitutive of transmittable signals. As can now be inferred from my last hypothetical scenario, the constitutive stupidity on my part, taken to the limit, means that the space of communication is most radically itself, most radically open to the coming of the other, when I am not even sure whether someone has come and said something. At the same time, and from a slightly different point of view, it also means that communication becomes virtual only when its space is heterogeneous, when it is invaded by an alien, an inscrutable other that embodies a void, a nothing as the I-know-not-what, which I, having been invited into that space, cannot ignore. It is this alien invasion that creates a crisis in me, and it is this crisis that causes the event of communication to occupy me, to take its place in me — in spite of its nothingness, in spite of the void it induces in me.

Here we arrive at the most radical of the conclusions about communication that I have tried to convey: The impossibility of communication is the birth *to* its possibility. Recall my visitor in the third situation. By uttering to me meaningless sounds, she might be trying to avoid being communicative. But her very attempt to avoid communication testifies to the force of its necessity and thus confirms the singular law of communication — communication cannot *not* take place — one of whose effects, as I became painfully aware, is my uncanny experience of feeling stupid. The communication of a void therefore does not and cannot avoid communication, for "a void of communication," as Fenves critically observes, "is communicated whenever communication is avoided."[4] Whether my visitor intended it or not, her avoiding communication nevertheless communicates a void to me. As long as she came to me, the "not" of her communication cannot not be, which is to say, her noncommunication is an impossibility.

That the impossibility of communication constitutes its possibility means that communication knows no negativity, that "a 'not' of communication is under every condition impossible."[5] This is not simply because there is a theoretical difficulty in literally and genuinely communicating about nothing, or that incommunicability, to the extent that it can be formulated into a concept, can always be communicated; rather, it is because even noncommunication, or successful refusal to communicate, such as deliberate silence, voluntary mutism, counterfactual fabrications, or a masterful feigning of stupidity, carries with it at every turn the promise, which is to say the threat, of its own negation.

This impossibility of annulling communication, taken to the limit, reveals that communication is governed—even before it begins—by (the force of) an imperative that binds the one to the other in an authorless contract. "When someone (?) comes (?) and says (?) something (?)," I immediately enter into the space of an imperative, just as he/she/it does.[6] Immediately and imperceptibly, there emerges an unsigned but effective contract between us, indispensable to what is taking place, namely, that you, the addresser, are addressing me, the addressee. This contract communicates to us, before our communication, its force—forcing us to obey, forcing upon us the demand to respond. Communicated to us as an imperative, this demand cannot be ex-communicated. It is a universal demand of exchange that interpellates the self and the other as communicating subjects by interpolating both into a measureless cycle of credit and debit, giving and returning, taking and keeping. As such, it demands our responsibility to respond to one another, despite the fact that I do not understand what you say, and that you are uncertain whether I will be saying anything back at all. By laying down the law for respons(e)ibility irrespective of the possibility that that response may not be forthcoming, this demand legislates promise, establishing a contract capable of having itself enforced in the future. This contract of anticipatory response, based on the decree of reciprocity, thus nullifies the possibility of any negativity of communication by bringing about a *contra*communication: a communication against (non)communication, a communication that crosses itself out by communicating.[7]

Seen in this light, we, as communicating subjects, can no longer be regarded as free agents who choose (or choose not) to communicate. For the exoteric autonomy of the subjects in communication, of my visitors and me, and of everyone else, too, is in effect a conditioned freedom bestowed on us by a prior contract. Agency, as the freedom *to* exchange, therefore means the universal responsibility to honor a contract delivered to us by we-know-not-what and from we-know-not-where. It is by obeying this imperative that we, as communicators, can be free *to* communicate as well as *not to* communicate.

Communication cannot not take place. This is the paradoxical freedom of communication, the unbearable freedom that one cannot not communicate, even if one chooses not to do so. One cannot not communicate; "communication cannot be avoided even when the void of communication, its negativity, is communicated."[8] This is the agony of communication, the ordeal of the *autonomos* of the communicating subjects, caused by what I called earlier the "postal paradox of communication." This agony, this ordeal, accompanies communication at every turn. As a result, we, the communicating subjects, are both autonomous and other-dependent—free to receive as well as to reject the other and yet bound to play this double role by the contractual force of an *an-archic* imperative. By the same token, communication theorists, to the extent that their metareflective statements say something—intelligible or not—about communication, are destined to reenact the same double play, exhibiting, in their very enunciations, the kind of duplicity that cannot not take place whenever one meets and says something to the other. That being the case, theorizing, particularly theorizing about communication, will never be more than an exploration. I choose the word *exploration* purposefully. Exploration does not entail end; it does not guarantee any final discovery any more than it predicts the attainability of some ultimate truth. Always *liminal*, that is, always *transitional*, communication theories, like any conversation worth its name, will never be able to have the last word on the subject matter they choose to address; their ostensive ending—whether it is caused by the addresser's avoidance of being communicative, by the addressee's stupid noncomprehension, or by the message's own vacuousness—is but a promise that another ending will come.

Ending, like beginning, cannot but take place. One way to end—arbitrarily and temporarily, of course—my argument in this book is to say that communication, like such philosophemes as presence, identity, origin, structure, and the like, is an *undecidable*. By focusing on the universal media of communication, sign and meaning, the purpose of my analysis has been to show that all communicative events, to the extent that they manage to transmit certain messages, are internally split and therefore thwarted by the very acts that materialize them. This, as Derrida reminds us, and as any deconstructive analysis worth the name demonstrates, "is something that happens — it just happens."[9] It happens in the ancient "quarrel" between philosophy and poetry (Plato's *diaphora*); it happens when philosophical heroism (Hegel) meets homoerotic fantasies (Genet); it happens when speech-act theory (John Searle) begins to speak to grammatology (Derrida); and I know it happens between conversing friends, as evidenced by my hypothetical scenario. Although its happening is never *thetic* (which in Greek means "to place," which is *ponere/positum* in Latin), it will certainly take place whenever someone comes and says something. So the best way for me to end this written communication is to repeat what I have been trying to say all along: Communication is possible and is impossible. If communication is anything at all, it is an *undecidable*. As you, my reader, can see now, I can only return in the end to where I began: "Il faut Parler. Parler sans pouvoir." One must communicate, communicate without the ability to do so.

Abbreviations

AR   Paul de Man. *Allegories of Reading.* New Haven, Conn.:Yale University Press, 1979.

BP   Martin Heidegger. *The Basic Problems of Phenomenology,* trans. Albert Hofstadter. Bloomington: Indiana University Press, 1982.

BT   Martin Heidegger. *Being and Time,* trans. John Macquarrie and Edward Robinson. New York: Harper and Row, 1962.

CM   Edmund Husserl. *Cartesian Meditations: An Introduction to Phenomenology,* trans. Dorion Cairns. The Hague: Martinus Nijhoff, 1973.

"DI"   Jacques Derrida. "Declarations of Independence." *New Political Science* 15 (1986): 7–15.

Diss   Jacques Derrida. *Dissemination,* trans. Barbara Johnson. Chicago: University of Chicago Press, 1981.

EGT   Martin Heidegger. *Early Greek Thinking,* trans. David Farrell Krell and Frank A. Capuzzi. New York: Harper and Row, 1975.

FTL   Edmund Husserl. *Formal and Transcendental Logic,* trans. Dorion Cairns. The Hague: Martinus Nijhoff, 1969.

Glas   Jacques Derrida. *Glas,* trans. John P. Leavey, Jr., and Richard Rand. Lincoln: University of Nebraska Press, 1987.

HCT   Martin Heidegger. *The History of the Concept of Time,* trans. Theodore Kisiel. Bloomington: Indiana University Press, 1985.

ID   Martin Heidegger. *Identity and Difference,* trans. Joan Stambaugh. New York: Harper and Row, 1969.

IOP   André de Muralt. *The Idea of Phenomenology: Husserlian Exemplarism,* trans. Gary L. Breckon. Evanston, Ill.: Northwestern University Press, 1974.

JD   Christopher Norris. *Jacques Derrida.* Cambridge, Mass.: Harvard University Press, 1987.

KP   Martin Heidegger. *Kant and the Problem of Metaphysics,* trans. James S. Churchill. Bloomington: Indiana University Press, 1962.

229

MP   Jacques Derrida. *Margins of Philosophy,* trans. Barbara Johnson. Chicago: University of Chicago Press, 1982.

OG   Jacques Derrida. *Of Grammatology,* trans. Gayatri Chakravorty Spivak. Baltimore: Johns Hopkins University Press, 1976.

OTB   Martin Heidegger. *On Time and Being,* trans. Joan Stambaugh. New York: Harper and Row, 1972.

OWL   Martin Heidegger. *On the Way to Language,* trans. Peter D. Hertz and Joan Stambaugh. New York: Harper and Row, 1971.

PC   Jacques Derrida. *The Post Card: From Socrates to Freud and Beyond,* trans. Alan Bass. Chicago: University of Chicago Press, 1987.

PLT   Martin Heidegger. *Poetry, Language, Thought,* trans. Albert Hofstadter. New York: Harper and Row, 1971.

Pos   Jacques Derrida. *Positions,* trans. Alan Bass. Chicago: University of Chicago Press, 1981.

PPH   David Carr. *Phenomenology and the Problem of History.* Evanston, Ill.: Northwestern University Press, 1974.

SP   Jacques Derrida. *Speech and Phenomena,* trans. David B. Allison. Evanston, Ill.: Northwestern University Press, 1973.

WD   Jacques Derrida. *Writing and Difference,* trans. Alan Bass. Chicago: University of Chicago Press, 1978.

"WM" Martin Heidegger, "What Is Metaphysics?" In *Basic Writings,* ed. David Farrell Krell. New York: Harper and Row, 1977.

Notes

Introduction

1. It can be argued à la Wittgenstein that "communication" is a "family resemblances" concept. There are phenomena and activities that we would describe as communicative (such as reading, conversing, watching television), but these phenomena and activities might not share any one characteristic. Like various forms of leisure activities normally called "games," they merely bear family likenesses to one another. An essential definition of communication is therefore impossible. See Ludwig Wittgenstein, *The Blue and Brown Books* (New York: Harper and Row, 1958), pp. 17–18.

2. In the following discussion, I make no distinction between "communication theory" and "theory of communication."

3. I borrowed the word *ex-timate*, meaning "external intimacy" (which also appears as the title of one of Jacques-Alain Miller's seminars, *L'extimate*), from Jacques Lacan. Lacan coins this neologism to describe a certain kernel in the symbolic order, the strange, traumatic, internal, and yet foreign element (for example, the death drive), which, though constantly articulating the individual's desire, can never be symbolized or integrated into the symbolic structure.

4. The notions of mimesis and castration are invoked by Derrida in relation to deconstruction at various places; see, for example, his *Positions*, trans. Alan Bass (Chicago: University of Chicago Press, 1981); hereafter referred to as *Pos*. Also see the discussion in Irene E. Harvey, *Derrida and the Economy of Différance* (Bloomington: Indiana University Press, 1986), pp. 28–36.

5. *Pos*, p. 67.

6. Jacques Derrida, *Of Grammatology*, trans. Gayatri Chakravorty Spivak (Baltimore: Johns Hopkins University Press, 1976), p. 162; hereafter referred to as *OG*.

7. Harold Bloom et al., *Deconstruction and Criticism* (New York: Seabury Press, 1979), p. 6.

8. See Jacques Derrida, *The Ear of the Other: Otobiography, Transference, Translation*, English edition ed. Christie V. McDonald, trans. Avital Ronell and Peggy Kamuf (New York: Schocken Books, 1985), p. 142.

9. See Jacques Derrida, "Plato's Pharmacy," in *Dissemination*, trans. Barbara Johnson (Chicago: University of Chicago Press, 1981); hereafter referred to as *Diss*.

10. The term "critical verisimilitude" is from Roland Barthes; see his *Criticism and Truth* (Minneapolis: University of Minnesota Press, 1987).

11. Jacques Derrida, *Writing and Difference*, trans. Alan Bass (Chicago: University of Chicago Press, 1978), p. 259; hereafter referred to as *WD*.

12. J. Hillis Miller, *The Ethics of Reading* (New York: Columbia University Press, 1987), p. 7.

1 / Phenomenology and After

1. John Sallis, *Spacings* (Chicago: University of Chicago Press, 1986), p. 1.
2. Ibid.
3. Ibid.

4. See Immanuel Kant, *Critique of Pure Reason*, trans. Norman Kemp Smith (New York: St. Martin's Press, 1968). Also see Sallis, *Spacings*, pp. 4–5.

5. Edmund Husserl, "Philosophy as Rigorous Science," in *Phenomenology and the Crisis of Philosophy*, trans. Quentin Lauer (New York: Harper and Row, 1965).

6. Ludwig Landgrebe, *The Phenomenology of Edmund Husserl* (Ithaca, N.Y.: Cornell University Press, 1981), p. 71.

7. Quoted in David Carr, *Phenomenology and the Problem of History* (Evanston, Ill.: Northwestern University Press, 1974), p. 52; hereafter referred to as *PPH*.

8. Quoted in Landgrebe, *The Phenomenology of Edmund Husserl*, p. 71, emphasis mine.

9. Ibid.

10. Edmund Husserl, " 'Phenemonology,' Edmund Husserl's Article for the Encyclopaedia Britannica," in *Husserl: Shorter Works*, ed. Peter McCormick and Frederick A. Elliston (Notre Dame, Ind.: University of Notre Dame Press, 1981), p. 32, emphasis mine.

11. See Herbert Spiegelberg, *The Context of Phenomenological Movement* (The Hague: Martinus Nijhoff, 1981), pp. 62–82.

12. See Emmanuel Levinas, *The Theory of Intuition in Husserl's Phenomenology* (Evanston, Ill.: Northwestern University Press, 1973), pp. 37–51.

13. *PPH*, p. 87.

14. Edmund Husserl, *Ideas: General Introduction to Pure Phenomenology*, trans. W. R. Boyce Gibson (New York: Collier Books, 1962), p. 183.

15. For a detailed discussion, see Harry Reeder, *The Theory and Practice of Husserl's Phenomenology* (New York: University Press of America, 1986), pp. 87–109.

16. For Husserl, the synthetic quality of the act results from a "unity of felt belongingness," a "unitary connection in continuous coincidence." See, for example, Edmund Husserl, *Logical Investigations*, 2 vols., trans. J. N. Findlay (Atlantic Highlands, N. J.: Humanities Press, 1970), vol. 2, p. 777. Also see Edmund Husserl, *Phenomenological Psychology*, trans. John Scanlon (The Hague: Martinus Nijhoff, 1977), pp. 58, 61.

17. J. N. Mohanty, *The Possibility of Transcendental Philosophy* (The Hague: Martinus Nijhoff, 1985), p. xxi.

18. See Paul Ricoeur, *Husserl: An Analysis of His Phenomenology*, trans. Edward G. Ballard and Lester E. Embree (Evanston, Ill.: Northwestern University Press, 1967), pp. 82–114.

19. Edmund Husserl, *Cartesian Meditations: An Introduction to Phenomenology*, trans. Dorion Cairns (The Hague: Martinus Nijhoff, 1973), p. 21; hereafter referred to as *CM*. It should be noted that Ricoeur's translation of Husserl differs from Cairns's. Unless specified otherwise, I have adopted Cairns's translation.

20. *CM*, p. 65.

21. Ricoeur, *Husserl*, p. 89.

22. Ibid., p. 10.

23. Joseph J. Kockelmans, "Husserl and Kant on the Pure Ego," in *Husserl: Expositions and Appraisals*, ed. Frederick A. Elliston and Peter McCormick (Notre Dame, Ind.: University of Notre Dame Press, 1977), p. 279.

24. Edmund Husserl, *Formal and Transcendental Logic*, trans. Dorion Cairns (The Hague: Martinus Nijhoff, 1969), p. 108; hereafter referred to as *FTL*.

25. See André de Muralt, *The Idea of Phenomenology: Husserlian Exemplarism*, trans. Gary L. Breckon (Evanston, Ill.: Northwestern University Press, 1974), pp. 86–113; hereafter referred to as *IOP*.

26. *CM*, p. 84, emphasis mine.

27. *IOP*, p. 108.

28. See *CM*, p. 117, and Kockelmans, "Husserl and Kant on the Pure Ego," p. 280.

29. In a conversation with Fink and Cairns, Husserl said, "The transcendental ego . . . is not a subject, but sui generis *the* subject." See Dorion Cairns, *Conversations with Husserl and*

Fink (The Hague: Martinus Nijhoff, 1976), p. 59. In this sense, transcendental ego and transcendental subject can be used interchangeably.

30. Ricoeur, *Husserl*, p. 89.

31. Ricoeur, *Husserl*, p. 107; see also *CM*, p. 118.

32. *IOP*, pp. 109–10.

33. See John D. Caputo, *Radical Hermeneutics: Repetition, Deconstruction, and the Hermeneutic Project* (Bloomington: Indiana University Press, 1987), p. 120.

34. Ricoeur, *Husserl*, p. 113.

35. Edmund Husserl, *The Crisis of European Sciences and Transcendental Phenomenology: An Introduction to Phenomenological Philosophy*, trans. David Carr (Evanston, Ill.: Northwestern University Press, 1970), p. 188.

36. Husserl's problem of intersubjectivity should be analyzed on three levels: (1) other egos as single subjects, (2) the formation of a community involving multiple subjects, and (3) the question of history and tradition. See Ricoeur, *Husserl*, pp. 115–42. Here I address only the first level.

37. *PPH*, p. 85.

38. Ibid.; see also *CM*, p. 89.

39. *CM*, p. 30, emphasis mine.

40. In addition to Ricoeur's detailed analysis in his book-length study on Husserl, see James Richard Mensch, *Intersubjectivity and Transcendental Idealism* (Albany: State University of New York Press, 1988). Representative articles on this issue include David Carr, "The 'Fifth Meditation' and Husserl's Cartesianism," *Philosophy and Phenomenological Research* 34, no. 1 (1973): 14–35; Harrison Hall, "Intersubjective Phenomenology and Husserl's Cartesianism," *Man and World* 12, no. 1 (1979): 13–20; Peter Hutcheson, "Solipsistic and Intersubjective Phenomenology," *Human Studies* 4, no. 2 (1981): 165–78.

41. *FTL*, pp. 272–73.

42. See Ricoeur, *Husserl*, p. 115.

43. Ibid., p. 118.

44. *CM*, p. 93.

45. Ibid. (Ricoeur's translation).

46. *CM*, p. 98.

47. Ibid., p. 106.

48. See, for example, the articles collected in John Perry, ed., *Personal Identity* (Berkeley and Los Angeles: University of California Press, 1975).

49. *CM*, pp. 110–11 (Ricoeur's translation).

50. Ibid., p. 112.

51. Ibid., p. 111.

52. Ibid.

53. Ricoeur, *Husserl*, p. 127.

54. See *CM*, pp. 114–15. The notion of "harmony" is not important for Husserl only at the interpersonal level; it is essentially related to intersubjectivity at all levels. In *CM* (p. 108), Husserl writes, "*The constitution of the world essentially involves a 'harmony' of the monads.*"

55. The notion of "indicative sign" is developed by Husserl in *Logical Investigations*. This is the point at which Derrida launches his attack on Husserl's logocentrism in his *Speech and Phenomena*, trans. David B. Allison (Evanston, Ill.: Northwestern University Press, 1973). This will be discussed in greater detail in later chapters.

56. *CM*, p. 114.

57. Ibid., p. 115.

58. Ricoeur, *Husserl*, p. 128.

59. *CM*, p. 132.

60. Ibid., p. 122.

61. I do not mean to suggest that perception is an act pure and simple, totally wrapped in presence. As long as perception takes place in time, it is inevitably determined by the tertiary structure of time-consciousness. See Edmund Husserl, *The Phenomenology of Internal Time-Consciousness,* ed. Martin Heidegger, trans. James S. Churchill (Bloomington: Indiana University Press, 1964).

62. *CM,* pp. 114–15, emphasis mine.

63. Ibid., p. 148, emphasis mine.

64. *PPH,* p. 89, emphasis mine.

65. See Michael Theunissen, *The Other: Studies in the Social Ontology of Husserl, Heidegger, Sartre, and Buber,* trans. Christopher Macann (Cambridge, Mass.: MIT Press, 1984), p. 161.

66. *PPH,* p. 89.

67. Ricoeur, *Husserl,* p. 131.

68. *PPH,* p. 97.

69. Near the end of *Cartesian Meditations,* Husserl writes: "phenomenological explication does nothing but *explicate the sense this world has for us all, prior to any philosophizing,* and obviously gets solely from our experience — *a sense which philosophy can uncover but never alter,* and which, because of an essential necessity, not because of our weakness, entails (in the case of any actual experience) horizons that need fundamental clarifications" (p. 151).

70. Louis Dupré, "Alternatives to the Cogito," *Review of Metaphysics* 40, no. 4 (1987): 690.

71. Ibid.

72. Ibid., p. 689.

73. Ibid., p. 690.

74. Ibid.

75. See, for example, Gilles Deleuze, *Kant's Critical Philosophy: The Doctrine of the Faculties,* trans. Hugh Tomlinson and Barbara Habberjam (Minneapolis: University of Minnesota Press, 1984).

76. Landgrebe, *The Phenomenology of Edmund Husserl,* pp. 118, 119.

77. *FTL,* p. 47.

78. See Richard J. Bernstein, *Beyond Objectivism and Relativism: Science, Hermeneutics, and Praxis* (Philadelphia: University of Pennsylvania Press, 1983), pp. 16–20.

79. See Jean-François Lyotard, *The Postmodern Condition: A Report on Knowledge,* trans. Geoff Bennington and Brian Massumi (Minneapolis: University of Minnesota Press, 1984).

80. For a discussion of the central themes of Husserl's phenomenology and their relevance to contemporary issues, see David Carr, "Husserl's World and Ours," *Journal of the History of Philosophy* 25, no. 1 (1987): 151–67.

81. *CM,* p. 157. Mark C. Taylor, for example, links the birth of philosophical modernism with the "death of God"; see his *Erring: A Postmodern A/theology* (Chicago: University of Chicago Press, 1984), pp. 19–33. One can also argue, following Jean-Joseph Goux, that Husserl's postulation of the transcendental subject represents the denouement of the Oedipal drama of Western metaphysics in which the theme/scene of *anthropocentering,* first expressed in Oedipus's answer to the Sphinx's riddle, "man," is restaged in purely secular terms; see Goux, *Oedipus, Philosopher,* trans. Catherine Porter (Stanford, Calif.: Stanford University Press, 1993).

82. See Michel Foucault, *The Order of Things: An Archaeology of the Human Sciences,* trans. Alan Sheridan-Smith (New York: Vintage Books, 1973).

2 / Communication before Deconstruction

1. Eugen Fink, "Die phänomenologische Philosophie Edmund Husserls in der gegenwärtigen Kritik," reprinted in *Studien zur Phänomenologie, 1930–1939* (The Hague: Martinus Nijhoff, 1966), p. 139.

2. Maurice Merleau-Ponty, *Phenomenology of Perception*, trans. Colin Smith (Atlantic Highlands, N.J.: Humanities Press, 1962), p. xiv.

3. On the idea of "discursive authority," see James Clifford's discussion with reference to ethnography, "On Ethnographic Authority," *Representations* 2 (1983, Spring): 118–46.

4. Roman Ingarden's two major works represent two different but complementary approaches: Taking a noematic point of view, *The Literary Work of Art*, trans. George G. Grabowicz (Evanston, Ill.: Northwestern University Press, 1973), anticipates text-oriented criticism, whereas *The Cognition of the Literary Work of Art*, trans. Ruth Ann Crowley and Kenneth R. Olson (Evanston, Ill.: Northwestern University Press, 1973), develops a noetic phenomenology of literary reception, thus laying the groundwork for the reader-oriented phenomenology of reading. Mikel Dufrenne's contribution to literary theory and aesthetics can be found in *The Phenomenology of Aesthetic Experience*, trans. Edward S. Casey et al. (Evanston, Ill.: Northwestern University Press, 1973).

5. Herman Rapaport, "Phenomenology and Contemporary Theory," in *Tracing Literary Theory*, ed. Joseph Natoli (Urbana: University of Illinois Press, 1987), p. 155.

6. It is not possible to document in full detail the recent history of philosophy of communication. In addition to well-known Continental critical theories by thinkers such as Karl-Otto Apel and Jürgen Habermas, representative works include Richard Lanigan, "Communication Models in Philosophy: Review and Commentary," in *Communication Yearbook 3*, ed. Dan Nimmo (New Brunswick, N.J.: Transaction, 1979), pp. 29–49; *Phenomenology of Communication* (Pittsburgh, Pa.: Duquesne University Press, 1988); and *The Human Science of Communicology* (Pittsburgh, Pa.: Duquesne University Press, 1992). Lawrence Grossberg has critically analyzed how recent Continental philosophies have shaped the thinking of communication scholars in his "Language and Theorizing in the Human Sciences," *Studies in Symbolic Interaction*, vol. 2, ed. Norman Denzin (Greenwich, Conn.: JAI Press, 1979), pp. 189–231; "The Ideology of Communication," *Man and World* 15 (1982): 83–101; "Intersubjectivity and the Conceptualization of Communication," *Human Studies* 5 (1982): 213–35; and "Does Communication Theory Need Intersubjectivity? Toward an Immanent Philosophy of Interpersonal Relations," in *Communication Yearbook 6*, ed. Michael Burgoon (Beverly Hills, Calif.: Sage, 1982), pp. 171–205. Given the heavy influence of phenomenology and hermeneutics on communication theory, it is no surprise that Robert White's *Philosophy of Communication* (London: Center of Communication and Culture, 1984) is essentially a book on several phenomenologists.

7. This is clearly reflected in the writings of the field. A recent case in point is the special issue of the *Journal of Communication: Ferment in the Field* 33, no. 3 (1983), which seeks to promote dialogue among competing paradigms in communication research.

8. Kant, *Critique of Pure Reason*, p. 27.

9. Althusser's conception of the problematic can be found in his *For Marx*, trans. Ben Brewster (London: Verso, 1979), and Louis Althusser and Etienne Balibar, *Reading Capital*, trans. Ben Brewster (London: New Left Books, 1970). By the phrase "discursive network," I do not mean to suggest any association with Friedrich Kittler's appropriation of Judge Daniel Paul Schreber's neologism, *Aufschreibesysteme*, usually translated as "discourse networks." See Friedrich Kittler, *Discourse Networks 1800/1900* (Stanford, Calif.: Stanford University Press, 1990).

10. Althusser, *For Marx*, p. 66.

11. It is not simply the influence of Freud that leads Althusser to characterize the problematic as "the unconscious" of scientific discourse. Through his "symptomatic reading" of Marx, Althusser becomes convinced that it is no longer the individual subject who thinks and develops scientific or philosophical theories. Rather, the problematic of the theory thinks through the theorist, and the theorist is but the vehicle of expression. In *Reading Capital*, Althusser writes: "The sighting is thus no longer the act of an individual subject, endowed with the faculty of 'vision' which he exercises either attentively or distractedly; the sighting is the act of its structural conditions, it is the relation of immanent reflexion between the field of the

problematic and *its* objects and *its* problems. . . . It is literally no longer the eye (the mind's eye) of a subject which *sees* what exists in the field defined by a theoretical problematic: it is this field which *sees itself* in the objects and problems it defines — sighting being merely the necessary reflexion of the field on its objects" (p. 25).

12. Mariam Glucksman, *Structuralist Analysis in Contemporary Social Thought* (London and Boston: Routledge and Kegan Paul, 1974), p. 3.

13. Althusser, *For Marx,* p. 32.

14. Steven B. Smith, *Reading Althusser* (Ithaca, N.Y.: Cornell University Press, 1984), p. 82.

15. The problematic could also be seen as a structure of vision, because as Althusser and Balibar describe, it "opens the way to an understanding of the determination of the *visible* as visible, and conjointly, of the invisible as invisible, and of the organic link binding the invisible to the visible. Any object or problem situated on the terrain and within the horizon, i.e., in the definite structured field of the theoretical problematic of a given theoretical discipline, is visible" (*Reading Capital,* p. 25).

16. Althusser, *For Marx,* p. 67.

17. Although not everyone would agree that the task of communication theory is to *explain* how individuality is transcended, my way of framing the question has the advantage of covering a wide theoretical terrain, thus encompassing the diverse theoretical positions in the literature. Moreover, I recognize that the notion of "explanation" is a complex one. Here I collapse the two types of explanation: explanation in terms of sufficient conditions (which addresses the question *Why necessary?*) and explanation in terms of necessary conditions (which addresses questions of the type *How possible?*). See Georg Henrik von Wright, *Explanation and Understanding* (Ithaca, N.Y.: Cornell University Press, 1971), pp. 132–67.

18. The perspective from which I frame the enabling question of communication theories is discussed in greater detail in Niklas Luhmann's "The Improbability of Communication," in *Essays on Self-Reference* (New York: Columbia University Press, 1990), pp. 86–98. Luhmann begins this essay by making a distinction between two different theoretical approaches whereby a scientific theory can be constructed. The first approach, exemplified by Francis Bacon and his followers, "looks for possible ways of improving the status quo. . . . They help to iron out flaws and gradually to improve the conditions in which people live. The second type of theory," represented by Hobbes and Kant, "is based on improbability" (p. 86). "The type of communication I am trying to advise," says Luhmann, "starts from the premise that *communication is improbable,* despite the fact we experience and practice it every day of our lives and would not exist without it. This improbability of which we have become unaware must first be understood, and to do so requires what might be described as a contra-phenomenological effort, viewing communication not as a phenomenon but *as a problem;* thus, instead of looking for the most appropriate concept to cover the facts, we must first ask *how communication is possible at all*" (p. 87, emphasis mine). According to Luhmann's classification, the traditional study of rhetoric would count as communication theory of the first type, whereas the kind of inquiry I am proposing corresponds to Luhmann's second type of scientific theorization. In *Mutual Misunderstanding* (Durham, N.C.: Duke University Press, 1992), Talbot J. Taylor provides an alternative analysis of theories of language by reading them as "rhetorical responses" to the challenge made by what he calls "communicational skepticism."

19. Paul Ricoeur, *Interpretation Theory: Discourse and the Surplus of Meaning* (Fort Worth: Texas Christian University Press, 1976), p. 15, emphasis mine.

20. See Grossberg, "Intersubjectivity and the Conceptualization of Communication."

21. For a brief discussion of the notion of the subject, see Paul Ricoeur, "The Question of the Subject: The Challenge of Semiology," in *The Conflict of Interpretations* (Evanston, Ill.: Northwestern University Press, 1974), pp. 236–66.

22. Rodolphe Gasché, *The Tain of the Mirror* (Cambridge, Mass.: Harvard University Press, 1986), p. 13.

23. Martin Heidegger, "The Age of the World Picture," in *The Question concerning Technology and Other Essays*, trans. William Lovitt (New York: Harper and Row, 1977), pp. 115–54.

24. Ibid., p. 117.

25. Ibid., p. 128.

26. *CM*, p. 6.

27. Ibid., p. 26.

28. One should not forget that for Husserl the "absolute subject" is the inner-time-flow itself, the absolute stream, the absolute streaming of the stream, the flux (*fluß*) itself. Husserl writes: "We can only say that this flux is something which we name in conformity with what is constituted, but it is nothing temporally 'objective.' It is absolute subjectivity and has the absolute properties of something to be denoted metaphorically (*im Bilde*) as 'flux,' as a point of actuality, primal source-point, that from which springs the 'now,' and so on. In the lived-experience of actuality, we have the primal source-point and a continuity of moments of reverberation. For all this, names are lacking." *The Phenomenology of Internal Time-Consciousness*, p. 100.

29. Paul Ricoeur, *The Conflict of Interpretations*, p. 257, emphasis mine.

30. The notion of subjectivity as privacy creates two different but interrelated questions for communication theory. First, there is the question of solipsism: If individuals are construed as isolated entities, there inevitably emerges the question of how their "egocentric predicament" can be overcome. In other words, if the communicative subject is defined in terms of its unique singularity, how could the certainty of that singular existence be extended to include other subjects? Second, there is the "hermeneutical question." To the extent that the enigma of communication emerges from a distrust of, from a suspension of belief in, ordinary communicative experiences, there emerges the question of how those phenomena or experiences should be interpreted. Now that the *appearances* of communication are not taken at their face value, interpretations of those appearances become crucial if the *reality* of communication is to be captured. These two questions are often conflated by communication scholars, and it explains why they so easily appropriate hermeneutics. The fundamental question of communication theory is therefore twofold. To resolve the existential enigma of communication, to overcome the egocentric predicament of those who participate in the exchange of meaning, any theoretical attempt at addressing this issue must not only account for how the gap between disparate realms of subjective experience is bridged, but it must also involve interpreting or reading the *phenomenon* of others, so that private subjective meaning can be freed from its precommunicative closure.

31. See Jacques Derrida, *The Post Card: From Socrates to Freud and Beyond*, trans. Alan Bass (Chicago: University of Chicago Press, 1987); hereafter referred to as *PC*.

32. Christopher Norris, *Jacques Derrida* (Cambridge, Mass.: Harvard University Press, 1987), pp. 192–93; hereafter referred to as *JD*.

33. *PC*, p. 206. In *Pos*, Derrida writes: "*Communication*, . . . in fact, implies the *transmission charged with passing, from one subject to the other, the identity* of a *signified* object of a *meaning* or a *concept* in principle inseparable from the process of passage and of the signifying operation. A communicates B to C" (p. 23, translation modified).

34. Jacques Derrida, "Sending: On Representation," *Social Research* 49, no. 2 (1982): 303.

35. *PC*, p. 12.

36. *PC*, p. 65, translation modified.

37. *Time Magazine*, November 14, 1988, pp. 68–69.

38. Gilles Deleuze and Félix Guattari, *What Is Philosophy?* (New York: Columbia University Press, 1994), p. 2.

39. Grossberg, "The Ideology of Communication," p. 85.

40. Jacques Derrida, *Margins of Philosophy*, trans. Barbara Johnson (Chicago: University of Chicago Press, 1982), p. 223; hereafter referred to as *MP*.

41. Ibid., p. 238, emphasis mine.

42. It should be pointed out that the practice of explication is full of obscurities. Not only is it logically problematic, but it also ultimately depends upon the unequal power relation between the student and the master. An insightful discussion of the "politics of explication" can be found in Jacques Rancière, *The Ignorant Schoolmaster* (Stanford, Calif.: Stanford University Press, 1991). He writes: "The logic of explication calls for the principle of a regression ad infinitum: there is no reason for the redoubling of reasonings to stop. What brings an end to the regression and gives the system its foundation is simply that the explicator is the sole judge of the point when the explication is itself explicated" (p. 4).

43. In "On Truth and Lie in the Extra-Moral Sense," Nietzsche gives his most famous statement on truth and metaphor: "What, then, is truth? A mobile army of metaphors, metonymies ... which have been enhanced, transposed, and embellished poetically and rhetorically, and which after long use seem firm, canonical, and obligatory to a people: truths are illusions about which one has forgotten that this is what they are; metaphors that are worn out and without sensuous power; coins that have their obverse effaced and now matter only as metal, no longer as coins" (Friedrich Nietzsche, *The Portable Nietzsche,* ed. W. Kaufmann [New York: Penguin Books, 1980], pp. 46–47).

44. Derrida writes: "Here, the metaphor consists in a substitution of proper names having a fixed meaning and referent, especially when we are dealing with the sun whose referent has the originality of always being original, unique, and irreplaceable, at least in the representation we give of it. *There is only one sun in the system.* The proper name, here, is the nonmetaphorical prime mover of metaphor, the father of all figures. Everything turns around it, everything turns toward it" (*MP,* p. 243).

45. Quoted in Derrida's "White Mythology," in *MP,* pp. 207–71.

46. Ibid., p. 213, emphasis mine.

47. According to Derrida, this is because "if one wished to conceive and class all the metaphorical possibilities of philosophy, one metaphor, at least, would always remain excluded, outside the system: the metaphor, at the very least, without which the concept of metaphor could not be constructed ... *the metaphor of metaphor*" (ibid., pp. 219–20, emphasis mine).

48. *MP,* p. 222.

49. For an excellent analysis of Derrida's notion of metaphor, see Irene E. Harvey, "Metaphorics and Metaphysics," *Journal of the British Society for Phenomenology* 17, no. 3 (1986): 308–30.

50. *MP,* pp. 228–29, emphasis mine.

51. Roland Barthes, *S/Z* (New York: Hill and Wang, 1975), p. 5.

52. Vladimir N. Volosinov, *Marxism and the Philosophy of Language,* trans. L. Matejka and I. Titunik (New York: Seminar Press, 1973), p. 86.

53. Ibid.

54. Michel Serres, "Platonic Dialogue," in *Hermes: Literature, Science, Philosophy,* ed. Josué V. Harari and David F. Bell (Baltimore: Johns Hopkins University Press, 1982), pp. 65–70.

55. Ibid., pp. 66–67.

56. Ibid., p. 67.

57. Ibid.

58. Alphonso Lingis, *The Community of Those Who Have Nothing in Common* (Bloomington: Indiana University Press, 1994), p. 81.

59. Serres, *Hermes,* p. 67.

60. Roman Jakobson, "Concluding Statement: Linguistics and Poetics," in *Style in Language* (Cambridge, Mass.: MIT Press, 1960), p. 353.

61. Jacques Derrida, "Signature Event Context," in *MP,* p. 315.

62. Leo N. Tolstoy, *Anna Karenina,* trans. Constance Garnett (Norwalk, Conn.: Easton Press, 1975), pp. 461–62.

63. Theodore R. Sarbin and Vernon L. Allen, "Role Theory," in *The Handbook of Social Psychology,* ed. Gardner Lindzey and Elliot Aronson (Reading, Mass.: Addison-Wesley, 1954), vol. 1, p. 225.

64. Robert Nisbet, *Social Bond* (New York: Alfred A. Knopf, 1970), p. 45.

65. See Michael L. Schwalbe, "Mead among Cognitivists," *Journal for the Theory of Social Behavior* 17, no. 2 (1987): 113–33.

66. Paul de Man, "The Epistemology of Metaphor," in *On Metaphor*, ed. Sheldon Sacks (Chicago: University of Chicago Press, 1978), p. 15.

67. Jonathan Culler, *On Deconstruction* (Ithaca, N.Y.: Cornell University Press, 1982), p. 139.

3 / The Inaugural Relation: Toward an Ontology of Communication

1. Paul de Man, *Allegories of Reading* (New Haven, Conn.: Yale University Press, 1979), p. 105; hereafter referred to as *AR*.

2. *AR*, p. 106.

3. Rodolphe Gasché, "Quasi-Metaphoricity and the Question of Being," in *Hermeneutics and Deconstruction*, ed. Hugh J. Silverman and Don Ihde (Albany: State University of New York Press, 1985), p. 168.

4. Timothy Clark, "No Motion, but a Mime of It: 'Rhythm' in the Textuality of Heidegger's Work," *Paragraph* 9 (1987): 71.

5. See Barthes, *Criticism and Truth*.

6. Barbara Johnson, "Taking Fidelity Philosophically," in *Difference in Translation*, ed. Joseph F. Graham (Ithaca, N.Y.: Cornell University Press, 1985), p. 146.

7. Paul de Man, *Blindness and Insight: Essays in the Rhetoric of Contemporary Criticism*, 2nd ed., rev. (Minneapolis: University of Minnesota Press, 1983), p. 9, emphasis mine.

8. *AR*, p. 105.

9. Ibid., p. 110.

10. Ibid., p. 113.

11. Martin Heidegger, *Identity and Difference*, trans. Joan Stambaugh (New York: Harper and Row, 1969), p. 106; hereafter referred to as *ID*.

12. Jacques Derrida, "From Restricted to General Economy: Hegelianism without Reserve," in *WD*, p. 271.

13. Jean-Luc Nancy, *The Birth to Presence*, trans. Brian Holms and others (Stanford, Calif.: Stanford University Press, 1993), p. 9.

14. Johann Gottlieb Fichte, *Versuch einer neuen Darstellung der Wissenschaftslehre* (Hamburg, p. 106), quoted in Peter Dews, *Logics of Disintegration* (London: Verso, 1988), p. 21.

15. Dews, *Logics of Disintegration*, p. 21.

16. I should point out that there are many phenomenologists (Aron Gurwitsch and Sartre, for example) who adopt the transcendental reduction without reifying the pure ego.

17. I should add that the Cartesian doubt itself, of which Husserl's "reduction" represents an extension, can be doubted. Charles S. Peirce, for example, questions the meaningfulness of the Cartesian doubt in no uncertain terms: "We cannot begin with complete doubt. We must begin with all the prejudices which we actually have when we enter upon the study of philosophy. These prejudices are not to be dispelled by a maxim, for they are things which it does not occur to us *can* be questioned. Hence this initial skepticism will be a mere self-deception, and not real doubt, and no one who follows the Cartesian method will ever be satisfied until he has formally recovered all those beliefs which in form he has taken up. . . . A person may, it is true, in the course of his studies, find reason to doubt what he began by believing; but in that case he doubts because he has a positive reason for it, and not on account of the Cartesian maxim" (p. 156). See his "Some Consequences of Four Incapacities," in *Collected Papers*, ed. Charles Hartshorne and Paul Weiss, vol. 5. (Cambridge, Mass.: Harvard University Press, 1934.)

18. See Alfred Schutz, "The Problem of Transcendental Subjectivity," in *Collected Papers, III: Studies in Phenomenological Philosophy,* ed. Maurice Natanson (The Hague: Martinus Nijhoff, 1966), pp. 51–84.

19. Jacques Derrida, *Edmund Husserl's "Origin of Geometry": An Introduction,* trans. John P. Leavey Jr. (Stony Brook, N.Y.: Nicolas Hays, 1978), p. 63.

20. José Ortega y Gasset, *Man and People* (New York: W.W. Norton, 1957), p. 127.

21. Alfred Schutz, *On Phenomenology and Social Relations,* ed. Helmut R. Wagner (Chicago: University of Chicago Press, 1970), p. 163.

22. Ibid., emphasis mine.

23. Karl-Otto Apel, "The Problem of Philosophical Fundamental-Grounding in Light of a Transcendental Pragmatic of Language," *Man and World* 8, no. 3 (1975): 240.

24. Ibid.

25. Ibid., p. 241.

26. Ibid.

27. Ibid.

28. Alfred Schutz and Thomas Luckmann, *The Structures of the Life-World* (Evanston, Ill.: Northwestern University Press, 1973), p. 3.

29. Ibid., pp. 3–4.

30. Alfred Schutz, *The Phenomenology of the Social World,* trans. George Walsh and Frederick Lehnert (Evanston, Ill.: Northwestern University Press, 1967), p. 74, emphasis mine.

31. Suzanne Bachelard, *A Study of Husserl's Formal and Transcendental Logic,* trans. Lester E. Embree (Evanston, Ill.: Northwestern University Press, 1968), p. 108.

32. Martin Heidegger, *Being and Time,* trans. John Macquarrie and Edward Robinson (New York: Harper and Row, 1962), p. 249; hereafter referred to as *BT.*

33. Martin Heidegger, *The End of Philosophy,* trans. Joan Stambaugh (New York: Harper and Row, 1973), p. 88.

34. Martin Heidegger, *The History of the Concept of Time,* trans. Theodore Kisiel (Bloomington: Indiana University Press, 1985), p. 107; hereafter referred to as *HCT.*

35. See Martin Kusch, "Husserl and Heidegger on Meaning," *Syntheses* 77, no. 1 (1988): 99–127.

36. *HCT,* p. 113.

37. Ibid., p. 110.

38. Ibid.

39. For Heidegger, phenomenology means the study of the *logos* of phenomenon. He stresses the meaning of *logos* in terms of its Greek origin *apophansis,* which is derived from *apophainesthai* (letting an entity be seen from itself): "Thus 'phenomenology' means *apophainesthai ta phainomena*—to let that which shows itself be seen from itself in the very way in which it shows itself from itself. This is the formal meaning of that branch of research which calls itself 'phenomenology.' But here we are expressing nothing else than the maxim formulated above: 'to the things themselves.' . . . To have a science 'of' phenomena means to grasp its objects *in such a way* that everything about them which is up for discussion must be treated by exhibiting it directly and demonstrating it directly. The expression 'descriptive phenomenology,' which is at bottom tautological, has the same meaning" (*BT,* pp. 58–59).

40. *BT,* pp. 383–84.

41. Ibid., p. 31.

42. Martin Heidegger, *The Metaphysical Foundations of Logic,* trans. Michael Heim (Bloomington: Indiana University Press, 1984), p. 196.

43. *BT,* p. 11. Also see Otto Pöggeler, *Martin Heidegger's Path of Thinking,* trans. Dan Magurshak and Sigmund Barber (Atlantic Highlands, N.J.: Humanities Press, 1987), pp. 33–50.

44. *BT,* p. 11.

45. Martin Heidegger, *The Basic Problems of Phenomenology,* trans. Albert Hofstadter (Bloomington: Indiana University Press, 1982), p. 128; hereafter referred to as *BP.*

46. Ibid.

47. Ibid., p. 24.

48. Ibid., p. 202.

49. Martin Heidegger, *What Is a Thing?* trans. W. B. Barton Jr. and Vera Deutsch (Chicago: Henry Regnery, 1967), p. 105.

50. Heidegger, *The Question concerning Technology,* p. 100.

51. Martin Heidegger, *Kant and the Problem of Metaphysics,* trans. James S. Churchill (Bloomington: Indiana University Press, 1962), p. x; hereafter referred to as *KP.*

52. Derrida, "Sending," pp. 308–9.

53. *BT,* p. 320.

54. Ibid., p. 157.

55. *KP,* p. xi.

56. See Jonathan Rees, *Philosophical Tales* (London: Methuen, 1987), p. 55.

57. Frederick A. Olafson, *Heidegger and the Philosophy of Mind* (New Haven, Conn.: Yale University Press, 1987), p. 124.

58. Martin Heidegger, "Letter on Humanism," trans. E. Lohner, in *Philosophy in the Twentieth Century: An Anthology,* vol. 3, ed. William Barrett and Henry Aiken (New York: Random House, 1962), pp. 271–302, emphasis mine.

59. *BT,* p. 11.

60. *KP,* p. 240.

61. Ibid., p. 200.

62. *BT,* p. 25.

63. Ibid.

64. Ibid., p. 26.

65. Ibid. Also see John Sallis, "Where Does '*Being and Time*' Begin?" in *Heidegger's Existential Analytic,* ed. Frederick Elliston (The Hague: Mouton, 1978), pp. 21–43.

66. *BT,* p. 27.

67. See Sallis, "Where Does '*Being and Time*' Begin?" pp. 28–35.

68. Ibid.

69. *BT,* p. 27.

70. Ibid.

71. Ibid., p. 206.

72. Ibid., p. 44.

73. Reiner Schürmann, *Heidegger on Being and Acting: From Principles to Anarchy,* trans. Christine-Marie Gros (Bloomington: Indiana University Press, 1987), p. 70.

74. See Michael Murray, "Husserl and Heidegger: Constructing and Deconstructing Greek Philosophy," *Review of Metaphysics* 41, no. 3 (1988): 501–18.

75. Stephen Watson, "Rationality and the Critique of Judgment," *Review of Metaphysics* 41, no. 3 (1988): 473, 474.

76. *HCT,* p. 196.

77. Watson, "Rationality and the Critique of Judgment," p. 474.

78. *BT,* p. 160.

79. Ibid., p. 155.

80. Ibid., p. 89.

81. Thomas Sheehan, "On the Way to *Ereignis:* Heidegger's Interpretation of *Physis,*" in *Continental Philosophy in America,* ed. Hugh J. Silverman, John Sallis, and Thomas M. Seebohm (Pittsburgh, Pa.: Duquesne University Press, 1983), pp. 137–39.

82. *BT,* p. 279.

242 / Notes to Pages 103–16

83. Ibid., p. 132.

84. Joseph Kockelmans, *Martin Heidegger: A First Introduction to His Philosophy* (Pittsburgh, Pa.: Duquesne University Press, 1965), pp. 63–65.

85. Martin Heidegger, "The Origin of the Work of Art," in *Poetry, Language, Thought,* trans. Albert Hofstadter (New York: Harper and Row, 1971), p. 67; hereafter referred to as *PLT.*

86. Martin Heidegger, "Introduction to Philosophy: 1929 Lecture," quoted in Walter Biemel, "Heidegger's Concept of Dasein," in *Heidegger's Existential Analytic,* ed. Frederick Elliston (The Hague: Mouton, 1978), p. 123.

87. *BT,* p. 120, emphasis mine.

88. Watson, "Rationality and the Critique of Judgment," p. 473.

89. Gerald Bruns, "On the Weakness of Language in the Human Sciences," in *The Rhetoric of the Human Sciences,* ed. John S. Nelson, Allan Megill, and Donald N. McCloskey (Madison: University of Wisconsin Press, 1987), p. 243.

90. Joseph Kockelmans, "Thanks-Giving: The Completion of Thought," in *Heidegger and the Quest for Truth,* ed. Manfred S. Frings (Chicago: Quadrangle Books, 1968), p. 170.

91. Charles Scott, *The Language of Difference* (Atlantic Highlands, N.J.: Humanities Press, 1987), p. 127. In *What Is Called Thinking?* trans. Fred D. Wieck and J. Glenn Gray (New York: Harper and Row, 1968), Heidegger writes: "as soon as I thoughtfully say 'man's nature,' I have already said relatedness to Being. Likewise, as soon as I say thoughtfully: Being of beings, the relatedness to man's nature has been named" (p. 79).

92. *BT,* p. 97.

93. Mark C. Taylor, *Deconstructing Theology* (New York: Crossroad, 1982), p. 55.

94. Plato, *Cratylus,* in *The Collected Dialogues of Plato,* ed. Edith Hamilton and Huntington Cairns (New York: Pantheon Books, 1961), pp. 421–74, here at p. 440.

95. G. W. F. Hegel, *Science of Logic,* trans. A. V. Miller (Atlantic Highlands, N.J.: Humanities Press, 1969), pp. 125–26.

96. T. J. J. Altizer, *The Self-Embodiment of God* (New York: Harper and Row, 1977), p. 37.

97. Jean Hyppolite, *The Genesis and Structure of Hegel's Phenomenology of Spirit* (Evanston, Ill.: Northwestern University Press, 1974), p. 116.

98. Taylor, *Erring,* p. 108.

99. Hegel, *Science of Logic,* p. 425.

100. Martin Heidegger, *What Is Philosophy?* trans. William Kluback and Jean T. Wilde (New Haven, Conn.: College and University Press, 1958), p. 49.

101. Emmanuel Levinas, *Collected Philosophical Papers,* trans. Alphonso Lingis (The Hague: Martinus Nijhoff, 1987), p. 70.

102. Taylor, *Deconstructing Theology,* p. 54, emphasis mine.

103. Jean-Paul Sartre, "Un Nouveau Mystique," in *Situations I* (Paris: Gallimard, 1947), p. 163.

104. Jacques Derrida, "The Original Discussion of 'Differance' (1986)," *Derrida and Difference,* ed. David Wood and Robert Bernasconi (Evanston, Ill.: Northwestern University Press, 1988), p. 85.

105. Philippe Sollers, *Writing and the Experience of Limits* (New York: Columbia University Press, 1983), p. 95.

106. I have explored this issue in more detail in my "Communication after Deconstruction: Toward a Phenomenological Ontology of Communication," *Studies in Symbolic Interaction* 7, A. (1986): 13–32.

107. Martin Heidegger, "Building Dwelling Thinking," in *PLT,* p. 152.

4 / The In-Difference of Being

1. John D. Caputo, "Gadamer's Closet Essentialism: A Derridean Critique," in *Dialogue and Deconstruction: The Gadamer-Derrida Encounter,* ed. Diane P. Michelfelder and Richard E.

Palmer (Albany: State University of New York Press, 1989), pp. 258–64. As readers familiar with Caputo's works can see, my discussion of Heidegger and Derrida is heavily indebted to him.

2. Ibid., p. 262.

3. Ibid.

4. Ibid., p. 263.

5. In "Force and Signification," Derrida discussed, among other things, the necessity of "elemental earth" (*terre*) as the indispensable medium through which airy ideas are materialized as "history" through inscription; see *WD*, p. 9.

6. I should point out that Derrida rejects the possibility of defining *deconstruction*. Responding to a Japanese scholar's inquiry asking how to translate the term *deconstruction* into Japanese, Derrida wrote, "All sentences of the type 'deconstruction' is X or 'deconstruction' is not X, a priori miss the point, which is to say that they are at least false. As you know, one of the principle things at stake in what is called in my text 'deconstruction' is precisely the delimiting of . . . the third-person indicative: S is P" (p. 4). See Jacques Derrida, "Letter to a Japanese Friend," in Wood and Bernasconi, eds., *Derrida and Differance*, pp. 3–12.

7. To define deconstruction, to describe its procedures, is to survey, as J. Hillis Miller remarks, "a region of the *Unheimlich* [the unhomely]"; it is an "attempt to reach clarity in a region where clarity is not possible" (p. 231). See his "The Critic as Host," in Harold Bloom et al., *Deconstruction and Criticism*, pp. 217–53. Any effort to give a general description of deconstruction can therefore be viewed only as a heroic but ultimately impossible task. The passages cited in the text are from the following sources: Jonathan Culler, *On Deconstruction* (Ithaca, N.Y.: Cornell University Press, 1982); Paul de Man, *Blindness and Insight: Essays in the Rhetoric of Contemporary Criticism*, 2nd ed., rev. (Minneapolis: University of Minnesota Press, 1983); Barbara Johnson, "Translator's Introduction," in *Diss*, p. xiv; Christopher Norris, *Deconstruction: Theory and Practice* (London and New York: Methuen, 1982).

8. *BP*, p. 23.

9. *ID*, p. 47.

10. *PLT*, pp. 183–84, emphasis mine.

11. Ibid., p. 185.

12. Otto Pöggeler, "Heidegger's Topology of Being," in *On Heidegger and Language*, ed. Joseph J. Kockelmans (Evanston, Ill.: Northwestern University Press, 1972), p. 108.

13. Michel Haar, "The End of Distress: The End of Technology," *Research in Phenomenology* 13 (1983): 50.

14. Martin Heidegger, *Early Greek Thinking*, trans. David Farrell Krell and Frank A. Capuzzi (New York: Harper and Row, 1975), p. 51; hereafter referred to as *EGT*.

15. Ibid., p. 51.

16. Ibid., p. 50.

17. For a discussion of the notion of *Ereignis*, see John Llewelyn, *Beyond Metaphysics? The Hermeneutical Circle in Contemporary Continental Philosophy* (Atlantic Highlands, N.J.: Humanities Press, 1985), pp. 18–29.

18. Quoted in Haar's "The End of Distress," p. 49.

19. *BP*, p. 319, emphasis mine.

20. Ibid.

21. The English translation of "The Anaximander Fragment" is collected in *EGT*.

22. *EGT*, p. 11.

23. The term "abnormal philosophy" is from Richard Rorty. See his "Derrida on Language, Being, and Abnormal Philosophy," *Journal of Philosophy* 74 (1977): 673–81.

24. Gilles Deleuze and Félix Guattari, *Nomadology: The War Machine* (New York: Semiotext(e), 1986), p. 5. Also see Paul Virilio, *Speed and Politics* (New York: Semiotext(e), 1986).

25. Martin Heidegger, *On Time and Being*, trans. Joan Stambaugh (New York: Harper and Row, 1972), p. 24; hereafter referred to as *OTB*.

26. Ibid., p. 24.

27. Ibid., p. 19.

28. Ibid., pp. 29–30.

29. Ibid., p. 24.

30. Ibid., p. 21.

31. Ibid., emphasis mine.

32. Ibid., p. 24.

33. Ibid., p. 41.

34. Martin Heidegger, *On the Way to Language*, trans. Peter D. Hertz and Joan Stambaugh (New York: Harper and Row, 1971), p.39; hereafter referred to as *OWL*.

35. Jacques Derrida, "The Ends of Man," *Philosophy and Phenomenological Research* 30 (1969): 53. According to Derrida, the desire to preserve and retrieve the meaning of Being is no less metaphysical than is presence. In "Ousia and Gramme," collected in *MP*, Derrida asks, "Is not the opposition of the *primordial* to the *derivative* still metaphysical? Is not the quest for an *archia* in general, no matter with what precautions one surrounds the concept, still the 'essential' operation of metaphysics? Supposing, despite powerful presumptions, that one may eliminate it from any other provenance, is there not at least some Platonism in the *Verfallen*? Why determine as *fall* the passage from one temporality to another? Why qual-ify temporality as authentic — or *proper* (*eigentlich*) — and as inauthentic — or improper — when every ethical preoccupation has been suspended?" (p. 63). To the extent that these questions can be posed in Heideggerian terms, Heidegger can arguably be accused of being logocentric.

36. Caputo, *Radical Hermeneutics*, p. 158.

37. Jacques Derrida, *Spurs: Nietzsche's Styles*, trans. Barbara Harlow (Chicago: University of Chicago Press, 1979), p. 119.

38. Caputo, *Radical Hermeneutics*, pp. 153–86.

39. "Time and Being," in *OTB*, p. 24.

40. Heidegger's letter is mentioned by John Sallis, *Echoes* (Bloomington: Indiana University Press, 1990), p. 43.

41. The starting point of deconstruction is the end of philosophy. But Derrida prefers the term *closure* to *end*. "End" is not the same as "closure." And Derrida uses the term *closure* because he refuses to speak of the "end" of philosophy in the sense of a termination. Early in *OG*, Derrida makes his point clearly: "For essential reasons: the unity of all that allows itself to be attempted today through the most diverse concepts of science and writing, is, in principle, more or less covertly yet always determined by an historico-metaphysical epoch of which we merely glimpse the *closure*. I do not say the *end*" (p. 4).

42. *WD*, p. 260.

43. *WD*, pp. 279–80.

44. Jacques Derrida, *Speech and Phenomena*, trans. David B. Allison (Evanston, Ill.: Northwestern University Press, 1973); hereafter referred to as *SP*.

45. Ibid., p. 96.

46. Barbara Johnson, "The Critical Difference," *Diacritics* 8 (1978 Summer): 3.

47. *WD*, p. 288.

48. *OG*, p. 24.

49. For a discussion on "strategy" and "stratagem," see Josué V. Harari, "Critical Factions/Critical Fictions," in *Textual Strategies: Perspectives in Post-Structuralist Criticism*, ed. Josué V. Harari (Ithaca, N.Y.: Cornell University Press, 1979), pp. 17–72.

50. *WD*, p. 280.

51. Jacques Derrida, *Limited Inc.*, trans. Samuel Weber (Evanston, Ill.: Northwestern University Press, 1988), p. 55.

52. *OG,* p. 24. In an interview addressing the issue of drugs and addiction, Derrida explicitly linked deconstruction to the notion of parasitism. He said: "This parasitism is at once accidental and essential. Like any good parasite, it is at once inside and outside — the outside feeding on the inside. And with this model of feeding we are very close to what in the modern sense we call drugs, which are usually to be 'consumed.' 'Deconstruction' is always attentive to this indestructible logic of parasitism. As a discourse, deconstruction is always a discourse about the parasite, a discourse 'on parasite' and in the logic of the 'super-parasite.'" See "The Rhetoric of Drugs: An Interview with Jacques Derrida," *1-800 Magazine* no. 2 (1991), p. 65.

53. *MP,* p. 135.

54. *Pos,* pp. 6–7, emphasis mine.

55. Ibid., p. 6.

56. *WD,* pp. 252–53.

57. *Diss,* p. 221.

58. Ibid., p. 194, emphasis mine.

59. Maurice Blanchot, *Le Pas au-delà* (Paris: Gallimard, 1973), pp. 48–49; quoted in Mark C. Taylor, *Altarity* (Chicago: University of Chicago Press, 1987), pp. 248–49.

60. Taylor, *Altarity,* p. xvi.

61. Jacques Derrida, *Glas,* trans. John P. Leavey, Jr., and Richard Rand (Lincoln: University of Nebraska Press, 1987); hereafter referred to as *Glas.*

62. *Diss,* p. 127.

63. Geoffrey H. Hartman, *Criticism in the Wilderness* (New Haven, Conn.: Yale University Press, 1980), p. 205.

64. Ibid., p. 213.

65. *MP,* p. 173.

66. *Pos,* pp. 41–42.

67. Ibid., p. 42.

68. Ibid., emphasis mine.

69. *Diss,* p. 221.

70. Ibid.

71. Ibid., p. 220.

72. Gasché, *The Tain of the Mirror,* p. 241.

73. *AR,* p. 131.

74. *Diss,* p. 221.

75. See Gasché, *The Tain of the Mirror,* pp. 142–54.

76. *Diss,* p. 221.

77. Ibid., p. 127.

78. Ibid., p. 222.

79. Ibid.

80. *Pos,* p. 43.

81. Ibid., p. 71.

82. The expression "What difference does it make?" as de Man pointed out, does not simply contain a duplicity of meaning. Rather, it simultaneously offers two meanings that annul each other. On the one hand, "What difference does it make?" conveys that it (whatever it is) makes no difference; yet on the other hand, the expression asks for the difference that the it (whatever it is) is supposed to make. See Paul de Man, "Semiology and Rhetoric," in *Textual Strategies,* ed. Harari, pp. 128–29.

83. *MP,* pp. 329–30.

84. Ibid., p. 38.

85. See *jd,* pp. 97–113.

86. Jonathan Culler, "Jacques Derrida," in *Structuralism and Since,* ed. John Sturrock (Oxford, U.K.: Oxford University Press, 1979), p. 168.

87. Martin Heidegger, *The Essence of Reasons,* trans. Terrence Malick (Evanston, Ill.: Northwestern University Press, 1969), p. 3.

88. Martin Heidegger, "What Is Metaphysics?" in *Basic Writings,* ed. David Farrell Krell (New York: Harper and Row, 1977), p. 100; hereafter referred to as "WM."

89. Ibid., p. 103.

90. Ibid.

91. Ibid., p. 105.

92. Ibid.

93. Ibid., p. 104.

94. Ibid., emphasis mine.

95. Ibid., p. 105.

96. W. B. Macomber, *The Anatomy of Disillusion* (Evanston, Ill.: Northwestern University Press, 1967), p. 102.

97. "WM," p. 106.

98. Ibid., p. 102.

99. Ibid., p. 103.

100. Gilles Deleuze and Félix Guattari, "Rhizome," trans. Paul Foss and Paul Patton, *Ideology and Consciousness* 8 (1981): 38.

101. *SP,* p. 159.

102. Derrida, *Edmund Husserl's "Origin of Geometry,"* p. 153.

103. *SP,* p. 136.

104. Ibid., p. 137.

105. The characterization of *différance* as "the productive and primordial constituting causality," however, must be immediately qualified. As Derrida writes: "But while bringing us closer to the infinitive and active core of differing, 'differance' (with an *a*) neutralizes what the infinitive denotes as simply active, in the same way that 'mouvance' does not signify in our language the simple fact of moving, of moving oneself or of being moved. . . . Here in the usage of our language we must reflect on the fact that the ending *-ance* is undecided *between* active and passive. And we shall see why that which lets itself [*se laisse*] be designated by 'differance' is neither simply active nor simply passive, but announces or rather recalls something like a middle voice, that it speaks of an operation which is not an operation, which lets itself [*se laisse*] be thought neither as a passion nor as an action of a subject upon an object, neither as departing from . . . an agent nor from a patient, neither from nor with a view to any of these *terms.* Now perhaps philosophy, constituting itself within this repression, began by hiving off into the active or the passive voice a certain non-transitivity, the middle voice" (*SP,* p. 137). Also see John Llewelyn, *Derrida on the Threshold of Sense* (New York: St. Martin's Press, 1986), pp. 92–94.

106. *SP,* p. 141, emphasis mine.

107. *WD,* pp. 113, 114.

108. *SP,* p. 158.

109. *Diss,* p. 157.

110. See Gasché, *The Tain of the Mirror,* pp. 121–77.

111. *OG,* p. 62.

112. *Diss,* p. 331. Through the notion of "trace," Derrida is responding critically to Heidegger's call to rethink "the forgotten of metaphysics," namely the oblivion to the difference between Being and beings: "What Heidegger wants to point out is that the difference between Being and beings, forgotten by metaphysics, has disappeared without leaving a trace. The very trace of difference has sunk from sight. If we admit that differance (is) (itself) something other than presence and absence, if it *traces,* then we are dealing with the forgetting of

the difference (between Being and beings), and we now have to talk about a disappearance of the trace's trace. . . .

"The trace is not a presence but is rather the simulacrum of a presence that dislocates, displaces, and refers beyond itself. The trace has, properly speaking, no place, for effacement belongs to the very structure of the trace. Effacement must always be able to overtake the trace; otherwise it would not be a trace but an indestructible and monumental substance. In addition, and from the start, effacement constitutes it as a trace — effacement establishes the trace in a change of place and makes it disappear in its appearing, makes it issue forth from itself in its very position. The effacing of this early trace (*die frühe Spur*) of difference is therefore 'the same' as its tracing within the text of metaphysics. This metaphysical text must have retained a mark of what it lost or put in reserve, set aside. In the language of metaphysics the paradox of such a structure is the inversion of the metaphysical concept which produces the following effect: *the present becomes the sign of signs, the trace of traces*. It is no longer what every reference refers to in the last instance; it becomes a function in a generalized referential structure. It is a trace, and a trace of the effacement of a trace" (*SP,* pp. 155–56, emphasis mine).

113. Jacques Derrida, "On Reading Heidegger: An Outline of Remarks to the Essex Colloquium," *Research in Phenomenology* 17 (1987): 181, emphasis mine.

114. *WD,* p. 230.

115. *OG,* p. 47.

116. In discussing the concept of "origin," I have drawn on Vincent Descombes, *Modern French Philosophy* (Cambridge, U.K.: Cambridge University Press, 1980), pp. 145–46.

117. The origin is always doubled and redoubled. Consequently, the beginning does not begin with count "one" but with "three." As Derrida writes, "Death is at the dawn because everything has begun with repetition. Once the center or the origin have begun by repeating themselves, by redoubling themselves, the double did not only add itself to the simple. It divided it and supplemented it. There was immediately a double origin plus its repetition. Three is the first number of repetition" (*WD,* p. 29).

118. *OG,* p. 167.

119. J. Hillis Miller, "The Disarticulation of the Self in Nietzsche," *The Monist* 64, no. 2 (1981): 249.

120. Derrida has more than once expressed his distrust of perception; see, for example, *SP,* pp. 103–4, and "Structure, Sign, and Play in the Discourse of the Human Sciences," in *WD,* pp. 278–93.

121. Jacques Derrida, "The *Retrait* of Metaphor," *Enclitic* 2, no. 2 (1978): 5–33. See also Rodolphe Gasché, "Joining the Text: From Heidegger to Derrida," in *The Yale Critics: Deconstruction in America,* ed. Jonathan Arac, Wlad Godzich, and Wallace Martin (Minneapolis: University of Minnesota Press, 1983), pp. 156–75.

122. *Pos,* p. 26.

123. *Diss,* p. 258; *Pos,* p. 66.

124. Gasché, *The Tain of the Mirror,* p. 280.

125. Jacques Derrida, "Living On: Border Lines," trans. J. Hulbert, in Bloom et al., *Deconstruction and Criticism,* pp. 75–176.

126. Oswald Ducrot and Tzvetan Todorov, *Encyclopedic Dictionary of the Sciences of Language,* trans. Catherine Porter (Baltimore: Johns Hopkins University Press, 1979), p. 357.

127. Ibid., pp. 357–58.

128. *Pos,* pp. 59–60.

129. Descombes, *Modern French Philosophy,* p. 150.

130. *MP,* p. 75.

131. Descombes, *Modern French Philosophy,* pp. 150–51.

132. Ibid., p. 151.

133. Ibid.
134. Martin Heidegger, "The Anaximander Fragment," quoted by Derrida in *SP*, p. 155.
135. Ibid., p. 157.
136. *BT*, p. 270.
137. Martin Heidegger, *Der Satz vom Grund* (Pfullingen: Neske, 1957), p. 188, quoted in Kees de Kuyer, "The Problem of Ground in the Philosophy of Martin Heidegger," *The Thomist* 47 (1983): 100–117.
138. De Kuyer, "The Problem of Ground in the Philosophy of Martin Heidegger," p. 114.
139. Derrida, *Spurs*, p. 121.
140. Ibid.
141. Richard Rorty, *Contingency, Irony, and Solidarity* (Cambridge, U.K.: Cambridge University Press, 1989), p. 135.
142. *MP*, p. 27.
143. See Caputo, *Radical Hermeneutics*, pp. 153–86.
144. *OWL*, p. 39.
145. *MP*, pp. 133–34. For this passage, I have adopted John Llewelyn's translation; see his *Derrida on the Threshold of Sense*, pp. 40–41.
146. Richard Rorty, *Contingency, Irony, and Solidarity*, p. 122.
147. Gayatri Chakravorty Spivak, "Revolutions That as Yet Have No Model: Derrida's *Limited Inc.*," *Diacritics* 10 (1980): 42.

5 / Deconstructing Communication: Derrida and the (Im)Possibility of Communication

1. John D. Caputo, "Heidegger and Derrida: Cold Hermeneutics," *Journal of the British Society for Phenomenology* 17, no. 3 (1986): 252–88. My discussion in this section is indebted to John Caputo.
2. Ibid., p. 264.
3. *BT*, p. 371, translation modified.
4. Jacques Derrida, "Ja, ou le faux-bond," *Diagraphe* 11 (March 1977): 103.
5. João Natali, "Communication: A Semiotic of Misunderstanding," *Journal of Communication Inquiry* 10, no. 3 (1986): 22–31.
6. Caputo, "Heidegger and Derrida," p. 254.
7. Natali, "Communication," p. 25.
8. Jakobson, "Concluding Statement: Linguistics and Poetics."
9. See Elmar Holenstein, *Roman Jakobson's Approach to Language* (Bloomington: Indiana University Press, 1976), p. 165. It should be noted that I am not criticizing Jakobson himself for promoting linear thinking; I am suggesting that his model has been appropriated by communication scholars to characterize communication as transmission.
10. See Jean Baudrillard, *Toward a Critique of the Political Economy of the Sign* (St. Louis, Mo.: Telos Press, 1981).
11. See Jean Baudrillard, *The Mirror of Production* (St. Louis, Mo.: Telos Press, 1976).
12. Emile Benveniste, *Problems in General Linguistics*, trans. M. Meck (Coral Gables, Fla.: University of Miami Press, 1971), p. 225. Benveniste forcefully articulates the relationship between language and the self: The I, he says, refers to "something very peculiar which is exclusively linguistic: *I* refers to the act of individual discourse in which it is pronounced, and by this it designates the speaker.... The reality to which it refers is the reality of the discourse. It is in the instance of discourse in which *I* designates the speaker that the speaker proclaims himself as the 'subject.' And so it is literally true that the basis of subjectivity is in the exercise of language. If one really thinks about it, one will see that there is no other objective

testimony to the identity of the subject except that which he himself thus gives about himself" (p. 226).

13. Similar ideas have been voiced within the phenomenological tradition. For example, Calvin Schrag has developed a theory of the decentered and situated subject through the notion of "hermeneutical self-implicature"; see his *Communicative Praxis and the Space of Subjectivity* (Bloomington: Indiana University Press, 1986).

14. Jean Baudrillard, "Requiem for the Media," in *For a Critique of the Political Economy of the Sign* (St. Louis, Mo.: Telos Press, 1981), pp. 164, 179. I have discussed this in "Mass, Media, Mass Media-tion: Jean Baudrillard's Implosive Critique of Modern Mass-Mediated Culture," *Current Perspectives in Social Theory* 7, no. 2 (1986): 158–81.

15. Baudrillard, *For a Critique of the Political Economy of the Sign*, p. 179.

16. Ibid., p. 178.

17. Michel Foucault, "The Order of Discourse," trans. Ian McLeod, in *Untying the Text: A Post-Structuralist Reader*, ed. Robert Young (London and Boston: Routledge and Kegan Paul, 1981), pp. 48–78.

18. Raymond Williams, *Keywords* (New York: Oxford University Press, 1983), pp. 62–63.

19. Cary Nelson, "Poststructuralism and Communication," *Journal of Communication Inquiry* 9, no. 2 (1985): 2–15.

20. See, for example, Diane Macdonnel, *Theories of Discourse* (Oxford: Basil Blackwell, 1986).

21. Deleuze and Guattari, "Rhizome," p. 53.

22. See Cary Saul Morson and Caryl Emerson, *Mikhail Bakhtin: Creation of a Prosaics* (Stanford, Calif.: Stanford University Press, 1990).

23. See Richard Rorty, "Nineteenth-Century Idealism and Twentieth-Century Textualism," *The Monist* 64, no. 2 (1981): 155–74.

24. In *Of Grammatology*, Derrida discusses how Heidegger's privileging of logos repeats the metaphysical insistence on the "proper," on self-proximity and nearness as embodied in the voice: "Metaphysics, ... not only from Plato to Hegel ... but also ... from the pre-Socratics to Heidegger, always assigned the origin of truth in general to the logos. ... Heideggerian thought would reinstate rather than destroy the insistence of the logos and the truth of being as 'primum signatum': the transcendental signified ... remaining irreducible to all the epochal determinations it nonetheless makes possible, thus opening the history of the logos; that is, *being nothing* before the logos and outside of it" (p. 20).

25. Ibid., p. 281.

26. See ibid., p. 73; also see *JD*, pp. 63–81.

27. *JD*, pp. 64–65.

28. *SP*, p. 76.

29. Ibid.

30. The example of *s'entendre-parler* is drawn from Christopher Norris; see *JD*, p. 71.

31. *MP*, p. 312.

32. *OG*, p. 281.

33. *MP*, p. 92; *JD*, p. 77.

34. *MP*, p. 313.

35. See "The Pit and the Pyramid: Introduction to Hegel's Semiology," in *MP*, pp. 69–108.

36. Ibid., p. 313.

37. Ibid., p. 314.

38. Ibid., p. 314–15.

39. Ibid., p. 315.

40. Ibid., p. 316.

41. On Derrida's reading of Austin, I have benefited from Frank B. Farrell. See his "Iterability and Meaning: The Searle-Derrida Debate," *Metaphilosophy* 19, no. 1 (1988): 53–64. It

should be noted that by "iterability" Derrida does not mean simply "repeatability." By retrieving the root meaning of *itara*, "becoming other," iterability means both repeatability and alterity. The aspect of alterity, of the sign's perpetually becoming other while functioning as the same, is overlooked by Searle.

42. *SP*, p. 92.

43. Ibid., p. 93.

44. Vincent Descombes, *Objects of All Sorts* (Baltimore: Johns Hopkins University Press, 1986), p. 64.

45. *SP*, p. 93.

46. Descombes, *Objects of All Sorts*, p. 64.

47. *SP*, pp. 96–97.

48. *MP*, p. 318. The constitutive role of re-petition for presence was emphasized by Derrida at various places. In *Speech and Phenomena*, Derrida discusses the necessity of repeatability, of the possibility of the trace as a return of the same, that renders possible the presence of the "now": "The possibility of re-petition in its most general form, that is, the constitution of a trace in the most universal sense — is a possibility which not only must inhabit the pure actuality of the now but must constitute it through the very movement of difference it introduces. Such a trace . . . is more 'primordial' than what is phenomenologically primordial. For the ideality of the form (*Form*) of presence itself implies that it be infinitely repeatable, that its re-turn, as a return of the same, is necessary *ad infinitum* and is inscribed in presence itself" (p. 67).

49. There is no denying the connection between the speaker's utterance and the intention that causes it, but this connection, as I have argued elsewhere, is *nontransitive*. See my "Empty Intention," *Text and Performance Quarterly* 12, no. 3 (1992): 212–27, and "Copies, Reproducibility, and Aesthetic Adequacy," *British Journal of Aesthetics* 31, no. 3 (1991): 265–67.

50. Harvey, *Derrida and the Economy of Différance*, p. 239.

51. Ibid., p. 320.

52. *WD*, p. 11.

53. See *JD*, pp. 68–69.

54. *MP*, pp. 95–96.

55. *WP*, p. 214.

56. *WD*, p. 12.

57. *MP*, p. 316.

58. Ibid., p. 294.

59. Ibid., p. 292.

60. *JD*, p. 25.

61. *Glas*, p. 41.

62. Hartman, *Criticism in the Wilderness*, p. 202.

63. *MP*, p. 210.

64. *WD*, p. 292.

65. *WD*, p. 11, emphasis mine.

66. Dews, *Logics of Disintegration*, pp. 12–13.

67. *Diss*, pp. 223, 258, emphasis mine. See also Rodolphe Gasché, "Nontotalization without Spuriousness: Hegel and Derrida on the Infinite," *Journal of the British Society for Phenomenology* 17, no. 3 (1986): 289–307. Derrida cautions against reading "undecidability" as equivalent to "indeterminacy." In "Afterword: Toward an Ethics of Discussion," in *Limited Inc.*, Derrida writes: "Undecidability is always a *determinate* oscillation between possibilities (for example, of meaning, but also of acts). These possibilities are themselves highly *determined* in strictly *defined* situations (for example, discursive — syntactical or rhetorical — but also political, ethical, etc.). They are *pragmatically* determined. The analyses that I have devoted to undecidability concern just these determinations and these definitions, not at all some vague 'indeterminacy.' . . . Which

is to say that from the point of view of semantics, but also of ethics and politics, 'deconstruction' should never lead either to relativism or to any sort of indeterminism. "To be sure, in order for structures of undecidability to be possible (and hence structures of decisions and of responsibilities as well), there must be a certain play, *différance*, nonidentity. Not of indetermination, but of *différance* or of nonidentity with oneself in the very process of determination. *Différance* is not indeterminacy. It renders determinacy both possible and necessary" (pp. 148–49).

68. "The Double Session," in *Diss*, p. 251.

69. Dews, *Logics of Disintegration*, p. 13.

70. *Pos*, p. 45.

71. *Diss*, pp. 333–34.

72. Dews, *Logics of Disintegration*, p. 30.

73. *SP*, p. 87.

74. Jean-Jacques Lecercle, *Philosophy through the Looking Glass* (La Salle, Ill.: Open Court, 1985), p. 34. See also his "Louis Wolfson and the Philosophy of Translation," *Oxford Literary Review* 11, nos. 1–2 (1989): 103–20.

75. Lecercle, *Philosophy through the Looking Glass*, p. 65. Also see Leonard Lawlor, "Event and Repeatability: Ricoeur and Derrida in Debate," *Pre-Text* 4, nos. 3–4 (1983): 317–34.

76. *Glas*, p. 1.

77. *JD*, p. 180.

78. Derrida, "Limited Inc. abc," *Glyph* 2 (1977): 199.

79. Jacques Derrida, "Declarations of Independence," *New Political Science* 15 (1986): 7–15, 8; hereafter referred to as "DI." See also *JD*, pp. 194–206.

80. "DI," p. 8.

81. Ibid., p. 9.

82. Ibid.

83. Jacques Derrida, "Desistance," in Philippe Lacoue-Labarthe, *Typography: Mimesis, Philosophy, Politics*, ed. Christopher Fynsk (Cambridge, Mass.: Harvard University Press, 1989), p. 2.

84. See David Couzens Hoy, "Dworkin's Constructive Optimism vs. Deconstructive Legal Nihilism," *Law and Philosophy* 6, no. 3 (1987): 321–56. I have benefited from Hoy's discussion. It is of interest to point out that Jacques Lacan also uses the notion of the future anterior to describe not only his own development but also the historicity of the subject in general. See Samuel Weber's discussion of this in *Return to Freud* (Cambridge, U.K.: Cambridge University Press, 1991).

85. Ibid., p. 335.

86. "DI," p. 10.

87. *WD*, p. 226.

88. Ibid., p. 227.

89. The word *proper* derives from the Latin *proprius*, meaning that which is one's own, special, particular, not held in common with others. For a discussion on the intricate relation among the meanings of *proper, property, propriety, possession, naming*, and *signature*, see Taylor, *Erring*, pp. 40–46.

90. Peter Brunette and David Wills, *Screen/Play: Derrida and Film Theory* (Princeton, N.J.: Princeton University Press, 1989), p. 180.

91. "*Envois*," in *PC*, p. 444, translation modified.

92. Ibid., translation modified.

93. David Wills, "Post/Card/Match/*Envois*/Derrida," *SubStance* 43 (1984): 23.

94. *PC*, p. 324.

95. Wills, "Post/Card/Match/*Envois*/Derrida," pp. 24–25.

96. For an excellent discussion on the notion of the "Hermeneutical Imperative," see Werner Hamacher, "The Promise of Interpretation: Reflections on the Hermeneutical Imper-

ative in Kant and Nietzsche," in *Looking after Nietzsche*, ed. Laurence A. Rickels (Albany: State University of New York Press, 1990), pp. 19–47.

97. *PC,* p. 64–65, translation modified.

98. Ibid., pp. 66–67.

99. Ibid., p. 21, translation modified.

100. Ibid., p. 48.

101. Ibid., p. 98.

102. Brunette and Wills, *Screen/Play,* pp. 188–89.

103. The notion of the "end of philosophy" has a special sense in Heidegger. In one of his final texts, "The End of Philosophy and the Task of Thinking," first published in 1966, Heidegger writes: "What is meant by the talk about the end of philosophy? We understand the end of something all too easily in the negative sense as a mere stopping, as the lack of continuation, perhaps even as decline and impotence. In contrast, what we say about the end of philosophy means the completion of metaphysics (*die Vollendung der Metaphysik*). . . . The old meaning of the word 'end' means the same as place. . . . The end of philosophy is the place, that place in which the whole of philosophy's history is gathered in its most extreme possibility. End as completion means this gathering" (*Basic Writings,* pp. 374–75). The end of philosophy is a matter of its being gathered into an end, not an end in the classical sense of perfection or termination, but rather end as extreme possibility.

104. In what is one of his darker apocalypses, Derrida writes the following in *Of Grammatology*: "The future can only be anticipated in the form of an absolute danger. It is that which breaks absolutely with constituted normality and can only be proclaimed, *presented,* as a sort of *monstrosity.* For that future world and for that within it which will have put into question the values of sign, words, and writing, for that which guides our future anterior, there is as yet no exergue" (p. 5, emphasis mine).

105. Jacques Derrida, "Of an Apocalyptic Tone Recently Adopted in Philosophy," trans. John P. Leavey Jr., *Semia* 23 (1982): 63–97.

Conclusion

1. Peter Fenves, *"Chatter": Language and History in Kierkegaard* (Stanford, Calif.: Stanford University Press, 1993), p. 2.

2. Geoffrey Bennington, *Legislations: The Politics of Deconstruction* (London: Verso, 1994), p. 2.

3. Ibid.

4. Peter Fenves, *"Chatter,"* p. 145.

5. Ibid., pp. 143–44.

6. Geoffrey Bennington, *Legislations,* p. 2.

7. Peter Fenves, *"Chatter,"* pp. 149–50. My use of the term "*contra*communication" differs slightly from Fenves's use.

8. Ibid., p. 146.

9. Gary A. Olson, "Jacques Derrida on Rhetoric and Composition: A Conversation," *Journal of Advanced Composition* 10, no. 1 (1990): 12.

Index

Compiled by Eileen Quam and Theresa Wolner

Affirmation, 203
Aletheia, 115, 125, 167
Alter ego: and intersubjectivity, 21–22, 24, 29, 79. *See also* Ego
Althusser, Louis, 36–38, 235n9, 235–36n11, 236n15
Analogy: and intersubjectivity, 22–23, 26, 64–65
Anthropocentering, 234n81
Anxiety: and nothingness, 150–52
Apel, Karl-Otto, 82–83
Apperception, 26–27, 76
Appropriation, 125, 130–33. *See also Ereignis*
Aristotle, 6, 51, 53, 70, 78; *De Interpretatione,* 189
Artaud, Antonin, 208
Austin, J. L., 196, 198, 200
Authenticity: in conversation, 223; of Dasein, 127

Bachelard, Gaston, 36–37
Bachelard, Suzanne, 85–86
Barthes, Roland, 55, 70
Baudrillard, Jean, 181–82
Being: as appropriation, 131–33; as beings, 123, 165–66, 168, 172; and consciousness, 8; versus Dasein, 87, 90, 98, 106, 166; defined, 115; destiny of, 124; *ekleipsis* of,

124; end of, 169–70; as *Ereignis,* 167; in-difference of, 115–70; and man's nature, 242n91; and metaphysics, 87–95, 99; nature of, 125; and ontological difference, 125–28; origin of, 126, 167; and projection, 171–72; as relational totality, 100–105; and text, 161–69; *there* of, 95–100; topology of, 123; and transcendental phenomenology, 7; true meaning of, 120–23; truth of, 115–17; void of, 147–52. *See also* Dasein
Being and Time (Heidegger), 87, 88, 90, 91, 100, 107, 115, 122, 127, 166, 171
Benjamin, Walter, xv
Bennington, Geoffrey, 224
Benveniste, Emile, 180
Berkeley, George, 31
Bloom, Harold, xiv
Boundaries: and nomadism, 129
Brentano, Franz, 115
Brunette, Peter, 215

Cage, John, 61
Capital (Marx), 36
Caputo, John, 133
Carr, David, 20
Cartesian Meditations (Husserl), 17, 31, 41, 234n69

253

Cogito, 4–5, 7, 13, 14, 15, 20, 22, 29, 40–41, 110. *See also* Ego

Communication: as abstract, 51; as bridge-crossing, 111–12; and commonality, x–xi; 58–59; and comprehension, 225; as convergence, 50; as coordination, 50; critical dogmatics of, 173–83; before deconstruction, 33–67; definition and usage of term, x–xi, 50–52; as delivery/return of messages, 46; and dialogue, 51; as enigmatic, 39–40, 66; as family resemblances, 231n1; impossibility of, 225–28; models of, 52, 176–79; as negotiation, 50; philosophy of, 34–35, 235n6; problematic of, 35–38, *45,* 55–61, 71; semantics of, 183–85; social relationships as paradigm of, 174, 186; surrogate ideas of, 51; theories of, xvi, xvii–xviii, 64–67, 71–72; as transmission, 48, 50, 57; triadic structure of, 61–62; verbal, 58

Confessions (Rousseau), 148

Consciousness: and Being, 8; as bipolar, 9, 14; and ego, 14–17; and immanence, 8, 9; intentionality of, 8–9; reductive, 8–9, 13; as reflexive, 9

Context, 198–200

Conversation, 221–24

Cratylus (Plato), 108

Crisis: and irrationalism, 6; and phenomenology, 6–9; and philosophy, 5–9

Crisis of European Sciences and Transcendental Phenomenology, The (Husserl), 6, 33

Critique of Pure Reason (Kant), 4, 92

Culler, Jonathan, 118, 148

Dasein: authenticity of, 127; versus Being, 87, 90, 98, 106, 166; disclosedness of, 95, 115; hermeneutics of, 87, 90, 98, 105; homecoming of, 122; and metaphysics, 99; and ontological difference, 128; as reflexive, 98; and relational totality, 100–107. *See also* Being

Declaration of Independence: Derrida speech on, 211–15, 219

Deconstruction, xii–xvii, xviii, 171–228; as antimetaphysical graphematics, xvi–xvii; and castration, xiii–xiv; communication before, 33–67; and counterreading, xiii–xiv; definition and usage of term, 118–19; versus destruction, 128–33;

double writing of, 141–43; duplicitous nature of, xiv; and mimesis, xiii–xiv; and ontological difference, 120, 125–28; and philosophy, xiv–xvi; as rewriting, 139–48; versus subjectivity, xiv; and syntax, 140; as text-dependent, xiii, xiv, 136–39; as textual violence, xiv, 137; and transgressive reading, xiii–xiv

Deleuze, Gilles, 38–39, 153, 184

de Man, Paul, 65, 69, 70–71, 118

Derrida, Jacques, 43, 61; on Being, 132, 169; on communication, 186–87; on Declaration of Independence, 211–15, 219; on deconstruction, xii–xiii, xiv, xv, xvi–xvii, 118–19, 136–47, 173; on *différance,* 154–58, 160, 163–65, 246n105; "Double Session," 140, 205; on end/closure, 244n41; "From Restricted to General Economy: Hegelianism without Reserve," 73–74; *Glas,* 141; and Heidegger, 116, 120, 128–29; on Heraclitus, 152; as hypertextualist, 188, 203; on iterability, 195–96, 250n48; as left-wing Heideggerian, 116, 128–29, 172; "Living On," 162; logic of deferral, 62; logic of paleonymy, 145, 146, 148; logic of the *supplément,* 147, 148, 152–53; on logocentrism, 116; on meaning, 203–5; on metaphor, 49, 52–55, 238n44, 238n47; on metaphysics, 43, 134; on origin, 159, 192, 247n117; on parasitism, 245n52; on phenomenology, 18, 73–74; on philosophy, xiv, xv, 53–54; on phonocentrism, 190; on postal principle, 46, 47, 48, 208, 210–20; *Post Card,* 208, 215; on self-reflection, 76; on solitude, 111; *Speech and Phenomena,* 134–35; on speech/writing, 134–35, 192–95, 200–202; on text, 161–69, 188; on trace, 158–60, 161, 246–47n112; on writing, 59–60, 202–7. *See also* Deconstruction

Descartes, René: on Being, 94; on *cogito*/ego, 29, 40–42; *Discourse on Method,* 3, 6; *Meditations,* 3, 4, 41–42; on metaphors, 53; on metaphysics, 53, 93; and rationalism, 29; on reduction, 13

Descombes, Vincent, 164, 197

Destruction: versus deconstruction, 128–33; of metaphysics, 120–23

Determinism, 56

Dews, Peter, 205–6
Dialogism, xii, xvii
Différance, 154–58, 160, 163–65, 217–18, 246n105; and writing, 203
Difference, ontological, 120, 124–28
Dilthey, Wilhelm, 90–91
Disclosedness: of truth, 114–15
Discourse on Method (Descartes), 3, 6
"Double Session, The" (Derrida), 140, 205
Ducrot, Oswald, 162–63
Dufrenne, Mikel, 34
Dupré, Louis, 29

Ecriture, 146, 148, 206–7
Ego: absolute certainty of, 5; and consciousness, 14–17; and intersubjectivity, 17–28, 29, 62; and other, 78–79; and self, 74–75; self-transparent, 179–80; as subject, 5, 29–30, 40–41; as transcendental, 13–17, 20, 232–33n29. *See also* Alter ego; *Cogito;* Individuality; Subject/subjectivity
Ekleipsis: of Being, 124; of metaphysics, 123
Enzensberger, Hans Magnus, 179
Epistemology: and metaphysics, 5, 88; and ontology, 88
Ereignis, 125, 126, 131–33, 167. *See also* Appropriation
Essence of Reasons, The (Heidegger), 149
Essentialism: and phenomenology, 11, 13
Explanation, 236n17
Explication, 238n42
Exposure, 98

Fantasy, 11–12
Fenves, Peter, 226
Fichte, Johann Gottlieb, 75
Fink, Eugen, 33
First Philosophy, 4, 6–7, 16, 18, 29, 33–34
Flux, 237n28
Formal and Transcendental Logic (Husserl), 17
Foucault, Michel, 32, 183
France, Anatole, 53
Frankfurt school, 179
Free variation, 11–12
Freud, Sigmund: *Nachträglichkeit,* 195
"From Restricted to General Economy: Hegelianism without Reserve" (Derrida), 73–74
Frye, Northrop, 34

Gadamer, Hans Georg, 116
Gasché, Rodolphe, 70
German Ideology, The (Marx), 36
Glas (Derrida), 141
Goux, Jean-Joseph, 234n81
Grossberg, Lawrence, 52
Guattari, Félix, 153, 194

Haar, Michel, 123
Harmony: and intersubjectivity, 24, 233n54
Hartman, Geoffrey, 142
Hegel, G. W. F., 42, 56, 73, 108
Heidegger, Martin, 95; on Being/Dasein, 79, 90, 98–99, 103, 120–28, 147–52, 167, 171–72; *Being and Time,* 87, 88, 90, 91, 100, 107, 115, 122, 127, 166, 171; on communication, xvi, 72, 111–12; on deconstruction, xv; on destruction of metaphysics, 120–23; on ego, 93; on end of philosophy, 252n103; *Essence of Reasons,* 149; on hermeneutical circle, x; on homeland, 133; *Identity and Difference,* 73; *Kant and the Problem of Metaphysics,* 92, 95; left-wing interpretation of, 116–17, 172; on metaphysics, 92, 134, 149; *On Time and Being,* 130; ontology of, 115–17, 169; relation to Derrida, 120; right-wing interpretation of, 116–17, 172; as storyteller, 169; on subject, 41; on transcendentalism, 89, 94; "What Is Metaphysics?," 149
Heraclitus, 152, 167
Hermeneutics: ambiguity in, 202, 206; hermeneutical circle, ix–x, 36, 72–73; ideology in communication theory, 174–75
Hitachi, 48–50
Hollier, Denis, 210
Homecoming: of Dasein, 122; versus nomadism, 128–33
Houdebine, Jean-Louis, 142
Hume, David, 22, 69
Husserl, Edmund, 9, 13; *Cartesian Meditations,* 17, 31, 41, 234n69; on *cogito*/subject, 42; on crisis, 5–9; *Crisis of European Sciences and Transcendental Phenomenology,* 6, 33; *Formal and Transcendental Logic,* 17; *Idea I,* 17; on immanence, 8, 9; *Logical Investigations,* 33; on natural attitude, 89; on pairing, 23, 26; on philosophy, 6–7; on sciences, 220; on sign, 134–35. *See also* Transcendental phenomenology

Idea I (Husserl), 17
Idealism: in communication theory, 179
Identity and Difference (Heidegger), 73
Immanence: and consciousness, 8, 9; and transcendence, 8, 9
Individuality: and intersubjectivity, 59, 61, 62, 64; transcendence of, 39, 40. *See also* Ego
Ingarden, Roman, 34
Intentionality: and consciousness, 8–9; versus transcendence, 9
Intersubjectivity: and alter ego, 21–22, 24, 29, 79; and analogy, 22–23, 26, 64–65; analysis of, 233n36; and apperception, 26–27; and communication, xii, 61; and ego, 17–28, 29, 62; and harmony, 24, 233n55; and individuality, 59, 61, 62, 64; and mediation, 61, 62, 64–66, 72–73; and metaphysics, 80, 82; and phenomenology, xvi, 17–28, 77, 83; and solipsism, 19, 25, 27, 28, 29, 64; and transcendentalism, 77–80. *See also* Subject/subjectivity
Irrationalism, 6
Iterability: and speech/writing, 195–96, 250n48

Jakobson, Roman, 58, 176–83
Johnson, Barbara, 70, 118–19, 135

Kant, Immanuel, 35; on apperception, 76; on Being and metaphysics, 87–95; *Critique of Pure Reason*, 4, 92; on knowledge, 10, 30; on rhetoric, 69; on subject, 30
Kant and the Problem of Metaphysics (Heidegger), 92, 95
Kierkegaard, Søren, 42
Kuhn, Thomas, 120

Lacan, Jacques, 231n3
Language: and meaning, 208–9; multiplicity of, 184–85. *See also* Rhetoric; Speech; Writing
Lecercle, Jean-Jacques, 208
Leibniz, Gottfried Wilhelm, 31
"Living On" (Derrida), 162
Logical Investigations (Husserl), 33
Logocentrism, xiii, 116, 192–210, 233n55
Logos; versus myth/*mythos*, 3. *See also* Reason
Luckmann, Thomas, 84–86; *Structures of the Life-World*, 84

Luhmann, Niklas, 236n18

Mallarmé, Stéphane, xv
Marx, Karl: *Capital*, 36; *German Ideology*, 36
Mead, George Herbert, 56
Meaning, 203–5, 208–10
Media practice, 179
Mediation: and communication, 35, 43–49, 56, 61; and intersubjectivity, 61, 62, 64–66, 72–73; and postal principle, 47–49
Meditations (Descartes), 3, 4, 41–42
Merleau-Ponty, Maurice, 79
Metaphor: in communication, 49–55; and metaphysics, 53–54; and philosophy, 54–55; in teaching/learning, 52
Metaphysics: and Being, 87–95, 99; to deconstruct, xiii; destruction of, 120–23; *ekleipsis* of, 123; and epistemology, 5, 88; and intersubjectivity, 80, 82; and metaphor, 53–54; representational, 106; single system of, 134; and subjectivity, 40–41; and transcendentalism, 42–43
Miller, J. Hillis, 119
Mimesis: and deconstruction, xiii–xiv
Misunderstanding, 174
Modernism: and phenomenology, 29–32
Mohanty, J. N., 13
Muralt, André de, 16, 18
Muttersprache, 116
Myth/*mythos*: versus *logos*, 3

Nachträglichkeit (Freud), 195
Naming, 136, 142–47
Narcissism: transcendental, 32
Natali, João, 173–76
Naturalism: and philosophy, 6
Nelson, Cary, 183
New Science (17th century), 35
Nietzsche, Friedrich, 238n43; on affirmation, 203; on deconstruction, xv; on metaphor, 53; and metaphysics, 92; on rhetoric, 69, 70–71
Nomadism: and boundaries, 129; and deconstruction, 130, 133, 135; versus homecoming, 128–33
Norris, Christopher, 119, 202
Nothingness: and anxiety, 150–52; and Being, 147–52

Occidental Reason, 53
Olafson, Frederick, 95
On Time and Being (Heidegger), 130
Ontology: of communication, xvi, 69–112, *112*; and epistemology, 88; fundamental, 87–96, 99, 129, 169, 172; matriarchal, 116; relational, 107, social, 81–87
Ortega y Gasset, José, 78–79

Paleonymy: logic of, 145, 146, 148
Parasitism, 245n52
Peirce, Charles S., 239n17
Perception, 26–27, 197–98, 234n61
Phaedo (Plato), 3
Phenomenology, xvi, 3–32; constitutive, 77; and crisis, 6–9; descriptive, 86; duplicity of, 18; egological, 13–17, 18, 25; eidetic, 16; and intersubjectivity, xvi, 17–28, 83; and philosophical modernism, 29–32; and philosophy, 33; as radical empiricism, 9, 11; and reduction, 8–17; and restriction, 74; as science of consciousness, 13; as study of *logos*, 240n39. *See also* Transcendental phenomenology
Philosophy: and crisis, 5–9; critical, 35, 76; and deconstruction, xiv–xvi; end of, 220, 252n103; and history, 3–4, 6; and humanities, 34; and metaphor, 54–55; and naturalism, 6; and phenomenology, 33; and rational science, 5; and reason, xiv, 3–5; as rigorous science, 6; and social sciences, 34; and text, 202–3; and thinking subject, 5, 35–36. *See also* First Philosophy
Phonocentrism, 190
Plato, 11, 13, 29, 42, 53, 56, 70, 91; *Cratylus*, 108; *Phaedo*, 3
Pöggeler, Otto, 123
Poincaré, Jules-Henri, 13
Polylogism, xvii
Positivity: as critical dogmatics of communication, 172–83; defined, 175–76; divergence after, 183–87
Postal paradox, 46–49, 210–20, 227
Post Card, The (Derrida), 208, 215

Rationalism, 5, 29
Reader response theory, 34

Reason: and knowledge, 35; and metaphysics, 92; occidental, 53; and philosophy, xiv, 3–5. *See also Logos*
Reconstruction: and transcendental phenomenology, 6
Reduction: eidetic, 11, 13; and phenomenology, 8–17; and transcendentalism, 78
Reid, Thomas, 22
Repetition. *See* Iterability
Rhetoric, 69–72
Richards, I. A., 34
Ricoeur, Paul, 17, 24, 39–40, 42
Rorty, Richard, 167–68, 188
Rousseau, Jean-Jacques: *Confessions,* 148

Santayana, George, 85
Sartre, Jean-Paul, 79, 111
Scarpetta, Guy, 142
Scholasticism, 5
Schürmann, Reiner, 99
Schutz, Alfred, 77, 79, 81–82, 84–86; *Structures of the Life-World,* 84
Scott, Charles, 106
Searle, John, 200
Self-reflection, 74–76, 80
Serres, Michel, 56–58, 61
Signature, 210–20
Signification, 179, 185
Social relationships/role: and interaction, 62–64; as paradigm of communication, 174, 186
Socrates, 3
Solipsism: and intersubjectivity, 19, 25, 27, 28, 29, 64; and subjectivity, 42; transcendental, 32
Solitude/solitary subject, 40, 43–44, 62, 111
Sollers, Philippe, 111
Space/time relation, 129–30
Spacing, 154, 216–17
Speech: as logocentric, 192–202; and writing, 189–95, 200–202
Speech and Phenomena (Derrida), 134–35
Spivak, Gayatri C., 170
Structures of the Life-World (Schutz and Luckmann), 84
Subject/subjectivity: and communication, 38–44, 46, 61–72, 111, 180–81; versus deconstruction, xiv; and metaphysics,

40–41; as privacy, 40, 237n30; and transcendentalism, 7, 16–17, 18, 42–43. *See also* Cogito; Ego; Individuality; Intersubjectivity; Solitude/solitary subject

Supplément, logic of the, 147, 148, 152–53

Syntax: and deconstruction of text, 140

Taylor, Mark C., 108, 234n81

Text: and Being, 161–69; deconstruction as text-dependent, xiii, xiv, 136–39, 140; Derrida on, 188; dissemination of, 205–7; and philosophy, 202–3; and syntax, 140; theology of, 162; violence to, xiv, 137. *See also* Writing

Time: space/time relation, 129–30

Todorov, Tzvetan, 162–63

Trace, 158–60, 161, 246–47n112

Tradition, 116

Transcendental phenomenology, xvi, 6–9, 11, 13–17, 76–77; and Being, 7; and immanence, 8, 9; versus intentionality, 9; and intersubjectivity, xvi, 17–28, 77–80, 83; and metaphysics, 42–43; and philosophical modernism, 29–32; and philosophy, 6–7, 33–34; and reconstruction, 6; and reduction, 78; and subjectivity, 7, 16–17, 18, 42–43. *See also* Husserl, Edmund

Truth: as *aletheia*, 167; as disclosedness, 114–15

Undecidables, 143–45, 154

Valéry, Paul, 202

Voice, 187–92

"What Is Metaphysics?" (Heidegger), 149

Williams, Raymond, 183, 184, 185

Wills, David, 215

Wittgenstein, Ludwig, 120, 231n1

Wolfson, Louis, 208

Writing: and *différance*, 203; double, and deconstruction, 141–42; and *écriture*, 206–7; rewriting, deconstruction as, 139–47; and speech, 189–95, 200–202; as transitive act, ix. *See also* Text

Briankle G. Chang teaches cultural studies in the Department of Communication at the University of Massachusetts, Amherst, where he is also the director of the Center for the Study of Communication. Previously, he taught at Rutgers University.